Paul Beyond the Judaism/Hellenism Divide

A dualism is a distinction drawn in such a way as to make unintelligible the relation between the two sorts of thing one has distinguished.

—Robert B. Brandom

PAUL BEYOND THE JUDAISM/HELLENISM DIVIDE

Edited by Troels Engberg–Pedersen

Westminster John Knox Press
LOUISVILLE
LONDON • LEIDEN

Book design by Sharon Adams
Cover design by Kathy York

First edition
Published by Westminster John Knox Press
Louisville, Kentucky

This book is printed on acid-free paper that meets the American National Standards Institute Z39.48 standard. ∞

PRINTED IN THE UNITED STATES OF AMERICA

02 03 04 05 06 07 08 09 10 11 — 10 9 8 7 6 5 4 3 2 1

Library of Congress Cataloging-in-Publication Data

Paul beyond the Judaism/Hellenism divide / Troels Engberg-Pedersen, editor.
    p. cm.
  Includes bibliographical references and index.
  ISBN 0-664-22406-7 (alk. paper)
    1. Paul, the Apostle, Saint. 2. Bible. N. T. Epistles of Paul—Criticism, interpretation, etc. 3. Christianity and other religions—Judaism. 4. Judaism—Relations—Christianity. 5. Hellenism. I. Engberg-Pedersen, Troels.

  BS2506 .P366 2001
  225.9'2—dc21   2001026264

Contents

Abbreviations

The list gives abbreviations employed in the book for commonly used periodicals, serials, reference books, and the like. Basically the abbreviations follow the Society of Biblical Literature system adopted in *The SBL Handbook of Style,* ed. P. H. Alexander et al. (Peabody, Mass.: Hendrickson, 1999). Abbreviations of biblical books, apocrypha, pseudepigraphical and early Patristic books also follow the SBL system. Abbreviations and editions of other ancient works, including Greco-Roman ones, follow generally accepted standards and may be unpacked by consulting the Index of Ancient Sources or, for instance, LSJ (9th ed. [1940] xv–xlv with revised supplement [1996] x–xxxi).

AAR	American Academy of Religion
AB	Anchor Bible
AGJU	Arbeiten zur Geschichte des antiken Judentums und des Urchristentums
ALBO	Analecta lovaniensia biblica et orientalia
ANF	Anti-Nicene Fathers
ANRW	*Aufstieg und Niedergang der römischen Welt: Geschichte und kultur Roms in Spiegel der neueren Forschung.* Edited by H. Temporini and W. Haase. Berlin, 1972–
APOT	R. H. Charles, *The Apocrypha and Pseudepigrapha of the Old Testament,* 2 vols. (Oxford: Clarendon, 1913)
BDAG	W. Bauer, F. W. Danker, W. F. Arndt, and F. G. Gingrich, *Greek-English Lexicon of the New Testament and Other Early Christian Literature,* 3d ed. (Chicago: University of Chicago Press, 2000)
BDB	F. Brown, S. R. Driver, and C. A. Briggs, *A Hebrew and English Lexicon of the Old Testament* (Oxford: Oxford University Press, 1907)

BDR   F. Blass, A. Debrunner, and F. Rehkopf, *Grammatik des neutestamentlichen Griechisch*, 14th ed. (Göttingen: Vandenhoeck & Ruprecht, 1976)

BETL   Bibliotheca ephemeridum theologicarum lovaniensium

BGU   *Berliner Griechische Urkunden* (*Ägyptische Urkunden aus den Königlichen [Staatlichen] Museen zu Berlin, Griechische Urkunden*), 15 vols. (Berlin, 1895–1983)

BJRL   *Bulletin of the John Rylands University Library of Manchester*

BT   Bibliotheca Teubneriana

CMG   Corpus Medicorum Graecorum

ConBNT   Coniectanea biblica, New Testament

CRINT   Compendia rerum iudaicarum ad Novum Testamentum

CurTM   *Currents in Theology and Mission*

DCH   D. J. A. Clines, *Dictionary of Classical Hebrew* (Sheffield: Sheffield University Press, 1993)

EDNT   H. Balz and G. Schneider (eds.), *Exegetical Dictionary of the New Testament*, 3 vols. (Grand Rapids: Eerdmans, 1990–93)

EPRO   Études préliminaires aux religions orientales dans l'empire Romain

ETL   *Ephemerides theologicae lovanienses*

FB   Forschung zur Bibel

FC   Fathers of the Church

FRLANT   Forschungen zur Religion und Literatur des Alten und Neuen Testaments

GCS   Griechischen christlichen Schriftsteller

GTA   Göttinger theologische Arbeiten

HBT   *Horizons in Biblical Theology*

HNT   Handbuch zum Neuen Testament

HNTC   Harper's NT Commentaries

HSS   Harvard Semitic Studies

HTR   *Harvard Theological Review*

HUT   Hermeneutische Untersuchungen zur Theologie

ICC   International Critical Commentary

IDBSup   K. Crim et al. (eds.), *Interpreter's Dictionary to the Bible, Supplementary Volume* (Nashville: Abingdon, 1962)

IE   H. Wankel, R. Merkelbach et al. (eds.), *Die Inschriften von Ephesos* (Bonn, 1979–81)

JBL   *Journal of Biblical Literature*

JECS   *Journal of Early Christian Studies*

JSNT   *Journal for the Study of the New Testament*

JSJ   *Journal for the Study of Judaism*

JSPSup   Journal for the Study of the Pseudepigrapha, Supplement Series

JTS   *Journal of Theological Studies*

LCL	Loeb Classical Library
LSJ	H. G. Liddell, R. Scott, and H. S. Jones, *A Greek-English Lexicon*, 9th ed. (Oxford: Oxford University Press, 1940)
MeyerK	H. A. W. Meyer, Kritisch-exegetischer Kommentar über das Neue Testament
Neot	*Neotestamentica*
NIDNTT	C. Brown (ed.), *New International Dictionary of New Testament Theology*, 4 vols. (Grand Rapids: Zondervan, 1975–85)
NovT	*Novum Testamentum*
NovTSup	Supplements to Novum Testamentum
NRT	*La nouvelle revue théologique*
NTS	*New Testament Studies*
OBO	Orbis biblicus et orientalis
OLD	P. G. W. Glare, *Oxford Latin Dictionary* (Oxford: Oxford University Press, 1982)
OTP	J. H. Charlesworth (ed.), *The Old Testament Pseudepigrapha*, 2 vols. (Garden City, N.Y.: Doubleday, 1983–85)
OtSt	Oudtestamentische Studiën
PG	J.-P. Migne, Patrologia graeca
PGiss.	O. Eger, E. Kornemann, and P. M. Meyer (eds.), *Griechische Papyri im Museum des oberhessischen Geschichtsvereins zu Giessen*, 3 vols. (Leipzig-Berlin, 1910–12)
PGL	G. W. H. Lampe, *Patristic Greek Lexicon* (Oxford: Clarendon, 1968)
PL	J.-P. Migne, *Patrologia latina*
PMich.	*Michigan Papyri* (1913–)
RAC	*Reallexikon für Antike und Christentum*
RB	*Revue Biblique*
RelSRev	*Religious Studies Review*
RSR	*Recherches de science religieuse*
RTR	*Reformed Theological Review*
SANT	Studien zum Alten und Neuen Testament
SBT	Studies in Biblical Theology
SBLBMI	SBL The Bible and Its Modern Interpreters
SBLDS	SBL Dissertation Series
SBLMS	Society of Biblical Literature Monograph Series
SBLRBS	SBL Resources for Biblical Study
SBLSBS	SBL Sources for Biblical Study
SBS	Stuttgarter Bibelstudien
SBT	Studies in Biblical Theology
SC	Sources chrétiennes
SCI	*Scripta Classica Israelica*
SJLA	Studies in Judaism in Late Antiquity

SJT	*Scottish Journal of Theology*
SNTSMS	Society for New Testament Studies Monograph Series
SNTSU	Studien zum Neuen Testament und seiner Umwelt
SVF	H. von Arnim, *Stoicorum veterum fragmenta*, 4 vols. (Leipzig, 1903–24)
TANZ	Texte und Arbeiten zum neutestamentlichen Zeitalter
TDNT	G. Kittel (ed.), *Theological Dictionary of the New Testament*, 10 vols. (Grand Rapids: Eerdmans, 1964–76)
TDOT	G. J. Botterweck and H. Ringgren (eds.), *Theological Dictionary of the Old Testament*, 8 vols. (Grand Rapids: Eerdmans, 1974-)
TLNT	C. Spicq, *Theological Lexicon of the New Testament*, 3 vols. (Peabody, Mass.: Hendrickson, 1994)
TPQ	*Theologisch-Praktische Quartalschrift*
TQ	*Theologische Quartalschrift*
TU	Texte und Untersuchungen
TZ	*Theologische Zeitschrift*
WBC	Word Biblical Commentary
WMANT	Wissenschaftliche Monographien zum Alten und Neuen Testament
WUNT	Wissenschaftliche Untersuchungen zum Neuen Testament
ZKG	*Zeitschrift für Kirchengeschichte*
ZAW	*Zeitschrift für die alttestamentliche Wissenschaft*
ZNW	*Zeitschrift für die neutestamentliche Wissenschaft*
ZTK	*Zeitschrift für Theologie und Kirche*

Introduction

Paul Beyond the Judaism/Hellenism Divide

Troels Engberg-Pedersen

A New Research Program

The point of this volume lies in its title. Let me explain.

In 1994 I edited a volume of essays entitled *Paul in His Hellenistic Context* (Edinburgh: Clark/Minneapolis: Fortress). A conference held in Denmark in 1991 under the title *Paul on His Hellenistic Background* formed the basis for that collection. The change from "background" to "context" emerged from insights reached during the conference. Participants perceived that Paul should not be seen against a "background" from which he would stand out in splendid isolation. Such a picture would not do justice to the many and complex ways in which he interacted directly with his cultural contemporaries. Instead, we should view Paul as one among them, as a coplayer within a shared "context" that would allow any player to stand out momentarily and for a specific issue of interpretation, but also to recede again later into the shared context.

Small as the change from "background" to "context" may initially appear, this change is in fact of the greatest importance. The shift in terminology encapsulates the fundamental insight that in comparative historical inquiry the observer must in principle look with equal attention and interest at each individual item that is brought into the comparison. This approach provides the only way of attaining a genuine understanding of each item on its own premises, and only on that basis will a comparison between them be genuinely fruitful; then an observer can see both similarities and differences, as it were, at the same level. Basically, the step claims that an adequate historical analysis must leave out the category of uniqueness. Methodologically, the presumption must always favor similarity rather than difference. Only on that basis will any claim about differences be valid. This fundamental perspective remains in place in the present volume, too.

The step from background to context went together with a special understanding of the term "Hellenistic" in the title of the first volume. The term was used there to refer to the comprehensive cultural melting pot that one finds in the lands first conquered and held by Alexander the Great and his successors and then by the Romans. This mixture was sufficiently similar across times and places for the culture to count as a single, comprehensive entity. Within the mixture there certainly were differences in different times and places, reflecting the use of different languages. Such differences might also result from different traditions with roots before the Hellenistic period proper. Thus Jews in Palestine or in the Diaspora would partially live within traditions that went far back; Greeks would do the same, and Romans, too, as would any unit among the many other distinct ethnic groups of which we have only little information. Still, they would all also live within the comprehensive mix of Hellenistic culture.

The previous volume attempted to do justice to this broad understanding of the term "Hellenistic." Under its umbrella term of the Hellenistic context, the book included essays intended to elucidate Paul by comparison with other cultural practices that had distinctly Jewish roots no less than distinctly Greek ones. And all through, the essays were dedicated to operating with the kind of open-minded contextualization identified above, one that took seriously in its own right any given cultural configuration that was brought in for comparison.

In 1997 I organized another conference at Rolighed in Denmark, intending to consolidate this approach and take it further. But I had not quite learned the lesson. The aim was once more to insist that scholars must not in advance give any value preference to any particular element or tradition in the broad cultural context within which Paul should be understood. Instead, one should address any specific issue about Paul in the light of all kinds of comparative material that might in itself appear potentially illuminating no matter where it is found, and in particular irrespective of whether it was originally Jewish or originally Greek (or Roman or . . .). To bring out this stance, I entitled the conference *Paul between Judaism and Hellenism*. Once more, however, problems with the title became clear during the conference. First, this title, too, could be read as envisaging Paul as a kind of disembodied mind operating altogether outside Judaism and Hellenism instead of within the context constituted by the two isms. Second, one could perceive the title as presupposing that the two isms should be taken to refer to two separate cultures instead of identifying different aspects of the same one. As against this, the conference only confirmed the approach that came out of the earlier one, as indeed was its purpose. Paul was a coplayer within a shared context, and that context was broadly Hellenistic in the manner identified above.

Another item also became clear. To avoid falling back into the traditional traps of presupposing uniqueness for Paul and playing out Judaism and Hellenism against one another, one should consider in some depth the ways in which the two isms have in fact been employed in readings of Paul throughout the ages. That approach would show the extent to which Judaism and Hellenism constantly appear as pawns in a power game, the purpose of which has almost always been to ensure Paul's uniqueness and conformity with the interpreter's own theological position. Thus it became clear that a fairly strong degree of scholarly self-consciousness about the hermeneutical categories that lie at the back of our minds and their ideological content is required to secure the new approach.

These lines of thinking have led to the new title of this book. Its purpose is to insist that as soon as one notices the strongly ideological content of any use of the terms "Judaism" and "Hellenism" (and "Hellenistic") in studies of Paul since antiquity, one will see the need to give up altogether operating with the dichotomy. Furthermore, one will see the same need as soon as one notices how skewed the dichotomy is in relation to the ancient historical facts.

The proposal of going beyond the supposed divide is intended to be quite radical: scholars must attempt to shed all unacknowledged, ideological, and historically unfounded presuppositions in addressing Paul in his context, by giving up altogether using any form of the Judaism/Hellenism divide as an interpretive lens. Instead, one must look entirely open-mindedly at the facts: the actual use of comparable ideas and practices in the cultural context no matter where and irrespective of their roots. Only by going self-consciously beyond the Judaism/Hellenism divide and giving up relying on it in any form will scholars be able to see Paul in the broad cultural context to which he belonged and to use that insight fruitfully for the comparative elucidation of his own ideas and practices.

The suggestion that we look at Paul from a vantage point beyond any Judaism/Hellenism divide proposes a new program for research, although its roots stretch far back in the scholarly investigation of Paul, e.g., in the approach adopted in the *religionsgeschichtliche Schule*. Still, such a viewpoint has distinctly contemporary applications. Scholars at the outset of the twenty-first century regularly bring in all sorts of comparative material for elucidating Paul. That is fine in itself. The problem is that the standpoint from which comparisons are made is often frightfully skewed, as if *either* the Jewish *or* the Hellenistic material is in the end the really important one. Only, this bias is now concealed by the comprehensiveness of the material that is quoted for comparison.

If the proposal is accepted, may we not continue to call Paul's cultural context Hellenistic in the broad sense? And may we not continue to speak of specific Pauline elements as having distinctly Jewish, Greek, or Roman roots? In both cases the answer should be "Yes," but only once scholars go about using those classifications with extreme care. We must constantly bear in mind that the term "Hellenistic" should be understood in the very broad, almost empty sense identified above. Similarly, when speaking of an idea or practice as having, for instance, a distinctly Jewish root, we must remember our focus on a single idea or practice that *we* have decided, for reasons of our own, to extract from the comprehensive cultural web in which it had its occurrent place and that it took its overall meaning, not primarily from its cultural root, but from its place within the contemporary cross-cultural web.

The Essays in Light of the Program

The authors represented in this volume clearly do not all share all parts of the proposed research program. Furthermore, even where they do, they often have different ways of stating the point. Nor would the contributors necessarily agree to speak of a new research program, not least because of its fairly old pedigree. Still, it is worth bringing out how the essays contribute to the proposal. We can do that by breaking the proposal down to some of its salient components and showing how the essays relate to them.

Questioning the Ideological Use of the Categories

In "Judaism, Hellenism, and the Birth of Christianity," Wayne Meeks provides an overview of how Judaism and Hellenism have been played out against one another in scholarly accounts of early Christianity since Ferdinand Christian Baur. Having described Baur's Tübingen view, Meeks comments: "'Judaism' and 'Hellenism' here are obviously code words for complex sets of ideas masquerading as historical entities." And he then goes on to show how the same is true of later scholarly developments— perhaps not so much in the *religionsgeschichtliche Schule*, though even here the cultural dichotomy between Judaism and Hellenism was accepted in an evolutionary scheme towards Christianity, but quite overtly in the later reaction to the *religionsgeschichtliche Schule*. "*Real* Christianity," these scholars urged, "was thoroughly *Jewish*. . . . The aim of this scholarship," Meeks notes, "was to demonstrate the distinctiveness of Christianity against its pagan environment, which meant the distinctiveness it shared with ancient Israel, while at the same time to demonstrate that Christianity climaxed and fulfilled what was true in Judaism." Meeks then proceeds to show how this ideological project has gradually crumbled under the pressure of historical studies that have brought out the complexities of Jews living in the Greco-Roman world and Christians doing the same.

Dale Martin broadens the canvas considerably in "Paul and the Judaism/Hellenism Dichotomy: Toward a Social History of the Question." Martin begins, like Meeks, with German scholarship from the beginning of the nineteenth century to the middle of the twentieth "because that is where and when . . . the Hellenic/Judaic dualism was invented and elaborated to its greatest extent." He shows how employment of the dualism at the time, often in connection with "the Jewish question," was deeply embedded in quite different projects—for instance, the attempts by intellectuals in the early nineteenth century to rally interest in German national unity. From there Martin moves back in time to discuss the meanings of Judaism in seventeenth- and eighteenth-century English scholarship in order to show that the dualism itself and the significations attached to it were not at all the only possible ones, which Martin further confirms with his brief look at post–World War II scholarship, mainly in North America. Not only is the Hellenism/Judaism dichotomy recent and of limited geographical range, but the meanings of the dualism and its constituent parts are also remarkably flexible and varied.

A full quote from Martin's conclusion is both revealing and deliciously overwhelming: "'Hellenism' has represented universalism, Christianity, rationality, freedom, abstraction, timelessness, barrenness, individualism, nationalism, antinationalism, culture, Protestantism, sophistry, human wisdom, philosophy, theology, dogmatism, asceticism, dynamism, and so on. Judaism, for its part, has been used to represent particularism, communalism, sterility, historicity, nonhistoricity, Roman Catholicism, Lutheran dogmatism, poststructuralism, effeminacy, feminism, revelation, nationalism, antinationalism, legalism, freedom, naturalism, simplicity, religion, prophecy, asceticism, nonasceticism, dynamism, and so on and on. Indeed, a history of scholarship on the topic shows that the terms in themselves are meaningless apart from specific contexts."

Philip Alexander, in "Hellenism and Hellenization as Problematic Historiographical Categories," agrees with the thrust of Martin's essay and himself aims to show how during the course of history the concept of Hellenism has acquired strong ideological associations that scholars must keep firmly in mind when employing the term in historiography. Alexander also focuses on the antithetical phenomenon of "Hebraism" within Christian tradition and shows how intertwined with apologetics and theology Christian Hebraism has been from the Renaissance onwards. The same goes, Alexander demonstrates, for Hellenism within the Jewish tradition. Here, too, an almost universal impression exists that Judaism and Hellenism as cultures are irreconcilably opposed, and Hellenism became a complex symbol in an ideological *Kulturkampf.* Alexander also gives examples of the status of Hellenism as a highly charged and value-laden concept in the discourse of post-Enlightenment European thought. Indeed, he claims, "the relationship between Hellenism and Hebraism is a live issue in the intellectual world in which we live." As an example, Alexander notes how Islam has now to some extent taken up the role previously given to Judaism within the European consciousness. The rhetoric with which the relationship between Islam and the West is depicted is reminiscent of the rhetoric that opposed Judaism to Hellenism or to civilized Christian Europe—the "old Hellene/Barbarian dichotomy," as Alexander puts it. "Islam rather than Judaism has become the bogeyman of Europe, the alien other against whom one defines one's own identity." Alexander concludes that "Hellenism is a highly charged ideological concept that should be handled with the utmost care. Historians are naive if they think they can safely use it and ignore its ideological overtones."

I placed the three essays by Meeks, Martin, and Alexander first in this volume because they bring out so strongly the ideological overtones of the concepts of Hellenism and Judaism. The basic ideas, but not the specific material, are well known already, particularly outside New Testament scholarship. But together the three essays point strongly in the direction of making scholars exorcize any use of the two categories when analyzing Paul in context, or at least of generating in scholars a very high degree of self-consciousness in their use. To me, the three essays point distinctly beyond the Judaism/Hellenism divide.

Questioning the Historical Facts Underlying the Two Categories

Most essays in the volume make a number of points under this rubric. According to Martin, the dualism misleads because it implies symmetry where none existed. Jews were one *ethnos*, like Lydians, Carians, Egyptians, Persians, Scythians. To contrast Jews with "Hellenism" (no matter how it is defined) in a dualistic relationship would have been seen by others as "crazy arrogance or wishful thinking." To imply that Judaism was in a symmetrical relationship with Hellenism is just "bad history."

Martin also makes the point that since all Judaism of the ancient world that would have had anything to do with early Christianity was already "Hellenized" and all forms of Greek culture in the same period had been influenced by "oriental" cultures, "to ask whether something is Hellenistic *or* Jewish would seem to be a misleading question." Meeks concurs: "The earliest Christian groups were simultaneously Jewish and Hellenistic."

Alexander, too, agrees and speaks of "a *broadly uniform culture* pervading the whole region" (my emphasis) as a result of cultural exchange that had been going on for at least a thousand years. Loveday Alexander, too, in "*IPSE DIXIT*: Citation of Authority in Paul and in the Jewish and Hellenistic Schools," repeatedly makes the same point. Employed at the usual level of abstraction, the distinction between Jewish and Hellenistic "seems to be virtually meaningless: what we are talking about are patterns of . . . activity that were more or less universal in the Eastern Mediterranean." She introduces the analogy of the global position of football (soccer) in today's sporting world and claims that, now as then, only when we move down to a more detailed level of comparison can we "identify distinctive cultural flavors within the broader structure." "Even where the two systems are treated more polemically as rivals"—and that, as we have seen, is the proper place of the dualism—"it seems meaningless to talk of anything distinctively 'Hellenistic' or 'Jewish' *in the structure itself:* we are talking about a common cultural pattern in the ancient Mediterranean, with recognizable equivalences" at the local level (my emphasis).

Stanley Stowers, in "Does Pauline Christianity Resemble a Hellenistic Philosophy?" also ranges over the whole of Philip Alexander's "broadly uniform culture" before identifying structural similarities between

Hellenistic philosophy and Pauline Christianity—"this phenomenon of a religion that looked in many ways like a philosophy." In fact, Stowers is quite prepared to find the shift in knowledge practices that he connects with Hellenistic philosophy also among Judean scribes and scholars, only the seven features of structural similarity that he identifies are more extensively present in Hellenistic philosophy.

In this connection Stowers raises an issue that comes through in several essays and belongs under the present rubric of how to understand the historical facts. In speaking of structural similarities, should we also think of borrowings and influence? Both Loveday and Philip Alexander decline to do so, and Stowers concurs. Margaret Mitchell, in "Pauline Accommodation and 'Condescension' (συγκατάβασις): 1 Cor 9:19–23 and the History of Influence," questions the picture of "tradition" that underlies any suggestion that one may find "a singular, discrete line of influence upon Paul." To Mitchell the word *tradition* "reifies and puts boundaries around what may be much more diffuse and disparate reflections on a related theme or cluster of themes." She therefore sets out to find another way of looking at the question of influence upon Paul, one that recognizes the "complex admixtures of Hellenism and Judaism present in Paul's thinking." She proposes to move beyond parallels to inquire about "the syntheses that Paul builds upon and creates." As it happens, for the particular motif she studies, Mitchell does end up identifying something like a singular, discrete line of influence upon Paul, one that is recognizably more Jewish than Hellenistic, but she insists that the (Jewish) motif that she identifies behind 1 Cor 9:19–23 is itself a complex mixture and fusion of Hellenistic and Jewish concepts; what's more, the motif may also have acted as "a conduit" for other motifs from a range of Hellenistic sources into Pauline thinking. In this way the question of borrowing and influence has indeed become complex, but that is only as it should be when Paul is being contextualized as operating within a broadly uniform culture.

Overcoming the Divide in Practice

In its determination to look around very broadly for comparative material, Mitchell's essay also exemplifies the principle highlighted in this third rubric. Meeks formulates the principle elegantly: "Again and again we find that the more broadly we cast our nets, the more interpretive fish we bring up."

David Aune and John Fitzgerald also adopt this approach. In his essay, "Anthropological Duality in the Eschatology of 2 Cor 4:16–5:10," Aune provides an exegesis of the crucial parts of this passage in order to lay bare the "problems inherent in focusing either on Hellenistic or early Jewish influences as mutually exclusive contexts for understanding Paul's thought." For instance, in discussing apocalyptic and Hellenistic eschatologies Aune claims that "Hellenistic eschatology was never culturally walled off from either early Judaism or early Christianity, and the eschatologies of both were inexorably subject to subtly modulated syncretistic pressures that led to the increasing assimilation of Hellenistic eschatological conceptions." In the rest of his essay Aune moves entirely freely back and forth between traditionally Jewish and traditionally Greek and Roman material in order to ascertain Paul's meaning. He thereby demonstrates in practice the falsity of the impression that "there was some sort of invisible cultural boundary separating one system from the other."

Fitzgerald, in "Paul and Paradigm Shifts: Reconciliation and Its Linkage Group," also ranges freely between traditionally Jewish and traditionally Greek and Roman sources. Two features of the particular way in which his essay overcomes the Judaism/Hellenism divide deserve special mention. One is that in studying the meaning of reconciliation in Paul, Fitzgerald does not in the least confine himself to material that is in any definable sense specifically religious. On the contrary, the more general areas of politics and social relations provide a rich field for Fitzgerald's search for comparative material. The other feature is the one identified in Fitzgerald's title under the term "paradigm shift." Margaret Mitchell spoke of moving beyond parallels to inquire about "the syntheses that Paul builds upon *and creates*" (my emphasis). Fitzgerald makes the same point when he speaks of Paul's penchant for making paradigm shifts: "when Paul makes use of an existing conceptual paradigm, he does not do so mechanically or uncritically. On the contrary, by changing key elements within a given paradigm, he creatively transforms it. The result is a paradigm shift."

Does Paul do this more than others? Perhaps, perhaps not. Fitzgerald does not discuss the issue. But he would probably agree that in principle, as it were, Paul is not to be seen as having been more creative than so many others who were working within the same broad context. In practice, however, he may have been so. Does that reflect his peculiar position "betwixt and between": as a Hellenized Diaspora Jew who was able both to make sense of the Jewish culture of Jerusalem and Judea when he encountered it as a young man and also later to take the teaching of a Palestinian Jewish sect to Greeks outside Palestine? (For this arresting image of Paul—neither one thing nor the other—see the concluding lines of Philip Alexander's essay.) The issue that is raised here concerns the relationship between our theme so far—Paul's objective position as a member of a Jewish-Greco-Roman culture that constitutes his context—and his own subjective perception of his role and position. More on that below. Here we should only emphasize the fruitfulness of the concept of a paradigm shift in describing Paul's handling of his contextual resources, as long as it is not misunderstood in a way that would once more tear him out of that context and place him on a pedestal and in splendid isolation.

Finally, Henrik Tronier's essay, "The Corinthian Correspondence between Philosophical Idealism and Apocalypticism," provides another example of how one may fruitfully move freely over the whole Jewish and Greco-Roman context in search for illuminating comparative material. Here the concern is the overall framework within which Paul aims to solve specific problems in the Corinthian congregation. Tronier illuminates this framework by drawing on both Philo as a representative of Hellenistic philosophical idealism and 1 Enoch as a representative of apocalypticism. At a high level of generalization, he concludes, the positions of Philo, the apocalypses, and Paul are similar in that they are all based on certain "interpretive structures that had been developed in Hellenistic episte-mology," ultimately with clear roots in Plato. Here is a claim for some form of direct borrowing or influence on the part of apocalypticism no less than Philo. But even if that claim is not accepted, the structural similarities across the invisible boundary between Greek philosophical idealism and Jewish apocalypticism remain striking. At a lower level of generalization, Tronier insists on the obvious differences but shows how they are basically two different ways of making closely similar points. By relating Paul in 1 Corinthians and 2 Corinthians to the two poles as found in Philo and 1 Enoch, Tronier ends up situating the Corinthian corre-spondence "somewhere between" a position like Philo's and that of the apocalypses. But this placement, as he emphasizes, does not mean "between Judaism and Hellenism." "For Philo as well as the apocalypses are themselves part and parcel of Hellenism since they are both rooted in interpretive structures developed in the Hellenistic world of ideas."

In this complex way of explaining Paul's use of certain important ideas in the Corinthian letters, Tronier's argument has structural similarities with Mitchell's.

The Specific Need Also
to Include Greco-Roman Material

In spite of their determined effort to overcome the Judaism/Hellenism divide in practice, one may detect a tendency in some authors (e.g., Love-day Alexander, Aune, Fitzgerald, and Stowers) to place special emphasis on comparative material that is not distinctly Jewish. Though these scholars in principle wish to range freely across any invisible boundaries, they are also keen to insist on the value for comparative purposes of the non-Jewish material. This fact is nowhere raised as an issue, but it seems sufficiently noteworthy to make us ask why.

Several answers may be given. The best is that due to deep prejudices in the Western consciousness concerning a set of intrinsic contrasts between religion and philosophy, religion and humanism, religion and secularism, an endemic tendency (at least at the present time) exists among New Testament scholars to think something like this: Christianity both is and was a religion. Philosophy, humanism, and even secularism have their roots in ancient Greece. Hence, for the elucidation of early Christianity, it is a priori likely that there is most to be gained by bringing in material that is Jewish. Only secondarily and somewhat peripherally may one then consider material that has no explicit connection with Judaism.

The quick and completely adequate answer to such a view is that everything said in the present volume goes directly against it. But since the view remains around and alive, there is very good reason to bring in also the non-Jewish material and to emphasize its interpretive yield.

From Etic to Emic Analysis: On Subcultures and Ethnic Identities

When he speaks of a broadly uniform culture pervading the whole region, Philip Alexander also adds that within that culture various groups adapted the dominant cultural patterns and structures "in order to create subcultures and establish ethnic identities." Both points evidently hang closely together. In his second essay, "Corinthian Christians as Artificial Aliens," Meeks may thus both describe the Corinthians as "most Jewish when they were most Hellenistic" and identify a "false paradox" here. Meeks also speaks of a wide range of modes of adaptation and self-identification, a range of "assimilation, adaptation, and acculturation . . . among people who still managed to think of themselves and . . . to be thought of by other members of the community as Jews." The etic and emic dimensions do not cancel one another out. On the contrary, *within* a broadly uniform culture specific groups may negotiate their own subcultures and outlooks.

John Barclay's essay, "Matching Theory and Practice: Josephus's Constitutional Ideal and Paul's Strategy in Corinth," makes a number of similar points. Searching for analytical tools in the cultural matrix of the first Christians for analyzing Paul's community-building strategies in Corinth,

Barclay first considers the potential value of the political philosophy of the Greeks and Romans. Eventually he settles for Josephus's account of the Jewish constitution in *Against Apion*, not because it is Jewish, but because, as Barclay takes it, when seen from the outside, "Jewish communities (at least those in the Diaspora . . .) were in many respects the closest social analogue to the churches founded by Paul." In any case, as Barclay also notes, Josephus himself utilizes the Greek political tradition for his broader depiction of the structural characteristics of the Jewish way of life. Thus, the comparison of Paul's strategies in Corinth with Josephus's account remains through and through contextual as an "experiment" or "heuristic exercise that at least helps us see how others might analyze and assess Paul's church-forming strategies."

That viewpoint is as seen from the outside. The patient, value-neutral, contextual comparison once more pays off. But then Barclay also gradually brings in the emic insider perspective in order to explain differences at various points between Josephus's account and Paul's strategies. For instance, in discussing the moral norms that Paul inculcates, Barclay shows how he insists on a discourse of difference that can persist despite obvious similarities with outsiders in moral norms and social practices. "Christians had to be made to *feel* different even when they were doing exactly the same as everyone else. A good deal of 1 Corinthians consists of the rhetorical affirmation of difference even where its moral norms conform to generally accepted standards" (Barclay's emphasis). All through, Paul presupposes a strong sense of differentiation between "brothers" and "outsiders."

Applying the etic and emic perspectives requires a delicate balance. The present volume emphasizes the etic outside view since the emic perspective is, of course, responsible for the traditional way of contrasting Paul with all his "backgrounds." But adopting the emic perspective is evidently also necessary in order to do justice to the historical facts. Paul himself did see things (at least also) in the way that Barclay and Meeks suggest. As Meeks noted, however, it would be false to detect a paradox here. Rather, the emic perspective should be adopted, in the way it is here, as part of the etic one. Only then will the views balance properly.

If scholars manage to keep these perspectives clear, they will also be able to see that there is no necessary contrast at all between the view favored here by Meeks and Barclay of the Pauline communities in Corinth and elsewhere and Stowers's point that Pauline Christianity resembles a Hellenistic philosophy. Even if the Pauline communities saw themselves, and were seen by Paul, as consisting of "resident aliens" (Meeks) on the analogy of those Jewish Diaspora communities with which they were most closely comparable (Barclay), they might also very well share fundamental structural features of the kind that Stowers identifies with the Hellenistic philosophies. For to begin with, at least, that is an etic observation. But furthermore, even though they probably would not see themselves from the emic inside as just another philosophy, they might well have adopted a range of social practices that they would themselves also have known from the contemporary philosophers and indeed have recognized as such if pressed. Loveday Alexander and Stowers abundantly demonstrate that point. Similarly, as I would claim, Paul himself might very well have made extensive use of ideas and practices that he knew from the philosophers without thereby in any way changing the fact that in his identification of himself and his groups, he would invariably stress difference in the manner explained by Barclay.

The Historical Facts and Paul's Perception of Them

Two fundamental viewpoints stand out in what has been said up to now. Viewed etically from an outside historical perspective, in his use of ideas and his social practices Paul ranges freely across any supposed invisible boundaries. Scholarship should honor this fact and adopt a corresponding perspective on him from beyond the Judaism/Hellenism divide. In Philip Alexander's memorable phrase, "we need an intellectual paradigm shift so that the presumption now is always in favor of similarity rather than dissimilarity." Viewed from the emic inside, Paul constantly employs a discourse of difference that persists despite obvious similarities with outsiders in moral norms and social practices. As Barclay said, "Christians had to be made to *feel* different even when they were doing exactly the same as everyone else." No inconsistency exists here, and Meeks is right to identify the suspicion of inconsistency as a false paradox. The Christian groups were most Jewish when they were most Hellenistic. To put the point in a different way, the etic perspective on Paul demands that his emic stress on difference be fully acknowledged.

This complex picture is true not only of Paul, but of many others. Philo is a good example. Another is Josephus, whom Barclay describes as a Diaspora-resident Jew whose loyalty to his Jewish tradition is expressed precisely in his creative use of an ancient Greek tradition, that of political philosophy. In Paul's case, however, an elusive extra dimension is added to the picture due to the fact that as a missionary to Gentiles of a message about a Jewish Messiah, Paul saw himself not just as a loyal Jew (he certainly thought of himself as that), but as one who struck an itinerary intended to lead to some place beyond a divide between Hellenism (certainly that) *and* Judaism as that would normally be identified from the outside (as tied to the law and certain specific practices). Paul, according to Barclay, was a "Diaspora-resident Jew whose social policy . . . *differs* from Josephus's at that point where he strives to enable a community of both Jew and Gentile, and attempts to forge them together into a new and culturally indeterminate (or at least, underdetermined) 'church'" (my emphasis).

This extra dimension is particularly elusive since it has clear contacts with all kinds of traditional, theological elaborations of how Christianity superseded anything in its cultural context, Judaism no less than Hellenism. Still, the dimension is there, and it must be acknowledged in any full account of Paul. As Loveday Alexander observes, "For Nock's Greek or Roman onlooker, . . . the cultural authorities Paul appeals to would be sufficient to identify him as 'Jewish.' But for Paul himself, to reduce the rhetoric of the gospel to a choice between Judaism and Hellenism would be to trivialize it. For him (here as elsewhere) the really profound questions can be asked equally within either cultural system, and their resolution must be sought 'beyond' rather than 'between' the two cultural flavors that dominate his world."

Once this dimension has been acknowledged, an interesting issue arises of Paul's own attitude at a somewhat less exalted, more down-to-earth level towards what he perceived as the two cultural flavors of his world. As hinted above, Paul was overwhelmingly positive (if that is the word) towards his own Judean heritage. Did he therefore distance himself specifically from Hellenism so that there is an imbalance in his own view of the two cultural flavors? This issue is not raised in the essays of this volume, but is worth exploring. A proper discussion would require some further definitional clarification. Still, a reasonable hypothesis is that whereas in some areas—for instance, the view of God—Paul would see a clear imbalance between the two poles, in many others he would be well aware that his argument was for a radicalizing extension of something also to be found both in his own Judaism *and* in non-Jewish Hellenism.

To give a single, intriguing example, in 1 Corinthians 1–2 Paul balances a contrast of his own *logos tou staurou* (word of the cross) as an expression of God's power and wisdom with both a Jewish perception of it as weakness and a Greek one as foolishness. Paul then proceeds to show in an equally balanced way how his initial preaching in weakness to the Corinthians was taken by them as a sign of power—and how to perfect Christ-believers the content of that preaching will also appear as a genuine case of wisdom. Such wisdom is evidently Greek wisdom transformed. But so is the power of the gospel God's Jewish power transformed. If one asks about Paul's own perception of the status of the two basic cultural forces within which he saw himself as operating, such a passage suggests that Paul himself fully recognized the cultural aspirations (if certainly not the actual performance) of *both*.

The Book's Organization

At the 1997 conference on which the volume is based, the aim was to focus on two comprehensive issues: that of Judaism versus Hellenism and that of religion versus ethics. In either case the focus was furthermore intended to be specifically on Paul's Corinthian correspondence.

To achieve maximum profile, the present volume concentrates on only the first and third foci. As such, the book falls into three parts. A first group of essays (by Meeks, Martin, and Philip Alexander) addresses the metareflective issue of how to handle the supposed Judaism/Hellenism divide. A second group shows how a focus on social history can overcome the divide. In this group, two essays (by Stowers and Loveday Alexander) range broadly over the Pauline letters, whereas two others (by Meeks again and Barclay) narrow the focus to the Corinthian correspondence. The third and final group (by Tronier, Mitchell, Aune, and Fitzgerald) shows how to overcome the Judaism/Hellenism divide in focusing on ideas and specific texts in the two letters to the Corinthians. The order of these four essays follows that of the two letters themselves, but they are not to be read merely as specimens of exegesis of specific passages. They are case studies intended to illustrate the wider issues identified in this introductory essay.

Thus the volume as a whole is not simply conference proceedings. All essays have gone back and forth several times between the editor and the contributors. In many cases the essays have undergone extensive changes since they were first presented. Also, some essays were not presented (or not at all in that form) at the conference. Meeks's first essay in this volume was given as a Term Inaugural Speech at Copenhagen University just after the conference. Philip Alexander's essay grew out of a much shorter response to Dale Martin's original paper. Stanley Stowers's essay was also originally a response, given in a quite different form, to Loveday Alexander's paper. Finally, John Fitzgerald's essay was especially commissioned after the conference.

The editor thanks all contributors for having put so much effort into producing a coherent and highly profiled volume.

Acknowledgments

The following scholars and research students from the United States, Canada, Great Britain, Belgium, Germany, and the Nordic countries attended the conference: Anneli Aejmelaeus (Göttingen), Lars Aejmelaeus (Helsinki), Loveday Alexander (Sheffield), Philip S. Alexander (Manchester), David E. Aune (Notre Dame), John M. G. Barclay (Glasgow), Hans Dieter Betz (Chicago), Lars Kjær Bruun (Aarhus), Gitte Buch-Hansen (Copenhagen), Samuel Byrskog (Göteborg), Ellen Juhl Christiansen (Aarhus), Anders Eriksson (Lund), Lone Fatum (Copenhagen), Clarence E. Glad (Reykjavik), Alexsandar Gusa (Copenhagen), Geert Hallbäck (Copenhagen), Lars Hartman (Uppsala), David Hellholm (Oslo), Sven Hillert (Uppsala), Birgitte Graakjær Hjort (Aarhus), Jonas Holmstrand (Uppsala), Gertrud Iversen (Copenhagen), Fredrik Lindgård (Helsinki), Dale B. Martin (Yale), Wayne A. Meeks (Yale), Margaret M. Mitchell (Chicago), Dieter Mitternacht (Lund), Halvor Moxnes (Oslo), Karl-Wilhelm Niebuhr (Jena), Johannes Nissen (Aarhus), Anders Klostergaard Petersen (Aarhus), John K. Riches (Glasgow), Lars Rydbeck (Lund), Turid Karlsen Seim (Oslo), James M. Starr (Lund), Stanley K. Stowers (Brown), Lauri Thurén (Aabo), Peter J. Tomson (Brussels), Henrik Tronier (Copenhagen), Leif E. Vaage (Toronto), Tor Vegge (Kristiansand, Norway), Erik Waaler (Bergen), and Reidar Aasgaard (Oslo).

Thanks also go to a number of foundations that contributed to the realization of the conference and indirectly therefore also of the present volume. G. E. C. Gad's Foundation (Copenhagen) came first. Next the Danish Research Council for the Humanities supported the conference very generously, as did the Nordic Academy for Advanced Study (under the Nordic Council of Ministers). It is to the great credit of these two major foundations that they helped in the first place to bring together a group of renowned Pauline scholars from the northern hemisphere. In this way they have also helped to consolidate through this volume a new scholarly approach to the study of Paul that has long been overdue.

Chapter 1

Judaism, Hellenism, and the Birth of Christianity

Wayne A. Meeks

Among those who have been baptized into Christ, wrote the apostle Paul, "there is neither Jew nor Greek" (Gal 3:28). Modern scholars have not believed him. For the past two centuries historians have been preoccupied with the question just how much of early Christianity is Jewish, how much of it is Greek, and what is the peculiar interaction between these two cultures, which are habitually taken as opposites. Here is a typical remark, by one of our leading scholars, from a standard reference work: "Christianity . . . became the intellectual and spiritual battleground on which the confrontation between Judaism and Hellenism was fought with unprecedented intensity."[1]

Why must it be assumed that when Judaism and Hellenism meet, it must be on a battleground? There are several reasons. One has to do with ancient history; the rest, rather more elusive, belong to the history of modern scholarship. The ancient events affecting our picture of Judaism confronting Hellenism are recounted in the books that we know as 1 and 2 Maccabees and, more cryptically, in the book of Daniel. The traditional reading of these stories is that the wicked king of Syria, Antiochus IV Epiphanes, undertook to destroy the religion of the Jews because it stood in the way of his grand program, as a true successor of Alexander the Great, to "Hellenize" his entire empire. This attempt at forced assimilation to Greek culture was prevented only by the heroic resistance of a family of rural priests, the Hasmoneans or Maccabees, who became guerrilla fighters.

As a matter of fact, the late Elias Bickerman showed many years ago that this description of the crisis depends on a credulous acceptance of propaganda from both the Syrian court and the adherents to the Hasmonean dynasty. In reality the issues were far more complicated, having more to do with internal tensions in the Jerusalem community than with Antiochus's ideology. The subsequent work of Viktor Tcherikover, Martin Hengel, John J. Collins, and others further complicated the historical picture and substantially undercut the traditional "Hellenism vs. Judaism" model.[2] For example, the books of the Maccabees are all in Greek, and the priestly state set up by the Hasmoneans when they succeeded, with Roman help, in freeing Jerusalem from direct Seleucid rule, was very like a typical Hellenistic microkingdom. The tract known as 4 Maccabees, which celebrates rather gruesomely the martyrdom of a family in the struggle, is a typical example of a well-known Greco-Roman genre, the Philosopher Resists Tyranny. Nevertheless, despite all these reasons for doubting the traditional picture, that picture endures and colors the way we think about subsequent Jewish adaptations to the dominant imperial culture.

The Tübingen School

The most influential application of this battlefield model to the history of earliest Christianity came just about 150 years ago, when a professor of Protestant theology at the University of Tübingen began trying to discover the underlying logic behind the various factions that appear in the New Testament, especially in the polemics of some of Paul's letters. The professor was Ferdinand Christian Baur. His proposals caused an uproar, but the Tübingen school, as his followers were called, profoundly altered the way modern scholarship conceived of the evolution of early Christianity. Baur found the key in the story told in Acts 6 about a controversy that arose between "the Hellenists" and "the Hebrews" among the Christians in Jerusalem over distribution of a dole for widows. Taking further clues from the speech attributed in Acts 7 to one of the leaders of the Hellenists, Baur proposed that the difference was not just a squabble over money, but was rather one of fundamental theology. On the one side was the original "Jewish-Christian" community led by Jesus' immediate apostles and his brother James. On the other side were "Hellenized" Jews who had a vision of a universal religion breaking through the boundaries of Judaism in a mission to Gentiles. Of the latter group the apostle Paul, after his conversion, was destined to be the leader. The conflict between these two groups, which Baur saw mirrored in Paul's chief letters, especially Galatians and 2 Corinthians, determined the development of the new religion. Baur made his discoveries just as Hegel's philosophy was becoming the rage in theological circles; it was easy for him to see "Judaism" or "Jewish Christianity" as the thesis that provoked among Jesus' more enlightened followers, and especially and uniquely the apostle Paul, the antithesis "Gentile Christianity." Efforts to resolve the conflict would eventually produce, as the synthesis, "early Catholicism."[3]

The ingenuity of the scheme is apparent. "Judaism" and "Hellenism" here are obviously code words for complex sets of ideas masquerading as historical entities. On the one side is the particularity of a national or ethnic religion; on the other side resides the universal religion for all humankind. On the one hand are the limited and conditioned facts of historical circumstance; on the other, the universal truths of reason. On the one hand flesh; on the other spirit. On the one hand "legalism"; on the other freedom. As Baur in one place could put it quite bluntly, "Judaism is nothing more than the religion of the law in contradistinction to Christianity, which is the religion of the spirit."[4]

Several things are going on here. The parody of Judaism assumed in Baur's schema is not simply direct anti-Semitism, though it has a great deal to do with the intellectual soil within which German anti-Semitism flourished. Rather, Baur's is an almost naive theological anti-Judaism. Its roots are in the *adversus Ioudaeos* literature of the ancient church, which of course looks much uglier when transposed from a minority group that sees itself under attack into a triumphant church backed by imperial power. But this traditional and originally defensive anti-Judaism had been transformed especially in Germany by the Reformation. Luther had identified his struggle against the laws of the church and hierarchical control by the papacy with Paul's campaign against "the Law" of his Jewish-Christian opponents. For a Baur, "Jewish legalism" stood not only for what was supposed to be characteristic of rabbinic Judaism through the ages, not only for Catholic ritualism and institutional authoritarianism, but also for Protestant scholasticism in his own tradition.[5]

"Hellenism," at the same time, clearly does not refer simply to the specific institutional and cultural forms that emerged in the eastern

Mediterranean world after Alexander the Great; the term is not "merely a convenient label for the civilisation of the three centuries during which Greek culture radiated far from the homeland."[6] Rather, it refers to certain principles of rationality and individualism that are taken to be characteristic of the philosophical and literary tradition of classical Greece, especially perhaps of Platonism. It was J. G. Droysen, a younger contemporary of Baur, who adopted the term *Hellenismus* for what he described as the beginning point of "the history of history," the epoch of Alexander and the Diadochoi. Informed by the use of the Greek word in 2 Macc 4:13 and, like Baur, the report of the dispute of the "Hellenists" in Acts 6:1—and also, again like Baur, indebted to Hegel's dialectical theory of history—Droysen saw in the confrontation between Judaism and paganism in the Hellenistic world "the last and deepest opposition." That opposition—not only between "Western" and "Oriental" civilizations, but also between the solidarity of human experience inscribed in tradition and the liberating but corrosive powers of reason—must be reconciled if the "history of human freedom" were ever to come to fruition. That reconciliation, Droysen asserted, was the task given by history to Christianity.[7]

The History of Religions

For another important group of scholars in the early decades of this century, "Hellenism" did not mean either the classical tradition or the "entzweite Welt" of Droysen's *Hellenismus*, but precisely the *syncretism* that characterized the culture of the successor kingdoms after Alexander and also the provinces of the Roman principate. These scholars belonged to the so-called "history of religions school," which began in the 1890s with a group of colleagues in the theological faculty at Göttingen.[8] For them neither the biblical and legal tradition of Israel nor the intellectual culture of classical Greece provided the best clues for understanding the rise of Christianity, but the influence in both the Jewish and the pagan worlds of "oriental" influences in the sphere of religion. What seemed typical of the Judaism out of which Christianity arose was apocalypticism, with its myths of cosmic warfare and its expectations of an immediate, cataclysmic transformation of the world. On the Hellenistic side, attention focused on the initiatory mystery religions that flourished in the Hellenistic and Roman periods, and on Gnosticism, which was now taken to be a pre-Christian religious movement sharing many of the sensibilities of the mysteries.

What the history of religions school had in common with the Tübingen school was an evolutionary perspective. Proponents tended to identify the phases in the development of Christianity with its expansion into successive geographical spheres, each with its own culture, beginning with the purely Jewish circle of the earliest Jesus movement and ending with the wide world of syncretistic Hellenism, with several intermediary steps. So Christianity was transformed from an apocalyptic sect of Judaism into a cultic mystery of Hellenism. The most important names in shaping this perspective, in the field of New Testament studies, were Wilhelm Heitmüller, Wilhelm Bousset, and Rudolf Bultmann.[9]

The claims of the history of religions school were profoundly threatening to many theologians. Now some of the most central values and institutions of the Christian religion—the sacraments, the concept of salvation, the representation of Jesus as a divine being, and even many of the stories of Jesus in the Gospels—were said to be additions to the "primitive" stock of Christian beliefs under the influence of Hellenistic syncretism.

Reaction

Not surprisingly, many students of early Christianity recoiled from the more radical proposals of the history of religions school. It is interesting that often those who reacted against the picture of Christianity as an example of Hellenistic syncretism accepted the cultural dichotomy on which that picture was based, but chose the opposite pole. *Real* Christianity, they urged, was thoroughly *Jewish*, not Hellenistic at all or Hellenized only in its outer forms or later corruptions. Among Christian scholars a new interest arose in the study of the sources and history of ancient Judaism—known in Germany as "*late* Judaism," the name embodying the common supersessionist perspective of most Christian theology of the day. The aim of this scholarship was to demonstrate the distinctiveness of Christianity against its pagan environment, which meant the distinctiveness it shared with ancient Israel, while at the same time to demonstrate that Christianity climaxed and fulfilled what was true in Judaism. The latter theme, of course, had been familiar since the apologies of the second century of the common era. The titles of two popular books from the "biblical theology" movement of a generation ago illustrate the point of view nicely: *The Old Testament Against Its Environment* and *The New Testament Against Its Environment.* Just as Israel was seen to be unique in comparison with the other peoples of the Ancient Near East, so early Christianity was found to be unique among the religions of the Roman Empire.[10]

This uniqueness could be construed in a couple of different ways, depending on what one took to be the characteristic form of Judaism from which Christianity emerged. Some scholars shared with members of the history of religions school the conviction that it was Jewish *apocalypticism* that gave birth to Jesus' vision of the kingdom of God and that his followers constituted an apocalyptic Jewish sect. In the English-speaking world, one of the great pioneers in the study of apocalyptic literature was the learned Canon and later Archdeacon of Westminster, Robert Henry Charles. As Charles saw Israel's history, all the creative energies that before the Babylonian Exile were expressed through the great prophets were in later centuries channeled into the new medium of apocalyptic visions. Apocalyptic differed from prophecy, however. "Whereas the scope of prophecy was limited, as regards time and space, that of apocalyptic was as wide as the universe and as unlimited as time."[11]

Thus, the "universalism" that Baur and his successors had found in the *Hellenistic* side of early Christianity Charles discovered within Judaism in the form of apocalypticism. Of course, this universal scope was taken as the antithesis of the "legalism" that Protestant scholars saw in other forms of Judaism: "the apocalyptic and the legalistic [forms of Pharisaism in pre-Christian Judaism] . . . were the historical forerunners respectively of Christianity and of Talmudic Judaism."[12]

Not everyone, however, found apocalypticism so attractive or the apocalyptic lineage of early Christianity so convincing. George Foot Moore, the great professor of the history of religions at Harvard from 1904 until 1921, directly challenged the viewpoint that Charles represented. In an important article published in 1921, Moore, himself a Presbyterian minister, castigated "Christian Writers on Judaism" for their blinkered histories, in which "Judaism serves as a background, an environment, and often, with a more or less conscious apologetic motive, as a contrast" to the beginnings of Christianity.[13]

It was those peculiarly Christian motives, along with the excitement of new discoveries, that led, Moore believed, to the emphasis on the apocalypses as sources for first-century Judaism. Moore insisted that, "inasmuch as these writings have never been recognized by Judaism, it is a fallacy of method for the historian to make them a primary source for the eschatology of Judaism, much more to contaminate its theology with them." Instead, "the primacy is properly given to those sources which are recognized by the religion itself as authentic."[14] "Those sources" meant the foundational documents of rabbinic Judaism, particularly the Mishnah, the two Talmuds, and the halakhic midrashim. For Moore, only the Judaism defined by those sources had any claim to be regarded as the "normative type of Judaism." Moore had several names for this mainstream Judaism, including "authentic," "normal," and "catholic," but the name that stuck was "normative Judaism."

Complicating the Picture

Space does not suffice for me even to mention the many variations of the Judaism-vs.-Hellenism theme that have appeared since the days of Charles, Moore, and the German historians of religions. Until quite recently most students of early Christianity continued to imagine a cultural chasm between Judaism and Hellenism, but the map of the country on either side of the chasm became more and more complicated. Today the chasm looks more like a wavering line drawn artificially and misleadingly across one huge and variegated map. Several things have happened to break up the old schemas. I will mention briefly examples of developments that have changed our picture of Judaism in antiquity, developments that have changed our picture of Hellenism, and new developments in our understanding of early Christian history.

Unnormative Judaisms

Moore's attempt to lead Christian scholars to study the normative sources of rabbinic Judaism in their own right and their own contexts was laudable and had profoundly helpful effects on later scholarship—though his advice was ignored by far too many. Nevertheless, his category "normative Judaism" could not survive a series of striking new discoveries and new ways of studying the evidence. Take, for example, the eccentric but important work of Erwin R. Goodenough, one of my teachers at Yale. Goodenough, a student of Moore, accepted the latter's "normative Judaism" category, but set out to show that it must have been some utterly different kind of Judaism that gave birth to the Christianity that was destined to become the religion of Constantine. It could only be, Goodenough reasoned, a Hellenistic, and indeed a "mystical" kind of Judaism. Goodenough found evidence for that kind of Judaism in several literary sources, especially in the writings of Philo of Alexandria. His most enduring contribution, however, was his collection of Jewish art. "Jewish art," of course, seemed from the point of view of normative Judaism a contradiction in terms: Jews were forbidden to make any "graven images." The discovery in 1932 of the great synagogue in Dura Europos suddenly revealed that some Jews in the Roman world understood that commandment quite differently. The dramatic paintings that covered every inch of the walls of the synagogue's assembly room confirmed Goodenough's hunch that had earlier started him collecting Jewish art; his eventual publication of thirteen large volumes of *Jewish Symbols in the Greco-Roman World* silenced critics who had scoffed at his project. By the time its last volumes appeared, synagogues even in Palestine had been found with floor mosaics portraying human and mythical figures. Other archaeological and inscriptional evidence as well, accumulating from points all over the Mediterranean basin, showed that Jewish interactions with their "pagan" environment were often of a sort that would have made the "normative" rabbis most unhappy. Normative Judaism was apparently not in fact normative in a practical sense in the time of the earliest growth of Christianity.[15]

The development of historical-critical study of rabbinic texts went further to suggest that the normative category could not be used as a descriptive category of Judaism in the first two centuries of our era. The American pioneer in this field was Jacob Neusner, whose prodigious productivity and fierce polemics provoked a radical reassessment of the traditional sources—the very sources to which Moore had directed attention. Ironically, Neusner began by adapting just the techniques of synoptic comparison, form criticism, and redaction criticism that had been so successful in the Bultmann school of New Testament studies—a school that had often proved most tone deaf in the use of Jewish sources. More and more scholars began to accept Neusner's argument that the reinstitutionalization of Judaism that constituted the rabbinic movement came about as a reaction to the failure of the two great revolts of the Judeans against the Romans, most decisively the second one led by Bar Kochba in 132–135 C.E. The rabbinic revolution was too late to explain what Judaism was like when Christianity was born.[16]

The Judaism at the time of Jesus began to look like a quite diverse family of ways of adapting the traditions of Israel to the Greco-Roman world. The bombshell discovery of the Dead Sea Scrolls in 1947 galvanized many people into recognizing this elementary fact that a few scholars had already intimated. This sect was as "apocalyptic" as any R. H. Charles could imagine, as it awaited the final "War of the Sons of Light with the Sons of Darkness" as the "community of the New Covenant" organized to live in "the end of days." At the same time, this sect defined its existence by detailed legal regulations—the opposite pole from apocalyptic in Charles's dichotomy. Furthermore, this sect reminded students in many ways of early Christianity itself: it seemed almost an older sibling.[17]

To make matters more confused, studies of language usage, trading patterns, political institutions, and other elements began to suggest to more and more scholars that Judea and the Galilee were far from being pure Jewish islands in a sea of Hellenism. Even the Maccabee revolt and its aftermath came more and more to look not like the ultimate defense of Judaism from Hellenism, but like a continuing struggle between different ways of adapting to Hellenism. Driven by the detailed and often polemical studies of such scholars as Morton Smith and Martin Hengel, the paradigms of scholarship gradually shifted to a recognition that, as Smith once wrote, "Palestine in the first century was profoundly Hellenized." The boundary between "Judaism" and "Hellenism" was not geographical. Indeed, "Judaism" was in some senses a Hellenistic religion.[18]

What Is "Hellenism"?

Events were occurring on the other side of the great divide as well. One of the persisting problems had been, as we have seen, vagueness about just what one meant by the word "Hellenism." Though for some historians the term was an epoch-marker in political history, as far as the study of early Christianity was concerned, "Hellenism" was a category of the history of ideas. This was true even of the history of religions school, despite its ostensible interest in ritual and myth. Since World War II, however, changes in historical fashion have brought significant new perspectives to the study of the time between Alexander and the decline of Rome. Building upon the pioneering labors of Mihail Rostovtseff and taking advantage of a vast and growing corpus of inscriptions, papyri, and archaeological finds, Roman social history became a robust discipline, turning our attention from the tiny elites of political and intellectual history to inquire about the world experienced by the other 99 percent of the population.[19] As we came to know more about the accelerating travels of diverse individuals and the migrations of peoples in the Roman era, we came to see the Diaspora of the Jews as no longer peculiar—however many distinctive features it might have—but part of a much broader phenomenon. To perceive what was special about the varieties of Jewish adaptation to this larger world now requires a much more concrete imagination.

Imagining the Early Christians

Grand schemes like the Tübingen School's Hegelian diagram of Christianity's evolution have enormous power to focus our attention and to call forth creative explorations. As we have seen, however, they also tempt us to gloss over contrary evidence and lull us sometimes into thinking we have understood when we have only classified. By contrast, we are presently in an era of atomistic scholarship. Many would-be paradigms contend, but none has the scope or perhaps the drama to mobilize troops of scholars. This may not be so bad. The best work being done today paints on a fairly small canvas, paying lots of attention to detail. On the other hand, much is busy work that lacks clear direction, just as some clear directions are palpably silly. Perhaps some new master paradigm will emerge and will run its time until it fossilizes, too, and has to be demolished by a later generation. In the meantime, a few things can be said about what we now think we know regarding the emergence of Christianity in the Greco-Roman world.

Christianity began its existence as one among several competing Jewish sects or movements. Judaism was not one thing, either in Judea and Galilee or in the Diaspora, nor were the boundaries among the varieties of Judaism fixed or impermeable. Not surprisingly, then, we see variety also in early Christian groups, from the earliest moment we can detect their character in our sources. The adjectives "Jewish" and "Hellenistic" are practically no help at all in sorting out that variety.

Like the other varieties of Judaism, the earliest Christian groups were simultaneously Jewish and Hellenistic. The questions that have to be asked are more particular: Which parts of the Jewish tradition were being assumed and reinterpreted by this or that group of early Christians? Which institutions were continued, which discarded? From the side of the larger society, what signs are there in a given Christian document that the author was employing a *topos* from the philosophical schools or a verbal strategy taught in the rhetorical schools? Or would a certain turn of phrase have reminded the hearers of commonplaces that we can learn at second hand from the magical spells and handbooks that have turned up in such abundance? Again and again we find that the more broadly we cast our nets, the more interpretive fish we bring up. Most people in antiquity, we must surmise, did not know that they were supposed to stay firmly in one or another of our ideal types.

The parade example, of course, is the apostle Paul, key player on the Hellenistic team for the Tübingen school and center of controversy in modern scholarship as in ancient polemics. "A Hebrew born of Hebrews," he tells us himself, "as to the law a Pharisee." Yet he wrote only and fluently in Greek. His rhetoric was peculiarly his own, and certainly not that of the new Atticistic high style that was just beginning to come into fashion. Nevertheless recent work by New Testament scholars who have immersed themselves in the Greco-Roman rhetoric of Paul's time—especially the students of Abraham Malherbe of Yale, of Hans Dieter Betz of Chicago, also of George Kennedy of Chapel Hill—has demonstrated that

Paul made recognizable, sophisticated, and original use of the strategies common to the orators. Some of these scholars and others are also making a strong case that Paul was more aware of the specifically philosophical school discussions of his day than we had previously guessed. Yet it is impossible to ignore the fact that frequently he also employs interpretive strategies and traditions of reading the Jewish scriptures that are strikingly like those found in earlier and later Jewish interpretations, both sectarian and rabbinic. Impossible, too, to erase the typically apocalyptic scenarios that intrude into Paul's argument, even in places where he is sounding most "Hellenistic" or "rabbinic." He was, it seems, all these things at once. However unique an individual Paul doubtless was, in this easy mixing of things that have seemed to us unmixable types, perhaps he was not so unusual.

Chapter 2

Paul and the Judaism/ Hellenism Dichotomy: Toward a Social History of the Question

Dale B. Martin

Twice in the opening paragraph of his monumental study *Judaism and Hellenism*, Martin Hengel suggested that the dualism he had chosen to study was unavoidable ("diese unvermeidliche Unterscheidung," "unumgänglichen Differenzierungen," both rendered as "unavoidable" in the English translation).[*][1] Though I had read over the paragraph many times, only recently did I realize how odd that claim really is. For not only is the Hellenism/Judaism dichotomy avoidable, the formulation itself is actually rather odd. In the first place, each side of the dualism contains its own

[*] Many people have provided help and suggestions toward the improvement of this paper. First, I am indebted to the different participants at the Danish conference at which a version of the paper was read, especially Troels Engberg-Pedersen and Philip Alexander. I owe thanks also to Kalman Bland, Bart Ehrman, Susannah Heschel, Andrew Jacobs, Hayim Lapin, Halvor Moxnes, and the "Late Ancient Studies Reading Group" of Duke University and the University of North Carolina at Chapel Hill for reading and commenting on the paper.

problems of definition. Today, most scholars of antiquity admit that both Hellenism and Judaism in the ancient world present important and irreducible complexities. Virtually anything related even remotely to Greek language and culture in the eastern Mediterranean from the time of Alexander to the time of Constantine could be classified as "Hellenism," and anything a Jew said, did, or believed could be taken as a form of Judaism. And since most scholars nowadays agree that all Judaism of the ancient world that would have had anything to do with early Christianity was already Hellenized, and that all forms of Greek culture in the same period had been influenced by "oriental" cultures, to ask whether something is Hellenistic *or* Jewish would seem to be a misleading question.[2]

Furthermore, the dualism leaves out too much. None of us would claim that these were the only two cultures in the eastern Mediterranean. What about, for instance, Syrian culture? After all, Paul did not come from Greece or Rome, but from Cilicia and Syria. Was nothing left of older (indigenous?) cultural elements in Tarsus, Antioch, or Damascus? It is possible that Paul understood, if not spoke, Aramaic.[3] Need we be reminded that Aramaic did not completely share the cultural history of Hebrew? And what about Rome? If Paul really was a Roman citizen, as many scholars believe, surely we should take Roman culture as important. In fact, I can think of several issues related to Pauline Christianity that should probably be pursued more in light of Roman than Greek "backgrounds," such as: slavery and its metaphors; the patron-client structure; household structures and symbols; roles of women and their access to public life; the imperial cult along with its ideology and public presence; and, indeed, the symbols of empire itself. Asking questions about "Hellenism or Judaism" either ignores Roman, not to speak of other, cultural factors, or collapses them into "Hellenism" in a way our more careful classicist colleagues would never do.

Finally, the dualism misleads by implying symmetry where none exists. No one in the ancient world, at least before Christianity, would have taken Judaism to be the "other" in a dualistic relationship with Hellenism or Greek culture—no one, that is, except maybe a Jew. Such a dichotomy would have been seen by others as crazy arrogance or wishful thinking. Jews were seen as one *ethnos*, like Lydians, Carians, Egyptians, Persians, and Scythians. They might have their own language, ancestral customs, peculiar practices, and religious rites. But already by the time of Jesus, Hellenism was considered by many people—certainly Greeks but other educated persons as well—to have transcended those smaller, ethnic boundaries. Hellenism was taken to refer to something like what the Germans would later call *Bildung*. A symmetry between Hellenism and

Judaism becomes conceivable only in late antiquity, when Christianity had itself attained a hegemonic position and *Christian* writers (appropriating earlier Jewish elite rhetoric) set up Hellenism and Judaism in a dualistic relationship—of course, only then to argue that Christianity had superseded both. But for the time of Paul, to imply that Judaism was in a symmetrical relationship with Hellenism is bad history.

So good reasons abound to avoid the dualism of Hellenism/Judaism. Perhaps, therefore, we should not be surprised when we realize that, in spite of Hengel's sense that the question is unavoidable, people had for centuries quite successfully avoided it. Up until nineteenth-century Germany, in fact, no one ever posited a dichotomy between Hellenic and Judaic culture or "mentalities" and then wondered how much each had influenced the content of Christianity or the thought of Paul. True, there were what we might think of as precursors to the question. Tertullian famously opposed Athens to Jerusalem, and his words have sometimes been quoted to portray the opposition of Greek to Jewish culture.[4] But such application misrepresents the function of the opposition in Tertullian's own rhetoric. The context makes it clear that Tertullian was opposing not Hellenism to Judaism, but Greek philosophy to Christian doctrine. As he says, "What does Athens have to do with Jerusalem? What does the Academy have to do with the Church? What do heretics have to do with Christians?" (*De praescriptione haereticorum* 7). This is one instance of Tertullian's famous denigration of Greek philosophy. Athens for Tertullian does not represent Greece as a whole, or Greek religion, or what we would call Greek or Hellenistic culture. Rather, Athens represents "human wisdom" as opposed to "simplicity of heart" or pristine Christian teaching. According to Tertullian, the philosophers are the "fathers of all heresy," and all heresies are traceable back to some particular philosophy.[5] Thus there is no Hellenism/Judaism dichotomy in Tertullian. For him, Athens stands for Greek philosophy and "human wisdom," and "Jerusalem," at least in this famous quotation, represents Christian faith uncorrupted by the sophistication of speculation and learning.

As I remarked above, some Christian intellectuals took over previous Jewish apologetics that opposed Judaism to Hellenism. Eusebius, in his *Preparation for the Gospel*, insists that Christianity is "neither Hellenism nor Judaism, but a new and true kind of divine philosophy, bringing evidence of its novelty from its very name" (1.5.16d). Generally for Eusebius, Hellenism stands for both Greek popular religion—which he sometimes terms "worship of the gods" or often more derisively *deisidaimonia* ("superstition")—and Greek philosophy with its, in his mind, bankrupt, "naturalistic" interpretations of the myths (see, e.g., 1.6.18b). Greek popular religious practices can stand in for all polytheism, according to Eusebius, because the Greeks had appropriated it all from other peoples anyway. Christianity is superior to Hellenism because it rejects idolatrous religion ("superstition"), and superior to Judaism because it rejects the Jewish "manner of living." Thus, we might see Eusebius as positing a "third way" between Judaism and Hellenism, a way identified with Christianity. But Eusebius's arguments have little in common with the modern debate about Hellenism and Judaism. For one thing, Eusebius is explicitly concerned about the worship of god or gods and the different ways different peoples do so—what Romans would call *religio* and Greeks would have designated by several different terms such as *eusebeia* or the *therapeia* or *latreia* of the gods. He does not mean the sort of wider category that we today call "culture." Furthermore, he is not interested in "influences." Eusebius is arguing that Christianity is neither Hellenism nor Judaism, but that it contains the best parts of both: it is the true "philosophy" on the one hand and the true faith of the Hebrew patriarchs on the other. If influence is to be considered at all, it is Christianity that has influenced both Hellenism and Judaism.

More ancient examples could be given, but these are enough to make my point: the question that seemed unavoidable for Hengel in the 1960s is eminently avoidable. But perhaps it *wasn't* avoidable to him at that time. It is the purpose of this essay to ask why—and to mark a tentative beginning toward historicizing the question itself.

Germany in the Nineteenth and Twentieth Centuries

As Wayne Meeks has remarked, our issue is related to the nineteenth-century question about the development of Christianity as a historical phenomenon: How did a movement deriving from Jewish followers of a Jewish teacher become "Hellenized"? This is "a distinctly post-Enlightenment question."[6] All histories of scholarship on the question give a central role to the writings and influence of Ferdinand Christian Baur (1792–1860). As Meeks notes, "In this discussion 'Jewish' became virtually a code word for 'particular,' 'limited,' 'historically conditioned,' while 'Greek' came to mean 'universal,' 'rational,' and 'ideal.'"[7] In order to appreciate the importance of historical context for Baur's biblical scholarship, though, it is important to pay close attention to his rhetoric.

In his *Paul the Apostle of Jesus Christ*, published in 1845 but incorporating essays originally published in 1835 and 1836, Baur begins with the problem of how a universal Christianity developed from the particularism of the Jewish nation.[8] Paul is the one most responsible for this development, though the Hellenists among the early Jewish Christians, as mentioned in the Acts of the Apostles, prepared the way.[9] Baur spends much of his book arguing that Acts is not historically reliable for the reconstruction of Pauline Christianity. Here we see his tendency, shared with his student D. F. Strauss (1809–1874), A. Schweitzer much later, and almost all scholars, it seems, of the nineteenth century, to pose problems in terms of either/or dualisms. As Strauss had insisted that one must choose either the Gospel of John or the Synoptics, so Baur insists that one must choose either Acts or Paul's letters on which to base any historical reconstruction.[10]

Baur's tendency toward dichotomies gives form to his historical account. The division between Hellenism and Judaism, though, is not between Greeks and Jews, but between Hellenistic Jews and Jewish Jews, the Hellenistic followers of Jesus on the one side and the "Mother Church of Jerusalem," or the "old cramping forms of Judaism," on the other (58–60). In the end, the important dichotomy will be between Pauline Christianity and Jewish Christianity (120). The most important characteristic difference is between Christianity, which is Hellenistic, universal, and spiritual, and Judaism, which is a particular race and nation characterized by limitation and legalism.[11]

Baur's ideas were expanded in his 1860 work *The Church History of the First Three Centuries*.[12] Baur reiterates his theory that the Hellenists in the early Jesus movement gave birth to Gentile Christianity, but he also explains why that development was inevitable after the death of Jesus. Jewish messianic ideas are, he says, "national ideas." A Messiah who has died and "been transfigured to a higher life" is not possible in "the limitations of Judaism." Jesus' death and elevation ran counter to "Jewish national consciousness" and could not be accepted by "the Jewish nation." That Christianity, after the death of Jesus, should transcend "the particularism of Judaism" was inevitable (48).

Part of the problem with Jewish particularism lay in its identity as a "nation," which in the nineteenth century carried connotations of both the nation-state and race. Christianity, however, cannot be identified with any particular race or nation, being spiritual and universal. Unfortunately, Jesus, as a Jew, had contained within himself this dualism.

> First, there was the moral universal in him, the unconfined humanity, the divine exaltation, which gave his person its absolute significance. On the other side there was the cramping and narrowing influence of the Jewish national Messianic

> idea. The latter was the form which the person of Jesus was
> obliged to assume if the former element was to have a point
> of vantage from which to go forth into the stream of history
> and to find the way on which it could pass into the general
> consciousness of mankind. (49)

Note the clear stream of influence in these remarks from Kant, through Hegel, and into mid-nineteenth-century thought. From Kantianism, Baur takes the idea that any morality worth the name must be universalizable.[13] From Hegel come themes such as the "absolute significance" that arises from *the* (not *a*) "stream of history" and comes to expression in "the general consciousness of mankind." We see here also the Hegelian thesis, antithesis, and synthesis, played out in the very mind of Christ.[14] As we will soon see, we can also hear echoes of other, more explicitly political and social issues.

But Paul is an expandable signifier. Besides his role as representing Hellenism, universalism, and spirit, his opposition to Judaism can also be narrated in tones that recall Luther's heroic opposition to the Roman Catholic Church. This fact is important, because for Baur and many of his colleagues, the enemy was not only Judaism but also Roman Catholicism, and the real savior was not Hellenism, but liberal Protestantism. Baur thus describes Paul's brave stand against his opponents at Corinth, who had behind them, Baur thinks, the support of the Jerusalem Church (the "Mother Church"), apostolic officialdom represented by the other apostles, and letters of recommendation. The "Mother Church" and Paul's opponents rely on "outward authority," whereas Paul must rely only on "his own independent self-consciousness" (64). Listen carefully, and we can hear someone crying, "Here I stand!"[15]

As is well known, Baur went on to portray Roman Christianity as the synthesis that reconciled the thesis of Jewish Christianity and the antithesis of Pauline Christianity (76–7, 147–52). But Baur, in good Hegelian fashion, would not really have left the developmental narrative there. Certainly, nineteenth-century Germany, with its critical theology, Kantian and Hegelian philosophies, liberal Protestantism, universal vision of its own *Kultur*, and Romanticism, represented a higher *Aufhebung*, a more refined and universal synthesis that had transcended the previous synthesis represented by Roman Christianity. Baur is not so clear about that historical dialectic, but its assumptions pervade his writings.

Baur's dualistic system retained its power all through the nineteenth century and well into the twentieth. Other writers would modify it in different ways, and some would highlight other elements.[16] For example, although we already have suggestions of modernist individualism in

Baur's accounts, we receive a much clearer indication of its importance in Harnack, who explains the connection of individualism to universalism for modern thought. In his *What Is Christianity?* he shows that individualism is the necessary obverse of the universal coin. "It was [Paul]," Harnack writes, "who perceived that religion in its new phase pertains to the individual and therefore to all individuals."[17] For something to be truly universal for all humans, it must be essentially available to the individual apart from any particular nation or race. The Christian religion, by being delivered from Judaism, is the only truly universal religion. (Harnack denies this attribution to Islam, Buddhism, or any other religion.) In order to achieve this universality, though, Christianity had to be transplanted from the East to the West. In fact, as counterintuitive as the argument may seem to us, Harnack insists that Christianity's thriving only in Europe was the proof of its universalism: "That the Gospel was transplanted from the East, where in subsequent ages it was never able to thrive properly, to the West, is a fact which we owe to Paul." Apparently, by making Christianity European, Paul made it "intelligible, not only to the Greeks but to all *men* generally, and united with the whole of the intellectual capital which had been amassed to previous ages" (177, Harnack's emphasis).

Harnack's volume, written in 1900, shows the durability of the Hellenism/Judaism dualistic scheme and its representations. Tinker with it though they might, German scholars throughout the nineteenth and early twentieth centuries were powerless to escape its grasp. And tinker with it they did. In Schweitzer's *Paul and His Interpreters* (1912), we have a fascinating account of the debates. Schweitzer chronicles the various ways scholars writing in German had placed Paul relative to the Hellenism/Judaism dichotomy (he admits that he ignored English language scholarship for the most part because of his poor skills in English). The important item to note is the ubiquity of the dualism throughout.

Many scholars reviewed by Schweitzer take the well-worn route of depicting Paul as the, or at least a, Hellenizer of Christianity. Holsten, Heinrici, and Havet see Paulinism as the first step in the Hellenization of Christianity: "the ethical series of ideas, the series dominated by the antithesis of flesh and spirit" are indications of Greek influence. Schmiedel and Harnack admit some Greek influence but claim that the Hellenistic ideas had no real impact on Paul's "doctrine of salvation." Lipsius, Bernard Weiss, and Weizsäcker don't make much of the Greek sources and try to explain Paul "from and by himself so far as possible."[18] Lüdemann (1872) had claimed two different "idea-complexes" of "flesh" in Paul, one Jewish and the other Greek. The "juridical" conception of redemption is Jewish, the "ethical" or "physical" is Greek. The "primitive Jewish system of thought with reference to Christ's vicarious suffering and righteousness by faith" is opposed to the later, and more really Pauline, "bolder realistic doctrine of righteousness," which is Hellenistic.[19]

Otto Pfleiderer (1887) had countered the Jewish "juridical" conception with the "mystico-ethical." For Pfleiderer, the atoning death is Jewish, but its universal application, Paul's anthropology, and the beginning of the process of its redemption in the resurrection of Jesus are all Hellenistic. Whereas Heinrici (1887) would speak of a synthesis of the Jewish and Hellenistic streams in Paul's thought, Pfleiderer would disagree and insist that the two strands were interwoven but unmixed in Pauline theology (31, 67, 71, 73). Scholars using what Schweitzer calls the "Comparative Method" (what we today generally refer to as the "history of religions" school) maintained that Paul translated his theology from Jewish thought into Greek language. Schweitzer takes Reitzenstein as an exception, since he tried to show that the entire "set of ideas" in Paul came from the mysteries and from a pre-Pauline, Hellenized form of early Christianity (218–19). In Schweitzer's view, the Baur and post-Baur school were unanimous in claiming that Paul had Hellenized Christianity. The Comparative School came to the same conclusions, but by using different materials than Hellenism, that is, from the mysteries and popular religious sources rather than Greek philosophy (229).

Schweitzer does note those who place Paul on the other side. Schürer and Ferdinand Weber had argued that Paul was "a child of late Judaism." Wellhausen had admitted that Paul had not been able to liberate himself from "Rabbinic methods of exegesis," although "the inner essence of his religious conviction was not affected by it" (45–6). Franz Delitzsch (1870), building on previous scholars reaching all the way back to John Lightfoot of the seventeenth century, traced much of Paul's language and thought to the rabbis (47). Schweitzer points out that some scholars emphasize the *non*-Greek character of Paul's thought in order to better enlist him for their own current theological interests. But then again, Schweitzer suggests that making Paul more Greek has also served apologetic, modernizing endeavors (158–9, 215).

Schweitzer delineates his own position in opposition to all these scholars he has examined. If anything, Schweitzer assumes an even stricter dichotomy between Hellenism and Judaism. For Schweitzer, the Jewish and the Greek represent "two different worlds of thought," and that both could have existed side by side in Paul is unthinkable (77). Schweitzer treats Hellenism as something that *must* have appeared "alien" to the earliest disciples of Jesus. If Paul's ideas had "grown up upon the soil of Hellenism," the other apostles would certainly have noticed it and attacked him viciously for it (79). (Note the presence of the traditional German motif of "soil" [*Blut und Boden*]. One wonders what "soil" would have been identified in Paul's day as "Hellenic"—and what not.) Schweitzer assumes that if something in Paul can be identified as Jewish, it must not be Hellenistic (e.g., 84, 230). Hellenism is "essentially foreign" to Paul (85). Schweitzer admits that Paul's terminology is often Hellenistic, but he denies that the meaning is shared at all. Language is held in common, but not "ideas" (238). Schweitzer thus takes over, from the debate of his time, the assumption of two cleanly separated worlds: Greek and Jewish. Moreover, a concern for "purity" *must* have been felt by the early Jewish Christians. The anxieties for pure racial-cultural boundaries that so preoccupied nineteenth and early twentieth-century German society *must* have been experienced by the ancients. But rather than those being experienced as German or Aryan and Jewish or Semitic, they were experienced as Hellenistic and Jewish.

Importantly, then, Schweitzer does not claim Paul for Hellenism. Paul's thought derives completely from Judaism. For Schweitzer, Hellenism is represented primarily by Greek philosophy and popular religion, such as the mysteries, on one side, and by later Christian doctrine on the other. The "primitive Jesus teaching" stands on one side of Paul, and "the Greek theology" on the other (viii, 92). According to Schweitzer, the Hellenization of Christianity begins only after Paul, in the second century (82–4, 190–1, 215, 229–30). Thus, for Schweitzer, "Greek" represents mainly doctrine, dogma, philosophy, or systematic theology.

Schweitzer recognizes that in order to show that Paul's thought comes completely from Judaism he must posit different kinds of Judaism: that from the Old Testament, Hellenistic Judaism, rabbinic Judaism, and apocalypticism. Schweitzer agrees with most other scholars that Paulinism cannot be derived directly from the Old Testament (45). Furthermore, since Schweitzer takes Hellenistic Judaism to be represented purely by such philosophical systems as that of Philo or high literature like Ezekiel's tragedies, he insists that Paul's thought cannot be attributed to Hellenistic Judaism either (92). Schweitzer also expends much energy arguing that the rabbis furnish no help in understanding Paul. Even if some scholars have been able to unearth "one parallel or another" between Paul and the rabbis, anyone can see that his thought is completely different from theirs (48). Rabbinic Judaism, in Schweitzer's portrait, is a "sunscorched plain," "yellow, wilted grass," "poor in ideas and unspiritual." We can understand the sterility of rabbinic Judaism if we consider the "decline of Christianity into dead Catholicism," or the decline of the freshness and true religiosity of Luther into the "Lutheran scholasticism of the sixteenth and seventeenth centuries" (49). Paul's religious experience reflects an earlier, fresher, spiritual Judaism before it fell into the deadness and sterility of rabbinism.

Schweitzer will find the source of that religiosity in Jewish eschatology. Beginning with the destruction of Jerusalem, though, that earlier form of Judaism became completely lost to human experience: "The destruction of Jerusalem interrupts the continuity of development of the Jewish people and of its thought. Its life is extinguished. Hellenism dies out. There arises a Rabbinism which is no longer borne on the tide of great national and spiritual movements. It becomes ossified, and confines itself to mere unproductive commentating upon the law" (51). The kind of Judaism Schweitzer is willing to attribute to Paul is one that has already disappeared from the face of the earth and certainly cannot be embodied by any actual Jews of Schweitzer's own society. For Schweitzer, in echoes of his previous book on the historical Jesus, Paul represents the lone, spiritual, religious, misunderstood, individualistic genius.[20]

Schweitzer's separation of later—and European—forms of Judaism from any "good" Judaism was a variant of a technique that had been developed over a century earlier, and that had become important in all sorts of Christian, and even some Jewish, scholarship. Now that we have seen the significance of the differentiation between earlier and later Judaisms, we must go back before Baur and Schweitzer to find the source for that strategy. In a recent dissertation on the topic, James Pasto traces the attempts to separate an earlier "Hebraism" from later, degenerate "Judaism," and locates the beginning of the enterprise in the influential work of W. M. L. de Wette, who entered the University of Jena in 1799 and completed his dissertation on Deuteronomy in 1804. In the early 1800s, de Wette published several works on the Old Testament and history of Israel. His most important thesis for our purposes was contained in his argument that ancient Israelite religion was radically different from post-exilic Judaism. The early period could be designated by terms such as "Israel," or "Hebrew," whereas terms like "Jew" or "Judaism" were reserved for some later, degenerate form that was taken as representing an essentially different people and religion.[21] Much of de Wette's scholarship was devoted to describing this "rupture" in the Israelite/Jewish past and in characterizing the two sides of the dichotomy.

De Wette's ideas were hugely influential, especially in nineteenth-century German scholarship. As Pasto has shown, Christian scholars repeatedly opposed an "Abrahamic covenant" to the "Mosaic Law," "Hebrews" to "Jews," and "ancient Israel" to "later Judaism." Different scholars would place the rupture at different times, perhaps at the Babylonian captivity, or the rise of Hellenism, or the time of Jesus, or soon thereafter. Ancient Israel might be identified with prophecy, freedom, covenant, or even universalism, while Judaism was identified with law, constraint, limit, and particularism. As Pasto explains, "This in turn is placed within a scheme of progress where the contradictory elements in Judaism are resolved through, and in, Jesus and early Christianity [including Paul, we should note]. The now separate universal, prophetic, and free elements serve as the foundational essence of Christianity, while the particularistic, legalistic, constraining elements become the foundational essence of post-Jesus Judaism."[22] This division between what we might label Hebraism and Judaism becomes important in debates about Judaism and Hellenism. For one thing, the themes of universalism and freedom, which were usually associated with Hellenism in its opposition to Judaism, were also in other systems associated with Hebraism in its opposition to Judaism. In either case, Judaism—that is, the form of Judaism embodied by actual Jews in modern Europe—is forced to play the inferior role.

To see how these various formulations signified, we must take a broader look at nineteenth-century Germany and "the Jewish Question." The story I am about to relate is familiar, but it is worth reminding ourselves of the ideological context in which Hellenism and Judaism were so "naturally" placed in a dichotomous relationship.[23] As is well known, in the eighteenth century the different lands that now make up Germany were divided among themselves. Holland had long before escaped Spanish control and had immediately begun constructing for itself a political and, gradually, cultural unity. Under Elizabeth I, England had created a growing national identity with a strong monarch as its focus. The Commonwealth of Cromwell and its aftermath in the seventeenth century, in spite of civil war and political chaos, did nothing to impede the growth of English, and then British, nationalism.

By the eighteenth century, French national identity and unity were also firmly established. The seventy-year reign of Louis XIV and then the almost sixty-year reign of Louis XV provided stability and the sense and politics of national unity. In the eighteenth century, France was a dominant power and had appropriated for its own propaganda self-comparisons with Rome. Germans gazed across the Rhine. German nobles spoke French in their courts. The Prussian court of Frederick the Great looked to France as its model for politics and culture. As Stephen Toulmin has put it, speaking of the late seventeenth and early eighteenth centuries, "For more than a century, Britain and France thus set the examples by which other nations measured themselves."[24]

As important as the French Revolution was, it did nothing in the long run to weaken France's hegemony. Indeed, Napoleon's defeat of Prussian forces at Jena in 1806 meant an increase of French influence in German lands. This victory also meant the partial and temporary emancipation of some Jews in some German lands from 1808 to 1813, supported by French rhetoric about political liberty and intellectual freedom. What followed in Germany was a concerted effort by intellectuals to rally interest in German national unity and consciousness. Johann Gottlieb Fichte's *Reden an die deutsche Nation* are one such example, and Schleiermacher's sermons are another. During this time Prussia put itself forward as the "enlightened leader" of the German lands.[25] Another important aspect of this period was the growing German interest in Greece: as France had portrayed itself as the "New Rome," so Germany would think of itself as the "New Greece."

A development in linguistics had prepared the way for this identification. In the eighteenth century, the "Indoeuropean" language group had been invented, along with several different terms to designate it (such as "Indo-German"). Gradually, this category was contrasted with the "Semitic" group (named after Shem, son of Noah). Apparently, the first scholars to use the term *Semitic* were Johann Gottfried Herder (1744–1803) and A. L. von Schlözer (1735–1809).[26] Although Herder would come to reject the category of "race" that had been recently invented and was growing in importance, and he argued against Johann Joachim Winckelmann (1717–1768) and others who advocated the superiority of the Greeks over the Hebrews or the Indoeuropeans over the Semites, he did not win the day. Increasingly in the nineteenth century, Indoeuropean and Semitic were placed in a dichotomy of unequal worth.

Ernest Renan (1823–1892) was an influential force in this development. His *General History and Comparative System of the Semitic Languages*, published in 1855, attempted to do for Semitic what had been done for Indoeuropean: show it to be a great system.[27] From these two systems, which he calls "two rivers," human civilization sprang. Nevertheless, the Semitic is always the inferior. The Hebrews, according to Renan, possess unique virtues, mainly monotheism. But they retain corresponding defects: they are primitive, vulgar, and "incapable of evolution."[28] The Semitic side of the dualism represents stagnation, a lack of historical development or evolution. Semites are closer to instinct, expressed in the simplicity of their language (Renan, 18–25). But that also implies a lack of refinement necessary for real culture. Even the Semites' monotheism, for which Aryans are in their debt, was merely the result of that instinct, and was dessicated, rigid, and unable to be appropriated by other races until the mediation of Christianity. Indoeuropeans or Aryans, on the other hand, are regularly depicted as youthful and noble. According to Adolphe Pictet (1799–1875), Aryans possess the "thinking element" as opposed to the "vital breath" of the Hebrews. They hold "the seeds of the spirit of liberty" and thus the beginnings of politics, science, and arts.[29]

The Greek War for Independence began in 1821, and philhellenism swept through the European intelligentsia. The enthusiasm of Shelley and Byron for the Greek cause is famous. They linked the new romanticization of Scotland with the struggles of little Greece. Both places were depicted as earthy, primal lands with rich traditions of native song, natural peoples, and, ironically in the case of Greece, "northern" naturalness and romance.[30] Many German intellectuals also became enthusiastic philhellenes.[31] Not that they were really much concerned about contemporary Greeks: apparently, most of the great German philhellenes (Winckelmann, Lessing, Goethe, Schiller, Hölderlin, Hegel, Nietzsche) never actually traveled to Greece.[32] Nor did these Germans want to imitate the *politics* of ancient Greek democracies. Not until the twentieth century did Athenian democracy become something modern political leaders would invoke as a respectable precursor.[33] The value of Greece lay neither in modern Greek culture nor in ancient Greek politics. Rather, the romanticized modern Greek battle for political freedom and independence (from the "dark and Asiatic Turks," yet) was wedded to a romanticized picture of ancient Greek literature, art, and philosophy to serve as a model of unified, national *Kultur*. To Wilhelm von Humboldt, for example, trying to rally all of Germany around the enlightened leadership of Prussia, Greece represented an integrated society that might be able to modernize while still avoiding the revolution of France. Judaism in this system was, of course, to serve as the foil. As F. A. Wolf, classicist colleague of de Wette in Berlin, wrote in 1831: "The Hebraic nation did not raise itself to the level of culture, so that one might regard it as a learned, cultured people. It does not even have prose, but only half poetry. Its writers of history are but miserable chroniclers. They could never write in full sentences; this was an invention of Greeks."[34]

It is easy to see the allure of Greece for these German intellectuals. Like Germany, Greece had also suffered from division into small, competing city-states. Greece had never attained the imperial status of Rome or Egypt, just as Germany, especially after the defeat at Jena, seemed unable ever to attain the imperial status of France or England. Yet all of Europe could be urged to look to Greece as the birthplace—and Germany as the steward—of European philosophy, philology, science, medicine, mathematics, poetry, and art.

Voices were sounded on the other side, too. Herder argued against Winckelmann's classicism, as mentioned earlier, seeking to raise the Hebrew over the Greek as a way of elevating *theo*centrism over *anthropo*centrism. For Herder, Hebraism represented coherent, organic, national-ethnic identity. As superintendent of schools, chief pastor, and court preacher in Weimar, he was more worried about English theology and the French Enlightenment than a supposed German lack of culture. He advocated the Hebrews as a true *Volk*, without the necessity of republicanism or monarchy. His vision of the Hebrew *Volk-Staat* excluded radical individualism, revolution, and classicism.[35] Later, in the nineteenth century, others attacked the dominant German philhellenism, often from a pietistic position. Rudolph Friedrich Grau (1835–1893), for example, defended the Hebrews as a way of defending Christianity against pagan Aryanism. Against Renan, he pointed out that Athens and Rome had fallen due to their decadence. Grau used Hebraism to counter secularism. Yet in the end, he advocated a synthesis. Hebraism represents an important religious and ethical element that Europe must retain, even if combined with Indo-German culture, represented as dynamism.[36]

We must also recognize that these pro-Hebraic views were seldom pro-Jewish. Due to the separation between Ancient Hebraism and contemporary Judaism made popular by de Wette described above, German writers could argue against Aryanists or radical philhellenes and praise Hebraism without implying any approval at all for rabbinic Judaism. We would certainly want to acknowledge those liberal Protestants (in the noble tradition of Lessing) who defended some forms of Judaism against the worst anti-Semitism of the nineteenth and twentieth centuries. But we must also recognize that they, and even some of the Jewish intellectuals fighting for emancipation, assumed that Jews would have to assimilate or eventually die out in a modern world that was becoming more and more enlightened and universal.[37] From a post-Holocaust perspective even the more liberal arguments are depressing.

The social position of Jews in nineteenth-century Germany and the contradictions within German culture and politics, it seems, conspired to create a remarkably monolithic and enduring ideology defining Judaism. Linguistic theories taught that language constructed identity, and thus specific languages constructed coherent identities and characteristics for entire peoples who shared the same language. Germans had something like a single language but without national unity. German intellectual writings of the period thus reflect a felt need for nation-state unity while simultaneously entertaining ambitions for transnational and perhaps even imperial influence. Emerging concepts of race sometimes identified race with nation, but they also allowed the category of race to encompass much broader groups of peoples. Combined with an academic propensity for dualisms, it seems almost inevitable that Indoeuropean, Semitic, Hebraic, Hellenistic, Greek, German, Jewish, Christian, universal, particular, free, and constrained would all eventually line up on one or the other side of a dichotomy. Finally, most people figured that there were only about three ways to deal with the significant Jewish minority: recognition as a "state within a state" (which most Germans were loath to accept since it seemed to destroy any hard-won national coherence), assimilation, or extinction. All these factors conspired to signify Judaism as the alien "other" within a problematic nationalistic development.

Unfortunately, World War II did not disrupt this ideological system. Although Martin Hengel's *Judaism and Hellenism* critiqued previous German scholarship and prejudices about Judaism, the work itself is still deeply implicated in self-serving Christian constructions of Judaism. True, Hengel goes some way toward disrupting the dualism by insisting that all Judaism of the Greco-Roman world was to some extent Hellenized. He argues further that the old notion of a "Palestinian Judaism" that can be opposed to a syncretized, Diaspora, "Hellenistic Judaism" should be rejected. Hellenism pervaded Palestine also. But in the end, Hengel reinscribes the old dualism with the same old prejudices. He speaks continually of the "Greek world of ideas" (e.g., 115) and the "spirit of Hellenism" (e.g., 107, 116, 126). Hellenism stands for both individualism and universalism (116–17). Hellenistic thought is "rational," "logical," and "critical" (126). In fact, Hengel's favorite designation for what he takes as "Hellenism" is actually "the Greek Enlightenment" ("die griechische Aufklärung," 121, 305, et passim). The Enlightenment received its greatest impetus from a combined Greek and Oriental "bourgeoisie" that proved to be an important social force of the Hellenistic period (126–7). The tendency of some Jews to resist universalism or assimilation is taken to be what triggered ancient "anti-semitism" (306). On one side were the Jewish "reformers," who were sympathetic to the universalizing message of the Greek Enlightenment and who were perhaps seeking just "to restore the original 'rational' form of worship without 'superstitious' falsification" (305, English translation altered slightly; "eine ursprüngliche »vernünftige« Form der Gottesverehrung ohne »abergläubische« Verfälschung wiederherzustellen" [German, p. 556]). Such reform, in combination with a missionary movement sponsored also by

Hellenistic Jews, set Judaism "well on the way towards becoming a *world religion*" (313, Hengel's emphasis).

But Pharisaism, with its reaction against Hellenization and its resulting "anxious and zealous fixation on the letter of the Torah," proved to be a powerful counter-reformation force. Moreover, "the almost complete fusion of religion and nationalism" prevented assimilation and hindered the universal tendencies of the ancient "prophetic" religion from escaping the limitations of Jewish national boundaries. Fortunately, Christianity arose to carry forward the torch of the "prophetic spirit":

> [T]he protective attitude of Judaism over against its environment, which had been developed in the controversy with Hellenism and was most strongly expressed by the absolutized place of the Torah, was shattered in pieces. Christology took the place of 'Torah ontology' as an expression of the free and sovereign saving revelation of God in history, which no longer recognized national or historically conditioned limitations. (313–14)

In Hengel's interpretation, the older Hellenism/Judaism dualism is simply shifted slightly, but not displaced. As John Collins has said, "Hengel has not entirely shed the negative view of Judaism which has been endemic in Christian biblical scholarship." In fact, in Hengel's system, "The rise of Christianity implies the failure of Judaism."[38] Moreover, Hengel's interpretation is problematic not only because it constructs Judaism as simply a *praeparatio evangelica*, but also because it construes ancient conflicts in the terms of nineteenth-century Germany.[39] Judaism, in the end, still represents particularism, limitation, reaction, and even extinction. Hellenism, or the "Greek Enlightenment," is the force for individualism, universalism, and freedom.

I have spent so much time rehearsing the German debate from the beginning of the nineteenth century to the middle of the twentieth because that is where and when, I believe, the Hellenic/Judaic dualism was invented and elaborated to its greatest extent. Moreover, that scholarship is important because of the great influence it has had on New Testament scholarship, especially in the United States. But I would like to give some attention to two other arenas of biblical scholarship in order to demonstrate that the dualism itself, and its significations sketched above, are not the only possible ones. First, I will briefly note the meanings of Judaism in seventeenth- and eighteenth-century English scholarship, and then I will turn to post–World War II scholarship, mainly in North America.

England in the Seventeenth
and Eighteenth Centuries

From the Middle Ages, rumors persisted that the Anglo-Saxons were actually the lost tribes of Israel or perhaps descendents of Noah through his son Shem, and throughout the early modern period these traditions had nurtured "Christian Hebraism" in England. It may have helped also that the Jews, for the most part, had been expelled from England in 1290 and did not begin trickling back until the last half of the seventeenth century.[40] With few (or no) real Jews to be perceived as a threat to developing English national identity, Jewish traditions could be, and were, much more freely appropriated for self-representation in England than they ever were in Germany or elsewhere in Europe.[41]

Some interest in Jewish studies was probably initiated by the Reformation and its advocacy of the study of Hebrew and Greek in opposition to the "medieval" and "Roman" concentration on Latin. The study of Hebrew was thus being introduced and promoted among the clergy and even educated laymen, first at Cambridge and then also at Oxford and even lower public schools. Scholars such as John Lightfoot in the seventeenth century and Bishop Robert Lowth in the eighteenth became famous even on the Continent for their studies of Hebrew. We should not overemphasize the Reformation in this development, however. The Humanists of the fifteenth century had already "discovered" Hebrew and its importance for biblical studies. We should also note that commitment to Hebrew did not mean pro-Jewish sympathies—among Continental or English scholars.[42] In any case, for a variety of reasons, England furnished an atmosphere for thinking about Judaism in varied ways—and ways different from those in Germany.

Although the Christian Hebraist traditions had already provided a mechanism with which to imagine English identity, the political events of the seventeenth century encouraged the tendency even more. As is well-known, the Cromwellian Commonwealth was often portrayed as a theocratic republic, taking Old Testament Israel as something of a model for a constitutionally ruled nation of God's people. The English Puritans who settled in the New World brought with them English republican propaganda and carried, at least initially, the confident demeanor of a people of God establishing a New Israel in the wilderness.[43] But the propagandistic appropriations of Israel by the republicans or Puritans did not preclude its use also by royalists or Anglicans.

The eminent Hebraist John Lightfoot (1602–1675) used his inherited humanist learning and expertise on Hebrew and ancient Judaism in a variety of ways. He advocated learning in general, arguing against radical Protestants who claimed that knowledge of the Bible alone was sufficient. He urged attention to Hebrew and nonbiblical Jewish texts of all sorts for the use they could afford for interpreting the Bible, including Paul.[44] But he also used Judaism as a symbol for the church of his own day, in fact, for the Church of England.

In a sermon preached on November 25, 1658, Lightfoot told his congregation that Jesus had been a faithful, upstanding member of "the Jewish national church." He notes that, according to John 10:22–23, Jesus observed the Feast of Dedication. Lightfoot points out that this feast celebrated the dedication of the restored purity of the Temple by the Hasmoneans. The narration of its establishment comes from texts taken by Lightfoot and his audience to be nonbiblical (Maccabean literature). This feast, therefore, is not mandated by God, Moses, the prophets, or divine warrant, "but it was only a civil and ecclesiastical sanction appointed by the higher powers in that generation."[45] Yet Jesus celebrated it. Lightfoot takes Jesus' actions as an important lesson for, as he says, "these times of our great divisions and separations" (215). They prove that Jesus "held communion in the public exercise of religion" with the "national religion" embodied in the "national church," and even in rites and celebrations that had no biblical warrant. In other words, Jesus was no Puritan. Lightfoot's message is clear: those nonconformists (note the term "conforming," 226), separatists, Dissenters, indeed, *Puritans* should follow the example of Jesus, give up their unreasonable biblicism, and return to the fold of the national church, established by tradition and the due mandates and leadership of national and ecclesiastical institutions. Jesus was a good Anglican. Judaism here represents the Church of England.

After the "religious wars" of the mid-1600s and the "Glorious Revolution" of 1688–89, some Englishmen were wary of theocratic rhetoric. Deists and other members of the "Radical Enlightenment" turned away from Israel and held up Egypt, other nations of the "Orient," or Rome as model nations and empires. Isaac Newton (1642–1727), on the other hand, opposed the (to him) alarmist tendencies of the Radical Enlightenment by reference again to Israel.[46]

Around the turn of the century, John Locke (1632–1704), continuing the tradition of John Lightfoot, emphasized the importance of Jewish learning for Paul. Paul had received his education from Gamaliel. His "information in Christian knowledge" he had received directly from God. According to Locke, Paul was not significantly influenced by either Greek philosophy or rhetoric, called by Locke, respectively, "man's wisdom" and "ornament." Greek philosophy influenced Christianity only later, and Greek interpretations of Paul arose only long after the time of the apostle.[47]

Around the same time, Edward Synge (1659–1741), in a different vein but without actually denying Paul's Jewishness, writes of Paul's battles defending his own "religion" against the "Jewish Church." Synge speaks of the "Jewish Church," the "Jewish Religion," and "Jewish Traditions." In Synge's book, Paul comes across as a Protestant defending himself against accusations of heresy and sedition. The "Jewish Church" becomes a type for the things taken by Synge to be inessential Roman Catholic beliefs and practices. If Roman Catholics want to hold onto such things, they shouldn't require them of other Christians, any more than Jews had the right to hold Paul to the expectations of their "inessential" traditions. Paul is thus a Protestant, and Judaism is the Roman Church.[48]

Finally, I must at least mention Bishop Robert Lowth (1710–1787)— if for no other reason than his influence on so many scholars after him, not the least of whom was Herder. Lowth's monumental *Lectures on the Sacred Poetry of the Hebrews* is a philological study of the poetry of the Hebrew Bible. It not only sparked interest in the study of Hebrew poetry, but also helped raise the estimation of Hebrew among generations of scholars to follow. Lowth does not address issues of Pauline scholarship: his importance for our purposes lies in the way he compares Hebrew to English. For Lowth, Hebrew, in contrast to Latin and Greek, represents both simplicity and sublimity. In fact, for Lowth, Hebrew is a great language precisely because its sublimity of expression of feelings is embodied in natural simplicity. "It is impossible to conceive any thing more simple and unadorned than the common language of the Hebrews. It is plain, correct, chaste, and temperate; the words are uncommon neither in their meaning nor application; there is no appearance of study, nor even of the least attention to the harmony of the periods."[49] For Lowth, the Hebrew language embodies traditional English virtues. The translator of Lowth's work from Latin into English captures a sentiment that was surely Lowth's as well when he compares the sublime simplicity of Hebrew to that of English. The translator's preface contains much talk about English "common sense." "So happily does the simple genius of the Hebrew language accord with our own," says the translator, that almost any English reader should be able to profit from Lowth's study (vii). What's more, this accessibility will be only improved by the translation of Lowth's Latin original into English, since English has much "greater analogy" to Hebrew than does Latin (viii). English common sense joins hands with the simple sublimity of Hebrew to overcome centuries of separation between the two nations of genius.

All this should not be taken as proof that the English were pro-Jewish in their politics or relations with actual Jews of their own time. Lightfoot, for example, along with many other Englishmen, expressed anti-Jewish sentiments.[50] My point is just that "Judaism" *as a symbol* represented many different things, not all bad, and was used in various ways in English rhetoric. Hebraism could represent English nationalism, virtuous monarchy, or antimonarchical, theocratic republicanism. It could represent the Commonwealth or the King. Judaism could stand for Puritan nonconformity or for the established Anglican Church, for Protestantism or Roman Catholicism, and as either a negative or a positive sign.[51] It could represent simplicity of style as opposed to Greek polish and sophistication. Judaism could be linked to English common sense and could represent the moderate piety of Newton against radical deism or atheism. Judaism always seemed to mean *something* in seventeenth- and eighteenth-century England, but its connotations were never as predictable or stable as in nineteenth-century Germany, and it was not placed in a regularly dualistic relationship with Greekness or Hellenism.

The writings of Matthew Arnold in the nineteenth century, however, catalyze a shift. In his *Culture and Anarchy*, Arnold takes over a Hellenism/Hebraism dichotomy that he borrowed, mostly, from Heinrich Heine.[52] Heine had contrasted the "Hellene" with the Jew (*Jude*) or Nazarene (*Nazarener*), the latter two representing Judaism and Christianity, respectively. The "Judaism of the Nazarenes" is "gloomy, gaunt, antisensual, overspiritual." The Hellenic is seen in "gaiety, love of beauty, and thriving zest for life."[53] As Peter Gay says, in a much-quoted statement that bears quoting again, "As the Enlightenment saw it, the world was, and had always been divided between ascetic, superstitious enemies of the flesh, and men who affirmed life, the body, knowledge, and generosity; between mythmakers and realists, priests and philosophers. Heinrich Heine, wayward son of the Enlightenment, would later call these parties, most suggestively, Hebrews and Hellenes."[54] I would like to point out that, in Heine's dualism, European asceticism is attributed to Judaism. This is interesting, I think, from the perspective of the twentieth century, which has seen so many attempts (mainly by Protestant Christians who reject sexual asceticism) to attribute early Christian asceticism to Hellenism in contrast to the (preferred) "Jewish" positive evaluation of the body and sexuality. At any rate, it is from Heine that Matthew Arnold takes his cue, renaming along the way Heine's "Jew" or "Nazarene" as "Hebraism," probably reflecting the long Christian Hebraist tradition in England.[55]

Arnold says that Hebraism and Hellenism ought to be evenly balanced in the English national makeup, but that they seldom are. When push comes to shove, though, Arnold clearly believes the English of his time have far too much Hebraism and far too little Hellenism; he comes across as favoring the latter. For Arnold, Hellenism represents thinking, knowing, and the "sponteneity of consciousness." Hebraism represents doing, acting, ethics, or the "strictness of conscience."[56] The aim of both Hebraism and Hellenism is "man's perfection or salvation," but the two go about striving for this goal in different ways (87–8). Both are taken by Arnold to be ascetic, that is, both the Greek and Hebrew "quarrel with the body and its desires." But for the Greek, the body hinders right thinking; for the Hebrew, the body hinders right acting. Arnold admits that one can quote Hebrew texts emphasizing knowledge and Greek texts emphasizing action, but he is strong enough in his convictions that he is able to resist mere evidence (see 89). Basically, he believes that the English middle class, the bourgeoisie, whom he labels "Philistines" (the aristocracy are "Barbarians" and the lower class the "Populace"), is so Hebraic as to have scarcely any culture at all. Yes, Hellenism was inadequate in its time, but Christianity, with its bit of Hebraism (ethical sense), triumphed over Hellenism in the ancient world. With the Renaissance, Hellenism triumphed over Christianity, but the time was too Hellenic—that is, too given to "perceiving and knowing" without sufficient attention to "feeling and acting" (94–5). The English Reformation effected a blend of the two, but with, apparently, a bit too much Hebraism. Puritanism and Nonconformism, which Arnold hates (calling all sorts of English groups "hole-in-the-corner" Christianity), constituted an unfortunate reaction against the Hellenism of the Renaissance. Arnold urges a Hellenic correction of the overly Hebraic (crass, overly serious, ethical, bourgeois) Reformation, arguing that the English middle class needs more reflection, more high culture, more "sweetness and light." Arnold retains the racism of much of the previous use of the terms: although he says that both forces exist in English history and character, he identifies the Hellenic with the Indo-European and the Hebraic with the Semitic (95).

For Arnold, therefore, Judaism, in his "cleaned up" form called Hebraism, represents action or ethics, and can be useful as a corrective to hedonism and effete degeneracy. Hellenism represents thought, high culture, perception, and is useful as a corrective to dull bourgeois moralism and crass attention to business or politics, both of which Arnold repeatedly scorns. In Matthew Arnold, therefore, we find the German Judaic/Hellenic dualism altered to fit the nineteenth-century English social situation with its battles between Anglicans and nonestablished Protestants, the growth of the power of the middle class, and intellectual concerns about "culture" in the face of advanced capitalism and industrialism.[57]

Post-War North America

The last group of texts I will analyze are studies of Paul since World War II, and I will concentrate on treatments from the United States. I should explain the unusual selection of examples I offer below. I have chosen to analyze one representative of what has been called the "Biblical Theology Movement" or neo-orthodoxy, and three Jewish writers on Paul. These examples, of course, do not exhaust the possibilities or represent anything like a comprehensive survey. I choose them because they illustrate the variety of uses to which "Judaism" and "Hellenism" have been put in North American intellectual culture, because they all present points of view different from the German scholarship examined above, and because they each reflect their own social environment in important ways.

By far the most important movement in post-war American biblical scholarship is one that is difficult to define because it was so large, diverse, and influential on scholars of different persuasions: dialectical theology or neo-orthodoxy and, what I take to be its spawn, the biblical theology movement, which took its beginnings mainly from German scholarship before the war but became important in America only afterwards.[58] Biblical scholars are familiar with the many studies from the post-war period that pitted the Greek against the Jewish conceptions of the body, time, death, or any other of a number of entities. Doubtless, these studies were influenced by the very structure of Kittel's *Theological Dictionary of the New Testament*, but they were also products of distinctly American theological, political, and ideological debates.

As an example of this sort of scholarship, I propose the short but representative essay by Earle Ellis, *Paul and his Recent Interpreters*, published in 1961.[59] Ellis correctly points to the nineteenth century as the time of the rise of the question, "Are Paul's thought patterns Jewish or Hellenistic?" (25). Ellis also notes that many arguments about Paul's Hellenism are dependent on concerns about the relation of Paul to Jesus. The more Hellenistic Paul is, the further he stands from Jesus and "the primitive Church" (29). Coming down firmly on the "Jewish" side, Ellis insists, "In interpreting Pauline concepts it is not the categories of a second-century Hellenistic Gnosticism (however easily they may be read back), but the categories of first-century rabbinic/apocalyptic Judaism which demand first claim upon the critical historian's mind" (30–1). Ellis cites W. D. Davies as having shown "that the relation of *Paul and Rabbinic Judaism* forms the background of many Pauline concepts formerly labeled Hellenistic" (31). Then, citing the work of Bultmann on anthropology, Cullmann on resurrection, and Robinson on the body, Ellis remarks, "It is widely recognized today that Paul views man in the Old-Testament-Jewish framework and not in the Platonic dualism of the Hellenistic world" (31). Paul's "participationist" language about the body of Christ reflects "Semitic thought patterns" (32). And Paul's notion of time is not the cyclic, static "Greek" view of time, but rather the "biblical" view that presents time as linear and historical. Paul's soteriology is also the "Old Testament-Jewish" view: rather than "spiritual deliverance" or the escape of the soul at death, Jewish salvation is the "physical redemption culminating in the deliverance of the whole man at the parousia." Rather than "Greek dualism," the Jewish view presents "man as a unified being." Rather than Hellenistic individualism, the Jewish view is one of corporate solidarity (which does, though, retain individual salvation [34]).

Several aspects of Ellis's treatment should be noted. For one thing, Ellis narrows the field of what counts as Greek and broadens the field of what counts as Jewish. Greek concepts are represented only by Platonic philosophy or second-century Gnosticism. Jewish concepts, on the other hand, may be derived from the Old Testament, apocalyptic literature, or the rabbis. This narrowing of the Greek field of reference and broadening of the Jewish makes it easier to argue that Paul's thought world is Jewish rather than Greek. Moreover, although he knows the work of Davies, who had cautioned against reading the rabbis as uninfluenced by Hellenism, Ellis takes rabbinic parallels in Paul to demonstrate the relative absence of Hellenistic influence.[60] But the most important thing to notice is the constellation of elements that differentiate the Greek from the Jewish: a cyclical view of time versus a linear historical view, implying that the Greek side may be represented by the word "static" while the Jewish side is "dynamic." Greek time is recurrent (that is, nonhistorical), whereas the Jewish is "historical," in line with biblical theology's interest in "salvation history." And the Greek view of the self—individualistic, dualistic, conceiving of salvation only as the escape of the soul from the body, and thus ascetic—is contrasted with the Jewish view that emphasizes the redemption of the body, the whole person, and the importance of community and corporate solidarity. It takes little imagination to recognize here mid-twentieth-century cultural anxieties. I would argue that the Greek side resembles the fractured state of modernity trapped in the timeless, non-Utopian end of history, whereas the Jewish/Pauline side represents a dream of a coherent Christian community peopled by integrated human beings saved from the disintegration of society and self. In addition, the emphasis on history reveals the conservative Christian concern to ground revelation in a real point in the past and to expect redemption, not in the social or political forces of liberalism, evolution, or gradualism, but in the eschatological inbreaking of God.[61]

I would go further and suggest that the American neo-orthodox inclination to portray Paul's thought as fundamentally Jewish rather than Greek reflects American pietistic concerns about revelation and culture. Hellenism comes to represent natural theology, whereas Judaism represents revelation. Hellenism stands for "culture," and Judaism stands for "Christ against Culture."[62] If truth could come from Hellenism, then liberals might be right in their notions of universalism, that God may be approachable through a variety of traditions. But if truth comes via Judaism, mediated of course by Christianity, then the epistemological and soteriological privilege of Christianity is preserved.

Note also how these post-war American assumptions are both like and unlike their nineteenth-century precursors. The Hellenic/Jewish dualism is retained, along with some of the significances of the different sides. Thus both earlier and later scholars identify individualism with Hellenism. But whereas that was a saving aspect for nineteenth-century Germans, for whom individualism was a valued commodity of both the Enlightenment and Romanticism, it was a problem by the middle of the twentieth century, when it could be made to symbolize the fractured, atomized, anonymous state of modernity with its loss of communities. And whereas individualism in conjunction with universalism represented truth to Kantian and Hegelian liberals, the same combination represented for American scholars, nurtured in pietism and evangelicalism, the loss of revelation or Christianity's claim to special access to truth. Judaism still represents the "particular." But in the twentieth-century American concern to counter liberal notions about the epistemology of universal religious experience, the particular is valued over the universal. In some respects, therefore, American scholars retained the earlier dualism and even its significations, but reversed the evaluations.

In other respects, though, the post-war assumptions also reversed the significations. Whereas it had been common in the nineteenth century to portray the Jews as static and lost in the past, now it became customary to use the word "static" for Greek time, with the corresponding Jewish side described as "dynamic," "historical," and "eschatological," that is, forward-looking. What is also interesting is that American scholars like Ellis recognize they are continuing a debate from the previous century, but they do not seem to recognize that the meanings of the terms of the debate have changed in important ways.

One of the important reasons for that changed environment, of course, is the Holocaust. The Holocaust and the war changed much about the meaning of Judaism no less in North America than elsewhere in the world. For one thing, simply the influx of European Jews into the United States, especially those in professional and intellectual careers, changed the way Judaism was presented publicly. The establishment of Judaic Studies in American universities and the prominence of Jewish scholars in the American academic scene have necessarily altered the representation of Jews and Judaism.[63] The shock over the Holocaust has led to increased Jewish-Christian dialogue, and many Christian scholars have become much more aware of the ideological effects of their interpretations of the Jewishness of Jesus, Paul, and early Christianity in general. One result of these changes has been the interest shown in interpretations of Paul by Jewish scholars.

An important influence on post-war revisionist readings of Paul has come from one Jewish scholar, albeit not an American. I give attention to Hans-Joachim Schoeps here because I see his portrait of Paul as representing a bridge between earlier German scholarship and post-war American portrayals. Also, Schoeps's view is an earlier point on a trajectory to the American Jewish scholarship analyzed below. Schoeps's treatment of Paul reflects his own Jewishness as well as what has been called his ambivalent relationship with other Jews. The *Encyclopaedia Judaica* (1971) describes Schoeps's thought as "a radical dialectical Jewish theology which excluded all nomistic as well as national-cultural elements, bringing Judaism very close to Christianity but stopping short of baptism" (14.991). Before the war, Schoeps had advocated German nationalism, suggesting that "German Jews" (as distinct from Zionists and eastern European Jews resident in Germany and the rest of Europe) should cooperate with the National Socialists. In 1938, however, Schoeps fled to Sweden, returning to Germany immediately after the war. He began teaching at Erlangen in 1947. In his autobiography, *Die letzten dreißig Jahre*, Schoeps regretted his mistakes about the Nazis; his parents were among the millions murdered in concentration camps.[64]

In 1959, Schoeps published *Paul: The Theology of the Apostle in the Light of Jewish Religious History*.[65] According to Schoeps, the study of Paul since Baur had fallen into three phases: the Hellenistic, the Judaic/Hellenistic, and most recently the Rabbinical. Schoeps insists that Paul was not influenced directly by Hellenism, which he takes as embodied mainly in the mysteries. In this argument, Hellenism is represented by myth, individualism, and degenerate syncretism. Pauline salvation, for instance, is historical rather than timeless or mythical, it is located in an event of recent experience rather than a projection or a distant myth, and it is corporeal and communal rather than individualistic (see 20).

Although Paul was not, therefore, influenced directly by Hellenism or, as Schoeps also puts it, by "pure" Hellenism, he was influenced by Hellenistic Judaism via the Septuagint. Schoeps reads the Septuagint as representing Hellenistic Judaism, which means evangelization and universalism. According to Schoeps, the Septuagint misleadingly translates *torah* as *nomos* and *berith* as *diathēkē*, which in Greek implies legalism for the former and a sort of authoritarian "last will and testament" for the latter. Thus, the Septuagint turns what in the Hebrew Bible must be understood as a mutual covenant into a concept of legalism. The Septuagint, in sum, replaced "the Old Testament religion of grace" with "a human religion of virtuous works" (28–32). In other words, Schoeps takes all those things for which Protestants had blamed Judaism and transfers them to the Septuagint as the corrupter of real Judaism, represented in the Hebrew Bible and, to some extent, the rabbis. Paul is presented as a Jew of the Hellenistic Diaspora, influenced by apocalypticism, and a "rabbinical exegete." But Paul, due to influence from Hellenistic Judaism mediated through the Septuagint, has tragically misunderstood the real Jewish notion of law and covenant.

Schoeps argues that the Septuagint misled Paul so that he failed to discern the true nature of the Jewish covenant. According to "the Biblical view," the law must be understood always in its relation to the covenant, that is, the intimate and mutual relationship of grace between God and Israel (213–14). "Because Paul had lost all understanding of the character of the Hebraic *berith* as a partnership involving mutual obligations, he failed to grasp the inner meaning of the Mosaic law, namely, that it is an instrument by which the covenant is realized. Hence the Pauline theology of law and justification begins with the fateful misunderstanding in consequence of which he tears asunder covenant and law, and then represents Christ as the end of the law" (218).

Oddly enough, Schoeps himself insists on maintaining a sharp distinction between "law" and "covenant." Whereas the covenant is timeless, the law has historical boundaries. Indeed, the covenant can have no history. The covenant (*berith*) is a matter of faith, although not a "confession of faith of any particular type" (293). That is, the covenant is faith but not doctrine or dogma. It is difficult to see how Schoeps is not involved in something of a contradiction here. He has insisted that Paul is a heretic—indeed, he repeatedly contrasts Paul with "all Jews everywhere"—and Paul's mistake is to divorce law from covenant and then proclaim the end of the law.[66] But then Schoeps, as a liberal Jew who argued against the necessity of "nomistic" Judaism himself (!), ends the book by suggesting that the really important thing for the Jews is the covenant, and that the law is relatively dispensable.

But perhaps the complexities of Schoeps's Paul are related to the complexities of Schoeps himself. Schoeps sees Paul as an urban Jew in a dual cultural environment. Like, as he puts it, "the Jewish communities of London, Amsterdam, Frankfurt, Leghorn, in the second half of the seventeenth century," all Diaspora Jewish communities would have held some beliefs in common, and they would all have been assimilated or acculturated to some extent with Hellenism. There are, therefore, two dominant forces: Hellenism and "rabbinic" or "biblical" Judaism. Paul represents a synthesis of both (note the phrase: "an integrated but composite cultural *milieu* such as his origins suggest")—like all Diaspora Jews in different ways. Ancient Jews were not "artificially confined to a ghetto" (35), so they necessarily shared in both cultures.

But Paul went too far. He became a heretic—albeit an understandable, Jewish heretic—and he did so because of a misunderstanding foisted upon Judaism by Hellenism. Hellenism misconstrued Judaism, essentially a religion of grace, covenant, and relationship, and made it seem legalistic, intellectualizing, and abstract. Schoeps has not at all broken out of the prewar dualism, but he uses it in a fascinating and novel way. The fundamental issue is who gets to define real Judaism. The context of the struggle is the confrontation between a dominant and subordinate culture. The danger is assimilation: some assimilation is unavoidable, but how much is too much?[67] And how does a Jew avoid the ghetto and live within and as part of another culture without losing his essential Jewishness? I want to avoid inappropriate psychologizing of Schoeps, but it is tempting to think that perhaps, chastened by events subsequent to his prewar commitment to intense German nationalism and even flirtations with National Socialism, Schoeps saw Paul as a Jew who had gone too far, and the reason Paul went so badly astray was that he made the fatal error of allowing the dominant culture to define Judaism.

As I have tried to show, although Schoeps began by disputing a rigid or pure Hellenistic/Jewish dichotomy, in the end the dualism proved to be indispensible for his criticism of Pauline Christianity. We find a similar situation, ironically, in a quite recent, though also quite different, interpretation by another Jewish scholar. Daniel Boyarin published *A Radical Jew: Paul and the Politics of Identity* in 1994.[68] Although Boyarin rejects any firm separation between Hellenistic Judaism on the one hand and Palestinian or Rabbinic Judaism on the other, admitting that all Judaism was Hellenized to some extent, he also retains the dualism as important for his understanding of Paul. Boyarin points to different degrees of acculturation of ancient Jews to Hellenism. The most important aspect of or key to Hellenism is the desire for "the One," univocity.

The Greeks themselves, with Platonism as the main culprit, saddled subsequent European civilization with an unfortunate desire for oneness, univocity, universalism. The essence of Greekness can be read off Greek interpretive strategies and theories: the mark of the Greeks is allegoresis or logocentricism (Boyarin uses the latter to gloss the former). Greek interpretive activity and theory are part and parcel of phallocentrism: "the Universal Subject as a Christian Male" (17).

The Hebrew side of the dualism is represented by an emphasis on difference, particularity, embodiedness. The particular Jew is opposed to imperialistic uniformity; the woman resists phallo-logo-male hegemony. The European search, through allegory, for oneness of meaning is the framework and driving force behind misogyny and anti-Semitism, and it all comes from the Greeks: "the same Hellenic search for univocity which the Universal Subject disembodies forth" (17). For Boyarin, Paul synthesizes "Greek and Hebrew culture," and this synthesis becomes the basis of "the later history of Europe," which we are certainly to understand, from Boyarin's tone, is not to be celebrated.

Boyarin recognizes that he is rehearsing the nineteenth-century debate, even reinstating Baur's account of thesis, antithesis, and synthesis, in which the synthesis is Christian Europe. Boyarin just renders an opposite judgment of value, condemning what the nineteenth-century Hegelians had admired. Boyarin's account is also very similar to the twentieth-century neo-orthodox high valuation of Jewish particularity, but for quite different reasons. Whereas Christian neo-orthodoxy emphasized Jewish particularity usually as a means of raising revelation over natural theology, Scripture over "universal human experience," Christ over culture, and, yes, Christian truth over that of all others, Boyarin's emphasis on particularity is in service of a more general postmodern, poststructuralist attack on modernism, the Enlightenment, and the "coercive universalism" of modern imperialism, whether militaristic, capitalistic, or cultural. For Boyarin, the universalism of Hellenism represents hegemony; the particularity of rabbinic Judaism, if it can avoid nationalistic Zionism, stands for peaceful multiculturalism in a postmodern, poststructuralist world.

The last of the post-war Jewish interpretations of Paul I will mention is Alan Segal's *Paul the Convert: the Apostolate and Apostasy of Saul the Pharisee.*[69] Segal's study may be considered out of place among these others because he does not really frame it in terms of a Hellenism/Judaism dualism (which is also perhaps why I find his study the most amenable to my own views).[70] I do include it here, though, because it reflects so clearly the current situation of American post-war pluralism and the constantly shifting situation of Jews within American society.

Segal self-consciously uses studies of modern religious conversion and their categories. He speaks of conversions from Anglicanism to evangelicalism, from being "an acculturated Jew" to becoming "a Lubavitcher Hasid." So his study stands clearly in an environment of contemporary religious volunteerism, denominationalism, and questions of unstable religious and ethnic identity—including questions about how religion and ethnicity relate to one another in the formation of identity. Jewish identity itself poses an intellectual *problem* in Segal's study: How is it to be understood? What is the relation between ethnicity, religion, and nationality? How much Judaism does it take to make a Jew? When does acculturation become complete assimilation, or conversion? In Segal's treatment of ancient Judaism, Hellenism represents acculturation to a dominant culture; Judaism is an ethnic-religious subculture.

According to Segal, Jews in the Hellenistic Mediterranean experienced a new situation of individual choice in which they had to redefine their identities as Jews.

> Instead of defining themselves merely as children of Israel, individual Jews among the developing cosmopolitan culture of Hellenistic cities, like all other peoples throughout the ancient Near East, began to look at themselves as individuals with unique personal histories. As the educated classes became aware of their unique histories among the varieties of cultures in the Hellenistic world, they exercised a new, broader choice in their religion and life-style. As in trade, the freer atmosphere brought new competition between religious establishments, which could no longer take for granted the allegiance of their population. As a result, the religious tradition, which had been an almost unconscious, self-evident assumption about the world, became a set of beliefs to be marketed. (32)

To understand how Jews reacted to the new cultural situation of Hellenism, Segal draws on modern studies of colonialism and subaltern groups: "Ancient Israel reacted to the influx of Hellenistic culture as colonized nations have always reacted to imperialism" (32). Two "sects" of Israelite culture thus developed (one more Hellenized and one more traditional), competing with each other for the loyalty of Jews. "But their interaction was absolutely essential to national unity in the cosmopolitan and individualistic Hellenistic world, for no one interpretation of Israel's traditional religious life could have satisfied the enormous spectrum of personal opinion that had developed. The sectarian rivalry, like the party system in the United States, allowed for an orderly expression of conflict." Paul should be understood as formed in just this environment, and, "In this atmosphere religious conversion was as common as it is today" (32).

Note the conceptual apparatus Segal uses to frame the ancient relationship between Hellenism and Judaism. He uses the language of individualism, colonialism, dominant and subaltern cultures, and pluralism. Ancient ethnic and religious "establishments" are spoken of as if they were American denominations "marketing" their commodified religious "options" to individuals who have recently experienced the collapse of traditional values and self-evident truths. Religions have become separated from traditional loyalties and ethnicity. Individuals are experiencing new freedoms, choices among several "life-styles." The commodification of religions and ideas becomes inevitable. Within this cultural pluralism, it is natural to expect that Judaism would reflect a wide spectrum of styles and theologies and that persons might move relatively freely from one to another, even with conversion to new religious movements a not uncommon occurrence. I'm not saying that this is a wrong historical account; I am saying that it looks remarkably like post-war America. In Segal's presentation, Hellenism and Judaism represent none of the predictable themes of previous scholarship. They are nonetheless symbols in a rather dualistic system, here representing the dominant culture on the one hand and the minority subculture on the other—in a way that is perfectly understandable in late twentieth-century America. Here at the end of the twentieth century, the Hellenism/Judaism dualism, developed with such different meanings in nineteenth-century Germany, may be doing different business, but it is still in business.

Conclusion That Is Not Conclusive

Even this superficial survey of a few instances of "Judaism" and "Hellenism" in the interpretation of Paul and early Christianity shows that a dualism that many have taken as "unavoidable," natural, or obvious in New Testament studies is dispensable after all. In fact, as a dualism, the Hellenism/Judaism dichotomy is recent and has a limited geographical range. It was invented in nineteenth-century Germany and imported into British and North American usage mainly from there. Furthermore, the meanings of the dualism and its constituent parts are remarkably flexible and varied. "Hellenism" has represented universalism, Christianity, rationality, freedom, abstraction, timelessness, barrenness, individualism, nationalism, antinationalism, culture, Protestantism, sophistry, human wisdom, philosophy, theology, dogmatism, asceticism, dynamism, and so on. Judaism, for its part, has been used to represent particularism, communalism, sterility, historicity, nonhistoricity, Roman Catholicism, Lutheran dogmatism, poststructuralism, effeminacy, feminism, revelation, nationalism, antinationalism, legalism, freedom, naturalism, simplicity, religion, prophecy, asceticism, nonasceticism, dynamism, and so on and on. Indeed, a history of scholarship on the topic shows that the terms in themselves are meaningless apart from specific contexts.

While I certainly would not want to contend that the exegetical or theological debates among scholars were unimportant or merely secondary to other, more "real" issues, it is nonetheless obvious that treatments of the Hellenism and Judaism of Paul and early Christianity are absolutely implicated in other contemporary debates. I do not mean to imply that we should attempt to extricate ourselves from our surroundings or work to be "objective" or "disinterested" in our research, as if we could keep our own concerns from affecting our historical work. I do suggest, though, that we might be better off, or at least less predictable and therefore more interesting, if we recognize our own interests and contingencies and acknowledge how they relate to our readings. I moreover believe it is important for us to be more aware of the categories we use in historical analysis. For example, once we look at the sort of historical survey here offered, we can see that the categories of meaning have shifted importantly over the last few centuries, suggesting that although we may be using the same terms as seventeenth-century English scholars, we do not mean the same things by those terms. At the beginning of modernity, for instance, "Judaism" was a category of religion (a *religio* linked to a particular people). Later, the term shifted and came to be a category of "nationality," which itself shifted to include notions of "race" either along with or in place of "nation." Since the Second World War, "Judaism" has lost its limited denotation as a "religion." Nor can it be limited to a "nation," since the state of Israel is not taken by most people to represent all of "Judaism." And since the racist underpinnings of Nazism have been so fully acknowledged, it is almost always assumed today that one should not understand "Judaism" as a term of "race." Rather, the dominant category has become "culture."

Since the middle of the twentieth century, "culture" has become an important category in Western intellectual circles. As two scholars have put it, "In explanatory importance and in generality of application it is comparable to such categories as gravity in physics, disease in medicine, evolution in biology."[71] The usefulness of the term is heightened, moreover, by the fact that it has become so important even outside scholarly contexts. Over thirty years ago, Margaret Mead could write, "The words 'in our culture' slip from the lips of educated men and women almost as effortlessly as do the phrases that refer to period and place."[72] But as has been well portrayed in recent scholarship, the category of "culture" has itself a short history. From its use before the twentieth century as a term referring to what we would call "high culture," as in the older German use of *Kultur*, its meaning changed, mainly in the hands of anthropologists.

Only in the twentieth century and initially among British anthropologists had "culture" come to be a complex and unified category, referring to social institutions, religion, politics, everyday practices, explicit and unacknowledged assumptions about eating, drinking, sex, family structures, the body, boundaries—indeed, the list is inexhaustible. The utility of the category of culture lay in its ability to provide some structure to an infinite and complex conglomeration of societal significations. Thus, just when scholars have become uneasy with the prejudices and limitations of the frameworks of nation, race, theology, and even religion for understanding Hellenism and Judaism, the category of "culture" offers a more comprehensive and, in the assumptions of most of us I think, more egalitarian, pluralist, and thus "fairer" way of structuring our thoughts.

Given the ubiquitous importance of the category of "culture" in modern culture, it may be inevitable that we use it to structure our current debates on Judaism and its relationship to early Christianity. But it is precisely in the use of the category of "culture" that I want to urge attention to current critical theory. Various critiques of the post-1920s concept of "culture" that have been mounted by postmodernist or poststructuralist writers have rightly emphasized that earlier anthropological notions of culture ignore important issues of historical change and conflict in the creation of culture. "Culture" has too often been taken as a stable, sometimes even essentialized entity.[73] Poststructuralists argue that the very instability of cultural formations must be recognized. Minority "subaltern" forces and systems must be seen not just as "others" to the "culture" but as part of the very complex that we are delineating as "culture." Contradictions and shifts must be taken into account much more than they were in the older, more "functionalist," anthropological studies of culture. Furthermore, Marxist criticisms have rightly argued that many uses of "culture" reify systems in ways that render political action difficult. Agency and politics can become irrelevant when "culture" takes on a life of its own. Some theories of culture, in other words, have committed the error of reifying an abstraction and then ignoring or implicitly denying the contingent, historical agency of actual people. Finally, I would highlight the poststructuralist critiques of older views of "culture" that assume relatively stable "selves" as existing in those relatively stable "cultures." Poststructuralism and postmodernism emphasize notions like "hybridity" and "bricolage" to characterize both social systems and individual selves. But these notions in turn render it more difficult to talk about Paul's Hellenism *or* his Judaism. Indeed, I would argue that, carried out properly, poststructuralist critiques of the "self" to a great extent undermine the meaningfulness of the older questions. I find that development salutary from a historical point of view. Our work, in my opinion, should now concentrate on the *complexities* and *instabilities* of both ancient "cultures" and "selves" rather than searching for a coherence, consistency, and stability implied by earlier uses of "culture."

In the end, I do not urge attention to current cultural theory because I believe that it will provide us with the "objective," "sufficient," or finally "accurate" portrait of early Christianity, Paul, or Judaism. Nor do I believe that disinterested history or exegesis is possible or, even if it were possible, desirable. I do believe that we will be better historians if we better understand our own interests and how they affect our research. And I certainly believe we will be more likely to avoid certain mistreatments of our fellow human beings if we recognize our own perceptual and epistemological limitations and contingencies.

Chapter 3

Hellenism and Hellenization as Problematic Historiographical Categories

Philip S. Alexander

Hellenism as an Ideological Construct

The concept of Hellenism has had a long and varied history in Western thought, starting with the Greeks themselves and coming right down to our own times.[*] I know of no single work that recounts this history in all its complexity, though aspects of it have been written up.[1] Besides looking at what the Greeks understood by "Hellenism," a full account of Hellenism would have to investigate the use of the term in four broad contexts—in Christian tradition, in Jewish tradition, in post-Enlightenment European thought, and in modern academic historiography. I would like

[*] The present essay began as a response to Dale Martin's paper on "Paul between Hellenism and Judaism: Toward a Social History of the Question" at the Copenhagen Conference in August 1997 (see pp. 29–61 of the present volume). While very much in agreement with the thrust of Martin's essay, this piece attempts to open up some ancillary lines of inquiry.

to offer here a few notes towards a history of Hellenism in order to demonstrate how the term has acquired strong ideological associations that must be kept firmly in mind when it is employed in historiography.[2]

One significant aspect of the history of Hellenism within the Christian tradition is the periodic resurgence of the antithetical phenomenon of Hebraism. This involves abandoning the vulgar translations of the Old Testament, and the apparatus of interpretation and theology which rests upon them, and returning to the original Hebrew, the *Hebraica Veritas*, and, in part, to the guidance of the Jewish scholars who were masters of that text.[3] Obvious cases of such Hebraism in antiquity are the *Hexapla* of Origen and Jerome's revision of the *Vetus Itala* in the light of the Hebrew. In the Middle Ages the Victorines and Franciscans such as Nicholas of Lyra also showed a strong interest in Hebrew.[4] The Reformation marked a further powerful upsurge of Hebraism within the church, which was followed in our own times by a second wave coinciding with the advent of historical-critical scholarship in the nineteenth century, though modern Christian Hebraists are less beholden to the linguistic authority of "the ancient Rabbins" than were their Reformation forebears.[5] We should be in no doubt that Hebraism in the Church has been for the most part ideologically driven. It might seem axiomatic to modern Christians that the original Hebrew is the inspired text of the Old Testament, but this fact was not so obvious to the early church, which, following Alexandrian Jewish tradition, seems to have accepted the Septuagint as equally inspired—a position that in principle is theologically defensible.[6]

A return to the *Hebraica Veritas* has raised difficult and possibly intractable theological problems for the church—for example, by weakening the link between Old Testament prophecy and New Testament fulfilment.[7] Moreover, the Christian scholars who have advocated Hebraism have usually not been motivated by any genuine desire to reach out to Judaism. Rather their aim has been to score points in inner Christian debates. Christian Hebraists, despite their considerable command of Hebrew and knowledge of Jewish literature, have often been highly critical, not to say contemptuous, of Judaism, and have used Jewish texts purely for their own ends. Indeed, there often seems to be implicit in their thinking as sharp a contrast between Hebraism (which is good) and Judaism (which is bad), as there is between Hebraism and Hellenism.

Two examples involving two of the greatest Christian Hebraists will illustrate how Christian Hebraism has been intertwined with apologetics and theology. Joseph Scaliger (1540–1609) was one of the most enlightened and learned scholars of the Reformation, and a formidable Hebraist.

The only complete surviving copy of the Talmud Yerushalmi (Ms. Scaliger 3 of the University Library, Leiden) was once in his possession. He took an interest, extremely rare at the time, not only in the Talmud but in the great Jewish opponents of the Talmud, the Qaraites, and wrote some brief but pioneering accounts of their ideas. Though all this seems highly commendable and scholarly, there may be a hidden agenda. When Scaliger begins to contrast the Qaraites favorably with the Rabbanites, we begin to wonder whether he saw an analogy between the Qaraites' rejection of the Talmud and return to the simplicity of the Hebrew Bible on the one hand, and the Protestants' rejection of Catholic tradition and their return to *Sola Scriptura* on the other.[8]

A somewhat similar story can be told about Johann Reuchlin (1454–1522). Reuchlin has earned enduring respect for his defense of the Talmud and other Rabbinic writings against the attacks of Johann Pfefferkorn and the Dominican friars of Cologne, but he too used Judaism for his own, very Christian ends. Reuchlin also found a "true" Judaism within Judaism, namely the Qabbalah, which he opposed to the Talmud, and which, accepting its claims to antiquity, he saw as anticipating Christianity. The Qabbalah served a twofold purpose in Reuchlin's thought. On the one hand he could invoke it to embarrass Jews and to challenge them to acknowledge that their most secret and authentic doctrines were actually more in accord with Christian teaching than they were publicly prepared to admit. On the other hand, the Qabbalah provided him with authentication for the distinctive views that he himself sought to advocate within Christianity.[9]

"Hellenism"[10] has also had a convoluted and ambivalent history within Judaism, which was shaped mainly by two factors: first, the struggle for Jewish national self-determination against the Greeks in the Hasmonaean era, an event annually recalled in the festival of Hanukkah, and second by the supposed Rabbinic ban on the study of "Greek wisdom" (חוכמת יוונית), a subject to which I shall return presently. These together have created an almost universal impression, both inside and outside Judaism, that Judaism and Hellenism as cultures are irreconcilably opposed. Certainly "Hellenism" has been used by orthodox Jewish writers in modern times as a highly negative term to denote secular culture antithetical to Torah Judaism. Orthodox apologists regard the followers of the Jewish Enlightenment in the nineteenth century—the Maskilim—as having sold out to Hellenism. Some of the advocates of Haskalah, like the poet Saul Tchernikowsky, wore the badge of Hellenism with pride, and saw it as their mission to introduce some Greek sunshine into the obscurantism of traditional East European Jewish orthodoxy.[11]

"Hellenism" in this *Kulturkampf* has become a complex symbol, which, although it has clear links with the historical civilization of classical Greece (Tchernikowsky was a pioneering translator of the Greek classics into Hebrew), also functions as a code word for modern European secular culture seen as derived in some sense from classical Greece. The Hellenizers wanted acculturation, even assimilation to contemporary European culture; the anti-Hellenizers opposed such acculturation as a betrayal of Judaism. The rhetoric of this dispute continues to resonate in the political discourse of contemporary Israel. Ultra-Orthodox (*Haredi*) groups in Israel when resisting secularization (such as the building of a sports stadium in Jerusalem) have regularly invoked the spirit of the Hasmonaeans. For them the struggles of Judas Maccabaeus and his brothers are still not over. Ironically secular Zionism, which in *Haredi* eyes is promoting Hellenism, also frequently invokes the image of the Hasmonaeans and has been responsible for a revaluation of the festival of Hanukkah that emphasizes the nation-building and the militaristic sides of the story.

Yet the ideological vehemence of this dispute clouds some simple historical facts. In antiquity Jewish opposition to things Greek manifested itself on a comparatively narrow front. It was first and foremost opposition to Greek political domination. Second, it was opposition to the idolatry of Greek popular religion. Third, it was opposition to certain Greek mores that the Rabbis loosely classified as "Ways of the Amorites."[12] But this approach leaves huge swaths of Greek culture untouched. Opposition to these aspects of Greek culture does not mean opposition to absolutely everything Greek. Take a work like the book of Jubilees. As I have argued elsewhere, this book was written partially to support the Hasmonaean revolution, yet its *Mappa Mundi*, which is fundamentally a piece of anti-Greek propaganda, is based on an Ionian Greek world map.[13] Jewish opposition to Hellenism is full of such ironies.

Take also the presence from time to time of creative fusions of Greek and Jewish thought. Philo is the most obvious example. It might seem easy, at first sight, to dismiss Philo from the standpoint of Rabbinic orthodoxy as a perversion of Judaism, until we recall that similar fusions of Greek and Jewish ideas were produced in the middle ages by Jewish theologians such as Sa'adya and Maimonides, who were pillars of Rabbanism and heirs of the Talmudic tradition. Or take the "Bible" of the Spanish Qabbalah, the Zohar, historically one of the most important religious texts in Judaism, which has manifestly been influenced, directly or indirectly, by Neoplatonism. Or take Ibn Gabirol's majestic poem the *Keter Malkhut*, which equally shows Platonic influence, and yet is part of the Sephardi liturgy for Yom Kippur. To call these "Hellenized Judaism," if by this we imply that the essence of Judaism has been fundamentally altered or distorted under the impact of Greek ideas, is facile, tendentious, and probably, in the final analysis, meaningless. It could be argued, with Yaacov Shavit, that the last act of the symbiosis of Judaism and Hellenism is being played out before our eyes. Those literary forms and genres that are peculiarly Greek in origin—plays, novels, lyric and epic poetry, belles-lettres and scientific history, scientific and technical writing of every kind—are now being produced in large quantities by Jews in the "Holy Tongue."[14]

Hellenism is also a highly charged and value-laden concept in the discourse of post-Enlightenment European thought. Two brief comments on the contemporary situation—one relating to the sphere of literary theory, the other to the sphere of politics—should suffice to illustrate this point. Hebraism has become a major issue in postmodernist literary criticism. Susan Handelman, José Faur, and others have argued that postmodernist hermeneutics are anticipated by Rabbinic ways of reading the Bible.[15] Faur claims that Greek modes of thought have so dominated European civilization that Rabbinic modes, especially as expressed in Rabbinic Bible commentary, have remained outside of, and opposed to, the cultural code of the West. However, he argues, in structuralism and post-structuralism ideas close to those of the Rabbis have begun to emerge in the mainstream Western tradition. A line runs from Rabbi Aqiba in Benei Beraq to Jacques Derrida in Paris, a link that Derrida himself seemed happy to affirm when he playfully referred to himself as "Reb Derrida."[16] Midrash has become a fashionable paradigm among literary critics for how one should read texts. I cannot rehearse here the arguments with which I would oppose these claims as historically incorrect.[17] Suffice simply to note them here to show how the relationship between Hellenism and Hebraism is a live issue in today's intellectual world.

The illustration from the contemporary political scene touches on the problem of "Orientalism" as analyzed by Edward Said and others.[18] The great European colonial powers in the nineteenth century played out in their own imaginations a variation of the Hellenism/Barbarism paradigm. This was certainly true in the case of many British colonial administrators, most of whom had been well trained in the classics at public school and read Latin and Greek. They pictured themselves as cultured Greeks or Romans bringing the light of law and civilization to the benighted barbarians, though a few, like some ancient Greeks, were seduced by the exoticism and the strange wisdom of the barbarians and "went native." A double intellectual construction was involved here: first classical antiquity was constructed in terms of law, rationalism, and "higher" cultural forms and identified with the culture of the colonial power; then native cultures were constructed in terms of the antitheses of these values. This view took on a deeply racist form in the case of thinkers such as Houston Stewart Chamberlain, who internalized it *within* Europe by arguing that the Indo-Aryans, and especially the Teutons and their German descendants, were the great civilizers of history and that the other peoples of Europe, especially Jews, were, in effect, "barbarians" within.[19]

Such language is, of course, unacceptable today in a post-colonial, post-Holocaust world. But the old Hellene/Barbarian dichotomy is by no means dead. Europe politically today finds itself facing, and feeling threatened by, an alien world across the Mediterranean Sea. That world is epitomized for the European media in what it calls "Islamic fundamentalism," a construct that includes a wide and highly diverse range of Islamic responses to the fear of continuing Western political and cultural imperialism. The rhetoric with which the relationship between Islam and the West is depicted is reminiscent of the rhetoric that opposed Judaism to Hellenism or to civilized Christian Europe. Complex cross-currents are flowing here. The Holocaust embarrassed most Christian critics of Judaism into silence, but to some degree the criticism has been displaced onto Islam. Islam rather than Judaism has become the bogeyman of Europe, the alien other against whom one defines one's own identity. Ancient memories and fears are invoked. Judaism and Islam have always been closely linked in the European imagination. Since the time of John of Damascus Christian theologians have tended to lump Judaism and Islam together as Christian heresies.[20] Europe has never finally exorcised the trauma of the loss of North Africa and the Levant to Islam. It is still haunted by the memory of the great pincer movement by which Islam, first surging through the Iberian peninsula and then later through the Balkans, almost brought Christian European civilization to an end. The threat of Islam has played a major role in the construction of the concept of Europe, a concept at the forefront of European politics since the founding of the European Union.[21] Theodor Herzl, the father of political Zionism, showed an uncanny appreciation of this when he said that if the European powers backed a Jewish state in Palestine, that state would function for Europe as a "bulwark against barbarism."[22] It is not hard to hear in this language the distant clamour of Marathon and of Greek pitted against Barbarian. But the ironies could scarcely be richer. Here was a Hellenized Jew proposing that a state comprised of European Jews, the archetypal "barbarians" of the Europe imagination, would act as a bulwark in the defense of European civilization. His words proved strangely prescient, since many Islamic thinkers see present-day Israel as an instrument of Western imperialism and as representing values that are alien to the culture of the Middle East.

There is obviously much more to be said on this complex subject, but I hope I have said enough to demonstrate that Hellenism is a highly charged ideological concept that should be handled with the utmost care. Historians are naive if they think they can safely use it and ignore its ideological overtones.

Hellenism Historically Deconstructed

Hellenism is only useful as a historiographical category if it can be defined clearly and demarcated from other cultures, such as Judaism, which are not-Hellenism. Such a definition remains elusive. Many have tried, but it is usually not difficult to show that their efforts are tendentious and subjective, and involve arbitrarily privileging one aspect of Greek culture over others. How can one begin to capture the essence of so diverse a phenomenon as Greek culture or civilization?[23] Capturing the essence of Judaism, or of Hebrew or Semitic thought, as distinct from Hellenism, is no more easy.

Behind the concept of Hellenism seems to lurk an assumption that Greek culture was in origin all but autochthonous. Within the fastness of their steep-sided valleys the ancient Greeks through their native genius produced a highly original and individualistic civilization, which was carried in the fullness of time into the Orient by Alexander the Great. If we set against the Greeks, as their mirror image, the fiercely xenophobic, exclusivist Jews, condemning and rejecting the cultures around them, at least from the time of Ezra, and clinging stubbornly to their own covenant God, then a picture emerges of two essentially monadic cultures that were destined to collide like billiard balls, and from whose collision, in Hegelian fashion, European civilization was to emerge. Of course I parody, but only a little. In fact, it is now clear from archaeology that all the cultures of the eastern Mediterranean and Near East were in constant contact and interchange at both the material and intellectual levels from earliest antiquity.[24] Martin West, one of the first to attack the "Hellenic solipsism" of classical scholarship, has shown that Hesiod had his Near Eastern forerunners, as had, more controversially, the Ionian Greek philosophers.[25] Stephanie Dalley and others have argued, with some plausibility, that Homer, the "prophet of the Greeks," may owe something to ancient Near Eastern epics such as Gilgamesh.[26] Interestingly, the Greeks themselves seldom claimed that their culture was autochthonous. Despite a streak of xenophobia, persistent traditions held that their civilization was derived from the East, usually from Egypt. And Greek intellectuals from time to time showed a profound interest in, and even respect for, non-Greek cultures, a phenomenon brilliantly analyzed by Momigliano in *Alien Wisdom*.[27] So when Alexander carried Greek culture to the Near East some of his cultural baggage may have originated there. It was, in effect, being repatriated, albeit possibly in altered form. It would hardly be surprising, then, if that culture found a ready home.

This fluid, interactive picture points to a more nuanced and dynamic model for understanding the relationship between Hellenism and Judaism in antiquity. Instead of thinking of the Levant and ancient Near East in terms of a set of essentially self-contained cultures that impinged on each other effectively only in times of historical crisis (such as invasion and conquest), we should envisage, rather, a set of cultures whose boundaries were always permeable to outside influences and allowed a constant flow back and forth across them of cultural exchange. Or rather, since by late antiquity such cultural exchange had been going on for at least a thousand years, accelerated latterly by the political unification of the Levant and Near East under the Persians, Greeks, and Romans, we should think of a broadly uniform culture pervading the whole region, within which various groups adapted the dominant cultural patterns and structures in order to create subcultures and establish ethnic identities.

This change of perspective has important consequences. A member of one society understands another society largely through a process of cultural translation, similar to the process of linguistic translation. He or she finds in his or her own society analogies to the elements of the alien society that they are trying to understand. The analogies are seldom exact, and will have varying degrees of validity, but without them comprehension is impossible. Within the broadly uniform cultural milieu of the Levant and Near East in late antiquity the analogies between the subcultures were numerous and strong, and cultural "translation" therefore relatively easy. Members of those subcultures, when in contact, could without too much difficulty find cultural structures and patterns in each other's societies to which they could relate. This was as true of the Greeks and the Jews as it was of everyone else. A simple example may help to clarify this point. When Josephus, writing for a Greek audience, correlates the sects of Second Temple Judaism with Greek philosophical schools, he is engaging in cultural translation.[28] In this case, the correlation is thoughtful and valid: he has correctly perceived a significant analogy between Greek and Jewish society. But it is somewhat pointless to speak of this analogy simply in terms of one group borrowing from another. The pattern itself is not intrinsically Greek or Jewish. Rather we should think of a cultural pattern generic to the whole region that has been specified in each subculture in slightly different ways.

This alternative model, which softens the dichotomy between Judaism and Hellenism, helps me solve a problem that I shall attempt to analyze a little more fully. I would argue that it was impossible for the Rabbis to be Hellenized in any strict sense of the term because they did not have a good command of the Greek language, nor did they attend Greek schools. Yet the more I study Rabbinic Judaism the more at home it seems to be as a cultural phenomenon in the Greco-Roman world of its day. The Rabbinic schools, for example—the quintessential Rabbinic cultural institution—show strong affinities to the Greco-Roman schools of law and medicine. Also, the development of Rabbinic law is significantly paralleled by the development of Roman law.[29] The reason is, I would suggest, that we are dealing here with cultural elements that by late antiquity were common to the whole region. Schools and scribes, law and lawyers, had been around in the Mediterranean and the Near East from time immemorial. To invoke a diffusionist model and to suppose that all the common cultural elements were Hellenistic in origin, and to conclude that the region was totally Hellenized, is tendentious and unwarranted. In fact it involves a *reductio ad absurdum* of the Hellenization model.

In one discipline the concept of Hellenism and Hellenization is noticeably alive, namely archaeology. Stand in the ruins of Gerasa (Jerash) and you cannot but be impressed by the Greekness of the city. Here, in Transjordan, in an historically Semitic milieu, is a city that has streets lined with Ionic and Corinthian columns, a Nympheion, theatres, and a huge temple dedicated to Artemis.[30] These artifacts are not historically native to this region. They come from elsewhere. Archaeologists digging through the mounds of the Near East notice a dramatic change of material culture when they come to the Hellenistic period. To them the process of Hellenization is tangible. At this level it may well be valid to talk of Hellenism and Hellenization. But we should be careful not to jump to conclusions. Cultural artifacts and material evidence require as much interpretation as do ancient written texts. We should not assume that what we are witnessing is some profound cultural upheaval—the imposition of an alien and uncongenial culture on the natives.

Moreover, here, too, we should observe the nuances. There is as much Romanitas in Gerasa as there is Hellenism. The city is laid out in the *Roman* fashion with a cardo and two decumani, following a pattern that was found throughout the Roman Empire all the way to Trier on the Mosel. At the southern entrance to the city stands a Roman arch erected in honor of Hadrian. In building in this fashion the natives were not so much expressing their admiration for things Greek as their aspiration to be part of the international world of the Roman Empire. Nor should we miss the local idiosyncrasies, such as the exuberant baroque style of decoration that is reluctant to leave any flat surface uncarved—a style that in terms of classical Greek aesthetics is definitely not *comme il faut*. And how can we tell from the material remains what the natives were *thinking*? Was it the *Greek* Artemis that they worshiped in their great temple or an ancient local Semitic goddess under that name? Was the Hellenism anything more than a superficial repackaging of a fundamentally unchanged local culture? Here a comparison with the Petra scrolls discovered to the south may help. These legal texts are written in Greek in a good documentary hand, but the names found in them are often Semitic (some, apparently, are to this day still to be found in the Wadi Musa region). More significantly, some of their legal formulae and usages are probably Nabatean and not Greek. Greek here is arguably only a veneer over continuing local custom and practice.[31] In short, the effects of Hellenization in the Transjordan may appear impressive and significant, but they may on closer inspection amount in cultural and historical terms to much less than we might at first suppose.

Hellenism and Judaism: A Revised Analytical Paradigm

Though I have argued for a broadly uniform culture throughout the Levant and Near East in late antiquity I do not want to over-homogenize the region nor deny the existence within it of cultural diversity. It undoubtedly contained quite distinctive subcultures. People, for example, identified themselves as Jews and as Greeks and vehemently, sometimes violently, defended those identities. How these subcultures interacted, how they understood and even influenced each other, is a matter of considerable historical moment. But how are we to analyze this interaction without falling into the trap of essentialism?

I would like to conclude this essay by considering briefly the problem of the Rabbis' relationship to Hellenism and by offering this analysis as a paradigm of the only valid way in which, as far as I can see, the modern historian can continue to use the categories of Hellenism and Hellenization. Two preliminary points are in order.

First, by the Rabbis I mean strictly the Palestinian Rabbis of the first five centuries of the current era—that is to say, the scholars who produced the Mishnah, the classic Midrashim and the Talmud Yerushalmi, and who are frequently quoted in the Talmud Bavli as well. I do not mean Judaism in any wider sense. Other forms of Judaism were present in late antiquity, some of which, like the Alexandrian Judaism of Philo, are more obviously Hellenistic than is Talmudic Judaism, but these forms are not my primary concern here, though they might be helpful comparatively, if one were attempting to measure the *degree* of the Rabbis' Hellenization.

Second, I take it for granted that there are *prima facie* significant parallels between Rabbinic Judaism and Hellenism. I have discussed these at length elsewhere.[32] The question is: how are such parallels to be explained? Are they due to the influence of Hellenism on Rabbinic Judaism? Was Hellenization a significant factor in the development of Rabbinic Judaism?

In tackling these questions we should avoid defining Hellenism in an abstract, and potentially tendentious, way. Rather we should break it down into its constituent cultural elements. We should also recognize that a hierarchical relationship pertains between these elements: elements of high cultural specificity—that is to say, elements that are distinctive to both systems—carry more weight than elements that belong to the common culture of the Levant in late antiquity. To speak more concretely we can resolve the problem of the Rabbis and Hellenism into a number of concrete questions, such as: (1) Did the Rabbis know the Greek language, and, if they did, what was the level of their knowledge? (2) Did they attend Greek schools, or did Greek studies form part of the curriculum in the Rabbinic schools? (3) Do the Rabbis in their writings display a knowledge of Greek literature, and if so what was the level of that knowledge? (4) Do they display a knowledge of Greek ideas or of Greek thought? (5) What were Rabbinic attitudes towards Greek art, and (6) Greek science? (7) Is there any clear evidence that Greek political or cultural institutions were adopted by Rabbinic society? Only when we have answered these kinds of questions will we be able to decide whether or not the parallels between Rabbinic Judaism and Hellenism are due to Greek influence. And even if they are, we will still not have answered the basic question of whether that influence was significant in the development of Rabbinic Judaism. Deep structural analogies between Greek and Rabbinic society may mean that all that we have uncovered is a somewhat superficial repackaging of Rabbinic cultural forms in Greek guise.

For purposes of the present brief analysis we can concentrate on the first two of our list of questions, because they are absolutely fundamental. A knowledge of Greek was the Oriental's indispensable entry-ticket into the Hellenistic club. Anyone who did not know Greek was effectively

locked out of Greek culture (we have not yet reached the era of translations from Greek into Oriental languages), and so could hardly have been
Hellenized to any significant degree. Greek language carries high cultural
specificity, but not *per se*. The *level* of knowledge is crucial: "street" Greek
will not do.[33] A higher knowledge of Greek, which shows evidence of
rhetorical training, could only have been acquired through participation
in Greek *paideia*, and that effectively meant attending Greek schools or
studying with Greek tutors. If there is doubt that the Rabbis knew Greek
well, or were involved in Greek *paideia*, then we must seriously question
whether they were Hellenized. The parallels between Rabbinic Judaism
and Hellenism will have to be explained in other ways.

Greek was probably widely spoken among the Jews of Palestine in the
first few centuries of the current era. Frey's *Corpus Inscriptionum
Judaicarum* (= CIJ) contains some 530 inscriptions from Palestine dating
from late antiquity.[34] Of these roughly 52 percent are in Greek, 40 percent in Hebrew/Aramaic, and 8 percent in a mixture of Greek and
Hebrew/Aramaic.[35] The conclusion seems obvious: many Palestinian
Jews spoke Greek, and, if this was the case, then there is surely a strong
presumption that the Rabbis, who were among the more educated members of Jewish society, would have known the language.

But such crude statistical arguments should be used with caution. Five
hundred thirty can be only a small proportion of the total number of Jewish inscriptions from Palestine in the period under review. Much of the
evidence comes from ossuaries. Ossuaries were probably made of two
materials, stone and wood. The former have survived whereas the latter
have perished leaving only, in some cases, telltale nails behind. Stone
ossuaries, being probably more expensive, would have been affordable
only by the more wealthy families, who for a variety of reasons are more
likely to have known Greek. Wooden ossuaries would have been used by
the poorer classes. If we had some inscriptions from the wooden artifacts,
then the statistics might well change significantly.

Bear in mind also that some of the Greek inscriptions belong to Jews
from the Diaspora, where Greek was, perforce, more widely spoken in the
Jewish communities. There is evidence that the necropolis at Beth
She'arim was used as a central burial place by the Jews of the East, after
Judah ha-Nasi made the town his residence and the seat of the Sanhedrin.
One of the catacombs appears to have belonged to the patriarchal family.
Several rooms contained Palmyrene ossuaries. Significantly burials from
this quarter ceased in 272/3 when Palmyra was destroyed by the Romans.
Another hall was reserved for Himyarite Jews from southern Arabia. It
would be rash to assume that all those names in Greek that are not asso-

ciated with some place abroad were local. We simply do not know. The settlement of Greek-speaking Jews from the Diaspora has also affected the picture in the coastal towns. We find Jews from Seleucia in Isauria at Haifa (CIJ 882); from Babylon at Caesarea Maritima (CIJ 889) and Jaffa (CIJ 902); from Cappadocia, Alexandria, Tarsus, Pentapolis (in Cyrenaica), Chios, Ptolemais, Diospolis, and Neapolis (though which Neapolis is uncertain), all at Jaffa (CIJ 910, 918, 934, 928, 931, 950, 915, 956, 957). Such inscriptions tell us more about the language of the Jews of the Diaspora than about the language of the Jews native to Palestine.

As I indicated earlier, it is important for our purposes to distinguish the Greek spoken by ordinary folk in every life, in business and trade, from the Greek of the more educated. The vast majority of the inscriptions exemplify Greek only of the former level. There are some longer inscriptions that betray some knowledge of Greek syntax, but only seven point to a deeper knowledge of the language. Two of these may be dismissed immediately as falling outside our precise period, viz., CIJ 1400 (the warning notice to Gentiles on the *tryphaktos* of the Herodian Temple), and CIJ 1404 (also from Herodian times, and anyway possibly erected by the archisynagogus of the Synagogue of the Libertines in Jerusalem mentioned in Acts 6:9). Of the others, one (CIJ 165) is in memory of the workmen who laid the mosaic in the synagogue at Beth Alpha. Possibly these workmen were from outside the region and were brought in as experts to lay the floor. The rest of the inscriptions in the synagogue are in Hebrew. Another inscription (CIJ 972), dated to 197 C.E., is in honor of Septimius Severus, but it is hardly surprising that an official inscription in honor of the emperor should be written in good Greek. Neither the Severus nor the Beth Alpha inscriptions prove much. Very different, however, are three long verse epigrams, two from Beth She'arim (second–third centuries C.E.) and one from Gophna (undated),[36] which show not only a good knowledge of the Greek language, but of Greek literature as well. These epigrams are so deeply pagan in tone that there must be some doubt as to whether they are, in fact, Jewish. If they are, then they constitute virtually the only substantial evidence for a significant level of Hellenization among Palestinian Jews in the Talmudic period that survives a rigorous sifting of the epigraphic evidence.

A similar conclusion emerges from a study of Greek loanwords in Rabbinic literature. Samuel Krauss's dictionary of Greek and Latin loanwords in the Talmud, Midrash, and Targum[37] lists some 2,370 Greek and 240 Latin loanwords in Rabbinic literature. But a large proportion of his identifications are wrong, and some are completely fantastic, as reviewers of the original work were quick to point out. When these doubtful elements are removed, the count drops to around 1,560. Since this constitutes the deposit of about a millennium of intensive contact with Greek (third century B.C.E.–sixth century C.E.) the number is hardly surprising against the total lexical stock of some 30,000 words for Rabbinic Aramaic and Hebrew. Moreover, some word-groups are hardly significant, e.g., proper names, both geographical and personal, and terms derived from the Roman administration. If such words are also deducted the number falls to around 1,100. A glance at the residue quickly shows that the majority of the words belong to the level of the street and the marketplace. More culturally significant terms relating to literature, thought, and religion are almost totally absent, as are verbal, as opposed to nominal, forms (only 17 out of the 1,100 items).

The channel through which Greek higher culture spread through the East was the gymnasium. As I have already observed, it is hard to see how anyone could have been deeply influenced by Hellenism without at least a basic Greek education. Is there any evidence either of Rabbinic Jews attending the gymnasium, or alternatively of the Rabbinical educational curriculum allowing the study of Greek subjects? This question brings us to a discussion of some much-debated Rabbinic texts that mention the so-called Rabbinic ban on the study of Greek language and Greek wisdom.

Tosefta 'Avodah Zarah 1:20 states: "They asked Rabbi Joshua: Is a man permitted to teach his son Greek? He said to them: Let him teach him at a time which is neither part of the day, nor part of the night, as it is written, 'You shall meditate therein day and night' (Josh. 1:8)."[38] Mishnah Sotah 9:14 offers a partial parallel: "During the War of Quietus they forbade the crowns to the brides, and that a man should teach his son Greek."[39] In both these quotations the reference is to teaching the Greek language to children. The imposing of the ban to teach Greek on the father is noteworthy. From time immemorial in the ancient Near East the duty of educating a son lay primarily with his father. If the father did not have the time or the ability to perform this duty himself, then he was obliged, at least so the Scribes said, to delegate it to teachers. The ban may, therefore, be logically addressed to the party seen as ultimately responsible for the child's education. On the other hand, given that there was probably a fairly well-developed Jewish school system by the time this tradition was formulated, it is rather strange that the father is brought in and not the teacher. The implication may be that if Greek *were* taught, then it would be a purely private matter and outside the official school curriculum. Whichever way we read the text, the father teaching his son Greek is not necessarily to be taken literally. One should not assume that the father himself knew Greek. "Is a man permitted to teach his son

Greek?" may be shorthand for "Is a man permitted to engage a tutor to teach his son Greek?" or "Is a man permitted to send his son to a Greek school so that he can learn to speak Greek?" The reference to the War of Quietus in Mishnah 'Avodah Zarah suggests that the ban may originally have been of limited duration. Quietus is Trajan's general Lucius Quietus who put down the Jewish revolts of 117–118 with great ferocity. However, the Tosefta passage points to an attempt to make the ban permanent by appealing to Josh 1:8.

Bavli Menahot 99b states: "Ben Dama, the son of Rabbi Ishmael's sister asked Rabbi Ishmael: Is a man like myself who has studied the whole of the Torah allowed to study Greek wisdom (חוכמת יוונית)? Rabbi Ishmael quoted him the verse, 'This Book of the Law shall not depart out of your mouth, and you shall meditate in it day and night' (Josh 1:8). Go, said he, and find a time that is neither part of the day nor part of the night and then study Greek wisdom." The precise wording suggests a different emphasis from Tosefta 'Avodah Zarah and Mishnah Sotah quoted above. Ben Dama's query concerns not Greek language, but Greek wisdom. However, just what this involved is not immediately obvious, though one thinks naturally of Greek thought or Greek philosophy.[40] Once again Josh 1:8 is invoked to make the prohibition in effect permanent.

These texts, though far from clear, point to some very tentative conclusions. They suggest that some Rabbinic authorities favored a ban on the study of the Greek language and Greek philosophy.[41] The ban may have begun under exceptional political circumstances during the revolts of 117–118, but then some tried to extend it and make it permanent. The fact that the ban was imposed suggests that some Palestinian Jews were actually studying Greek and Greek wisdom, but we do not know how widespread this practice was, nor how effective the ban may have been in curtailing or stopping it.

What of the possibility that Greek Studies formed an element in the Rabbinic curriculum? Bavli Bava Qamma 83a is a key text: "Was Greek wisdom banned? Did not Rav Judah say that Samuel stated in the name of Rabban Shim'on ben Gamliel: The verse, My eye has been left like a gleaning grape alone of all the daughters of my city (Lam 3:51),[42] could be applied to the thousand young men of my father's house, five hundred of whom studied Torah, while the other five hundred studied Greek wisdom, and out of all of them there remain only myself here and the son of my father's brother in Asia. It may, however, be said that the family of Gamliel was an exception, as they had associations with the government, as indeed it is taught: He who trims the front of his hair in Roman fashion is acting in the way of the Amorites. Yet Abtolmus ben Reuven was permitted to cut his hair in Gentile fashion because he was in close contact with the government. So also the family of Gamliel were permitted to study Greek wisdom because of their association with the government."

Lieberman has made much of this text, inferring from it that "an academy of Greek wisdom existed in Palestine under the auspices of the Patriarch,"[43] but such a conclusion is too bold. The tradition hardly inspires confidence. It comes from a late stratum of a late source: the parallels in Bavli Gittin 58a, Yerushalmi Ta'anit 4:8 (69a), and Eikhah Rabbati III 51 §9 (ed. Buber, 138) make no reference to Greek wisdom, and it is clearly extraneous to the story. The two balancing groups of five hundred have a legendary ring. Lieberman grants that the numbers cannot be taken literally but then tries to argue that "we have here explicit testimony to the effect that the young men belonging to the House of the Patriarch who studied Greek Wisdom were numerically at least approximately equivalent, and whose [*sic*] numbers must have been considerable."[44] But this is over-literal special pleading. If the tradition is historically accurate, it presumably refers to the situation before 135 C.E., but far from recording the persistence of this supposed academy of Greek wisdom it refers to its destruction and dispersal, probably in the aftermath of the Second Revolt.[45] Yet it is not implausible, as the Bavli notes, to suppose that Greek *was* studied by members of the House of the Patriarch for diplomatic purposes. As much is explicitly stated in Tosefta Sotah 15:8 (ed. Zuckermandel 322, 6). A knowledge of Greek would also have been necessary for the *shelihim*, the *apostoloi*, who acted as mediators between the Palestinian Rabbinate and the Jews of the Hellenistic Diaspora. It is probably in this context that we should view the traditions about the Greek learning of the children of the later Patriarchs.[46] Bavli Bava Qamma 83a, which dates from the later Amoraic period, is uncertain whether Greek Wisdom had ever been banned. It is inclined to think that it had. The evidence to the contrary relates to special circumstances. But it is noticeably relaxed about the issue. Whether or not there ever had been a ban seems to be a matter of indifference to the redactor. This indifference is most plausibly explained by supposing that no one in the redactor's milieu bothered to study Greek Wisdom. The question whether or not such study was permitted was, therefore, no longer a burning issue.

If a good knowledge of Greek and a good Greek education are the necessary conditions for Hellenization, then the conclusion seems inevitable that the Rabbis were not in any meaningful sense Hellenized. I know of no compelling contradictory evidence. The Rabbis show no real knowledge of Greek literature (Homer is the only Greek author they mention by name),[47] nor is there any evidence that they were influenced significantly by Greek ideas, nor that any aspect of their political institutions—their law courts and legal system, their schools, the Patriarchate—can be explained only by invoking Greek influence. Some Rabbis were probably rather tolerant of Greek figurative art, more tolerant than their forebears in the Second Temple period had been, but others continued to oppose it implacably.[48] All in all Hellenism probably had little cultural influence on Rabbinic Judaism. Yet, as I noted earlier, Rabbinic Judaism as a culture is very much at home in the Greco-Roman world of late antiquity. The significant parallels remain. The parallelism, however, will have to be, and as I suggested earlier can be, explained in other ways.

Conclusions

What can we conclude from this brief, exploratory discussion? First, I would suggest that it calls into question whether the Judaism/Hellenism divide is meaningful, at least in the sense in which it has commonly been understood, namely, as a *Kulturkampf* between quintessentially antithetical cultures. This dichotomy is based on dubious historical assumptions and is shot through with ideological presuppositions that must be challenged from a post-colonial perspective. However, this is not to deny that Jews and Greeks in late antiquity constructed for themselves recognizably different ethnic identities and created distinctive cultures and societies that interacted in a variety of ways. Tracing the history of that interaction is a meaningful task, but it must not be done in terms of cloudy generalizations about the essence of each culture, but in terms of concrete cultural phenomena (language, literature, institutions, and so forth), and of how these functioned to form national identity. "Culture" must always be broken down into its constituent parts. We must always remember, also, that by late antiquity these cultures had been interacting already for hundreds of years, within the framework of a common culture that spanned the whole of the Levant and the Near East, and that had been evolving dynamically throughout the region for some two millennia. We should be more surprised, therefore, to find fundamental, unparalleled differences between adjacent cultures than to find similarities. We should concentrate on studying in what ways Judaism translated into Hellenism and vice versa, on noting and nuancing the analogies between the subcultures. In short, we need an intellectual paradigm shift so that the presumption now is always in favor of similarity rather than dissimilarity.

Where does Paul fit into this revised picture? Obviously seeing him in terms of a radical Judaism/Hellenism divide is no longer helpful, or even meaningful. Thus it makes little sense to ask how he may have fused Judaism and Hellenism (as if these were clearly different entities) to make something new (Gentile Christianity), or whether he should be considered more Hellenistic than Jewish (or vice versa). Instead we should focus on how Paul, a Hellenized Diaspora Jew, would have been able to make sense of the Jewish culture of Jerusalem and Judea when he encountered it as a young man, on how he took the teaching of a Palestinian Jewish sect and "translated" it for the benefit of Greeks outside Palestine, on what cultural resources those Greeks had at hand to make sense of his message. In asking these questions we should constantly bear in mind that, given the overall cultural situation, Paul's path into Palestinian Judaism would not necessarily have been strewn with hurdles, nor (despite his protests to the contrary)[49] would the Greeks, had they set their minds to it, have found the Christian gospel all that difficult to grasp.

Chapter 4

Does Pauline Christianity Resemble a Hellenistic Philosophy?

Stanley K. Stowers

Introduction

Scholars have rightly judged that in order to properly describe early Christian groups they must compare these groups to other social formations in the environment of the early Christians.[1] But to which group or groups are the Christians best compared? The most frequently appearing candidates are synagogues, voluntary associations, mystery religions, and philosophical schools.[2] Scholars are apt to point out that all of these groups had a religious or cultic element, requirements for membership, meetings, common meals, and a mode of organization and leadership.[3] A moment of reflection, however, ought to give us pause about basing comparisons on these characteristics, especially when abstracted from the particular web of beliefs and practices of the groups. The Senate of the United States, a Hasidic community in Brooklyn, Bob and Shirley's trucking company dedicated to Jesus, and the New Age–oriented Bristol Bird Watching Club all can be said to have a religious element, requirements for membership, meetings, common meals, and a mode of organization and leadership. Comparisons made on this basis do not indicate which practices are most important to the particular groups and what goods the members of the groups consider to be internal to those practices rather than external or incidental.

Part of the instinct, I suggest, that impels scholars toward this set of features for comparison derives from a twentieth-century Western notion that religious groups are naturally voluntary associations. Definitions of a Greco-Roman voluntary association given by scholars in 1936 and 1993, respectively, are "a group which a man joins of his own free will, and which accept him of its free will, and this mutual acceptance creates certain obligations on both parties" and "a coherent group, which could be recognized as such by outsiders, with its own rules for membership, leadership and association with one another."[4] Such definitions express the modern Western conception of social contract. In groups of this sort, free individuals are said to consciously and freely enter into rationally articulated modes of association with other individuals for the pursuit of a limited and specified set of purposes that the individuals agree to pursue jointly. In the early nineteenth century, Alexis de Tocqueville was amazed at how characteristic such groups and an attendant ideology had become in the young United States.[5] For de Tocqueville, these groups were precisely what distinguished the new nation from old Europe with its, in his description, organic solidarity based on family and an interdependent hierarchy of social ranks.[6] The definitions of a voluntary association given above rather naively lack one half of the equation for understanding the phenomenon historically, a certain conception of the person that does not fit antiquity. An influential version of this modernist conception was articulated in the philosophy of Immanuel Kant. The person is an autonomous self-legislating and universalizing agent whose identity and activity is based on fully conscious choice. I would argue that the ancient association members were more like de Tocqueville's romanticized medieval people than the Kantian individual.

An important recent collection of essays places various Greek and Roman religious and trade groups, Jewish synagogues, philosophical schools, and Christian groups all in the category of voluntary associations.[7] I want to challenge the appropriateness of the criteria of comparison implied in the conception of voluntary associations and propose another approach.[8] In order to illustrate the approach, I will first do some ground clearing with remarks on synagogues and Greek and Roman groups and then focus upon philosophical schools. Because many different early Christian groups seem to have differed rather widely in character, I will choose one for which we do have some evidence, the assemblies of Paul's letters. In this case, it is important to remind ourselves that we have only Paul's representation of these groups.[9] I am skeptical about inferring much concerning the Pauline groups themselves and thus will focus on Paul's conceptions in the letters.

Toward Reassessing "Synagogues" and Associations

Many New Testament scholars have held that the Pauline groups were modeled upon "the Jewish synagogue."[10] A host of highly complex and hotly debated issues surround the definition of and evidence for synagogues in the period before 70 C.E. and after.[11] Everyone agrees that the term "synagogue" can refer to some sort of meeting or assembly of Jews or even to institutionalized, if not locally uniform, meeting practices. But when did the term designate a building for specific meeting practices? In the fifth century and later, synagogues look like institutions and buildings that are comparable to and in my opinion clearly influenced by churches. But, of course, in the fifth century as compared to the period before 70, the situation of Judaism had changed dramatically, and we ought to expect a different type of institution.[12] With the decisive redating of important synagogues and challenge to the traditional typology by Jodi Magness and the critique of the picture dominant in New Testament studies by Howard Kee, one can only characterize scholarly opinion as in transition.[13] I will not enter directly into this debate about evidence for synagogues. Instead, I want to refocus the issue of comparison.

In basing comparison on categories such as meeting places, meetings, membership, and organization, I suggest that our modern instincts about religious institutions keep us from contextualizing synagogues and from selecting the practices that were most important to the ancient Jews in question. We must remember that first-century Jews were Judeans. Interpreters should not, in principle, segregate Judeans from Greeks, Romans, Egyptians, and so on by creating something suspiciously like a modern religion called Judaism.[14] Even Jews who lived permanently in Rome or Alexandria were Judeans living outside of their traditional homeland and therefore similar to Syrians, Greeks, or Egyptians who lived abroad. A synagogue is a meeting place or meeting practices of Judeans. In our language, Judeans were an ethnic people. Unfortunately the idea of "the synagogue" as the Jewish church still haunts much scholarship.

Instead of the criteria of rules of membership, meetings, and so on that are instinctive for moderns who think of religions as associations of individuals, I want to ask what these Judeans considered to be their most important religious practices. On the basis of their discourses, their articulated conceptions, and the social organization of their practices, which religious activities ranked highest in the hierarchy of practices? The best answer, I believe, are the practices of the temple in Jerusalem and practices that related Judeans to the temple.[15] The religious practices of synagogues or of communities of Judeans were to a large extent activities that oriented those Judeans, no matter where they lived, toward the temple. I can only suggest an outline for this case here, but let me note that the claim goes against much of traditional interest in the synagogue by New Testament scholars. The synagogue has appealed to scholars precisely because it has been understood as a religious institution that is independent of the temple and the temple's cultus and locative ethnic nature, a preparation for Christianity. I want to argue that orientation toward the temple was central in the period before 70 C.E.

Evidence exists for the celebration of the great temple festivals in the Diaspora.[16] These celebrations suggest that Jews in the Diaspora were attempting to participate from a distance in festivals of the temple that had a strong agricultural and local orientation.[17] The connection between the gifts of land and lineage and rituals of reciprocity with God was not lost on Judeans of the Diaspora. Temple time with its agriculturally oriented calendar shaped the calendar of Jews in general. Pilgrimage to Jerusalem for the festivals and sacrifices was a major feature of the period.[18] Many Judeans of the Diaspora directly participated in the temple cultus sometime during their lives. The temple tax that supported the daily sacrifices in the temple and the first fruit offerings that signified the ancient pattern of reciprocity and divine giving of productivity were among the major yearly efforts of Diaspora communities.[19] Rome recognized these collections to be so significant for Judeans that they made a major and economically risky exception to the prohibition on exporting large quantities of money from one province to another.[20] When Philo wants to argue (*Legat.* 156) that the emperor supported Judean rights, his illustration falls into two parts: Judean philosophy and Judean religion. Let me urge the usefulness of taking seriously Philo's typical Greek and Roman distinction between intellectual activity (e.g., philosophers, philological and rhetorical teachers and scholars)—even if the gods sometimes might also be discussed by philosophers—and religious practice. First, Philo says that the emperor allowed the Judeans to meet on the sabbath in houses of prayer for instruction in "their ancestral philosophy." Second, the emperor knew with approval that "they collected sacred dedications from first fruits and sent them to Jerusalem by those who would offer the sacrifices (*taś thysiaś*)." Evidence shows that prayer, which could take place almost anywhere and was not tied to an institution called the synagogue or house of prayer, was sometimes said facing Jerusalem and often timed to coincide with the offering of the *tamid* in the temple.[21] Some evidence exists for the practice of sacrificing the passover lamb in homes rather than only in the temple or Jerusalem as Deut 16:1–8 directs.[22] If widespread, this practice would have been a very important extension and linking of sacrificial religion.

Experts on synagogues seem to agree that study or reading of scripture was important. The Torah, Prophets, and Psalms are, in my view, absolutely dominated by the centrality of the temple, priesthood, and cult. The epics and myths of Judeans were about land, people, and socio-economic reciprocity with God and other Judeans. Even in the extreme case of the Judean philosopher, Philo, he still reads scripture in terms of temple, people, land, and reciprocity, but finds additionally stories about the soul and the nature of the cosmos. For Judeans, unlike for Christians, to study scripture was to be oriented toward an actual temple, a place where reciprocity with the divine was enacted in the imagined exchange of produce from the land and shop, womb and market. Although a culture of imagination, Judaism at the same time involved the exchange of economic and social goods. The resulting cultus of the imagination was so powerful that the framers of later Judaism would write with attention to the minutest detail of its operation as if the temple still existed centuries after its demise.[23] These and other practices, I would argue, allowed Judeans living outside of Judea to participate in the practices of the temple cult.

Christianity of the fourth and fifth centuries recreated itself by imagining that it and not the Jews were carrying on the true cult of the temple and its priesthood, but in a "spiritual" way. Earlier Christian myth and ritual was bizarre by ancient Mediterranean standards in not explicitly relating the practitioners to land, lineage, and economy.

What more concretely, then, were the practices in the temple to which the local activities of Jews both in Judea and elsewhere linked? The dominant activities of the temple were sacrificial offerings of grain and animal products. Judeans shared these practices with Greeks, Romans, and most peoples of the Mediterranean world. Josephus proudly proclaims that Judeans share the practices of sacrificing domestic animals with "all the rest of humanity" (*Ag. Ap.*, 2.137). I have elsewhere argued that sacrificial practices were central to the constructions of ethnic peoplehood in the ancient Mediterranean cultures.[24] At the heart of my thesis lies the claim that through sacrificial practices the productivity of the land was interpreted in terms of reciprocity with God or the gods. Productivity included not only the products of agriculture and—by extension down a hierarchy of gifts—even the products of artisans, but above all, the offspring of animal and human lineages. Ethnic peoples are groups that understand themselves to be organized by kinship and descent from common ancestors and to have traditional homelands. As if mirroring the principle of descent, the finest specimens of animal lineages were the highest in the hierarchy of gifts from God or the gods that humans returned as offerings. The great range of offerings, cleansings, and strategic circumstances for offerings produced a highly complex and life-encompassing order of reciprocity with the divine and within the social order that had a marked local character.[25] Judeans living at a distance from the temple ranked these practices connected with the temple and practices involving social/economic/religious reciprocity with the divine—no matter where they lived—as their most important.

Jews in the Diaspora also developed a whole range of local religious practices—from rites described as magical that Judeans practiced in common with other groups to very specific local festivals like those celebrated in Alexandria. But I would make two points. First, most of these practices would have had a local and ethnic character fitting the larger patterns of sacrificial religion. Second, insofar as the practitioners maintained an identity as Judeans, they would have ranked higher the core of practices linking them with the sacrificial cultus of the temple. My case would thus not be an argument for uniformity or systematic coherence of practices, but a case for loose and variable networks of activities with a hierarchy that ranked some practices as most important.

Known early Christian groups did not look very much like religious groups because they were almost entirely missing this whole set of practices related to sacrifice, intergenerational continuity, and productivity. In Pauline Christianity, there are no temples on the land, no ties to or concern for the land, no animal or other types of sacrifice, and no agricultural festivals or festivals of other types of productivity. For the ethnic peoples, ritual activities and settings for sacrificial rituals that relate to intergenerational continuity were absolutely essential. Ritual and other practices related to intergenerational continuity have no place in the Pauline groups. Paul's representation of these groups lacks rituals of birth and death and sacrificial practices for purification from birth and death pollution. Without sacred spaces on the land—that is, altars—purity and pollution became moral metaphors. One finds nothing like circumcision or the sacrificial initiation of the ephebes and no Christian marriage rituals.[26] Indeed, Paul does not even encourage marriage except as a remedy for passionate desire.[27] All that is missing here constituted the heart of ancient religion. Paul has no altar to Hephaestus in his shop and he does not belong to an association of leather workers with a calendar of sacrificial feasts. He does not tell myths about how God or the gods gave to humans crafts, land, and agricultural skills so that they could possess the goods of human life. Nor does he instruct members of his churches to collect first fruits and tithes for the temple in Jerusalem. He tells those who have business dealings to act as if they were of no importance (1 Cor 7:30–31).[28] He does not see his work as a source of goods for supporting a valued way of life organized as a household, but as an instrument to aid his work in teaching others the Christ myth (1 Cor 9:1–27; 4:11–13; 1 Thess 2:9). The Christians did not develop their own versions or replacements for such practices until centuries later. When they did, a land-owning Christian elite appeared along with holy places and attendant festivals scattered across the landscape of the empire.

Whatever kind of community center or assembly that the synagogue was for Judeans, it must have supported these practices. In regard to these activities, Judeans differed most from Greeks and others in that the transport of first fruits, tithes, and other offerings was a long-distance project, and that orientation by imagination played a large role. But, in principle, the religion of a Judean who lived five hundred miles from Jerusalem did not differ radically from one who lived twenty miles away. The comparison reads differently when one understands that the synagogue was an instrument of the practices that constituted the ethnicity of the Judeans. Framed in this way, the synagogue does not seem to be the best model for Pauline groups. The contrast, it should be emphasized, is not between the supposedly primordial natural ties of families or ethnic groups and opposing consciously human-made and chosen groups (as in Weberian theory and some folk belief).[29] Rather, I will draw a contrast between different sorts of practices that hang together in patterns of social formations that cannot be reduced to the inherited/chosen dichotomy.

Scholars who argue that Greek and Roman voluntary associations that were organized by common trade, a particular deity, or by household are the best model for comparison also often fail to focus on the practices most central to these groups, and show how these activities tie into larger ways of life.[30] Joining a *thiasos* of Dionysus or a *collegium* of the wool workers was not like a Methodist becoming a Baptist or converting to Buddhism. The deities were deities that—in principle, even if not necessarily in practice—had always belonged to the devotee's religious universe, even for a foreign deity like Isis who had characteristics that made it possible for Greeks and Romans to place her somewhere in the family of gods. Scholars who emphasize that a person, when joining an association dedicated to a particular deity "chose devotion to that deity" simply fail to understand the way that Greek and Roman religion worked. Such language seems to echo the modern idea that what is important about a religious act or choice is that one chose it for oneself. Dionysus of the association and Athena of the woolworkers make no sense as objects of devotion isolated from the family of gods. In Greek and Roman conceptions, the basic unit of the religion was not the cult of a particular god, but primarily the gods and rites of a particular city and secondarily of the corresponding ethnic people. On the other hand, unlike what some have thought, Greek or Roman polytheism was not a massive body of systematic beliefs upon which one consciously drew in order to act.[31] Rather, although practices could involve prior conscious reflective thinking, more basically situations—environments and the contexts of events—evoked what Wittgenstein called reactions (*Reaktion*).[32] Reciprocity with the gods was embedded in the practical skills for coping with life that were evoked by the situations and contexts that these ancient polytheists encountered. The family of gods, therefore, had to be as complex, multivalent, and locally particular as the web of lived lives. Whether offering a libation to the Zeus or the Good Daimon of a household, placating Poseidon before travel, merchants sealing a contract with an oath by sacrifice, the pageantry of celebrating the city's gods, the creation of divine comradeship and mutual honors in an association or countless other contexts, the responses drew on the practical know-how for dealing with everyday life.

A Greek was someone who had Greek parents and whose life was shaped by patterns of reciprocity with other Greeks and with Greek gods. An aristocracy of elites defined the religion and politics of the Greek city and was defined as elite precisely by the ownership of enough land to support the surfeit of animals required for the city's sacrificial victims. As with Judeans, a host of ritual practices helped to construct Greek ethnicity, including patterns of intergenerational continuity, and wove religion into areas that moderns cordon off as economic, political, and social.

A way of summarizing a number of these observations is to say that the goods of traditional Mediterranean religion, including Judean religion, were the varied, complex, and conflicting goods of the traditional ethnic peoples. The network of religious practices helped to maintain a complex balance of potentially conflicting goods by giving each good its own bounded place. The proverbial exuberant sociality of Dionysus and the cool deliberation of Apollo each had a place along with numerous other oppositions. Judeans, I believe, maintained a similar complexity through the intricacy and interplay of cult, festival, rites of orientation toward the temple, and legal interpretation. Precisely on this point the Hellenistic philosophies and the groups advocated by Paul organized themselves differently than the ethnic peoples. Both, of course, worked from a context of ethnic heritage, but reduced and reordered the complexity of traditional goods by creating ways of life that focused on a somewhat different and more limited range of goods.

Toward Comparing Paul and Hellenistic Philosophy

I have identified at least seven closely connected areas in which the Hellenistic philosophies and Pauline Christianity possessed similar features. I want to be clear about what I mean by "similar features."[33] First, I am not making claims about origins, that is, genetic relations. The question of how the similarities seen in the Pauline groups came about is a different and more difficult question. Second, similarity is not sameness. I do not think that Pauline Christianity was a philosophy, and differences are as important as similarities. Third, the similarities with the philosophies are not exclusive of similarities with other social formations. I do, in fact, think that it is worth comparing the Christian groups to Judean communities and to so-called voluntary associations.[34] Similarities do exist, but for the reasons given above, overall I judge differences to be greater than the similarities. Comparison is thus a complex, multitaxonomic activity.[35]

First, the Hellenistic philosophies conceived themselves as distinct and mutually exclusive *haereseis*, choices, or sects.[36] The schools developed conceptions of the good characterized by a unitary focus on a central value. Anthony Long has pointed out that our English words "cynical," "stoical," "skeptical," and "epicurean" reflect the nature of the Hellenistic philosophies as mutually exclusive attitudes toward life.[37] By contrast, "Aristotelian" has no such connotation because Aristotle's philosophy rejected the idea of a unitary good and accepted what I have characterized above as the traditional ethnic view that the good consisted of a balanced accommodation of different and often conflicting values. For a Stoic, virtue is the only good. This focus on a single good means that traditional goods like marriage, family, ethnic heritage, possessions, and everyday pleasures have only a relative and, in some circumstances, quite dispensable value. This way of thinking often tends to put concrete relations into opposition with abstract ideals. Epictetus says (*Diss.* 3.3.5), "For this reason, the good must be preferred above every relation of kinship. My father is nothing to me, but only the good." Epicureans made freedom from pain and friendship the focusing goods, and so on with the other schools. Because of the focus on different unitary goods, the schools were mutually exclusive and tended to define themselves over against other alternatives in a way that made totalizing claims on their adherents.

Paul also constructs life in Christ as a distinct and mutually exclusive choice with a unitary good. In 1 Corinthians 7, Paul counsels "undistracted devotion to the Lord" (7:35) instead of marriage. He gives no indication that marriage, procreation, and running a household are central goods in their own right. He does not want the divided interests that marriage entails (7:32–34). In light of the approaching day of the Lord, wives, possessions, and business dealings have no intrinsic significance (7:32–35). Members of the group who make up the audience of this advice are those who have called upon the name of the Lord (1:2). Christ is the only foundation for the group (3:11) and there is only one God, not the many of Greco-Roman religion (8:1–6). Although the beliefs about the one God, mutually exclusive loyalty to the one God, and apocalyptic intensification of these beliefs are Judean in origin, they function differently in Paul's letters where they are freed from the ethnic, cultic, and legal contexts that instantiate a range of human goods. Paul's difficulties in relating the law to his Gentile churches reflects this shift of context. In 1 Cor 7:19 where he relativizes matters of ethnicity and status, he writes "circumcision is nothing and uncircumcision is nothing, but only keeping the commandments of God matters." The reduction of goods becomes evident when one realizes that circumcision *is* a commandment of God for Judeans according to the scriptures that Paul holds as authoritative. Indeed, circumcision is a central ritual of intergenerational continuity, procreative promise, and ethnic identity. For Paul, the teaching about Christ's faithfulness meant that even earlier commandments of God were relativized and refocused on the new good, at least for Gentiles. Thus, although one sees a very different content to the sense in which Pauline groups were choices, a structural similarity remains with the Hellenistic philosophies.

Second, the choices of the Hellenistic philosophies were paradoxes in the sense going back to the pre-Socratics of being *para doxa*—that is, contrary to conventional thinking.[38] They asserted that the happy life could not be founded on ordinary civic virtue.[39] The modified beliefs created by critical reflection changed one's motivations, desires, and needs, resulting in a tension between conventional life and post-reflective life. I have discussed possible implications of such a change above in terms of departures from the complex goods of ethnic peoples. I believe it no accident that the founders of the Hellenistic schools were not married and that Jesus and Paul were also not married. Ancient Christianity thus interpreted Paul primarily as the great ascetic. Early Christianity shared a strong ascetic impulse with the Hellenistic philosophies.[40] The ascetic impulses of both stem from a reduction and focusing of more conventional goods and goals. The positive side of this feature is the seventh characteristic discussed below, a tendency toward radical social formations.

Pauline Christianity claimed to oppose itself to traditional thinking on moral matters and regarding religious belief and practices. For Gentiles, at least, Paul conceived an ethical field that corresponded neither to the traditional norms of Greek or other Gentile cultures nor to the traditional norms of Judean culture.[41] Paul sets God's wisdom in opposition to the wisdom of the world, both Greek and Judean (1 Cor 1:22–25). Again, the structural similarities with the philosophies are obvious.

Third, the change to the new life might be described as a conversion in the sense of a dramatic reorientation of the self. Scholars speak of conversion to Judaism, but important distinctions tend to be lost. How is it that we speak of conversion to being a Judean, but not for becoming a Greek, Roman, or Egyptian? An Egyptian who became a citizen of a Greek polis changed religious practices and adopted a whole range of cultural and social relations, but we do not call this "conversion." I judge it fruitless to look for some essence to the way that scholars have employed the concept of conversion. For my purposes it is helpful merely to point out that the letters of Paul share a very specific tradition of describing the process of conversion, a rhetoric of conversion.[42] Admittedly, conversion in Hellenistic philosophy has been oversimplified, including in A. D. Nock's famous discussion.[43] The Stoics, for example, emphasized that the attainment of virtue was grounded in one's nature and the conventional goodness habituated by participation in ordinary social life. If one were very bad, then transition to virtue would be impossible or extremely unlikely. The acquisition of virtue—in the Stoic sense of virtue (dispositions to perform proper functions perfectly)—they claimed was instantaneous and might not even be noticed by the person undergoing the change.[44] Epicureans and Platonists ridiculed these teachings and said that coming to virtue was ordinarily a process of progress in intermediate steps of relative virtuousness.[45] Scholars have suggested conceptions of conversion that range from repentance of past life and the beginning of moral progress to a commitment to a particular school or even to the acquisition of virtue and wisdom. I would also argue that Christian conversion contains an element largely unparalleled in the philosophies in making submission to a divine being part of conversion.[46] In spite of these problems, there is a literary tradition that becomes most prominent in the early empire in which writers give vivid descriptions of the turmoil and changes in the soul of those who convert to philosophy. Paul uses exactly the same language for conversion to the gospel.

Conversion relates closely to the fourth mark of the Hellenistic schools: Namely, this choice made possible and required a technology of the self. Socrates is the first to have detailed the notion that one could reconstitute the self on a new basis and that the self could have an authority and power to take complete charge of life and its goals by mastering passions and desires.[47] The Hellenistic schools presented differing technologies for asserting this new self formed around its sharply focused goals. The schools agreed that people had unhealthy desires due to false beliefs about the nature of the world. True beliefs would reorder the soul, turning it from vice to virtue. Epicureans, for example, asserted that the primary impediments to moral health were fear of death and fear of the gods. Eradicating these false beliefs and destructive desires might begin with a dramatic reorientation, but typically also required a sustained and conscious process of rehabituation with the help of fellow Epicureans.[48] The early empire seems to have been a time that saw an increasing specification of techniques for self-care and self-scrutiny.[49]

Paul's basic teaching began with the call to turn from idols to a true God and included the idea that worship of the false gods entailed bondage to passions and desire (1 Thess 1:10, cf. 4:1–5; Rom 1:18–32). Turning to the true God meant a dramatic reorientation and mastery of passions and desire, but also a continuing struggle for self-mastery. In 1 Cor 9:24–27, Paul presents himself as a model for the Corinthians, "Do you not know that all those in a race compete but only one receives the prize? So run that you might win! Everyone who is an athlete exercises self-mastery in all things. They do it to win a perishable wreath, but we for one imperishable. So then I pummel my body and subject it to slavery, lest after preaching to others I myself not meet the test." Self-mastery allows him to order his life around the unitary *telos*: "I do it all for the sake of the gospel, so that I might share in its blessings" (9:23). The important work of Abraham Malherbe and of Clarence Glad on Pauline psychagogy concerns Paul's technology of the self.[50]

Fifth, the Hellenistic philosophies developed the notion of the wise man.[51] The wise man was someone like Socrates who stood against conventional society and exhibited a redefined paradigm of human excellence seen in his unitary focus and extraordinary self-mastery. Similarly, the authority of the founders of Pyrrhonism, Stoicism, Epicureanism, and Cynicism was seen to stem not only from their teachings, but also from their exemplary focus and self-mastery. Such founders and sages of the past might become the subject of mythmaking and exemplary anecdote by schools. Diogenes Laertius (7.27) tells us that a proverbial saying arose, "more self-controlled than the philosopher Zeno." He was known for his extreme frugality and poverty, toughness, and independence from social convention.[52] The paradigms of Pyrrho, Epicurus, and Diogenes the Cynic are well known. Again Aristotle makes a useful contrast. His philosophy has no place for a wise man since his model of excellence is the Athenian gentleman. Because ideal wise men, founders of school traditions, and devoted followers must exhibit their unconventional choice of life, one sees a certain theatricality among members of the Hellenistic schools.[53] Both Stoics and Epicureans said that the wise man would remain happy and tranquil under torture on the rack.[54] Aristotle had pronounced this idea absurd (*EN* 7.1153b19). One could make a great list of the dramatic episodes of philosophers from Socrates' trial and death to the Cynic Proteus who burned himself and many less destructive but equally showy acts. How would the story of Jesus' attack on the money changers at the temple and his death have seemed to Hellenistic audiences? Surely Paul's long lists of sufferings fall into the same genre.[55] Paul writes (1 Cor 11:1), "Be imitators of me, as I am of Christ."

Sixth, encompassing the previous five characteristics, the central practices of the Hellenistic schools and of Pauline Christianity were intellectual practices and practices that made reference to mind. The most basic move in creating a technology of the self is articulating a self. Of what functions, faculties, and parts does a person consist? What is the proper ordering and functioning of these parts? What part of the person is the true self? Traditional Greek, Roman, and Jewish religion went along quite well without articulating a human psychology, but the philosophies and Pauline Christianity made central discourse about the self. Moreover, the chief practices of both emphasized types of speaking, writing, and interpretation. Both were centrally concerned with the reading, writing, transmission, and interpretation of texts: on the one hand, the writings of the chief authorities of the particular philosophical school and, on the other hand, the Greek translation of the Judean sacred writings.[56] Teaching, learning, and moral training were also central to both. Whatever else they were, Jesus and Paul were teachers. The existence of Pauline social groups depended on his textual interpretive skills, his expertise in forms of esoteric knowledge, and his teaching abilities.[57] In this regard, Paul resembled the teacher of a philosophical school.

The centrality of mind and self becomes apparent when one compares the major rituals of Pauline Christianity to the sacrificial rituals of the Greeks, Romans, and Jews. In animal sacrifice, there might be nothing said at all; no speech and no text.[58] There was interpretation, but not interpretation of the soul or of texts. The animal's body was divided, distributed, manipulated, and interpreted. Did its opened body give signs of the god's disposition? Had the deity received the burned gift? If so, some designated group of participants might share in the occasion by making a festive meal from a portion of the animal's flesh. In the Lord's Supper, according to 1 Corinthians 11, the meal recalls a foundational myth of the group, and certain words and actions in the ritual make reference to that story. Participants are to examine their motivations and attitudes toward the community in light of the story and of God's knowledge of their inner condition. Unlike the first ritual, the second requires speaking, interpretive, textual practices, and an articulated technology of the self. Romans 12:1–2 nicely illustrates the point with its reinterpretation of sacrifice as a metaphor that concerns the care of the self: "present your bodies as a living and holy sacrifice (*thysia*) acceptable to God which is your rational worship. Do not be conformed to this age but have your form changed by the renewal of your mind so that you might test what is the will of God."

Seventh, the goals and practices of the Hellenistic philosophies and Paul's "Christianity" might give rise to nontraditional and radical social formations. This characteristic is a tendency and not an invariant feature of the two groups. For Epicureans, one sees this feature in their ideal of the garden, a return to a simpler, earlier phase of human social evolution based on friendship rather than the patriarchal family and city that, in their view, had led to conflict and empty competition by overly concentrating power and wealth. The radical proposals of Zeno's *Politeia* are well known. Malcolm Schofield has done much work to clarify the nature of this writing as antiutopian.[59] Zeno wanted to contrast his attainable society of friends characterized by wisdom and virtue to Plato's unrealizable ideal society. Some scholars have found evidence that early Stoics fomented revolts and advised politicians in attempts to implement Stoic social and political ideals.[60] Sphaerus, for instance, a student of Zeno and Cleanthes, may have been the thinker behind the Spartan revolution of 220 B.C.E., in which land was redistributed according to egalitarian principles, the wider population was enfranchised with citizenship, and a common citizens' mess was instituted. Zeno's state had no slavery, marriage, or traditional families. Men and women performed the same occupations, wore the same clothes, exercised naked together, and had sex and children in common. Zeno abolished temples and large public buildings, traditional Greek education, and money. People took common meals, and the glue that held the city together would be rational eros and friendship. The second-century Christian, Epiphanes, who tried to institute a community similar to Zeno's, believed that he was following Paul.[61] Later Stoicism shifted to the idea of a world society that transcended cities and might be interpreted in either a conservative or a radical way. Philo and Josephus cast the Essenes and Therapeutae as radical philosophical communities.[62] I labor these examples to illustrate that the focus on a single good and mind/character/intellectual practices of the Hellenistic philosophies tended to give rise to experimental and alternative social formations. All of these groups share the principle that economic and other "ordinary" practices must be demoted and serve only purposes that are instrumental to the virtue, friendship, and intellectual practices upon which the group is to focus. One might interpret what I describe below as "the Pauline household" along these lines.

These seven features are not just incidental, but relate closely to what the philosophers and Paul himself understood to be the goods internal to their central practices. A. D. Nock was correct in arguing that early Christian groups would have typically appeared more like philosophies than cults. But in my view, Nock based his conclusions on an analysis that did not take seriously the goods of the practices that the participants valued. He also sent scholarship down the wrong road with his description of cults, philosophies, and Christianities in terms of the psychological needs that the groups supposedly met. For Nock, external similarities clothed incommensurable essential contents.[63]

I have come to a different conclusion. Pauline Christianity and probably other kinds of Christianity did resemble Hellenistic philosophies, but not necessarily because they derived from philosophies or directly borrowed much. Troels Engberg-Pedersen has recently argued impressively that Pauline thought owes some central features to Stoicism.[64] I have sympathies with that claim, but my major point is different, although also compatible with Engberg-Pedersen's conclusions: Aside from the question of borrowings, the network of practices that Paul conceived as assemblies of Christ had structural similarities to the Hellenistic philosophies because both organized themselves by similar practices and goals.[65] First, the central practices of both were intellectual practices and practices relating to mind and self or soul. But this first similarity alone would not have made earliest Christianity like a Hellenistic philosophy. Ancient rhetorical and legal schools, for instance, also focused on intellectual practices, but they did not much resemble Hellenistic philosophies because they lacked the second feature: Namely, the practices were ordered by a tightly focused and totalizing understanding of a unitary good. These two structural features of Pauline Christianity together made it resemble a Hellenistic philosophy. Formulated from another perspective, the structure produced a life that resembled a philosophical life, especially for Christian teachers.

In order to understand the unitary good in Paul, however, one must attend to the fifth characteristic, Jesus Christ as a model of human excellence. Even early Christian sources attest that whatever Jesus and his students were about, it concerned the way of life and future of the Judeans and must be understood in the context of Judean culture and politics. In Paul's letters, however, probably in virtue of reinterpreting Jesus for Gentiles, whatever vision Jesus had for Judeans gets displaced by mythmaking about Jesus as the Christ who died and rose to rule from above and serves as a model for imitation. Paul ignores Jesus' teachings and focuses on the paradigmatic character of Christ, especially as exhibited in his death.[66] In dying, Jesus exhibited self-mastery, trusting loyalty or faithfulness (*pistis*) to God, and mercy toward both Judeans and non-Judeans.[67] Jesus showed that character and mind oriented toward God are invulnerable, while ordinary products of human activity fail. You can kill the teacher and forget his teachings, but the idea of the martyr and his virtues lives on. Paul thus makes Jesus into a model of human excellence that is characterized by self-mastery, trusting loyalty, mercy, and invulnerability. The goods of Pauline Christianity focus intently upon these and loyalty to the continuing mission of the risen Christ who is a pioneer of the ideal life to come.[68] In this way, Paul interprets the unitary good in terms of certain virtues or excellencies as do the Hellenistic philosophies.

Josephus was able to represent (*Ant.* 13.171–173, 18.12–20; *J.W.* 2.119–166) Essenes, Pharisees, and Sadducees as Jewish schools of philosophy by attributing the two major structural features to them. According to Josephus, they were all occupied with intellectual practices relating to the sacred texts and the teaching and promotion of certain doctrines. Second, the schools like Hellenistic philosophies distinguished themselves as mutually exclusive choices by centering on particular doctrines. The Pharisees resembled dogmatic Stoics attributing everything to fate and providence; the Sadducees, like skeptical Epicureans, made humans free and removed God from dealings with the world (*Ant.* 2.162–166). Not only do Josephus and Philo in this way construct certain groups as Jewish philosophers, but they also tend to present Jews and Judaism in general as philosophical.[69] This approach has made them wonderful sources for Christian readers, writers, and theologians, but makes their depiction of Judaism and Judeans highly unrepresentative.[70]

The oddity of Pauline ritualization and mythmaking in comparison to ancient Mediterranean religion is to be explained by the different practices and relations to types of production of each. The typical sacrificial religion of the Greco-Roman world was closely intertwined with economic production and made no sense apart from that production. This holds true of associations, the Judean temple, and the religious practices of dispersed Judean communities. The ideal economic production in this Mediterranean religion is the fruit of the land, but artisanal, trade, and other sorts of economic production were also included in the structuration effected by the linking of shared practices. Even the potter and the shoemaker made offerings at the workshop shrine and at meetings of associations of fellow workers from plants and animals received from landowners. The potter, of course, did not see that in honoring the gods with the products deemed most natural to the gods, he was reproducing—among other forms of sociality—an order that gave power to the landowners and ranked artisans with slaves. Paul may have been a leather worker, but he had no workshop altar and was alienated from local communities of Judeans who made a great corporate effort of collecting and delivering to the temple in Jerusalem first fruit offerings gleaned from trades such as leather working. Pauline offerings were not translated into the plant and animal products of Judean landowners. Paul describes the proper offering to God as a disciplined body and a renewed mind (Rom 12:1–2) with virtues productive of a certain ideal sociality (Rom 12:3–21). Paul, like the model Cynic, Simon the Shoemaker, probably used his workshop as a place for teaching, the activity that he ranked as important.[71]

The Christ followers rejected offerings from the land and cultivated other activities. The cultural production, including mythmaking and ritualization, of Paul's Christ groups hid or even explicitly renounced connections with economic production. Christ, unlike Dionysus, Diana, or Demeter, was not "worshiped" with the return of products (e.g., of land, of workshop) given by him to Paul and his followers as producers. The foundational myth of a teacher who "died for us" and traveled to heaven for a temporary stay does not open a space for reflection on the relation between economics and sociality. No matter what else Greek and Roman myths did, they dwelt on that relation. The Judean epic is about a land flowing with milk and honey given to a certain people by a god who dwells in that land.

I have already spoken of ritual, but let me add that what is entirely missing from early Christianity in comparison with ancient religion is huge in terms of cultural space. One example is the aesthetics of produce and production that is so massively important to sacrificial religion. Greeks customarily summed up what a successful sacrifice meant with the expression *ta hiera kala*, "the holy things are beautiful." The Roman attitude was the same. The most beautiful animals decked out in ribbons and garlands, perfect fruits and grains, finely formed loaves of bread, sacred groves of olive trees, temples of marble and bright colors, processions of beautiful youths in the best clothes carrying flasks of oil, jars of honey, baskets of golden wheat, sumptuous tables for joyous feasts shared with the gods, and on and on suggest the aesthetics of ancient religion. The Hebrew Bible waxes eloquent about the beauty of the temple and the sacrifices, and the sweet smell that God enjoys. Philosophers were known more for their ragged dirty clothes and their foul smell than an aesthetic. If one wants to call it an aesthetic, then theirs was one of dialogue, books, self-mastery, and endurance in suffering. Even the kinds of philosophers who valued the ordinary goods ranked the latter higher.

Not only is the meat missing from the Lord's Supper, but Paul says that the event is not even about eating. If the Corinthians want food and feast, they have their own homes (1 Cor 11:20–22, 34). The food in the Supper is not important as food, but as something that symbolizes and points to something else. There is virtually no place in ancient Mediterranean religion for putting enjoyment of the food of meals into opposition to devotion to God. Such practices as the following constitute the proper activities of the Lord's "meal": Reflecting on the suffering of a martyr (11:24–26), examining oneself (11:29), practicing living in view of God's judgment (11:30–32), cultivating virtues of sociality with an egalitarian strain, or perhaps more precisely, an emphasis on solidarity (11:18–22, 29), and reflecting on the ideal of the community brought into existence by the teacher's words (11:17–26, 29).

How different were the sacrificial feasts and drinking parties of associations. Both groups had food on the table, but the activities that counted for Paul's people were to be exercises of mind and character distinguished from and made more important than ordinary practical activities like feasting and the exchange of goods and honors, e.g., thinking something, reflecting on a text, examining, discerning, judging, acting with solidarity. The Lord's Supper does not even have an offering or an offerer. In the foundational story, Jesus does give thanks for the food, but no food is given back. Words and thoughts are enough. Philosophers knew that the gods did not need food. Pure mind does not need flesh. In sacrificial religion there is always an offerer, and the offering indicates something about the wealth of the offerer. The fine cattle or the dove is his and was given to him by the god. The same principle holds true for collective offerings made by groups. But just as the Lord's Supper is not about food or eating, neither is it about anyone's wealth made natural by the gods.

When Paul mentions reciprocity that involves wealth, it is not of material for material, but material for spiritual (Rom 15:25–28).[72] Work for Paul is not an activity through which God provides the goods for a valued way of life, but a form of suffering for a higher purpose (1 Cor 4:11–13). In 1 Cor 7:30–31 he tells his audience to focus only on Christ and not to give any value to their buying, selling, and economic activities.[73] In chapter 9, he treats his work not as productive of its own goods that belong to a way of life, but as an instrument for the preaching of the gospel. The ancient household was the locus for almost all of the economic production in Greco-Roman antiquity. The *kyrios* ruled his household and participated in civic and cultural activities because of the leisure opened up for him by the labor of wives, children, slaves, and other dependents. The *ethos* inside the household was, ideally at least, to be one of family affection and a sharing of goods according to the roles given by nature and fate. Outside of the household, the *kyrios* forged friendships with male peers. What we might reasonably call the Pauline household had no wife to manage the labor of the children and slaves. There were no children and probably no slaves. He wishes that all Christ people were unmarried like him—free for important activities. Paul probably lived with friends and fellow workers for the gospel, who on occasion might also happen to share his trade. The economic engine is missing from the Pauline household. The only labor and goods that he values are those related to his teaching, assembly-building, and leading activities. Paul's social formations resembled those of Hellenistic philosophers because they were productive of "mind goods" in a way that subordinated other goods. In sum, Paul's groups were constituted by social formations that "exalted" discursive practices over nondiscursive practices and tended to treat nondiscursive practices and affects as valuable to the extent that agents could attribute discursiveness to them (e.g., that eating bread *symbolizes* X; one's sufferings *indicate* that Christ will soon return).

Conclusions

My conclusion, I hope, will help explain an important feature of ancient Christianity. From at least early in the second century there appear Christians like Justin and Athenagoras who with all seriousness style themselves philosophers and Christianity a philosophy. This identification became a major characteristic of ancient Christianity. I would argue that this claim made sense to many people because, as early as Paul, certain types of Christianity focused on intellectual practices and ordered these around a totalizing unitary vision of the good. Even though Christianity did not derive from philosophy in any direct way, but from Judaism, it shared the structural features that made it philosophy-like. Eventually the church would solve the problem by dividing Christian life into two types: those who lived the compromised conventional life and those who lived lives as monks and ascetics focused only on the ultimate good. The hierarchy of the two ways reflected the powerful new arrangement that the Hellenistic philosophies pioneered in making life a choice focused on a limited good or set of goods produced by intellectual practices.

Three caveats are in order. First, Pauline Christianity was not a neat package, fully integrated and consistent. A major tension seen most clearly in his letter to the Romans reveals him continuing to accept and to understand himself as working within Judaism even as, being the apostle to the Gentiles, he adapts himself to the life of a Gentile who is in Christ.[74] While Christ and the new age of the Spirit certainly modify traditional forms of Judaism in some ways, the change for Gentile culture is much more radical. In Paul's thought, Gentiles in Christ must undergo a radical modification of the self because they have been fundamentally and consistently shaped by idolatry and *porneia*. They do not, like Judeans, merely receive a "messiah" and a new moment in history. Rather the culture of the Greek, Roman, Egyptian, and so on must be largely abandoned and reread in terms of a new version of the master narrative of the Judeans (although Gentiles are not to adopt Judean religious practices that relate to the temple) and a recreated self. The resemblance to a Hellenistic philosophy would thus apply most clearly to Paul's Gentile groups and presumably less so or not at all, for instance, to Judean Jesus people in Jerusalem who were led by James. The future of Christianity, of course, would lie in Paul's direction.

Second, Hellenistic philosophers tend to associate as friends. In Pauline Christianity, however, one finds the language of fictive kinship.[75] Since the kinship is fictive and not "real," it in many ways resembles friendship and draws upon the language of friendship.[76] Paul also writes about the Gentile adoption into the lineage of Abraham through Christ.[77] The dominant metaphor of a family—albeit an oxymoronic family not founded on marriage, descent, and property—might be counted as a dissimilarity from the Hellenistic philosophies, but needs to be better understood.[78] No matter how often one utters the word "brother" or "father," using the language of family is not the same thing as the practices of a family, which include much more than the language. Some later Christian writers made an easy move from speaking of Christianity as a "brotherhood" to Christianity as the third ethnicity, a *genos* or *ethnos* that is neither Greek/Roman nor barbarian/Judean.

Third, specific rituals play an intrinsic role in Pauline Christianity that they do not for the Hellenistic philosophies, except possibly for Epicureans. Again, let me emphasize that the philosophies assume to various degrees that the practices, institutions, and virtues of the Greek city are a basis that the philosophy modifies and rectifies by critical reflection. Thus, a Stoic does not throw out traditional religion and ritual of the city but obtains a modified critical understanding of it that is less local. But only the Epicureans developed their own rituals.[79] Evidence also exists for ritual among later Pythagoreans and Platonists that needs study.[80] To even further diminish the force of the caveat, one should remember that the Christian rituals dispensed with animal sacrifice and almost all of the other practices central to ancient ritual, except for public prayer and ritual washing. But in traditional religion, the latter only had its sense in relation to temples and sacred places, where purity had to be maintained in order to sacrifice. Christian ritual in the first two hundred years was an odd sort of ritual by ancient standards. Its form decisively broke the link with land and lineages of peoples that was intrinsic to traditional Mediterranean ritual.

Finally, let me very briefly suggest a context in ancient Mediterranean cultural history for this phenomenon of a religion that looked in many ways like a philosophy.[81] The traditional religion and wider cultures of Greeks, Judeans, Romans, and so on were based on the local knowledges of face-to-face communities led by aristocrats who administered the lore and practices, e.g., how to sacrifice an animal, calculate when to have a festival, read events for signs from the gods of the place. Led by the so-called Greek enlightenment, the centuries before the common era saw a massive growth in the specialization of knowledge that was no longer local. Greek philosophy led this trend for many areas of knowledge. The particular character of the Hellenistic philosophies derived from creating specialized knowledge and practices about the soul or "how to live an entire life." In place of the local morals of peoples, they claimed a universal expertise regarding character and mind. Judean scribes and scholars also attained a similar authority as specialists in knowledges that were becoming increasingly important to Judean culture. The shift in knowledge practices also meant a shift in authority toward the specialists and away from the local knowledges of the aristocrats who now had to employ specialists themselves. Christianity was a new form of religion based on the new shape of knowledge that depended on expert interpreters and teachers like Paul.[82] It is not surprising, then, that Pauline Christianity might in many respects have more in common with the Hellenistic philosophies than with the traditional religions based in the landed aristocracies of Rome, Greece, and Judea.

Chapter 5

IPSE DIXIT: Citation of Authority in Paul and in the Jewish and Hellenistic Schools

Loveday Alexander

Arthur Darby Nock, in a famous passage from his classic study on conversion in the ancient world, speculates on the impression that interested Greek or Roman observers might gain if they were to stray into a Christian meeting:

> Christianity had no outdoor ceremonies capable of catching the eye. Their own private worship was not likely to attract interest. . . . The group which met for these purposes in any place would be composed of people who knew one another, and while there would be visitors from other communities they would have letters of introduction. Of course in the larger bodies, as for instance at Rome, it would no doubt have been possible for an inquisitive person to find his way in, as Burton did to Mecca. If he did, he was probably very disappointed. He saw no orgies, and he saw little which would suggest to him worship as he knew it. . . . He heard scriptural readings,

> a little wearisome, perhaps, by reason of their length, an
> exhortation like those of the synagogue, and his impression
> here also may well have been that this was of the nature of a
> philosophical school.[1]

We might call this a kind of "ancient reader-response" criticism, and in an earlier paper I have tried to set out an agenda for exploring Nock's insight, building on the observations of the second-century medical writer Galen, who records very much the kind of impression Nock hypothesized.[2] This "reader-response" approach, I would suggest, provides a useful way of approaching the topic of "Paul beyond the Judaism/Hellenism divide." Rather than trying to define either entity ontologically, this stance allows us to focus on the perceptions of the contemporary Greek or Roman observer. Our question then becomes, What would Nock's inquisitive cultural tourists find familiar about the Pauline communities, and what would they find strange? And would the strangeness reflect something standing out as distinctively "Jewish" in a cultural world dominated by "Hellenism"?

At first sight, the comparison with the philosophical schools appears to push the early Christian groups firmly towards the Hellenistic side of the comparison. One of the most substantial comparative studies along these lines is that of Clarence E. Glad, who focuses on the psychagogy of the Pauline communities and sees significant similarities with the practice of the Epicureans. Glad is not seeking to demonstrate "either a pattern of influence and cultural borrowing or direct influence or reaction" but arguing for a "basic congruity" between the two groups that provides at the very least "a rationale for comparing the hortatory and psychagogic practices of the two communities."[3] His work builds on the pioneering studies of Abraham Malherbe (himself a pupil of Nock), who has argued for some time that Paul's work needs to be seen in continuity with the popular philosophers of his day; but where Malherbe would look to contemporary Stoic and Cynic practice, Glad would argue that the Epicureans provide a better analogue. Nevertheless, Glad is happy to concur with Malherbe's presentation of Paul as "a Paul who is at once *Paulus christianus* and *Paulus Hellenisticus,* one who is thoroughly familiar with the traditions of his philosophic contemporaries and who knows these traditions first-hand."[4]

But this does not seem to be the point of the comparison either for Nock or for Galen. If early Christian meetings included a combination of scriptural readings and sermonizing, as Nock suggests, this would be something they shared with sabbath-day meetings of the Jewish community: the practice has as much right to be labeled "Jewish" as "Hellenistic." For Galen, similarly, the unit of comparison is simultaneously Jewish and Christian: to this ironic observer, the quarreling adherents of the medical and philosophical schools of his day are comparable with the disciples of "the school of Moses and Christ."[5] Galen is not concerned here about the details of particular teachings:

> The parallel is conceived phenomenologically, in terms of social structures, rather than in terms of any similarity at the conceptual level. It is the teaching activities of Jews and Christians, and the traditions which by implication lie behind them, which qualify both groups to be regarded as "schools": there are "teachers" and "pupils" in the present, and their teaching is traced back to a revered founder in the past through either written or oral tradition.[6]

As I argued in my earlier paper, this comparison, put forward in passing by a dispassionate ancient observer,[7] presupposes a basic congruity between the two kinds of group at a structural level: whatever the details of their behavior or doctrines, they were seen in some way as belonging to the same category, being a similar kind of group. What Galen is doing here, in modern academic terms, is developing a cross-cultural model (understood as a framework for helping the observer to organize large quantities of nebulous data).[8] He is drawing on a pattern that can be observed throughout the history of the schools in the Hellenistic and Roman periods (and indeed throughout the Eastern Mediterranean), though its individual components may be combined in different ways: and it is a pattern onto which we can quite easily map the Judeo-Christian groups. Far from being distinctively Hellenistic, in fact, this basic school structure was common to a number of cultural groups across the Eastern Mediterranean.

The key features of the model are represented schematically in Table 1. This table intentionally represents a highly abstracted matrix for organizing the structural components of a range of social structures (within the broad cultural framework of the ancient Mediterranean world) that could support the description "school." This model need not account for every aspect of these groups. On the contrary: part of its usefulness lies in its potential for pointing up significant differences between comparable groups. Nevertheless, for the purposes of this paper, the tabular format allows us to see at a glance the basic structural parallels between different cultural groups.

Table 1
"The School of Moses and Christ"
Hellenistic, Jewish, and Christian School Structures.

A: **Founding Teacher**	Plato	Hippocrates	Moses	Christ
B: **Tradition** a) written b) oral	Dialogues oral teachings exegesis	Corp. Hipp. oral teachings exegesis	Torah oral Torah exegesis	Scripture word of the Lord exegesis
C: **Tradents**	Academy	Cos school	"Great synagogue"	Disciples/family
	DISCIPLE CIRCLES			
D: **Teachers**	local Platonist teacher	local medical teacher	rabbi **or** synagogue leader	"apostle"/"prophet" /"teacher"
E: **Students**	philosophy student	medical apprentice **or** *philiatros*	talmid **or** any Jew	apprentice **or** any Xtn
F: **Community context**	philosophy class	master's house **or** lecture **and/or** professional guild	rabbinic "academy" **or** synagogue	"school of Paul" **or** *ekklesia*
	IN THE BROADER SOCIAL CONTEXT OF THE			
	polis	*polis*	Jewish community	Christian community

Patterns of Authority
in Jewish and Hellenistic Schools

What is a "school"? As I have remarked elsewhere,[9] the minimal requirements are a teacher and some pupils—not necessarily many pupils, and not necessarily all taught at once. These are in fact the only indispensable elements to constitute a school in ancient terms: schools did not require special buildings, institutions, public support, or elaborate constitutions. All that was required was a teacher able and willing to give instruction, and a number of pupils (disciples/apprentices/students) willing to learn; for much of antiquity this was all there was. The point is well made by David Goodblatt in his valuable study of the Rabbinic academies in the Geonic period,[10] where he argues that the norm up to this period is not the "academy" or "school" in the modern sense, but the "disciple circle." The "academy" (in this sense) may be described as an institution which transcends its principals. It has a staff, a curriculum, and, most important, a life of its own, a corporate identity. Students come and go, teachers leave and are replaced, the head of the school dies and a new one is appointed—the institution goes on. A disciple circle, on the other hand, does not transcend its principals. Disciples meet with a master who may have teaching assistants; the group may meet in a special building. But when the master dies, the teaching circle disbands. Some of the disciples will attach themselves to a new master. Others may consider themselves no longer in need of a master and may even take on students of their own. What I have in mind is a relationship similar to that of a group of apprentices and a master craftsman.

In fact the "disciple circle" is the norm for the vast majority of schools in antiquity: the more famous "academies" are the exception rather than the rule, even in the Hellenistic world.

Thus if we ask the question, What did Galen know of second-century Jewish and Christian groups that would make him think of them as "schools," we should naturally expect to start with the visible, on-the-ground essentials: these groups had people who "taught" and people who "learned" in a particular community context. Galen clearly knows of contemporary Jews and Christians who teach and have "pupils":

> If I had in mind people who taught their pupils in the same way as the followers of Moses and Christ teach theirs—for they order them to accept everything on faith—I should not have given you a demonstration.[11]

In my earlier paper[12] I examined how those teachers might have operated, and how they could be compared with the teachers and pupils of the Hellenistic schools (table 1, sections D, E, F). But Galen's description also implies that these Jews and Christians resemble a "school" in another sense, in the way they derive their ultimate authority from the more distant founder-figures of Moses and Christ. This essay concerns these less visible aspects of ancient school life—the founding teacher, the tradition, and its tradents (table 1, sections A, B, C).

The Founding Teacher

Galen's perception settles one question right at the outset: he does not speak of the "school" of Clement, Justin, Pantaenus, or any contemporary Christian teacher, but "of Christ." The term *diatribē*[13] is attached to the name of a teacher of the past, not of a living teacher, and so cannot here (as it might in other cases) be translated "lecture." Moses and Christ, in other words, are equated functionally with the long-dead founders of other schools, with Plato or Hippocrates, Zeno or Epicurus. The primary unit of comparison is the movement as a whole, the "school of thought," rather than the intermediate circle of an individual teacher or any contemporary local community.

The particular point made in Galen's comparison is not a flattering one: Jewish and Christian teachers, he complains, encourage their pupils to accept everything on faith, with the result that no amount of logical demonstration can persuade them to change their minds. But it is misleading to interpret this (as Walzer does) in terms of a fundamental conflict between "Judaism" and "Hellenism":

> There is no question that these passages point to a deep divide—Galen on one side and the Jews and Christians on the other. But to interpret this as a divide between "Hebraism" and "Hellenism" is to overlook the fact that, on the specific point at issue, Galen places most of his Greek and Roman contemporaries, including the adherents of the philosophical and medical schools, on the same side of the gulf as the Jews and Christians. The essential point of [these] passages is that the "followers of Moses and Christ", whatever their deficiencies as philosophers, are *in this respect* no worse than—in fact may even be superior to—the adherents of the schools. Dogmatic adherence to a particular school or "sect," whether philosophical or medical, is Galen's own personal bugbear; the Christians and Jews are only introduced as incidental ammunition in the real debate.[14]

Excessive reliance on "faith" coupled with excessive loyalty to the beliefs of one's own sect is a serious fault for Galen, but it is not a uniquely Jewish fault.[15]

Still less is there anything distinctively "Jewish" or "Hellenistic" about the underlying structural pattern presupposed by the comparison, which sees a functional analogy between Moses and Christ and the founders of the Hellenistic philosophical and medical sects. The functional equation of Moses with the founders of the Hellenistic schools should occasion no surprise. Moses' reputation as a wise and ancient lawgiver was well established among pagans before Galen's time,[16] and Hellenistic Jewish writers like Philo and Josephus were assiduous in promoting Moses as a philosopher to rival the brightest and best founders of the Greek schools:[17]

> That the wisest of the Greeks learnt to adopt these conceptions of God from principles with which Moses supplied them, I am

> not now concerned to urge; but they have borne abundant wit-
> ness to the excellence of these doctrines, and to their conso-
> nance with the nature and majesty of God. In fact, Pythagoras,
> Anaxagoras, Plato, the Stoics who succeeded him, and indeed
> nearly all the philosophers appear to have held similar views
> concerning the nature of God. (Josephus, *Ag. Ap.* 2.168)
>
> An infinity of time has passed since Moses, if one compares
> the age in which he lived with those of other legislators; yet it
> will be found that throughout the whole of that period not
> merely have our laws stood the test of our own use, but they
> have to an ever increasing extent excited the emulation of the
> world at large. Our earliest imitators were the Greek philoso-
> phers, who, though ostensibly observing the laws of their own
> countries, yet in their conduct and philosophy were Moses'
> disciples, holding similar views about God, and advocating
> the simple life and friendly communion between man and
> man. (Josephus, *Ag. Ap.* 2.279–281)

This presentation is matched by the internal logic of the literature of the
rabbinic schools, where Moses is consistently cited as paramount and
incontestable authority.[18]

It might be objected, however, that the status of Christ in the early
church is higher than the status of the founder of a philosophical school.
Theologically speaking (that is, from an insider's viewpoint), the title
"teacher" captures only a part of the significance of Christ for the church;[19]
but from the outsider's point of view the reverence accorded to the founder
of a school would in many cases be difficult to distinguish from that
accorded to Christ by Christians. This is especially—and notoriously—
true of the Epicureans. When Lucretius speaks of Epicurus as a god,[20] this
was not simply poetic exaggeration; Cicero mentions this religious vener-
ation of the founder as a feature of the school (*Tusc.* 1.21.48; *De nat. deor.*
1.16.43). Cicero also witnesses to the Epicurean practice (said to derive
from a provision of Epicurus's will: Diogenes Laertius 10.18) of celebrating the founder's birthday (*De fin.* 2.31.101–103). Plutarch, a century
later, describes the charismatic fervor of such a gathering:

> your "roars" of ecstasy, and "cries of thanksgiving" and tumul-
> tuous "bursts of applause" and "reverential demonstrations,"
> all that apparatus of adoration that you people resort to in sup-
> plicating and hymning the man who summons you to sus-
> tained and frequent pleasures. (Plutarch, *Adv. Col.* 1117A,
> Loeb trans.)

Another Epicurean, Metrodorus, speaks of "the holy mysteries of Epicurus which are in very truth the revelation of a god" (Plutarch *Adv. Col.*

1117B). For Philodemus, writing in the first century B.C.E., Epicureans who criticize the views of the sect's founding fathers are guilty of a crime "little short of parricide."[21] Thus, when Lucian speaks of the "mysteries" founded by the "crucified sophist" and "lawgiver" whom the Christians "worship" (*Peregrinus* 11, 13) he is using the same blend of religious and scholastic language that was used, by both friends and enemies, of the Epicurean school.

But it would be erroneous to suppose that the Epicureans were alone in treating the founder of their school in a manner that could be called "religious." In an important article on "Philosophical Allegiance in the Greco-Roman World,"[22] David Sedley claims that "in the Greco-Roman world, especially during the Hellenistic and Roman periods, what gives philosophical movements their identity is less a disinterested quest for the truth than a virtually religious commitment to the authority of a founder figure." Sedley's prime examples of this phenomenon are taken from the Epicureans, but he insists that all the Greek philosophical schools follow the same pattern, with only occasional exceptions. Despite the concern for open enquiry that characterized the original Academy, Platonists of later generations "presented themselves as loyal to Plato's thought."[23] Even the "emancipated, freebooting Stoics" are careful not to disagree with the founder: "It was every bit as unthinkable for a Stoic to criticise Zeno, or to question his authority, as it was for an Epicurean to show such disrespect to Epicurus. . . . I can think of no instance in which any of Zeno's successors in the school is reported as ever suggesting that Zeno had been *wrong* about anything."[24] The criticisms of Galen and other second-century writers, in other words, were perfectly justified:

> Those who were first came into contact with philosophy and thus became famous. Their successors followed them blindly without any search for truth; they were simply impressed by their predecessors' perseverance and self-discipline and by the unusual quality of their sayings. They believed that what each had learnt from his teacher was true. They handed these doctrines on to others and were named after the father of the system by their adherents.[25]

Matters were little different in the medical schools, where the sects contended jealously for the reputation of their own teachers: few, as Galen many times laments, were prepared to take his own eclectic, independent line:

> For there are some people amongst them, who are led to do so by their inclination to the sort of thing that would carry

conviction to Erasistratos; and so they praise Erasistratos' view and reject the views of all other people, calling themselves, for this reason, Erasistrateans; and band themselves together like capable soldiers who are led by a single leader. Other people, again, assert Praxagoras' view to be good and right; so you find that by their belief in him they are convinced by what carried conviction to Praxagoras. A fitting motto for these people would be what Homer said about Odysseus: "Greatly do we desire to be companies of Praxagoras, the noble, the great-hearted." Then you will find a third army, the disciples of Asclepiades, and you will find other people who have made Herophilos their leader, master, and director in all their affairs, others again accord Hippocrates this position.[26]

As with the philosophers, the occasional exception merely underlies the strength of the normal pattern:

All doctors who are followers of experience, just like the philosophers who are called Sceptics, refuse to be called after a man, but rather want to be known by their frame of mind. And accordingly they say that, though the other doctors are called Hippocratics or Erasistrateans or Praxagoreans or Asclepiadeans or by some other name of this kind, they themselves are not. [27]

Hippocrates, like Socrates among the philosophical schools, held a special position as one whose authority all the schools (including the empiricists) sought to claim for themselves. Herophilus of Alexandria was a notable exception:[28]

The shadow of Hippocrates loomed large in Alexandria. . . . Having been trained by a physician from Cos—Praxagoras—Herophilus undoubtedly was familiar with some Hippocratic texts . . . [and] with Hippocratic theories. . . . Herophilus' explicit responses to these texts are striking for their unorthodoxy. Unlike the Alexandrian Empiricists and numerous other ancient physicians, both early and late (including Galen), Herophilus did not succumb to the temptation to invoke the sanction of "Hippocrates" to legitimate his own views. Instead, he faced the spell of the Hippocratic tradition squarely, if not always successfully. . . . Contentious though the Greeks were, Herophilus' polemics represent an unprecedented step in the history of medicine. Previous physicians had abandoned individual Hippocratic positions silently and implicitly, but no one had confronted the Father of medicine with open criticism. The absence of traditional inhibitions, along with the spirit of scientific frontiersmanship in a new city, Alexandria, may have emboldened Herophilus to risk open confrontation, to question the dominant authority, and thus to clarify and enhance his own status as the initiator of a new tradition.

The Tradition

As Goodblatt points out, the death of a teacher creates problems for the survival of the school: if teaching was the product of an individual, not an institution, it would not ordinarily survive the teacher's death:

> [W]hen the master dies, the teaching circle disbands. Some of the disciples will attach themselves to a new master. Others may consider themselves no longer in need of a master and may even take on students of their own.[29]

Where we hear of the "school" of a long-dead teacher, then, it is clear that some additional (often quite mundane) mechanism must have come into play. The "Garden" where the Epicurean school held its meetings was actually the master's private property, and its fate after Epicurus's death was determined, as the fate of private property usually is, by a will.[30] More important, however, and more universal (not all the schools had private meeting places) was the role played by written and oral tradition—teaching was passed down from master to pupils, who in turn passed it on to their own pupils. Thus, within the Jewish tradition, the later projection of Moses as founder of a "school" is dependent on the function of the Mosaic writings as scripture within the Jewish community. It is hardly necessary to document this. For Philo, for example, "Moses says" means effectively "scripture says"—and vice versa. In the rabbinic academies, similarly, Moses is the ultimate authority: the scriptures embody his teachings. And alongside the written text of Torah is the "oral Torah," the unwritten "traditions of the fathers," derived—according to the classic doctrine—from *Moshe Rabbenu* himself (*b. Meg.* 19b):

> R. Hiyya bar Abba said in the name of R. Yochanan: What is the meaning of the verse (Deut. 9:10) "and on them was written according to all the words which the Lord spoke with you in the Mount"? It teaches us that the Holy One, blessed be He, showed Moses the minutiae of the Torah and the minutiae of the scribes and the innovations which would be introduced by the scribes, and what are these? The readings of the Megillah.[31]

David Sedley has argued that things were not significantly different in the philosophical schools of the Hellenistic world. The writings of Epicurus became canonical texts for his followers, just as the writings of Zeno did for the Stoics.[32] Plato's writings, and even more his unwritten teachings, formed the backbone of the Academic tradition.[33] In fact, Sedley can go so far as to say that a school could not survive the loss of its master's teachings. When Aristotle's successor Strato allowed the library of the founder to pass into private hands, the Peripatetic school "rapidly declined in importance, virtually vanishing as a cohesive force in the remainder of the third century. . . . The Peripatos' fall from prominence under Strato only serves to re-emphasise the indispensable cohesive force exerted by a school's commitment to its scriptures. Without them, there was no school."[34]

It was not only written texts that had this cohesive force. The major part of a teacher's activity was oral instruction (*catēchēsis*), and this might never be put into written form at all: Diogenes Laertius lists a number of philosophers who wrote no books. Sometimes the students took notes that were then passed on, sometimes without the teacher's knowledge or sanction (Galen and Quintilian both provide examples of this phenomenon; Arrian's notes on the *Discourses of Epictetus* are perhaps the most famous surviving example, but the literature of the schools provides many more).[35] In this process, whether written or oral, the names of intermediate teachers tended to be submerged in the broader school allegiance: cf. Galen's own account of his education, where the name of the teacher is not given, only his school affiliation:

> After I had completed my fourteenth year, I attended lectures by philosophers from my own city—mostly under a Stoic who was a disciple of Philopator, but for a short time, also, under a Platonist, a disciple of Gaius. . . . Meanwhile, I studied under another teacher from my home town, a disciple of Aspasius the Peripatetic, on his return from a long sojourn abroad. After him I had another teacher from Athens, an Epicurean.[36]

In this case, the local teacher is perhaps too insignificant to mention: what is important is the link with a larger tradition.

It is no surprise, then, to find that quotation and exegesis of both oral and written tradition becomes a vital task in the preservation of a school's identity. This was only partially linked with the Alexandrian literary tradition of textual criticism and lexicography.[37] The canonical texts were not simply dead monuments of the founder's thought: "the role of scriptural authority was to provide a philosophical movement with a *raison d'être* and a framework within which it could preserve its cohesion *while* continuing to inquire and debate."[38] In fact, the framework of exegesis allowed a wide diversity of interpretations of the master, which often became the focus of inter-sect polemic:[39] Galen provides good examples of this phenomenon.[40] Herophilus himself underwent a similar process after his death: "Throughout these three and a half centuries [sc. from 300 B.C.E. to 50 C.E.] the sanction provided by the common label 'follower of Herophilus' was sought and shared by numerous distinguished physicians, but this nominal uniformity cannot conceal the diversity and the fierce, often contentious individualism accommodated within the 'school'."[41]

Loyalty to the tradition, then, did not impede individualism in interpretation. Neither did it prevent an ongoing process of innovation and correction to meet changing circumstances. This ability to adapt and modernize the tradition was particularly important in medicine and other practical disciplines, where improvements in practice were constantly rendering earlier authorities out of date, but a similar process went on in philosophy.[42] This updating was relatively easy to manage in an oral tradition, or with the unpretentious, agglomerative school handbooks that could easily be expanded by successive copyists.[43] Updating was harder where a body of texts had earlier achieved "canonic" status, especially if the texts themselves were relatively explicit. In this respect, as David Sedley puts it, the Stoics were blessed with a founder who was "an inspirational rather than a systematic teacher, leaving vast areas of unclarity about his teachings for his successors to illuminate, and much virgin territory . . . for them to colonise."[44] The Epicureans had to cope with a much more detailed written corpus: textual criticism provided one method of dealing with it, but paradoxically the Epicurean respect for the words of the master also encouraged pseudepigraphy as a means of adapting the tradition to changing needs.[45] The more certain classic texts came to be accepted as authoritative, the more ingenuity was required to find the truths that were hidden in them. We can see already here a pattern that was to dominate the philosophical and medical schools down through the medieval period and beyond. Pierre Hadot describes the predominantly exegetical activity of the philosophical schools in these terms:[46]

> The fact that authentic texts raise questions is not due to any inherent defect. On the contrary: their obscurity, it was thought, was only the result of a technique used by a master, who wished to hint at a great many things at once, and therefore enclosed the "truth" in its formulations.[47] Any potential meaning, as long as it was coherent with what was considered to be the master's doctrine, was consequently held to be true. Charles Thurot's remark about the commentators on the grammarian Priscianus is applicable to all philosopher exegetes:

"In their explanations of a text, the glossators did not seek to
understand the author's thought; but rather to teach the
doctrine itself which they supposed to be contained in it.
What they termed an 'authentic' author could neither be mistaken, nor contradict himself, nor develop his arguments
poorly, nor disagree with any other authentic author. The
most forced exegesis was used in order to accommodate the
letter of the text to what was considered the truth."[48] It was
believed that the truth had been "given" in the master's texts,
and all that had to be done was to bring it to light and expli-
cate it. . . . Each philosophical or religious school or group
believed itself to be in possession of a traditional truth, communicated from the beginning by the divinity to a few wise
men. Each therefore laid claim to being the legitimate depos-
itory of the truth.

The Tradents

Tradition implies tradents: the claim that a tradition represents "Torah to
Moses on Sinai" necessitates an explanation of the mechanism by which
it was transmitted from Sinai to the speaker. Hence the importance of
"succession-lists" like that of *Pirke Aboth* 1.1:

> Moses received Torah from Sinai and delivered it to Joshua,
> and Joshua to the Elders, and the Elders to the Prophets,
> and the Prophets delivered it to the men of the Great
> Synagogue. (R. H. Charles, *APOT* 2.691)

The role of these succession-lists in the rabbinic tradition is well documented: cf. especially Bikerman's classic article.[49] In the Hellenistic
schools, equally (as Bikerman demonstrates), tradition is authenticated by
a knowledge of the means by which it is passed across the generations.
Diogenes Laertius's compilation on the philosophical schools is probably
the best-known example of this type of Hellenistic succession literature,[50]
but in fact all the Hellenistic schools told their history in terms of who
taught whom. Compare, as an example taken at random, this account of
the Alexandrian medical schools:

> At the head of the rationalist school stood Hippocrates of Cos,
> who was also the principal leader of the school and first estab-
> lished this rationalist school, and after him, Diocles of Carys-
> tus, Praxagoras of Cos, Herophilus of Chalcedon, Erasistratus
> of Ceos, Mnesitheus of Athens, and Asclepiades the Cian of
> Bithynia, also called Asclepiades of Prusias. . . . At the head
> of the Empiricist school, on the other hand, stood Philinus of

> Cos, who was the first to have severed it from the rationalist
> school, after getting the impulse for doing so from Hero-
> philus, whose pupil he was.[51]

Note that this process does not of itself imply the existence of an institutional "academy": the succession is created simply by the individual teachers and their concern to pass on their own teacher's received tradition to
their pupils. Pupils in their turn were keen (as we have seen) to make it
clear that they had studied with the right teachers: cf. this example from
a medical textbook dating from the first century B.C.E.:[52]

> Some of these operations I have performed myself, while oth-
> ers I observed as a student of Zopyrus in Alexandria. And Posi-
> donius, who studied with the same doctor, would testify with
> us that this man practised medicine with the highest degree of
> fidelity to Hippocrates.

The importance of tradents is most obvious where an oral or practical
teaching tradition was at stake. Note also that the majority of school writings had no formal "publication" independent of their school setting; they
were "esoteric" (as opposed to "exoteric") writings, passed around from
pupil to pupil or from teacher to pupil and preserved only in the context
of the school. Direct acquaintance with published philosophical writings
was rare in antiquity: in Sedley's words, "a school member's response to the
text he reveres, although it may in a few instances (as many have suspected
in the case of Lucretius) be a direct one, is more likely to have been mediated and shaped by his own living teacher."[53] Even where a canonic text
was widely known outside the school, as for example in the case of the Platonic dialogues (which are not strictly speaking "school" literature at all),
the important knowledge to be gained from them was mediated through
the living voice of a teaching tradition: Dillon makes this point about the
Platonists, and Galen gives us a good example of the thinking behind this
widespread phenomenon, which was equally operative in medicine.[54]

Citation of Authority in Paul

It is not difficult to find parallels to these patterns of authority in early
Christianity. I have argued elsewhere[55] that Papias's allusion to the "living
voice" proverb (which Galen also uses) puts the bishop of Hierapolis
squarely within the Hellenistic school tradition, and his interest in
quizzing the associates of the disciples clearly fits within that context.
Clement gives a similar list of tradents (which includes Paul):

> These men preserved the true tradition of the blessed teach-
> ing straight from Peter, James, John and Paul, the holy apos-
> tles, son receiving it from father—how few are like their
> fathers! By the grace of God, they came right down to me, to
> deposit those ancestral apostolic seeds. (Clement in Eus. *Hist.*
> *Eccles.* 5.11)

But it is misleading to identify this interest purely as a post-first-century
phenomenon. The New Testament at several points shows an interest in
the passing-on of tradition and the identification of tradents. The major
claim in Luke's preface is the accurate following of the "tradition" passed
down by the "eye-witnesses and ministers of the word,"[56] and the narrative of Acts shows a clear interest in presenting the Jerusalem apostles in
this role;[57] but there is no sign that this was in any way innovatory.
Arguably, in fact, all the Gospels in their different ways bear signs of being
structured to underpin the authority of Jesus' disciples as bearers of
authentic tradition. Moreover, there are clear indications that Christian
teachers of subsequent generations were explicitly discouraged from setting up on their own authority as teachers: "But you are not to be called
Rabbi: for you have one teacher, and you all are brothers" (Matt 23:8). In
other words, Christ was and remained the sole authoritative teacher of the
school.[58]

Our immediate concern, however, is not with the Gospels but with
Paul. How does 1 Corinthians—one of the earliest documents of the New
Testament—fit into this pattern? How would Nock's cultural tourist
reconstruct the chain of tradition in this "school"? No Greek or Roman
observer of Paul's interchanges with the Corinthian church could fail to
observe (as Galen did of a later generation of Christians) that the cultural
matrix in which this discourse operates is distinctively "Jewish," in the
sense that the classic text on which it draws is the Jewish scriptures. The
classical bias of the Greek and Roman educational systems meant that "an
educated Roman was a man who knew his Virgil, as a Greek knew his
Homer, as a treasury of wisdom and beauty buried in the depths of his
memory, lines of which came back to him whenever he needed to express,
or insist on, or stand up for, any feeling or idea."[59] This common educational heritage leaves a very decided mark on contemporary moralists and
philosophical writers (Dio, Plutarch, Epictetus, Lucian), but there is no
trace of it in the New Testament, nor any explicit citation of the acknowledged founders of the philosophical schools.[60] Paul never quotes any
Greek writer by name in his letters: the closest we come to it in 1 Corinthians is the Menander epigram cited as a commonplace (without attribution) at 1 Cor 15:33.[61]

Instead, Paul makes constant reference, explicit and implicit, to the body of literature that both Jews and Greeks knew as "Moses." This source is most commonly cited with the formula "it is written" (see below), amplified at 1 Cor 9:9 to "it is written in the law of Moses." Moreover, as a closer study makes clear, Moses is the implicit authority for many of the key ethical statements in 1 Corinthians, e.g., in chapters 5–6.[62] Whatever Paul may say explicitly about the contrast between Moses and Christ (Rom 10:5–6; 2 Cor 3:7–15), his constant citations make it clear that the Jewish scriptures continue to play a vital part in forging the identity of the new sect—or, in the terms of the Hellenistic schools, that "Moses" still functions as a prime source of authority for Paul and his readers. This ambivalence suggests, indeed, that Galen's rather puzzling phrase "followers of Moses and Christ" may simply be a way of referring to a Christian group whose use of scripture identifies them, to the outsider, as a "school" with two poles of authority. In this sense, the "school" represented by the Corinthian community would almost certainly be identified by outsiders as "Jewish," not because it cites the authority of a revered teacher (all schools did that) but because of its choice of teacher: because it is "Moses" who is cited rather than Plato or Hippocrates.

Alongside this written tradition, Paul draws on a less clearly defined body of apparently oral material passed down within the community as "the word of the Lord."[63] Two striking passages in the epistle identify Paul as a tradent of *paradosis* received "from the Lord," one narrative (15:1–11) and one liturgical (11:23–25). "The Lord" is also cited as an authority on behavioral matters: on divorce (7:10) and on support for preachers (9:14). Despite the fact that Paul never uses the common Gospel description of Jesus as a teacher, this material identifies "Christ" as the second pole of the complex authority-structure of 1 Corinthians. Whether Paul himself would have accepted Galen's description of the Christian movement as a kind of "school" must be open to question.[64] But Paul would certainly not find fault with the all-important structural perception implicit in the comparison, namely that for the Christian movement Christ is both founder and living master. This is precisely the point he strives to clarify in 1 Corinthians 1–4: Paul, Cephas, and Apollos are not rival teachers but servants of the one master—and that, under God, is Christ. In terms of the Hellenistic schools, this passage suggests that Paul would be happier with the model of a philosophical or medical school with its overreaching allegiance to a founder-figure than with the eristic teaching style of contemporary sophists, whose "star" performances encouraged loyalty to individuals and whose adherents can be likened to the fans of a modern pop star.[65]

Strikingly, Paul is also quite explicit in 1 Corinthians about giving an opinion in his own name where he does not have a "word of the Lord": cf. 7:12 "to the rest I say, not the Lord"; 7:25 "now concerning the unmarried, I have no command of the Lord, but I give my opinion (*gnōmē*) as one who by the Lord's mercy is trustworthy." Equally striking is Paul's refusal to name any intermediate tradents between himself and "the Lord." The list in 15:5–9 looks at first sight like a "succession-list," but in point of fact there is no succession. Paul may be "last of all" (15:8), but his vision comes direct from the Lord: it is not (as Paul is at pains to point out in Galatians 1–2) mediated by Cephas or James. The argument of the first few chapters makes the same point in reverse: Cephas, Paul, and Apollos stand on the same level (1:12–13; 3:22), fellow-workers sharing the same divine commission (3:9; 4:1). This insistence on Paul's direct contact with Christ gives an added dimension to the intricate argument of chapters 1–4. Ostensibly addressed to factionalism within the church, these chapters also have the effect of bolstering Paul's authority to speak in his own right (4:1–5), as "your father in Christ Jesus through the Gospel" (4:15). Paul's apparent readiness to speak and pronounce judgment in his own name, in other words, is not presented as a way of establishing a rival locus of authority to the founder (1:13), but is so structured as to emphasize Christ's overarching authority. The divine wisdom imparted by the Spirit does not confer the independent status of *sophos* (2:1–5), but the privilege of speaking in the name of the founding teacher: "we have the mind of Christ" (2:16).

At the purely verbal level, Paul's citations of scripture seem to use a mode of expression that is as distinctively Jewish as their object. Not that there is anything distinctive about the habit of referring to an authoritative body of written texts: as we have seen, this is just as characteristic of the Hellenistic schools as it is of Judaism. But Paul's regular habit of introducing quotations with "as it is written" (*kathōs/kathaper gegraptai*) sounds strange to a Greek ear.[66] The Greeks tend almost universally to use verbs of saying rather than writing, even when they are citing written texts: "Hippocrates says," or "Epicurus makes clear."[67] This formula is so widespread in Greek literature that it is hard to believe the choice of verb (present tense, oral mode of presentation) has any particular force; nevertheless, it does tend to reinforce the idea that authority lies in a living, present teaching tradition rather than in a dead text written in the past. Moreover, it may be linked to a broader cultural pattern to which Josephus draws attention in *Against Apion:* the Jews, like other peoples of the ancient Near East, could boast a more reliable, authoritative body of written historical documents than the Greeks, who learned the art of writing relatively late (*Ag. Ap.* 1.10) and failed to devote proper care to the main-tenance of written archives (*Ag. Ap.* 1.19–22). Even where written records existed, Greek historiography showed a marked preference for oral tradi-tion. We might therefore posit a cultural distinction here that goes back to the essentially scribal nature of some ancient Near Eastern societies, and which was reinforced and maintained by the Rabbis in their insis-tence on the firm distinction between oral law and written law. Unfortu-nately for this neat distinction, the standard Rabbinic formula for citing scripture, though it is often translated "as it is written," actually means (like the Greek formulae, though using the passive rather than the active) "as it is said"—*she ne'amar.* "It is written," however, does occur in the Damascus Document alongside "he said" and "that which is said."[68] It would be an interesting and worthwhile study to examine the citation for-mulae of the differing school traditions in more detail in order to deter-mine whether Paul's formulation (which is common in the whole New Testament) is closer to Jewish than to Hellenistic terminology.

The language Paul uses of tradition, on the other hand, is much less distinctive. Cullmann isolates the formal nature of the terms used of the transmission of tradition at 1 Cor 15:3ff and 11:23ff and identifies it as definitively "Jewish": "it is clear that these are Jewish formulae, by which the rabbis refer to the *halakha* and the *haggada.*"[69] But in fact this termi-nology can be readily paralleled in Greek school texts. Philo of Byzantium, for example, introducing the fourth book of his *Mechanike Syntaxis,* promises to describe his techniques for building engines of war "just as we received the tradition (*kathoti kai autoi pareilēphamen*) both in Alexandria, where we were introduced to most of the craftsmen who con-cern themselves with this subject, and in Rhodes, where we were made known to not a few master-carpenters. . . ."[70] Vitruvius reproduces the Greek phrase exactly in the recurrent formulae that punctuate his *De Architectura:* "as I received it from my teachers"; "as it has been handed down to us from the ancients."[71] Philodemus speaks of the *paradoseis* of the rhetorical schools (*Rhet.* 1.78). Hero, a mechanical writer of the first century C.E., uses *paradosis* of the content of his manual of artillery con-struction, while his contemporary Dioscorides uses it of botany.[72] In fact, as I have argued elsewhere, the language of *paradosis* is widespread across the whole of the Hellenistic school tradition:[73] it is also characteristic of the more antiquarian side of Greek historiography (cf. e.g. Dionysius of Halicarnassus, *De Thucydide* §7). In this respect, then, there is nothing particularly Jewish about Paul's language.

How far we should seek to parallel the more distinctively Christian for-mulae for referring to "the Lord"—especially those that seem to presuppose a charismatic background—is a more difficult question. Clearly, many of the different schools in the Hellenistic world developed their own sectarian idiolect: the "*Ipse dixit*" formula of the Pythagoreans is a notorious example.[74] In this sense there would be nothing unexpected in the discovery that many of Paul's phrases display an idiolect that is (in the purely linguistic sense) distinctively "Christian." But the underlying phenomenon of referring sayings of individual prophets or teachers back to the founder is much more widespread. Here Paul's practice, as we have noted, seems less like that of the rabbinic schools (which like to articulate the succession by citing a chain of individual authorities within the tradition) and more like the practice of, say, the Epicurean school. But even here it would be misleading to claim this as evidence of Paul's "Hellenism": differences of practice between Paul and the rabbinic schools should be seen not as a mark of Hellenism but as a variant coloring within the common culture. The Hellenistic schools themselves were conscious of differences in this matter, particularly the Stoics:

> And suppose we did want to separate out individual aphorisms from the mass, whom should we attribute them to? Zeno? Cleanthes? Chrysippus? Panaetius? Posidonius? We Stoics are no monarch's subject; each asserts his own freedom. Among Epicureans whatever Hermarchus or Metrodorus says is credited to one man alone; everything ever said by any member of that fraternity was uttered under the authority and auspices of one person.[75]

Whatever Seneca may imply by this, the practice of retrospective attribution was not unique to the Epicurean school. The whole Hellenistic process of canonization, and the collection and cataloguing of school treatises into written *corpora*, tended to lead to the attribution of later texts (and later versions of tradition) to the head of the school: Hippocrates is an obvious example of this, and the same process seems to have affected the Aristotelian tradition.[76]

Jewish or Hellenistic?

What are we to do with these parallels? When Saul Lieberman, in a famous study,[77] drew attention to some of the resemblances between the rabbinic academies and the Hellenistic schools, he discussed them under the general rubric of "Hellenism in Jewish Palestine," and argued that he could identify clear cases of "Hellenistic influence" on the rabbis.[78] Similarly for Bikerman, the "houses" of Hillel and Shammai "étaient des

Écoles, et des Écoles hellénistiques."[79] However, Lieberman was also careful to point out that not all parallels entitle us to speak of "borrowing" or "influence":

> The early Jewish interpreters of Scripture did not have to embark for Alexandria in order to learn there the rudimentary methods of linguistic research. To make them travel to Egypt for this purpose would mean to do a cruel injustice to the intelligence and acumen of the Palestinian sages. [80]

> The methods applied in the understanding of dreams were invented neither by the Jews nor by the Greeks. They go back to hoary antiquity. The ingenuity of the diviner or the seer produced the most complicated solutions of dreams, oracles and magic, which lent themselves to similar ways of interpretations; they borrow from one another and supplement one another.[81]

Talking about "influence" in this kind of case, in other words, is arguably missing the point. At this level of abstraction, the distinction between "Jewish" and "Hellenistic" seems to be virtually meaningless: what we are talking about are patterns of academic activity that were more or less universal in the Eastern Mediterranean. Where they arose and how they may have been carried from one cultural setting to another are questions of some historical interest: the lasting influence of educational patterns associated with "wisdom" in the ancient Near East must be part of the picture, and only a severe form of Hellenic diffusionism can seriously contemplate the proposition that all patterns of intellectual activity in the region were derived from Greek models.[82] But these genetic questions are not our concern here. For the purposes of a diachronic study, it would be important to take full account of the widely divergent historical roots of the different school traditions in the ancient Mediterranean, but for our limited purposes they can be ignored. What is more important is the synchronic perception that ancient observers are able to use the related terms "school" and "sect" as mutually meaningful models for conceptualizing what is going on in one cultural community in terms of what is going on in another.[83] This kind of observation comes both from outside the Jewish community (Galen) and from inside (as in Josephus's famous description of the sects of first-century Judaism in terms of Greek philosophical schools).[84] So we might argue that whatever parallels we may find in Paul to the practice of the schools, at this level of abstraction it really does not make sense to label them as either "Jewish" or "Hellenistic." We might use the analogy of the position of football (soccer) in today's sporting world.

Although the game originated in England, it is meaningless at the end of the twentieth century to label the game itself "English" (much as some English football fans would like to do so). The game has become an aspect of a global sporting culture, a universal code understood and played with enthusiasm and skill across Europe and the world. National distinctives operate not at the level of the system itself but within it, both formally (national anthems, team uniforms) and stylistically (in the idiolects that give variety and character to the playing style of different national teams). Similarly with the Jewish and Hellenistic schools: only when we move down to a more detailed level of comparison can we identify distinctive cultural flavors within the broader structure. It is not the appeal to authority in itself that is "Jewish" or "Hellenistic" but the choice of authority (Plato or Moses, Socrates or Jesus), and further perhaps the distinctive idiolects that mark the development of individual hermeneutical styles.

But perhaps matters are more complex than that. Within this broad Near Eastern framework, the parallel between Greek and Jewish academies was not simply inert but had the potential to be exploited at any time for the purposes of one side or the other. On the Greek side, as I have pointed out in an earlier paper (cf. n. 2), it was exploited polemically by Galen not for the purpose of attacking the Jewish and Christian groups but as a weapon against his Greek contemporaries. The wider perception of the parallel between Moses and the Greek founding philosophers is a recurrent motif within the history of the ambivalent love affair between Greek philosophy and the "alien wisdom" of the Jews and other barbarian races.[85] Some of this material (as in Josephus) can be seen as part of a linguistic struggle to find mutually comprehensible categories to describe parallel social systems—"models," in the modern sense. Josephus must be at least partly disingenuous in describing the Sadducees as a "sect" (how did one join?), but *hairesis* is a perfectly reasonable category for the Pharisees, and conveys well a sense of the plurality of first-century Judaism, which was (as modern scholars increasingly emphasize) not a monolithic system but one that could support a diversity of emphasis and interpretation. In the absence of political parties, the Greek philosophical sects provide arguably the best social analogue to this situation in the ancient world.[86]

But the model also has the potential to be exploited for more polemical purposes, as in the intercommunal apologetic which may be ostensibly directed to an external audience but which actually appears to be designed for internal consumption.[87] Much of the rhetoric of Philo's obsession with Greek philosophy serves to underline that there is no need to leave the Jewish community and its scriptures to find a depth of philosophical reflection that can match anything the Greeks have to offer.[88] Some of the rabbinic parallels with Greek school material may have a similar exhortatory function. Judah Goldin has argued that "the School of Rabbi Johanan b. Zakkai, one of the chief links in the chain of Pharisaic tradition as represented by the *'Abot,* was also engaged in discussion of a strictly philosophical kind, and, in particular, in the exploration of ethical problems which were characteristic of the Hellenistic philosophical schools."[89] Goldin argues that *'Aboth* 2.14 ("Be diligent in the study of Torah, and know how to answer an Epicurean") should be taken seriously as "a kind of anti-epicurean polemic, . . . some as-it-were Stoic (I emphasize as-it-were) remark" directed not at the all-purpose *epiqurus* of later rabbinic texts, where the word is used "indiscriminately to suggest any kind of heretic or unbeliever," but at real Epicureans, albeit probably Jewish ones: "he very likely did have in mind such Jews as had become epicurean more or less in outlook, not just any heretic at all."[90] And Goldin goes on to argue a possible locus for such "as-it-were Stoic" views in the school of Johanan, which seems to have been willing both to construct the ideal disciple in terms reminiscent of the Stoic school[91] and to discuss the essential components of the good life in a distinctively Stoic manner.[92] This seems to be more a kind of first-century "Jewish Continuity"[93] than simply a matter of noting an interesting parallel: it demonstrates that whatever you thought you could find in the Greek philosophical schools can be found in the Torah-centered study of the rabbinic academies. The rabbinic debates on the propriety of studying "Greek wisdom," on this view, should be seen (despite Galen)[94] not so much in post-Enlightenment terms of the assault of Reason on traditional faith, but in terms of something much more aggressive, the totalizing claims of Greek philosophy to provide a way of life answering to humanity's deepest ethical and religious needs.[95] Clarence Glad makes a similar point, noting the common tendency in the second century to lump together Christians and Epicureans as groups characterized by "atheism, separateness and secrecy, misanthropy, social irresponsibility, the disruption of familes, sexual immorality and general moral depravity": "The early Christian attitude towards the Epicureans was understandably polemical as they attempted to dissociate themselves from the Epicureans."[96]

If Goldin's interpretation of the rabbinic material is even partially right, his view of its consequences must, I think, also be taken seriously:

> We certainly have no evidence that the Palestinian sages read Plato or Zeno, much less studied them. But one result seems to me inescapable: living in the Hellenistic-Roman world the

Tannaim could not remain unaffected by that world. It is not simply a matter of loan words: it is something much more profound. Not only did the Palestinian sages appropriate the terminology for some hermeneutic rules from the Hellenistic rhetors, but inside the *bet ha-midrash,* the rabbinic academy, apparently one did take up from time to time philosophical questions, and one did from time to time attempt to answer these questions in the current philosophical idiom. Study of the Law of course remained paramount. But along with such activity went an awareness, at least in the School of Johanan ben Zakkai, of the subject and style popular in intellectual circles generally.[97]

The fact of this awareness puts an unexpected spin on the persistent rabbinic stories about philosophers being routed in argument with rabbis. These stories do not express a Jewish attitude which is "anti-philosophy as such": "in no way do such stories demonstrate that philosophy, and the current manner of discussing what was generally regarded as philosophical questions, were repugnant to the talmudic sages." Rather they express "a typically recurring popular attitude: anything they can do, we can do better . . . indeed there is in such stories a distinct acknowledgement that among the Gentiles the wisest are the philosophers; but of course the *hakam* is superior since he is a master of the Torah."[98]

I would suggest that we might do well to reexamine Paul's arguments about "wisdom" in 1 Corinthians 1–4 against this background, and especially the key verses at 1:19–25. Paul, too, has commonly been taken (by commentators from Celsus onwards) to be presenting an argument that is "anti-philosophy as such": but perhaps he is simply using the rhetoric of the popular antiphilosophical debate to enhance the claims of a rival philosophy. Paul's claim here is that Christians are privy to a "secret and hidden wisdom of God," a wisdom that has been hidden from "the rulers of this age" (2:6–7). The language would perhaps strike a Greek auditor as idiosyncratic, but it is not too remote to be comprehensible as a rival claim to that of, say, the Platonists, who also proclaimed a "hidden" wisdom defined as "the science of those things which are the object of thought and really existent, the science which . . . is concerned with God and the soul as separate from the body." For Plato, Diogenes Laertius tells us, "wisdom" (*sophia*) means "philosophy, which is a yearning for divine wisdom" (Diogenes Laertius 3.63). But what does "wisdom" mean for Paul?

It is not too difficult to identify the biblical roots of the composite web of quotations and allusions of 1 Cor 1:19–20,[99] which clearly forms part of a widespread early Christian barrage of *testimonia* demonstrating the power of "babes" to understand mysteries hidden from "the wise."[100] The Hebrew of Isa 33:18 is "Where are the scribes? (*sopherim*)," and Paul's choice of *grammateus* as an equivalent suggests a ready identification with the "scribes" of the Gospels, that is, with the local repositories of wisdom in the Jewish community.[101] If we push the identification in a "Jewish" direction, the *sophos* can be read as the *hakham,* the rabbinic sage, and the *suzētētēs* as the *darshan* or exponent of the classic rabbinic school activity of *midrash.*[102] But Paul's words also have a Greek currency, and it would be perverse, in a context where he is speaking both of "Jews" and of "Greeks," to ignore their Greek connotations.[103] Lieberman rightly points out that the *zētēsai* word group is widely used in the technical language of the Hellenistic schools, but the compound form is much less common. *Suzētētēs* is actually a *hapax legomenon,* but the cognate noun *suzētēsis* and the adjective *suzētētikos* may have had particular associations with the Epicurean school.[104] In this context, Paul's reference to the *sophos* could take on an added piquancy. The word is of course widely used in Greek, but it has a particular resonance for the followers of Epicurus, who reserved the title for his sole use: Plutarch makes the point ironically that Colotes failed to earn the title "wise man" even after he had gone to the lengths of throwing himself at Epicurus's feet and clasping his knees in an attitude of reverence normally reserved for the gods (Plutarch, *Adv. Col.* 1117B). In this school, "we discern a veritable pyramid of reverence, each grade of disciples looking up with due respect to the smaller numbers in the grade above, until the peak is reached, where the inspired leader reigned alone, the sole sage, the unique discoverer of the true philosophy and the ethical father."[105] Paul is writing for internal consumption, not head-on polemic: but to the Greek reader even remotely aware of this notorious feature of the Epicurean school (and why should not some Corinthian Christians have had such an awareness?),[106] his words provide forceful propaganda against what was obviously a powerfully attractive rival philosophy. Unlike the Greek philosopher, Christ not only proclaims divine wisdom but embodies it—and all Christians, however ignoble their social status, have access to this divine wisdom through the Spirit.

Here again we can see that the categories "Jewish" and "Hellenistic" seem to be more or less irrelevant as descriptions of the structures themselves. The game being played here, as we have seen, is one that straddles the cultural divide: the "school" concept has the capacity to function synchronically as a mutually comprehensible model for describing parallel social systems. Paul's carefully balanced language in 1 Cor 1:18–26 suggests that he himself saw the two as parallel systems, equally visible on both sides of the cultural divide. Even where the two systems are treated

more polemically as rivals, it seems meaningless to talk of anything distinctively "Hellenistic" or "Jewish" in the structure itself: we are talking
about a common cultural pattern in the ancient Mediterranean, with recognizable equivalences on both sides. The parallels between rabbinic and
"Hellenistic" school systems perceived by Lieberman and Bikerman
should not be read in terms of "influence" in either direction but as testimony to broad cultural patterns in the ancient Mediterranean; only at the
intermediate level of the specific cultural authority appealed to (and perhaps in the specific hermeneutical idiolect of a particular school) does the
distinction between Judaism and Hellenism make sense. For Nock's Greek
or Roman onlooker, as we observed earlier, the cultural authorities Paul
appeals to would be sufficient to identify him as "Jewish." But for Paul
himself, to reduce the rhetoric of the gospel to a choice between Judaism
and Hellenism would be to trivialize it. For him (here as elsewhere) the
really profound questions can be asked equally within either cultural system, and their resolution must be sought "beyond" rather than "between"
the two cultural flavors that dominate his world.

Chapter 6

Corinthian Christians as Artificial Aliens

Wayne A. Meeks

It is difficult to rid ourselves of the assumption that "Judaism" and "Hellenism" name cultural antitheses. That dichotomy is deeply lodged within the collective psyche of modern New Testament scholarship, thanks to the theological program of the Tübingen School and subsequent reactions to it.[1] The polarization was still manifest in the original topic of the 1997 Rolighed conference, "Paul *between* Judaism and Hellenism," and in much of our discussion there; the title of the present volume calls us to think in a new way. Moreover, we tend to think of Judaism as "a religion"—an anachronism unconsciously drawn from our experience of modern Western societies. One way to clear our heads of these large cultural abstractions is to focus on the specific ways that groups of ordinary people in antiquity lived their lives, though in practice we will find that surviving evidence is rarely adequate to give as clear a picture of those ordinary lives as we would wish.

The Jews of the Roman colony of Corinth were, from the outset, resident aliens: immigrants or children of immigrants from Judea.[2] Their decision to settle in a Greco-Roman city, in this case a Roman colony, outside the land of Israel placed them within the world of "Hellenism," as that term is understood in New Testament scholarship. Their everyday language, for example, was Greek.[3] However, it is doubtful they thought in those terms. Perhaps a rare intellectual among them would have had the leisure, like the great Philo of Alexandria, to muse on ways the *politeia* of Moses resembled or differed from that of Plato. Most of them simply focused on the practical issues of daily life: how to participate in the crafts and businesses of this very commercial colony without compromising the essential marks of their identity as Judeans? How to compete in this quite competitive young society—in which even some families of servile origin were joining the ruling class after a few generations—without sparking dangerous conflict with other groups? How to balance the assimilation necessary for survival and flourishing with the ancient traditions of their homeland that set boundaries and preserved identity?[4]

The Judeans of Corinth were not alone in facing these challenges. To various degrees, every immigrant group had to find a balance between identity and assimilation. In the period after Alexander and especially in the early Roman principate, travel became easier, cities grew, positive reasons for temporary or permanent migration increased, and every city saw the influx of aliens from places all around the Mediterranean basin. Those immigrants developed common strategies for holding on to some measure of separate identity in the cosmopolitan environment. Central to these strategies was the organization of associations of immigrants from each homeland. One focal point of such an association was the cult of the gods of the homeland, though that focus did not make the association a "religious community" in the sense that we use that phrase. The island of Delos shows us, in the physical relics of such groups, some graphic examples. The group of Jews (as we assume them to be) who made dedications to "God Most High" were in that respect like not only their neighbors the Samaritans, "Israelites who send their first fruits to sacred Mount Garizim," but also like the better-endowed immigrants from Beirut, who dedicated their large and elegant community center to Poseidon, identified with their native Ba'al.[5]

Unfortunately we know little about the specific situation of Judean settlers in Roman Corinth. Archaeology has produced little evidence—a crudely lettered, broken inscription of uncertain date and provenance, a lamp or two—and apart from the New Testament, the literary evidence is equally meager. We are left to extrapolate their strategies of balancing identity and assimilation by comparison with other immigrant groups and with Jewish communities in other, better-documented places. We may then compare those strategies with what we know, from Paul's letters and from Acts, of the formation of the Christian groups.

Meeting Places

Immigrant associations, like other private associations, depended on benefactors, either within their own community or from interested outsiders, to help them obtain suitable space for their various communal activities. Such patronage is amply documented by dedicatory inscriptions; in the case of Jewish groups, the collection by B. Lifshitz shows the range of services rendered.[6] The typical pattern was to begin as guests in a private house; eventually the house might be given or bequeathed to the association, remodeled more or less extensively for the exclusive use of the group, or finally replaced by a more public and specialized structure. L. Michael White has analyzed the pattern and collected much of the evidence for Mithraists, Jews, and Christians for the period of the early Empire.[7] We do not know whether the Judean immigrants in Corinth followed this common pattern, though that is a reasonable guess, nor, if they did, to what stage they had progressed when Paul arrived on the scene. The author of Acts assumes a single meeting place that was in a residential quarter: the house of Titius Justus, a "worshiper of God," was adjacent. Titius became the first patron of those who responded positively to Paul's preaching (Acts 18:7). Paul mentions neither Titius Justus (unless one accepts the ingenious suggestion that these are the nomen and cognomen of Gaius, "host of the whole meeting" according to Rom 16:23)[8] nor Crispus the *archisynagōgos*, first convert according to Acts 18:8. Nevertheless, the importance of householders and patrons is clearly underscored by Paul, who names in this category not only Gaius but also Stephanas (1 Cor 16:15), perhaps Stephanas's companions Fortunatus and Achaicus (16:17), and of course the indispensable Prisca and Aquila (16:19; Rom 16:3; cf. Acts 18:2–3). Whatever the state of the Jewish community of Corinth when Paul and his coworkers arrived, the latter followed the pattern ordinarily used by Judean and other immigrant associations for obtaining space of their own when they withdrew or were banned from the Jewish space.

Organization, Leaders

The internal organization of immigrant groups seems to have varied from place to place, and the little we know of the details does not help us much in our comparison with the early Christians of Corinth. Like smaller clubs of various purposes, the immigrant associations sometimes mimicked civic offices; whether that was the case in colonial Corinth we cannot be sure. Until recently it has been commonly assumed in modern scholarship that *politeuma* was the standard term for a formally recognized body of resident aliens, particularly Jews, with certain rights similar to those of citizens. Detailed analysis of papyrological, literary, and epigraphic evidence, however, has undermined that assumption.[9] It is nevertheless true, as Louis Feldman has noted, that, whatever they were called, and whether they were more like a citizen body or more like a voluntary *collegium*, the Judean immigrants in each city were organized.[10] Moreover, in most places there seems to have been some unifying organization of Jews in the entire city, however many individual meeting places may have existed.[11] We have seen that the author of Acts assumes that only a single synagogue existed in Corinth. Be that as it may, the several household groups founded by Paul and his assistants seem to have been able to meet together occasionally in the house of Gaius (Rom 16:23), so the Christians, too, had some sense of being a single community.

From inscriptions we have a fairly wide range of titles of offices or functions within Jewish communities; none of these, except *didaskaloi*, corresponds precisely with any of the leadership roles mentioned or alluded to by Paul (cf. 1 Cor 12:29f.).[12] Leadership of the young Christian household groups in Corinth seems to have been quite fluid in the time of Paul's writings, and some aspects of it were notoriously problematic—not least the role of women. That women did exercise leadership roles in some Jewish communities is now established; whether that was true in Corinth, of course we have no way of knowing.[13]

Boundary-Setting Rituals

Interpreting the oracle of Balaam, "Behold a people shall reside (*katoikēsei*) alone, and shall not be reckoned among the nations" (Num 23:9), Philo explains that Israel is not physically separate from other nations, but set apart by its distinctive customs (*Mos.* 1.278). Every ethnic community in a Greek or Roman city, to the extent that it would maintain its identity, must have had some marks of distinctiveness, but the Judeans were undoubtedly more self-conscious about their ethnic boundaries, on the whole, than were most. Their tendency to keep apart is one of the characteristics often mentioned in pagan comments about the Jews.[14] The Deuteronomistic program of centralized worship and separation of Israel from "the nations round about," the disdain of "idolatry" by the exilic and postexilic prophets, the reforms of Ezra and Nehemiah, and the experience of generations in the Diaspora had combined to provide in both scripture and custom a tradition of separateness. The tradition was by no means univocal, however, and practice varied widely in the Diaspora communities. Philo complains about other Alexandrian Jews who, sharing his taste for allegorization, see no point in his insistence on observing the literal commandments (*Migr.* 89–92). The Jews who, two centuries later, had reserved seats in the theater of Miletus (along with the "God-worshipers")[15] were evidently "liberal" in their interpretation of proper Jewish customs, but nevertheless clearly identified as Jews. Other examples of the range of construals of the proper way to draw the boundaries could be multiplied.

There are obvious echoes of Jewish ways of drawing boundaries in Paul's Corinthian correspondence. To be sure, there is no sign of the circumcision controversy that was central in the disputes in Galatia, but people who insist on avoiding "meat offered to idols" are certainly following a Jewish precedent. Paul's rather complex reply to this question draws also on Jewish traditions about idolatry and includes a midrash on the central biblical text on this topic, the Golden Calf episode in Exod 32:6.[16] When Paul speaks of the man living with his father's wife as representing a kind of *porneia* found "not even among the Gentiles," he reveals that his own sense of the group's place in the world is shaped by the Jewish Diaspora experience, and he backs his directive with allusions to Jewish ritual traditions and, finally, with a direct quotation from Deuteronomy (1 Cor 5:1–13). The Jewish Diaspora experience is also clearly evident behind the following admonitions about pursuing lawsuits in pagan courts, although the warrants advanced in support of these admonitions are specifically Christian (6:1–11).

In another way as well—the matter of proselytes—the Jews differed from other immigrant associations, as far as our sources reveal, and this difference also became central to the self-definition of the early Christian groups. While an interested Gentile might apparently enjoy a wide spectrum of possible relationships with the Jewish community,[17] to become a full proselyte entailed a change of social location that was more radical. To understand the difference, consider religious initiation into the cult of an ethnic community's god. Lucius, in Apuleius's fictional account of initiation into Isis (*Met.* 11), did not become an Egyptian by that act. Indeed, despite the profound devotion to the goddess depicted in the remainder of the novel, Lucius did not by initiation become a member of a community of any sort. So, too, it was possible to attribute power to the God of Israel—"God Most High" or "Iao"—without "conversion" or exclusive attachment or becoming in any sense a "Jew." Think, for example, of the popularity of Iao among the divine names invoked in the magical papyri. There seem to have been in some places and some times (Aphrodisias and Panticapaeum most clearly) formal arrangements for recognizing "worshipers of God" who were attached in some way to a synagogue or formally recognized by a synagogue, but not or not yet "proselytes." But to go the whole way, to "turn from idols to serve the living God" (as Paul would describe it to the Thessalonian converts, using language that clearly came from Jewish practice, 1 Thess 1:9), was an act that entailed a profound resocialization, a change of identity and primary allegiance.[18]

In all his letters, Paul presupposes that the people he is writing to have experienced that radical transfer into a new community. Thus the process of incorporation that focused in and was symbolized by baptism resembled the reception of proselytes by the Jewish community rather than initiation into the mysteries. A disciple of Paul, recognizing this functional equivalent, fittingly describes baptism as "Christ's circumcision," "a circumcision not made with hands" (Col 2:11f.). Obviously baptism had great significance for the Corinthian Christians, and while Paul distances himself from an understanding of baptism that promotes factionalism (1 Cor 1:14–17), he strongly reaffirms the Spirit's creation by baptism of one community out of those formerly separate (12:13).

These facts are perhaps so familiar that we do not recognize how extraordinary they are. Judean emigrés, in order to preserve their identity, followed the pattern that other immigrant groups also developed in the Hellenistic and Roman periods, forming associations centered in the cult of their native god and observing certain of their ancestral customs that both preserved their link with their place of origin and set boundaries around their transplanted community. But the Judeans also reinterpreted the biblical injunctions about incorporating resident aliens (*gērim*) into Israel's cultic life to apply to their new situation now that they were resident aliens themselves. Thus the *prosēlutoi*—the term the LXX translators coined to translate *gērim*—became those individuals who for whatever reason were drawn from the cosmopolitan environment into the transplanted Judean community. But now the sect of those who are initiated into Messiah Jesus separates out of that Judean association of emigrés, becoming a distinct cult and one no longer with a single ethnic identity. The separation seems to have happened quickly in each of the places Paul worked; we know that the process was not uniform elsewhere.[19] At the writing of Paul's Corinthian letters, the dominant majority of the new cult are no longer Jewish, but Gentile—at least in Paul's perception (1 Cor 12:1–3). This multiethnic association nevertheless looks and acts in some ways like an ethnic, that is, an immigrant association—and specifically like the Judean association in the way that it receives "proselytes." In a way of speaking, they are all of them "proselytes," "whether Jews or Greeks." Baptism is a ritual of *disassimilation*, if the term be allowed, creating boundaries where none was before, signaling the joining of people from diverse origins into a single "body," a new clan of "brothers and sisters," an ethnic-like association of artificial aliens. And in the Corinthian correspondence, Paul speaks of the other major distinctive ritual of the Christ cult, the Lord's Supper, as having similar functions (1 Cor 10:16–21; 11:23–34).

The Pauline groups in Corinth thus mark themselves off from the surrounding society in ways that are quite "Jewish"—but these "Jewish" strategies come about only within a "Hellenistic" environment. Further, those strategies are used not only to create an artificially alien association, but one that is separate from Judaism in its social reality, however much Paul (at least the Paul who would later write Romans 9–11) might wish theologically that were not the case.

By suggesting that the new social form invented by Paul and his converts in Corinth (and elsewhere) owes much of its practical inspiration to the time-tested strategies of Judean immigrant groups, who in turn were adapting the techniques of other immigrants, I by no means discount the growing consensus that the shape and language of Paul's letters, and therefore presumably also the habits and expectations of his audience, owe far more than we had once recognized to the conventions of Greco-Roman rhetoric, the topics discussed in Greco-Roman philosophical schools, and the patterns of Greco-Roman paraenesis.[20] Take, for example, the fact so elegantly demonstrated by Margaret Mitchell that the whole of 1 Corinthians may be read in analogy with speeches supporting the civic virtue of *homonoia* and decrying factions that lead to *stasis*.[21] This represents a point of view entirely appropriate to a group that conceives of itself on the model of an immigrant association, a kind of city within the city or a transplanted *politeia,* that calls itself by the term *ekklēsia,* borrowed by the LXX translators from the political language of democratic Athens to describe Israel assembled at Sinai, "God's civic assembly." If we had writings from the Jewish community of Corinth, we might well find similar rhetoric, which only *seems* paradoxical: like the more famous and extreme case of Philo in Alexandria, perhaps they were most Jewish when they were most Hellenistic.[22]

Moral Formation

The false paradox is also exhibited in the moral exhortation and advice that fill Paul's letters. An ethnic group could use social artifacts of the common, dominant ("Hellenistic") culture to help maintain its own distinctiveness. The Judean immigrant community could use such strategies to accomplish ends shared by many immigrant groups in that culture and could adapt those strategies to their own special needs. Then the Christian movement could further adapt similar strategies to its own, even more special case. So, too, the movement could take this approach in its moral formation. The mores of an ethnic group are a primary dimension of its (sub)culture, and preserving a sense of continuity of ethos is central to maintaining ethnic identity in a multicultural environment. In all of the literature that has survived from Greek-writing Jewish authors of the Hellenistic and Roman periods, we see an energetic and varied process of adaptation, blending both form and substance of Israel's traditions and scriptures and communal experience with those of the Greek and Roman world. Through the voices of those writers, we hear speaking an Israel that has an intensely moral conception of its identity: to be Israel is to have a certain moral shape to the community, certain obligations imposed by Israel's God. In the public spaces of the Greco-Roman world's crowded cities, such a moral vision must inevitably both clash and merge with other visions, with manifold and constantly changing results. For an outsider to engage in that communal experience of Israel, to any degree from interested observer to "god-fearer" to proselyte, involved some measure of resocialization, the reconstruction of one's moral universe.

So, too, the formation of a conversionist sect at the periphery of the Jewish group, becoming a quasi-Jewish transethnic cult, entailed such resocialization. I have written about this process at some length elsewhere, so I will not repeat what I have said.[23] One point to be kept in mind is that such moral formation or resocialization is not ordinarily the job of "religion" in the ancient world. It is something that happens in every natural community, between the generations in every transplanted community (complicated by the interaction with other reference groups in a complex culture), and, by extension, in every artificially constructed community of "converts" like the Pauline Christians.

City and Empire

There is one more fundamental dimension of the immigrant's life in the Greco-Roman city that I will mention only in passing, for there is very little in Paul's Corinthian letters that is directly connected with it. That dimension is the intricate interplay between Rome's power and authority and legal institutions, on the one side, and local authorities, the power of various local groups, and local laws and traditions on the other. Many potential conflicts were hidden in this dynamic power field, but there was also room for maneuver, for playing one kind of patronage or one kind of legal authority against another. The most obvious example is the appeal to the Roman governor or, eventually, the Roman emperor, for redress of grievance against some local wielder of power. The instance we know best, thanks to Philo's first-hand (though hardly objective) account and the happy discovery of Claudius's decree in a papyrus letter, is the appeal of the Jewish community of Alexandria to Gaius and, on his death, to Claudius about the pogroms of 38 C.E. and the surrounding issue of Jewish rights in that city. But Josephus records a number of other instances of such appeals, including the successful appeal of Jews in Antioch for protection at the particularly dangerous time of the revolt in Judea and Galilee in 66 C.E.[24] It has long been recognized that Paul's advice in Rom 13:1–7 presupposes this kind of relationship on the part of the Jewish community with Rome and assumes that Christians, as an artificially alien community, can trade on the same balance of power. I see little in the Corinthian correspondence, however, to which this situation is relevant— the avoidance of pagan courts urged in 1 Cor 6:1–11 is another matter altogether.

Conclusion

My point can be stated quite simply. As we discuss the delightfully complex and fascinating question—which of Paul's rhetorical strategies, which of his modes of argument, which of his argumentative warrants, which of his evocative metaphors are Jewish and which are Hellenistic—it will help to keep our feet on the earth if we consider the practical lives of immigrant groups in a Roman colony. I have argued that the household groups organized by Paul under the patronage of Stephanas, Gaius, Prisca, Chloe, and others, all together gathering occasionally at Gaius's place as the "civic assembly of God in Corinth," was like an association of, as it were, artificial immigrants—made aliens by their conversion to the God of Israel and baptism into Messiah Jesus. While the form of their community was in many ways necessarily unique, it drew from its closest model, the Jewish immigrant associations of the Diaspora cities, probably including the one closest at hand, in Corinth itself. But the strategies of those Jewish associations were entirely "Hellenistic" not only in the sense that they used Greek language and cultural forms, but also because they became necessary only by virtue of transplantation out of their homeland (itself exhibiting more and more signs of "Hellenization") to rub elbows with immigrants from other places who were also trying to find the proper balance between identity and assimilation. If they remained Jewish, they would be Jewish in a Hellenistic way. So the groups founded by Paul would be "Christian"—a word Paul did not yet have—in a Christian-Jewish-Hellenistic way.

A final word of caution may be in order. In the 1930s and even more recently, conservative Protestant scholars sought to rebut the history-of-religions schools' case for "Hellenistic" influence on early Christianity and its consequent "syncretistic" nature by emphasizing Christianity's *Jewishness*. Recent scholarship, much of it summed up by essays in the present volume, has made not only that strategy untenable, but also the underlying assumption of both sides in that debate, that "Judaism" and "Hellenism" were fundamentally antithetical. It would be doubly ironic, then, if I were understood to be arguing that the Jewish organizations of resident aliens in the various cities of the eastern Empire provided some kind of *standard* model for the nascent Christian sect. On the contrary, if we look closely at the array of evidence we have about Jewish interaction with the larger culture in many places, we are struck again and again by the wide *range* of modes of adaptation and self-identification deployed by Jews at different places and in different times. Moreover, where the evidence is sufficient to give us a fuller look at a particular community, we are struck by the range of assimilation, adaptation, and acculturation from one individual or family to another, among people who still managed to think of themselves and, except for extreme cases, to be thought of by other members of the community, as Jews. So we should not be surprised to find jostling one another in Paul's communities and even within Paul himself some ways of thinking, talking, and acting that our scholarly constructs would have segregated into separate worlds.

Chapter 7

Matching Theory and Practice: Josephus's Constitutional Ideal and Paul's Strategy in Corinth

John M. G. Barclay

Comparing Josephus and Paul

It is no surprise that Paul's letters to the church in Corinth continue to attract the interest of historians and theologians. The issues that Paul addresses in these letters reveal so much in detail about the social realities of an early Christian community that they invite historical and sociological reconstructions of Corinthian church life from many different angles. But they also reveal much about Paul. Precisely because he faced so many and such disparate difficulties in Corinth, Paul was forced here to reinscribe the contours of the Christian community in both theoretical and practical terms. By their very nature, Paul's letters represent follow-up, rather than initiatory, activity; they show us how he built on foundations that he and others had already laid. Yet, in these letters to Corinth, Paul feels himself forced so often to return to basics that we are given here a rare glimpse of his strategic priorities in the forging and forming of a

Christian community. Here he is not so much nurturing the mature as feeding the newborn with their baby milk (1 Cor 3:1–4). Thus, although some of the issues addressed in these letters may be peculiar to the Corinthian church, the principles with which Paul responds are more general than the case to which he applies them. Hence these letters provide a rich insight into Paul's social and symbolic construction of a Christian community (in theological terms, his ecclesiology).

Paul's strategies for the establishment of his socially anomalous "assemblies" (ἐκκλησίαι) are not easy to analyze. Comparison with contemporary social phenomena, such as the vastly diverse "clubs" and "associations," can be illuminating to a degree, but it is difficult to identify the key structuring elements that should form the focus of comparison between a "church," on the one hand, and the numerous varieties of club, society, synagogue, or religious association on the other. They are always alike in some respects and unlike in others, but it is hard to establish which of these is socially most significant. It is perfectly proper to sharpen this historical analysis with the aid of perspectives developed in sociology and anthropology, as has sometimes been achieved to great effect. But these latter perspectives can be distorted by their refinement in cultural and social conditions (whether Western or pre-industrial) which are very remote from the world inhabited by the earliest Christians. Thus, the question arises: Are any useful analytical tools for social analysis available in the cultural matrix of the first Christians? In particular, can Paul's strategies in the formation of his churches be illuminated with the aid of culturally contiguous analyses of social formation?

One obvious candidate here is the Greco-Roman tradition of political philosophy focused on civic constitutions. This tradition came to its full flowering in Plato's *Republic* and *Laws*, and in Aristotle's *Politics*, though it continued to develop in derivative ways in later Greek and Roman political analysis.[1] At first sight this tradition appears less than pertinent, since these constitutional analyses cover topics such as political systems of government, suitable terrain for cities, appropriate terms for citizenship, and proper systems of education, all of which seem far removed in scale and function from Paul's house-churches. Although Paul can give these churches a quasi-political label (ἐκκλησίαι), and can utilize other political *topoi* in battling against their endemic disunity, the structures and goals of his communities are very different from the "city-states" discussed in the classical tradition, and if they have a πολίτευμα it is, he says, in heaven (Phil 3:20).[2]

Nonetheless, some forms of "constitutional" analysis are less remote than we might imagine. The term πολιτεία was elastic, ranging in meaning all the way from "form of government" to something as loose as "pattern of social life"; and the ancient Greek tradition of "political" analysis was correspondingly adaptable. Thus, if we could identify examples of such "constitutional" analysis that are broad enough to apply to societies less extensive and less complex than states, they might suggest fruitful questions for the analysis of Paul's community-formation.

The example that I wish to use in this essay is found in Josephus's apologetic work, *Against Apion*. Josephus is clearly conversant with the Greek political tradition, and at several points may be drawing more or less directly on Plato's *Laws*.[3] Earlier, in his *Antiquities*, he had presented his summary of the laws as Moses' "constitution" (4.196–301), and at several points referred to Israel's political system with reference to the debate about the best system of government (e.g., *Ant.* 4.223–224).[4] However, in *Against Apion* Book 2, the specifically political dimensions of this topic are reduced, and Josephus utilizes the tradition for a broader depiction of the structural characteristics of the Jewish "way of life." This partially depoliticized version of the "constitutional" tradition might, therefore, be of greater value for our purposes than its original application to city-states or nations.

Josephus's use of this tradition is slanted by his apologetic interest in demonstrating that Jews have the best and most balanced constitution of all. In one respect this makes his material all the more interesting for our comparison with Paul, since Jewish communities (at least those in the Diaspora, where Josephus writes) were in many respects the closest social analogue to the churches founded by Paul, and the histories of synagogue and church were in many places intertwined. In another respect, allowing Josephus to set our agenda may be problematic if it does not raise some of the questions relevant to Paul, or raises them in ways that place undue emphasis on distinctively Jewish features. Nonetheless, I believe the experiment is worth conducting as a heuristic exercise, which at least helps us see how others might analyze and assess Paul's church-forming strategies.

Such an experiment also raises some of the questions concerning Paul's cultural placement that permeate this volume. On one side of our comparison we have a Diaspora-resident Jew whose loyalty to his Jewish tradition is expressed precisely in his creative use of an ancient Greek tradition (a use that is also perhaps slanted specifically for Roman readers); such a cultural mix clearly defies neat categorizations such as "Hellenism" and "Judaism." On the other, we have another Diaspora-resident Jew whose social policy, I shall argue, differs from Josephus's at that point where he strives to enable a community of both Jew and Gentile, and attempts to forge them together into a new and culturally indeterminate (or, at least, under-determined) "church."

Josephus and the Jewish Constitution

Josephus's *Against Apion* is the last of his extant works, written at the very end of the first century C.E. This work is designed to make up for the less-than-enthusiastic reception of his *Antiquities* and to refute, in a systematic manner, some of the most influential critics of Jews and their culture. After the lengthiest of these refutations, directed against Apion (2.1–144), Josephus turns to face "Apollonius Molon, Lysimachus and certain others" (2.145), but changes tactic from a point-by-point defense to a positive portrayal of Moses and the "constitution" he founded. Apollonius appears to have engaged in derogatory comparisons between Jewish customs and the laws or constitutions of other nations (*Ag. Ap.* 2.150, 238, 270), so Josephus takes the opportunity to engage in a comparative exercise of his own. In this context he can afford to abstract this analysis from the historical vicissitudes of Jewish history, and he here provides a generalized and idealized portrait whose focus is less on political governance, and not only on the content of the Jewish laws, but also on the structure or framework in which the constitution operates.[5]

When Josephus outlines the accusations leveled at Moses and the laws, he announces his plan to defend the latter by describing in brief both "the whole structure of our constitution" (ἡ ὅλη ἡμῶν κατάστασις τοῦ πολιτεύματος) and its individual parts (2.145).[6] Thus, after a short presentation of Moses' virtues (2.151–163) and before his summary of the particular laws (2.190–218), Josephus outlines the "structure" of the Mosaic constitution in terms that are of particular importance to our inquiry (2.164–189).[7]

The most famous feature of this outline is Josephus's coinage of the term θεοκρατία (2.165), which is clearly intended to trump all other constitutions, pure or mixed. The term is often taken to signify the rule of the priests ("hierocracy"), and Josephus does finish this section with reference to their putative political control (2.185–188). Its primary meaning, however, is something far more abstract and philosophical. Ascribing the sovereignty and power (τὴν ἀρχὴν καὶ τὸ κράτος) to God (Josephus's *definition* of "theocracy," 2.165) means recognizing God's universal (and particular) providence (2.166), and acknowledging his omniscience (2.166), oneness, and transcendence (2.167). Hence, Josephus claims, the chief and central virtue in Judaism is piety (εὐσέβεια, 2.170–171). This viewpoint already indicates that Josephus's primary interest here is not political theory in the narrow sense (the distribution of power within the Jewish "state"), but the shape of Jewish life as governed by its monotheistic beliefs and God-given laws.[8]

Josephus was conversant enough with Greek philosophy to recognize that Judaism was hardly unique in affirming the providence and transcendence of God. He accepts that Pythagoras, Anaxagoras, Plato, and the Stoics held similar views on the nature of God, though he hints (following an old Jewish contention) that they borrowed such truths from Moses (2.168). However, he immediately identifies the locus of Jewish superiority in this matter: where others kept their philosophical discoveries to the elite, Moses embedded such truths in the lives of the masses. The statement Josephus makes at this point skillfully combines the themes he will develop in the rest of this section of his discourse, and is worth quoting in full:[9]

> (169) But our legislator, by making practice conform to the laws,[10] not only convinced his contemporaries but also implanted this belief about God in their descendants of all future generations, such that it could not be shaken (ἀμετακίνητον). (170) The reason is that the very shape of the legislation makes it long-lasting and continually accessible to everyone. For he did not make piety (εὐσέβεια) an element of virtue, but viewed and established the other virtues together as elements of piety—that is, justice, moderation, endurance, and harmony (συμφωνία) among citizens in all affairs. (171) All activities and occupations, and all speech, have reference to our piety towards God: he did not leave any of these unscrutinized (ἀνεξέταστον) or imprecise (ἀόριστον).

Several points are made here at once: that Moses ensured a match between the theory enshrined in the law and the practice of that law, that his legislation was transmitted to future generations, and that it remained permanently unalterable. The last two are dependent on the first, in that the embedding of belief or rule in action is what ensures its transferability and permanency. Josephus himself unpacks these intertwined claims in the paragraphs that follow (2.170–183), whose logical interconnection may be set out as follows:

The Principle:	Matching Theory and Practice
The Mechanisms:	1. Thorough Education in the Laws
	2. Comprehensive Application of the Laws
	3. Unquestioning Adherence to the Laws
The Result:	Harmony in Belief and Practice

Josephus is clearly describing an ideal, which we know, even from his own writings, was hardly realized in practice; the Josephus who here claims total harmony in belief and practice elsewhere describes fundamental differences in both spheres between the four Jewish "philosophies" (e.g., *Ant.* 18.11–25)! Nonetheless, it is worth examining in more detail how he thinks this ideal is enshrined in the Jewish "constitution," so that we can compare it with the structural ideals to be found in Paul's letters to Corinth. Our aim is certainly *not* to contrast Josephus's ideal with Paul's problems in the church in Corinth, but to juxtapose the aims and characteristics of Josephus's Jewish constitutional ideals with the comparable ideals expressed or implied in Paul's letters. If the constitutional shape of Paul's churches is different in theory and/or practice, it is important to perceive how and why this is so.

1. Josephus immediately explains the foundational principle of *matching theory and practice* in 2.171–174. There he distinguishes two possible modes of παιδεία (education) or κατασκευὴ περὶ τὰ ἤθη (moral formation): one utilizes λόγος (verbal instruction) and the other ἄσκησις τῶν ἠθῶν (practical moral training, 2.171).[11] Following a well-established topos in Greek literature, he illustrates this distinction by contrasting Spartans and Cretans on the one hand, with Athenians and "almost all the rest of the Greeks" on the other. Spartans and Cretans employ ἔθη (customs), not λόγοι (words) in their education, while Athenians and the rest give instructions about what one must or must not do through laws (νόμοι) but neglect accustoming people to these requirements through deeds (τοῦ δὲ πρὸς αὐτὰ διὰ τῶν ἔργων ἐθίζειν ὠλιγώρουν, 172).

"Word" and "deed" are a standard pairing in Greek, as in many other traditions (elsewhere in *Ag. Ap.* at 2.233, 241, 292). The contrast "in word but not in deed" was a common way of expressing unreality (e.g., 2.241), while the harmony of word and deed was a recognized sign of a fully rounded character.[12] Josephus here combines two aspects of a hackneyed contrast between Spartans and Athenians. In the first place, the Spartans were famous for their pithy but unsophisticated style of speech; their image was as people of deeds (especially military deeds) but few words.[13] On the other hand, the unique system of Athenian democracy fostered an image of Athens as the scene of continual debate and intense competition in rhetorical prowess. The contrast could be variously evaluated: were the Spartans simply uneducated, or were they admirably short on words and long on disciplined obedience?[14] Second, Josephus builds on the contrast between the Spartan lack of written laws and the Athenian fetish for the recording and publication of theirs. Plutarch sums up a long line of commentators in insisting that Lycurgus (the Spartan legislator) did not put his laws in writing, since "he reckoned that the guiding principles of most importance for the happiness and excellence of a state would remain securely fixed if they were embedded in the citizens' character and training" (ἀγωγή, *Lycurgus* 13).

Josephus's exploitation of these clichés is rhetorically effective, since he can combine the near universal admiration of the Spartan constitution with the widespread assumption that laws are more secure if fixed in writing (cf. 2.155). On the one side he lines up λόγος (word, speech, articulation) and νόμος (law); on the other, ἔργα (actions), ἄσκησις (practice/training), and ἔθη (customs). Jews, he claims, are guilty of neither form of one-sidedness since Moses took great care to combine both features (2.173): he did not leave ἄσκησις "dumb" (κωφή, that is, without verbal support), nor did he leave the verbal articulation of the law (ὁ τοῦ νόμου λόγος) "ineffectual" (ἄπρακτος, that is, without practical instantiation). Thus the Jews' constitution avoids the pitfalls of other constitutions while combining their strong points.[15]

Josephus's rhetoric artfully exploits the breadth and ambiguity of his terms, but his main point is clear enough: the theory that Jews embrace (about God, themselves, or their moral norms) is not merely talked or written about, but enmeshed in the practices and customs of Jewish life. This principle of matching theory with practice is, for Josephus, the foundation of all that follows: It is because the Jews have an articulated system of "theory" (the laws/scriptures) that it can be thoroughly learned; it is because they are concerned to apply it that it is practiced with comprehensive range; it is because it is fixed both in writing and in custom that it remains unalterable; and it is because of their commonly agreed doctrine and commonly practiced norms that Jews enjoy such harmony. Indeed, Josephus ties theory with practice even more securely by showing that the content of the "theory" (the belief that God watches over everything) provides, in Jewish piety, the strongest sanction and the ultimate goal for every detail of Jewish practice. As he puts it at 2.181 (cf. 2.171, cited above):

> Nor will anyone see any difference in our living habits: we all share common practices and all make the same affirmation about God, in agreement with the law, that he watches over everything. As for the habits by which we live, that everything is geared towards piety one could gather even from the women and slaves.

2. If theory and practice are to match, the practitioners must clearly know the theory, and Josephus thus devotes a paragraph to the topic of Moses' laws as the focus of a *thorough education* (2.175–178). As we saw,

Josephus's programmatic statement presented Moses' achievement as "implanting" the law in the lives of his people (ἐνέφυσεν, 2.169), and Josephus can go on to claim that Jews need no legal experts since everyone knows the laws "more readily than his own name": they are so thoroughly learnt, from the very first moment of consciousness as to be "engraved on our souls" (ἐν ταῖς ψυχαῖς ὥσπερ ἐγκεχαραγμένους, 2.178). The reference in this sentence to the first moment of consciousness (ἀπὸ τῆς πρώτης αἰσθήσεως) indicates that Josephus is thinking in the first place of those crucial stages of primary socialization that take place in childhood. Later, in his summary of the law, he boasts of the Jews' concern for the reading ability of children, with its twin focus on "the laws and the exploits of our forebears": the latter are to be imitated, while the former are the basis of an education that guarantees against transgression or ignorance (2.204; cf. 1.60).

All constitutional theorists were concerned, of course, with the education of citizens, especially those who were to take leading political roles.[16] Here the virtues necessary for the good functioning of the state were to be learned. Josephus's reference to the education of children in the exploits of the "forebears" (οἱ πρόγονοι) reflects the importance of ethnic continuity, by which the "ancestral customs" (τὰ πάτρια, 2.182, 237) are passed down from generation to generation, especially within the household (2.169).[17] But if in this respect the Jews had much in common with non-Jews (Josephus refers to the Athenians' πάτριος πολιτεία at 2.264), Josephus wishes to claim superiority in another. At 2.175 he boasts in the Jewish use of the law as teaching-material (παίδευμα) which is heard, not just on an occasional basis, but every week, since the Sabbath affords freedom from work for the purpose of gathering to hear and accurately learn the law (ἀκριβῶς ἐκμανθάνειν, 2.175; the verb is repeated in 2.178).[18] Like Philo (e.g., *Legat.* 156–157, 312–313; *Spec.* 2.63–64), Josephus celebrates the Sabbath gathering as an educational institution, signaling the Jews' unique concern to internalize the laws of their constitution.[19]

Josephus's claim that this system of education means that "it is rare to find a transgressor and impossible to excuse oneself from punishment" (2.178) is an obvious idealization. But our concern is to delineate his ideal, and the important point is that Josephus's ideal constitution contains educational instruments as routine events embedded in the rhythm of Jewish life.

3. The matching of theory with practice requires that, for Josephus, the internalization of the laws involves not just the acquisition of knowledge about them, but also their *comprehensive application* in daily life. We have seen him make a claim to this effect in general terms: that "all activities

and occupations, and all speech" have reference to piety (2.171, cited above; cf. 2.156). However, he also spells this out in revealing particularity in 2.173–174 where he illustrates the practical effect of the law from the earliest stages of infancy:

> Starting from the very beginning of our upbringing and from the mode of life practiced by each individual in the home (ἀπὸ τῆς κατὰ τὸν οἶκον ἑκάστων διαίτης), he [Moses] did not leave anything, even the minutest detail, free to be determined by the wishes of those concerned. Even in relation to food, what we should refrain from and what we should eat, the company we keep in our daily lives, and our application to work and, conversely, rest, he himself set the law as the boundary and rule, so that we might live under it as if it were our father and master and commit no sin either willfully or from ignorance.

The three items given special mention here are perhaps of particular importance: dietary rules, limits in social intercourse, and the regular Sabbath rest.[20] These all concern aspects of domestic routine that, as regular and intimate features of everyday life, have a marked and pervasive influence on life patterns. What is more, the effort required to maintain these (cf. 2.234–235), especially as a minority cultural tradition, would do much to enforce the social distinctiveness of the community that practices such rules. Their special function as "boundary marks" is thus clear. Outsiders confirm, in their comments on Jewish food, marriage, and Sabbath laws, that these distinctive Jewish practices made a considerable social impact.[21] Their significance is also recognized by Josephus when he affirms (against detractors) the readiness of Jews to show kindness to outsiders and to "welcome those who wish to come and live under the same laws as us," but adds the significant proviso that "he [Moses] does not want those who approach us on a casual basis to mix with us at an intimate level" (2.209–210).

It is its imprint on the regular intimacies of daily life which makes the law's comprehensive application of such importance. It is not just the detailed definition of the law which matters here, but its hold on features of life which determine the everyday lifestyle of a Jew. Josephus is thus right to say that, according to his ideal, the Jewish constitution contained the means by which it could be made broadly effectual.

4. An important supplement to the above is the significance that Josephus attaches to *unquestioning adherence to the law*. This theme was adumbrated in Josephus's programmatic statement that the law is ἀμετακίνητον (2.169; cf. 2.234, 254). The term seems to imply both that

the laws cannot be altered over time and that it is not an option for individuals to interpret or circumvent them at will. The first sense is taken up in the continual refrain of *Against Apion*, that the Jews are ever faithful to their laws, willing even to die rather than transgress them; they see no benefit in updating their constitution or abandoning their laws (e.g. 2.232–235, 271–275, 277; cf. Philo, *Mos.* 2.12–16). Indeed, Josephus uses this virtue to counter the otherwise damaging charge that Jews have been signally lacking in cultural creativity (the charge is mentioned in 2.148 and countered in 2.182–183). The second sense implies that the law cannot be subverted by individual choice or "freedom of opinion." We have seen this point spelled out in 2.173, where Josephus insists that Moses "did not leave anything, even the minutest detail, free to be determined by the wishes of those concerned" (οὐδὲν οὐδὲ τῶν βραχυτάτων αὐτεξούσιον ἐπὶ ταῖς βουλήσεσι τῶν χρησομένων κατέλιπεν, cf. 2.234).

The key term here, αὐτεξούσιον, is highly charged. Josephus uses it elsewhere for the failure of military discipline (*J. W.* 3.86; 5.556) and for the dangerous freedom of autocratic power (*Ant.* 15.266), but its most potent use is in his expanded analysis of the revolt of Zimri (Zambrias) concerning intermarriage with Midianite women (*Ant.* 4.131–155, based on Numbers 25). The space that Josephus gives to the seductions of the Midianite women, and the speech he accords to Zambrias justifying his revolt against Moses' laws, indicate the paradigmatic significance of this episode for Josephus, and we may surely detect here echoes of debates in Josephus's contemporary Judaism.[22] Zambrias accuses Moses of accumulating tyrannical power and taking away from his people "the sweetness and independence of lifestyle, which is enjoyed by free men who have no master" (τὸ ἡδὺ καὶ τὸ κατὰ τὸν βίον αὐτεξούσιον, ὃ τῶν ἐλευθέρων ἐστὶ καὶ δεσπότην οὐκ ἐχόντων, *Ant.* 4.146). Josephus sees this independence ("self-determination") as the polar opposite to submission to the law, and it is not surprising that in extolling the strict discipline of the Jews, Josephus should hail the law as κανών, πατήρ and δεσπότης (*Ag. Ap.* 2.174). His ideal Judaism does not accord value to individual freedom in interpretation or adaptation of the law: it binds the community together precisely by binding them all to a single authority.

5. Thus we reach Josephus's constitutional goal: *harmony in belief and practice*. The importance of this theme is indicated not only by the fact that Josephus here devotes a paragraph to its explication (2.179–181), but also by his subtle alteration of the list of virtues in 2.170, so that the last is not φρόνησις or its equivalent (as we might expect from the Greek tra-

dition) but συμφωνία (harmony). The "unanimity" that Josephus here describes (ὁμόνοια, 2.179, 283, 294) matches the traditional concern among constitutional theorists that the state not descend into discord or factionalism (στάσις), but is internalized to an extraordinary degree by his insistence that it is operative in belief as well as in practice. Tying together his twin themes of "theory" and "practice," Josephus locates the unity of Jews both in their shared affirmations about God (εἷς λόγος περὶ θεοῦ—e.g., his existence and providence) and in their common practices (κοινὰ ἔργα). Although remaining at a high level of generalization, the breadth of this claim is striking.

It is not difficult to trace how, on Josephus's account, such constitutional harmony comes to be. Because theory and practice match, both spheres are equally affected and mutually reinforcing. Because all Jews are educated in the law, all have the same outlook. Because the law covers every department of life, the unanimity in practice is comprehensive. And because no freedom of will is allowed, all bear allegiance to a common authority. This vision is, of course, Josephus's utopian scenario. He gives no recognition here to the Jews who strayed from the law to varying degrees, or, more significantly, to the necessary role of interpretation with regard to the common authoritative tradition, which helped make Judaism in antiquity so diverse. But Josephus's ideal is our present concern, and one may grant him at least that his portrait of the Jewish constitution is carefully and consistently worked out, and that he puts his finger on certain structural elements in the Jewish way of life which at least bear the potential to function in the ways he describes.

Paul and the Constitution of the Church in Corinth

In turning to Paul, we may recall that our purpose is not to contrast the difficulties Paul encountered in his church in Corinth with the ideal constitution delineated by Josephus: that would be manifestly unfair to Paul, or to his converts. Rather, our task is to place Paul's ideals alongside those of Josephus, to compare their aims and structural characteristics. For instance, Paul clearly places as high a value on unity, even unanimity, as Josephus: Paul's aim is that his converts be "of one mind and one opinion" (1 Cor 1:10). As Margaret Mitchell has shown, this concern for concord within the church permeates not only 1 Corinthians 1–4, but also the rest of that letter, and is treated by Paul in terms closely resembling the discussion of this topic in politics.[23] Thus it is reasonable to ask: do

Josephus and Paul agree about the means towards this shared goal, or are their constitutional ideals differently structured?

Since Paul is not writing a treatise on this subject, we will have to discern his intentions in rather more subtle ways than was necessary in the case of Josephus. For our purposes it is fortunate that, as noted above, the Corinthian church forced him to redescribe the basics of his ecclesiology and to define his ideals of church life on a wide range of topics. Thus we have many explicit comments from which to work and can view his social edifice from enough angles to gain an adequate view of its shape. On occasion we may wish to supplement the material from the Corinthian correspondence with insights from other Pauline letters, but we will take as our starting point in each case the blueprints, goals, and programmatic statements that Paul offers to the Corinthian believers.

Where we find Paul differing from Josephus it is important to inquire whence this difference arises. Does Paul's constitution match that of Josephus in general shape, differing only in its departure from particular Jewish practices, like Sabbath readings of the law or dietary restrictions? Or do these surface differences represent deeper structural discrepancies? Comparing Paul with Diaspora Judaism in general, Michael Wolter has recently put forward an interesting argument for a fundamental difference in the way Paul matches (or fails to match) the "ethos" of his communities with their "identity."[24] Whereas in Diaspora Judaism, the exclusive identity of Jewish communities is matched and instantiated in a range of practices (the ethos-defining "works of the law"), whose function is to represent their distinctive Jewish identity, Wolter finds no such straightforward symmetry between ethos and identity in the case of Paul's prescriptions for his churches. Although Paul describes his converts as an exclusive social entity (with many terms borrowed from Judaism to emphasize their difference from "Gentiles"), he does not develop an exclusive range of practices to match; although the ban on idolatry and sexual immorality is retained from Judaism, other boundary-defining Jewish practices are not expected of his Gentile converts. Moreover, Paul's moral prescriptions that correlate ethos with identity either are so general as to lack specific content or inculcate moral norms whose function is not exclusive but *inclusive*: they match general moral norms in the wider society, such as love, joy, and peace, and provide no alternative habitualized lifestyle. Thus Wolter concludes that "the correlation of ethos and identity in Paul and in his communities is in many areas asymmetrical and deficient" ("die Korrelation von Ethos und Identität bei Paulus und in seinen Gemeinden auf mehreren Ebenen asymmetrisch und defizitär ist," 438).

Wolter finds an explanation for this "asymmetry" in the fact that Paul's communities united Jewish-Christians and Gentile-Christians whose unity could not be expressed in common practices, on which they continued to differ. What unites them rather is their faith in Christ, and here Wolter locates the role of Paul's doctrine of "justification by faith" as a legitimating symbol-system. Since faith is the central qualifying and distinguishing attribute of those "in Christ," Wolter argues that Paul detaches the discriminating function of ethos from the level of practice and transfers it to faith.[25] Because the Christians' exclusive ethos takes expression only in faith, the way they lead their lives can be freed from the burden of distinguishing themselves from outsiders through habitual practices; only the (inherited) concern to withdraw from "idolatry" and "sexual immorality" forms an exception to this general pattern.[26]

I find Wolter's analysis stimulating, and many of my own comments on Paul will run parallel to his. However, some important questions arise. Why do the bans on idolatry and sexual immorality stand out as exceptions in this pattern? Would Paul have recognized them as such? Since, as we shall see, Paul's arguments against immorality and idolatry are given a distinctively Christian foundation, can they be integrated into the structure of Paul's thought? And would Paul have drawn such a sharp distinction between faith on the one hand and habitualized practice on the other? That is, if Paul relativizes the significance of many Jewish practices (ἔργα νόμου), does he also downgrade the importance of ἔργα in general, or does Christian faith have its own concomitant practices? If these are less socially discriminating than some Jewish practices, does that make them less significant *for Christians themselves* as distinctive expressions of their faith?

We will return to these and related issues as we proceed with our analysis of Paul.

1. We may start with *the matching of theory and practice*: in what ways was the articulation of Christian identity (in preaching, exhortation, regulation, and confession) made consonant with social practice?

Josephus, we may recall, castigated "constitutions" that left activity "dumb" (unexplained or uninscribed in law) or which, alternatively, left speech unenshrined in practice (*Ag. Ap.* 2.173). As to the first potential fault, one of the most striking features of 1 Corinthians is Paul's extensive effort to offer explanations for the practices of the community. Although he can lampoon rhetoric (1 Cor 1:18–2:5; cf. *Ag. Ap.* 2.292) and claims to prefer power (δύναμις) to speech (λόγος, 1 Cor 4:19–20), he actually invests much in the articulation of the gospel, whether that be represented in his own preaching (λόγος and κήρυγμα, 1 Cor 2:4; 2 Cor 2:17, etc.), in the creedal formulae he cites (e.g., 1 Cor 8:6; 11:23; 15:3–5), or in the scriptures he quotes (e.g., 1 Cor 1:30; 10:1–12; 15:54–55). Paul's "constitution" thus has plenty of foundational documents and oral traditions on which to draw, and his letters themselves continue the provision of such resources. At several points in 1 Corinthians Paul is concerned to provide the rationale for practices that he does not (or cannot) leave to be learned simply by habit. Thus in 1 Cor 11:2–16 he provides elaborate justification for his insistence that women should pray or prophesy only with their heads covered, a practice which it seems he has hitherto taken for granted (as a cultural token of female modesty), but now has to buttress with multiple theological and cultural supports. Similarly in 1 Cor 6:12–20 his previously assumed prohibition of sex with prostitutes is given an explicit theological rationale, the ban made articulate in a form that links it to foundational Christian beliefs.

Here, then, one may say that Paul goes to some lengths to provide the λόγοι which Josephus considered necessary: the rules of the community are not just ingrained by habit but spelled out and explained. Of course, the novelty of the Christian community made particular demands in this regard, since for Gentile converts little if any reliance could be placed on inherited traditions. As Paul repeatedly found, Gentile converts could not be expected to assume his Jewish moral sensibilities, while the special revolutionary features of the movement could lead some converts to call into question even quite generally held cultural assumptions. Early urban Christianity needed considerable articulation in order to support, explain, and rationalize its "customs," and the Corinthian correspondence shows us how complex and controverted that discourse might be. It is not surprising, perhaps, that gifts of well-founded speech are so highly regarded by Paul (1 Cor 1:5; 12:8) and his instructions in 1 Corinthians 14 show him regulating but nonetheless encouraging an extraordinarily loquacious community. Of course, the bandying of words could have its own dangers (the sort of λογομαχία for which Athens was notorious, cf. 1 Tim 6:4; 2 Tim 2:14), but at least Josephus could not have complained that Paul's polity was "dumb."

What about the other side of Josephus's equation, the concern not to let the λόγος of the constitution remain ineffective (ἄπρακτος)? How successfully did Paul embed his verbal (oral or written) definitions of Christian identity in practical activity? Again, the Corinthian correspondence shows Paul's special concern to link gospel to conduct. The message of the cross should make a direct impact on the evaluation of rhetorical prowess and human boasting (1 Corinthians 1–4). The resurrection of Christ, and thus the resurrection of the body, have immediate and far-reaching implications for the use of the body in the present (1 Cor 6:12–20). The gospel of grace should inspire and channel the generosity that springs from faith (2 Cor 8:1–9). These and many other examples of the appeal to "come to your right minds and sin no more" (1 Cor 15:34) indicate Paul's concern to channel the application of Christian symbols in particular directions, matching the desired practical outcome with the theoretical resources of the Christian community.

The fact that Paul has to work so hard at this task in the Corinthian correspondence might, however, give us pause. In these letters we find Paul combating not a wholly different set of symbols but *an alternative interpretation of the same.* There is no reason to think that the Corinthian Christians doubted or denied the common creedal confessions to which Paul draws attention in 1 Cor 8:4–6 and 15:3–5. But they clearly saw different practical consequences arising from these beliefs. Why not hold, on the basis of the resurrection of Jesus, that death is defeated, the richness of life begun, and the fullness of Spirit acquired (1 Cor 4:8, etc.)? Why not celebrate the Lordship of Christ by bold forays into the territory of shadowy "no-gods"? Thus although Paul continually draws connections between Christian master symbols and definite patterns of life, we may wonder whether the links were always logically or theologically persuasive. If not, does this merely represent a failure on the part of the Corinthians to carry through the constitutional ideal, or does it signal that the structural correlation between Christian convictions and actions was not as clearly defined as Josephus's ideal might require?

This question concerning the match of word and deed may be pressed at certain points. In 1 Cor 7:19 Paul claims that the Christian duty is "keeping the commandments of God" (τήρησις ἐντολῶν θεοῦ), but makes that assertion in a context where he relativizes circumcision as a cultural token, though it was naturally regarded in the Jewish tradition as one of God's commandments. A Jewish reader of 1 Corinthians might also sense that in 10:23–26 Paul suggests an alarmingly casual attitude to the Jewish food laws, a suspicion that would be supported by close attention to 1 Cor 9:21 and 2 Cor 3:6–18 (cf. Rom 14:14). It might thus seem legitimate to complain that Paul's traditional Jewish language such as "keeping the commandments of God" is belied by his practical neglect of key features of the law. According to its normal meaning, honed by Jewish tradition, Paul's claim (λόγος) at this point does not seem well matched by practice (ἔργα). On a more general level, Paul claims for his converts an identity very different from their former Gentile selves. They are no longer, in a certain sense, ἔθνη (1 Cor 12:2); they have been washed, sanctified, and justified (6:11), they are righteousness in contrast to sin, light in contrast to darkness (2 Cor 6:14). Yet Jewish observers, conscious of what distinguished *them* from "sin," "darkness," and the "Gentiles," would naturally voice the complaint raised by Trypho:

> This is what we are most at a loss about: that you, professing to be pious (εὐσεβεῖν λέγοντες), and thinking yourselves better than others, are not in any way distanced from them, and do not alter your way of life from the Gentiles (κατ᾽ οὐδὲν αὐτῶν ἀπολείπεσθε, οὐδὲ διαλλάσσετε ἀπὸ τῶν ἐθνῶν τὸν ὑμέτερον βίον), in that you observe neither festivals nor Sabbaths, and do not practice circumcision; and further, resting your hopes on a crucified man, you still expect to obtain some good from God, although you do not keep his commandments (μὴ ποιοῦντες αὐτοῦ τὰς ἐντολάς). (Justin, *Dialogue with Trypho*, 10)

How would Paul respond to this charge? In relation to the particulars mentioned here by Trypho, he would have to concede that he did not regard circumcision as a rite to be enjoined on all the people of God, although he would insist that even the uncircumcised could still be considered "pious" (cf. Rom 2:25–29). Although he marks time by Jewish festivals (1 Cor 16:8), and expects his converts to know when it is the first day after Sabbath (1 Cor 16:2), he has given the Passover a new meaning by its association with Christ (1 Cor 5:7) and can hardly expect his Gentile converts, who seem unattached to synagogue assemblies, to celebrate Jewish festivals and Sabbaths in the proper Jewish manner.[27] Thus Paul would define "piety" and "obeying God's commandments" in terms confusing to a Jew, just as elsewhere he decouples the Jewish notion of "righteousness" from its standard association with Jewish dietary laws (Rom 14:17).

Could Paul's strategy here be construed simply as a redefinition of terms? Does he differ from Josephus only in the content he gives to abstract terms like "piety" or "righteousness," or does the difference here suggest a more significant discrepancy? We must stress that Paul has *not* reduced Christian difference to faith alone, since it is important for him that faith is made effective in practical activity of many kinds ("work" as in 1 Cor 3:10–15; 2 Cor 5:10; 9:8, etc.). On the other hand, Paul's polity tends towards less cultural specificity in the "practice" that he links with his "theory," since his own mission, and the churches which he founds, cross the cultural boundaries between Jews and Gentiles. His programmatic statement on this matter in 1 Cor 19:20–21 is revealing: he can afford to live sometimes ὡς ὑπὸ νόμον and sometimes ὡς ἄνομος, since his true position is neither ὑπὸ νόμον nor ἄνομος θεοῦ but what he describes as ἔννομος Χριστοῦ. What this latter entails is left ill-defined, but it clearly cannot contain the cultural commitment of submission to the Jewish law, nor the absence of moral obligation which Paul associates with Gentile "lawlessness." This culturally adaptable morality is evoked as the paradigm for Paul's converts in 1 Cor 10:31–11:1, where their dietary practices are left deliberately undetermined, so long as they represent giving glory to God (cf. Rom 14:5–12). As in 9:19–23, Paul here refers to the varying cultural contexts in which his converts live (10:32), thus signaling (as Wolter rightly suggests) that the cross-cultural mission and multicultural identity of Paul's churches places a *structurally necessary* limit on the specificity with which Christian obligation can be detailed. We will return to this point below, but may note here that while Paul is indeed concerned to match theory and practice, in line with Josephus's constitutional ideal, the ways in which he does this may be necessarily different from those enshrined in the Jewish "constitution" that Josephus describes.

2. If we turn now to the mechanisms by which the constitution operates, we may inquire first into the *educational* means by which the Pauline norms are to be learned. The first thing which might strike us by comparison with Josephus is that Paul too refers to an "engraving on the heart." Josephus, we may recall, considered the laws to be engraved on the soul from the child's first moments of consciousness (see above, p. 146). Paul, on the other hand, uses this metaphor with reference to the work of the Spirit, by whose means the Corinthians constitute a letter ἐγγε–γραμμένη ἐν ταῖς καρδίαις (2 Cor 3:2–3). What is more, he consciously *contrasts* this Spirit-operation with the inscribing of the law by pen on paper, or chisel on stone, evoking the biblical narratives of the giving of the law only in order to emphasize the *superior* glory of the "new" covenant.[28] If this contrast is more than merely rhetorical, it suggests that Paul's strategy of moral formation depends greatly on the work of the Spirit, whose effect is not only to inspire and energize but also to bring about a "transformation" of the believer (2 Cor 3:18). Paul makes comparable statements elsewhere in the Corinthian correspondence, claiming, for instance, access to "the mind of Christ" and "the deep things of God" through the Spirit (1 Cor 2:6–16). The expectation of instruction through Spirit-inspired prophecy (1 Corinthians 14) points in the same direction: that Paul's prime educational aid is the guidance and instruction of the Spirit, effective both in individual and in communal formation.

In order to assess how large a difference this constitutes from Josephus's educational strategy, we may examine if Paul has any equivalent to the two phenomena that Josephus identified as the prime agents in the internalization of Jewish norms: the raising of children and the Sabbath readings of the law. Since he was founding new communities made up largely of Gentile converts Paul could not rely, of course, on their "ancestral traditions" or childhood training. In fact, he places a symbolic gulf between their past and present (1 Cor 6:9–11; 2 Cor 6:14–7:1), since he has endeavored to wean them from what 1 Peter would call "the futile life-pattern inherited from your ancestors" (ἐκ τῆς ματαίας ὑμῶν ἀναστροφῆς πατροπαραδότου, 1:18). In its place he grafts them into an alternative family tree (1 Cor 10:1) and, like Josephus, appeals to the exploits (or failings) of their adopted "forebears" (10:1–16). But this adopted ancestry cannot reproduce the emotional and practical impact of a real one: the Corinthians' "Israelite" identity is not genuinely inherited and was not a factor in their primary socialization. Thus the Corinthians, like all converts, lacked that childhood security of inherited norms.

Nonetheless, Paul might expect them to transmit their traditions and norms to the next generation. What is striking, however, is how little interest Paul shows in this matter. His instructions on marriage in 1 Corinthians 7 are famous for their higher evaluation of celibacy, and even if he regards marriage as "no sin" and sex within marriage as proper and necessary, he shows remarkably little interest in the offspring of such marriages. Children are mentioned explicitly only in 1 Cor 7:14, and then as a subsidiary argument for something else. The theological context of this chapter reveals an important cause of this omission: the imminent collapse of "the form of this world" (1 Cor 7:25–29). It appears that the short-termism generated by early Christian eschatology militated against embedding Christian socialization into the structure of family life: it is not until Ephesians that we find our first reference to children in relation to the παιδεία κυρίου (Eph 6:4).[29]

Josephus's other medium of instruction was the weekly reading of the law. Was there anything equivalent, or similarly effective, in Paul's constitutional provision? In relation to the law itself, Paul's frequent citations and allusions might presuppose that he expects his converts to be regularly exposed to its contents. Nothing is said on this topic, however, even in 1 Corinthians 14, where prophecy, teaching, revelation, and tongues are mentioned, but no reading of scripture; even in 2 Corinthians 3, the "reading of Moses" is associated only with "them" (Jews), and the Spirit's unveiling is said to enable not a clearer or better reading of Moses but a perception and reflection of the glory of the Lord (2 Cor 3:14–18). In practical terms, it is not clear whether Paul could rely on the availability of a copy of scripture in the Corinthian, or any other, house-churches: the

rolls were bulky, expensive, and obtainable only from Jews. Thus he pre-
scribes nothing equivalent to the weekly reading of the scripture.

However, the scriptures were not the only, or even the main, form of
"training" within the Corinthian church "constitution." Presumably Paul
thought, as their "father" (1 Cor 4:14–15; 2 Cor 12:14–15), that he had
provided what education they needed, through his example and teaching;
further reinforcement was provided by παιδαγωγοί, by his letters and by
delegates such as Timothy, who could remind them of his "ways in Christ"
(1 Cor 4:16–17). Since he appeals repeatedly to his earlier instructions,
"as I teach them in every church" (1 Cor 4:17; 11:2, 16; 14:33 [?];
15:1–5), Paul seems to think of early Christian "catechesis" as a sufficiently authoritative and integrated body of material to enable his converts to find their moral bearings.

What is unclear is how these norms would be regularly and effectively
instilled, especially as Paul cannot control their interpreters—the Corinthians' παιδαγωγοί and πνευματικοί. These latter in particular highlight the
authority which Paul's constitutional ideal accords to the Spirit, and the
problems which that authorization could entail. There is massive potential
here for immediacy, creativity, and adaptability, but the concomitant lack
of fixity would certainly by judged by Josephus as a disadvantage.

3. As we saw, Josephus's constitutional ideal emphasized not only
knowledge of the law, but also its *comprehensive application* in daily life.
Does Paul expect the same in relation to the ethos of his communities?

On the one hand, Paul clearly expects his theological and moral norms
to influence every dimension and every aspect of life. The range of moral
and social topics dealt with in 1 Corinthians speaks eloquently for this
conclusion: here we find the believers addressed on matters as diverse as
the conduct of common meals, covering (or not covering) one's head, eating meals in non-Christian company, buying meat in the market, and
even sexual relations between husband and wife. Indeed, 1 Corinthians 7
demonstrates Paul's attempt to apply Christian convictions to every form
of sexual status (single, married, betrothed, divorced), and the illustration
of his central point by reference to slave and free, Jew and Gentile
(7:17–24) further confirms the comprehensiveness of his moral vision.
Just as he is concerned to take *every thought* captive for the gospel (2 Cor
10:5), so he wants his converts equipped for *every* good work (2 Cor 9:8),
so that *everything* they do is done for the glory of God (1 Cor 10:32). Correspondingly, Paul's central virtue, love, is of universal application: it πάντα
στέγει, πάντα πιστεύει, πάντα ἐλπίζει, πάντα ὑπομένει (13:7),
and without it every action is worthless (13:1–3). This singular virtue is
given shape by the many related individual injunctions (*Einzelgebote*),

covering such matters as sex, social etiquette (food offered to idols), and financial responsibility.[30] If Josephus's crowning virtue is εὐσέβεια, and Paul's is ἀγάπη, both could claim that every feature of their respective "constitutions" embodies the virtue to which the whole is dedicated.

It is important to observe the significance of this comprehensive vision from the viewpoint of believers. As we noted above, Wolter has emphasized that the most socially distinctive features of Paul's moral rules (the ban on idolatry and sexual immorality) actually derive from Judaism, while much else was held in common with outsiders and was not in their view distinctively "Christian"; few, for instance, would find Paul's depiction of love morally peculiar. Yet from Paul's point of view, and from the point of view of the insider, all these practices are marked as distinctively "Christian" by their connection to key features of Christian identity. Thus, while Paul's rules on idolatry and sexual practice may differ little from those in Judaism, it is noticeable and important that he connects them to specifically Christian beliefs and the special allegiance of the believer to Christ (1 Cor 6:12–20; 10:14–22). Thus, from the insider's perspective, these practices are not inherited Jewish practices but the expression of Christian faith. Similarly, the virtues of honesty and love, which were quite unobjectionable to outsiders, do not thereby necessarily function *for insiders* as links that include them in the wider society, but could serve as part of their specifically Christian commitment. Thus it is not impossible for Paul to build a complete moral universe founded on a distinctively Christian identity, even where the majority of its components are not in practice socially distinctive. In such a case what will be required is the continual affirmation of distinctive Christian identity, a discourse of difference that can persist despite obvious similarities with outsiders in moral norms and social practices. In other words, Christians had to be made to *feel* different even when they were doing exactly the same as everyone else. A good deal of 1 Corinthians consists of this rhetorical affirmation of difference even where its moral norms conform to generally accepted standards.

In general terms, Paul could thus justifiably claim that his constitution was comprehensively applied. Josephus, however, might press Paul on those areas where, as a Jew, he found his "constitution" having particular effect. We may recall that Josephus referred especially to Jewish rules concerning diet, social intercourse, and the regular Sabbath rest (*Ag. Ap.* 2.173–174). As we noted, the common characteristic of these practices is their regularity, their intimate connection to the natural, repeated processes of life. Paul's polity is different, and somewhat less defined, in each area. As regards food, he advocates a bold acceptance of anything sold in the *macellum* (1 Cor 10:25–26) and regards the consumption or noncon-sumption of food as a matter of less than central concern (1 Cor 8:8; cf. 6:13; Rom 14:17). Moreover, in 1 Corinthians 8–10 he allows for differ-ent perceptions of food offered to idols, giving the food itself less empha-sis than one's obligations to the "weak." This suggests a complex and variable assessment of how, in such cases, one gives glory to God (1 Cor 10:32), rather than the more predictable reinforcement of social differ-ence necessitated by Jewish dietary laws.

Paul's expectations regarding social intercourse are harder to compare with those of Josephus, since the latter does not clarify what aspects of social interaction he has in mind. Paul ridicules the notion of social iso-lation and sees no problem in Christians eating with sexually immoral, unscrupulous, or idolatrous non-Christians (1 Cor 5:9–11). But as this passage makes clear, this apparent laxity is workable only because it presupposes a strong sense of differentiation between "brothers" and "out-siders." Whatever social contacts are maintained with unbelievers (neces-sarily so in the case of mixed marriages, 1 Cor 7:10–16), an ideological differentiation requires that they be regarded quite differently from believers, as an alien entity on the outside of the circle (cf. 1 Cor 6:1–8). Thus, Paul knows, as well as Josephus, that "bad company ruins good manners" (1 Cor 15:33), and given a choice would always encourage a Christian form of endogamy (1 Cor 7:39). But the subtleties of his social policy require a repeated emphasis on the church's ideological boundaries, a constant reminder to believers of their identity and how they differ from the "outsiders" with whom they continually mingle.

The regular Sabbath rest is, however, a significant point of difference from Josephus's constitution, at least for Paul's Gentile converts. What-ever Paul himself or his fellow Jewish converts may have practiced, there is no reason to think that his Gentile converts either would or could observe the Jewish Sabbath in abstention from work.[31] While Paul may presuppose that they counted time in Sabbaths (1 Cor 16:2), it is not clear how Sabbaths (or other Jewish festivals) could be anything more than names of days, rather than real alterations in routine. The (regular?) celebration of the Lord's Supper (cf. Pliny, *Letter* 10.96, "on a fixed day" [*stato die*]) and the mention of "the first day after Sabbath" (1 Cor 16:2) might signify the rudiments of an alternative time-structure, but by social necessity this could hardly have changed the patterns of daily life as sig-nificantly as Jewish observance of the Sabbath. Thus, while *every day* can be lived in honor of the Lord (Rom 14:5), it seems that Paul had noth-ing equivalent to Josephus's mechanism for routine reinforcement of social identity.

Paul's difference in this regard could be taken to represent his failure to supply adequate compensation for the loss of specifically Jewish customs as the common repertoire of the Christian community. Perhaps the accumulating body of Christian rituals, major and minor, could go some way to meet this lack.[32] Yet it is doubtful that Paul intended the comprehensiveness of his moral vision to attain the specificity we might anticipate. In his treatment of "food offered to idols," Paul appears to sanction, within limits, the different perspectives and different practices of the "weak" and the "knowledgeable," as if it was important to recognize that "giving glory to God in everything" might mean variable dietary practice (1 Cor 10:32). The same passage indicates the importance of knowledge in this matter, as tempered by love (1 Cor 8:1–13). In other words, Paul's "constitution" seems to leave some room for moral discernment, under the guidance of the Spirit, not as a necessary evil (since all rules require interpretation), but as an integral characteristic of the moral task. If, compared to Josephus's ideal, Paul's comprehensiveness appears less predictable in its effects, he might have regarded this as a strength rather than a weakness.

4. This suggestion might be further illuminated by asking how Paul's polity compares with Josephus's virtue of *unquestioning adherence to the law*. For Paul, the situation is complicated, of course, in relation to the law itself, since his emphasis on "keeping the commandments of God" (1 Cor 7:19) and the slogan "not beyond what is written" (1 Cor 4:6) must be balanced against his statement that he is no longer "under the law" (ὑπὸ νόμον, 1 Cor 9:21) and his disparaging comments about Moses' ministry of death (2 Cor 3:6–10; cf. 1 Cor 15:56). I take these latter comments, which would have been unthinkable for Josephus, as a sign that the law, although at times a theological resource, is no longer the unquestioned point of departure for his theology or ethics. He has, of course, other norms to which he can appeal, such as the creeds he cites, his own traditions, and the commands of Jesus (1 Cor 7:10; 9:14). But it is unclear whether any of these provide that fixity and non-negotiability for which Josephus looks, since Paul shows an extraordinary ability to modify or disregard even the commands of Jesus according to circumstance. Yet there clearly are certain fixed points for Paul on which he will not allow dispute: sexual immorality and participation in idolatry are obvious examples.

We may be able to gain some insight on this question by comparing Josephus's horror of τὸ αὐτεξούσιον (see above) with Paul's reception of the Corinthian (?) slogan "all things are lawful for me" (πάντα μοι ἔξεστιν, 1 Cor 6:12; 10:23). As we noted above, Josephus introduced the motif of "self-determination" into his depiction of the Midianite disaster, allowing Zambrias (Zimri) to offer his defense for exogamy and the worship of Midianite deities, only to applaud Phinehas's ruthless suppression of this rebellion against the law. At first glance this seems parallel to Paul's warning against sexual immorality and religious compromise, a warning he also illustrates by Israel's disasters in the wilderness (10:1–22), including the Midianite episode (10:8). Yet Paul does not refute the Corinthian slogan, nor deny that they have in this matter a large measure of "freedom/authority" (ἐξουσία).[33] The question is not whether they have this authority/freedom, but what they do with it, and the initial modifications of the slogan in 6:12 and 10:23 look surprisingly weak. There Paul insists only that freedom is limited by a paradoxical danger of enslavement, or by expediency (οὐ πάντα συμφέρει), which seems to mean specifically what is expedient for the community (10:23–24: οὐ πάντα οἰκοδομεῖ). To this extent, Paul's notion of "freedom" is not αὐτεξούσιος, since the individual's interests are subordinated to those of the church, here particularly with regard to the "weak" (8:9–13).

As the broader context shows, Paul in fact had other grounds on which to limit the range of the Corinthians' ἐξουσία. When he illustrates from his own ministry what it means to forfeit (or apply) that freedom (9:1–23), he brings into play not just the interests of the community but also the purposes of the gospel (9:12), his concern to "gain" converts (9:19–21), and above all his sense of obligation to God (μὴ ὢν ἄνομος θεοῦ) and Christ (ἔννομος Χριστοῦ, 9:21). It is here that Paul locates what Josephus would have called his κανών (*Ag. Ap.* 2.174; cf. Gal 6:14–16). Yet, within this framework, and subject to these limits, Paul not only allows but positively encourages a degree of "polyphony" (Meeks), in which different Christian convictions, of the "weak" and of the "knowledgeable," can be heard, and the community can come to its decision not simply by the interpretation of a rule but through a process of moral discovery.[34] In other words, while sometimes Paul can allow only his own voice to determine the Corinthians' decision (1 Cor 5:1–5), at other times he seems to want his converts to take responsibility for their own ethical decisions (11:13, 28; 14:29), to come to their own right minds and "sin no more" (15:34).

This conclusion tallies well with our observations on the other features of Paul's constitutional mechanisms. We have suggested above that certain aspects of Paul's strategy necessitated a limit on the degree of specificity with which Christian obligation could be detailed, and we have found a concomitant emphasis on the direction of the Spirit, and an apparently conscious disinclination to spell out what purchase the gospel should have on some aspects of daily life. While faith clearly has important practical effects (cf. Paul's descriptions of conversion in 1 Cor 6:9–11 and 14:25), not all of these can be predictably fixed: some space is accorded to "freedom" not simply as an interpretative necessity, but as a structural *desideratum*.

5. For these reasons, Paul's goal of *communal harmony* is more complex than that articulated in Josephus's ideal. As we noted earlier, the unity of the Corinthian church is one of Paul's prime objectives in 1 Corinthians, as he strives to eliminate the factionalism and self-regard that vitiate its life. The interdependence of the body and the "upbuilding" of the community are thus among the leading themes of the letter. However, Paul's prescription for unity also allows for a measure of diversity in the church—not only the diversity of different spiritual gifts and different forms of marital status, but also the principled acceptance of cultural diversity such that "neither circumcision nor uncircumcision counts for anything" (1 Cor 7:19; cf. 12:13). To put the matter in Josephus's terms, while Paul might endorse Josephus's goal of "uniform speech" (εἷς λόγος), he might give less than complete support for the notion of "common practices" (κοινὰ ἔργα, *Ag. Ap.* 2.181), not because he is concerned only with faith, rather than works, but because the instantiation of that faith in works is to a certain degree under-determined, and deliberately so (cf. the strategy of permitted difference in Romans 14). Paul's constitutional strategy has a built-in "uncertainty principle" that allows for different expressions of a common faith.

The dangers inherent in this strategy are obvious. Its permission for difference could encourage fissure, and the effort that Paul has to invest in keeping the Corinthian church together, and in keeping his Gentile churches in fellowship with Jerusalem (1 Cor 16:1–4), is testimony to the difficulties he faces. Insensitivity and judgmentalism, as displayed by the "knowledgeable" in Corinth and the "strong" in Rome, are further and associated risks. At the same time, Paul's strategy allows a degree of flexibility and adaptability that could be important factors in the church's growth and cultural penetration.[35]

Josephus's constitutional ideal thus helps raise significant questions concerning the aims and characteristics of Paul's church-formation. Even if Josephus's ideal is artificially utopian and its characterization of Judaism exaggerated for apologetic purposes, it helps set a grid against which to place Paul. Our purpose has not been to identify deficiencies in the Pauline constitution, but to submit it to analysis from a new perspective capable of revealing its structural characteristics. We have discovered a social strategy that is culturally under-determined in certain aspects of the practical outworking of faith, a strategy which, to succeed, will need to rely on the repeated assertion of difference from outsiders (in the face of extensive similarity), and which will require skillful negotiation to enable the community to hold together, despite permissible internal difference.

If Paul refuses to compel his Gentile converts to "judaize" (cf. Gal 2:14), neither does his policy amount to a subtle "Hellenization" of his Jewish tradition. While conscious of this (simplified) social distinction between "Jews" and "Greeks," Paul places himself and his converts paradoxically both within their own cultural traditions and beyond them. People who believe in Christ crucified inevitably distance themselves from the "wisdom" valued by "Greeks" and the "signs" sought by "Jews" (1 Cor 1:22–23), and yet they remain as the "called" still properly labeled "Jews and Greeks" (1:24). At certain points Paul appears to suggest that "the church" constitutes a third category beyond "Jew" and "Gentile" (1 Cor 10:32), yet it is clear from his own example that this church entails not some new cultural package of its own, but an "obligation to Christ" that can be expressed in variant cultural forms (1 Cor 9:19–21).[36] We have found that Paul's constitutional strategy involves a commitment to allow this obligation to affect every dimension of life, even in everyday habits, but also a restraint against determining what this obligation will mean for diverse individuals, in diverse circumstances, under the differential guidance of the Spirit. In these respects Paul would have recognized his own policy in the description of the Christians' paradoxical πολιτεία found in the Epistle to Diognetus: although not distinguished by country, language, and custom, and following local custom in their dress, food, and lifestyle, whether Greek or non-Greek, Christians yet retain their sense of difference paradoxically as "strangers" and "sojourners" whose identity is based outside any specific culture (5:1–5). It is clear that the transcultural communities that Paul attempted to build required a similar degree of flexibility to accommodate their diverse members and to situate themselves appropriately in their various social contexts. If that rendered them sometimes unstable, and vulnerable to multiple distortions, it also made them peculiarly adaptable and creative environments for the development of moral discernment.

Chapter 8

The Corinthian Correspondence between Philosophical Idealism and Apocalypticism

Henrik Tronier

Introduction

In 1994, David E. Aune published an important essay on "Human Nature and Ethics in Hellenistic Philosophical Traditions and Paul: Some Issues and Problems."[1] In opposition to a widespread view among New Testament scholars, Aune argued that it is impossible to maintain a dichotomy between Hellenistic anthropologies on the one hand and a Pauline, more genuinely Jewish view of human nature on the other. Rather, like several Jewish writers of his time, Paul made use of terms and concepts from a variety of Hellenistic anthropologies. Although he did not take over any one specific Hellenistic model of anthropology, his view of human nature was deeply influenced by his Hellenistic context.

Aune continuously stressed the complex nature of the issue: "Paul has more to say about human nature than any other early Christian author, yet he never deals with the subject directly, nor do the fragmentary expressions of his views of human nature exhibit internal consistency."[2] This caused Aune to consider the possibility that other ideas of crucial importance to Paul might have given rise to his statements on human nature. In a quite tentative way, he pointed to Paul's apocalyptic cosmology and eschatology as possible generative ideas.

> In some respects this is a chicken-and-egg problem—did Paul's mythological view of eschatological dualism give rise to a homologous view of human nature in which the old and the new are juxtaposed until the eschatological consummation, or did his mythological view of the structure of human nature provide confirmation for his Christian understanding of Jewish apocalyptical eschatology? Neither of these possibilities is quite satisfactory, for the answer is probably more dialectical. It is more likely that Paul linked his Christianized apocalyptical outlook with current conceptions of the human person, since the former is far more unified than the latter.[3]

Unfortunately, Aune did not follow up on this point. Yet he was here touching upon problems of crucial importance, not only with respect to the specific issue of Paul's use of Hellenistic anthropologies, but even more to questions of methodology that ought to be seriously addressed in order to move forward the discussion of Paul in context. Often the discussion has been narrowly focused on bringing together a single, isolated idea in Paul's theology with comparable ideas in his context. As has become abundantly clear, such studies have been both necessary and highly illuminating. Nevertheless, this kind of approach raises at least two obvious problems for readers who presuppose the traditional Judaism/Hellenism divide. Selection of some ideas might lead to the emergence of a "Hellenistic" Paul, but selection of others (for instance, the eschatological ideas) might lead to the emergence of a more "Jewish" Paul. So where does that leave Paul? Furthermore, suppose Paul's anthropological terms are tangential only to the structures of his apocalyptic eschatology, which are basic, but that they nevertheless get whatever meaning they have from being cast in the mold of a Jewish apocalyptic framework. Should one then draw another conclusion on Paul in context than if one does an isolated study of his anthropological terms?

Thus, if the aim is to situate Paul in context, a mere continuation of cumulative studies of separate ideas will not help us out. Instead, I propose that we attempt to elucidate the comprehensive system of ideas in Paul's construction of theology, the overall structure of meaning or inner logic that holds together the individual ideas within the argument and worldview of a given Pauline letter. Which ideas are of the greatest importance and which seem to be brought in by Paul in a more tangential manner only? Furthermore, do the former give meaning to the latter by operating as a mold in which the latter are cast?

In terms of criteria, the degree of internal consistency, hinted at by Aune, may be a helpful initial tool for unearthing the hierarchical order of ideas. The relative lack of consistency in some ideas may indicate that others, developed elsewhere in the letter, have actually been at the front of Paul's mind all through.

By comparing whole systems of ideas and employing the criterion of internal consistency, we shall hopefully be able to give the basic ideas the necessary weight when placing Paul's theology in its Jewish and Hellenistic context.

The conclusion of this essay will be twofold: The basic ideas and structures of meaning in Paul's theology belong to Jewish apocalypticism. Paul is thus a genuinely Jewish writer, to be situated firmly within his immediate Jewish context. But Jewish apocalypticism is itself a particular version and variation of certain basic ideas in the Hellenistic world at large, Jewish as well as non-Jewish. Thus, what I am offering is a reading of Paul within Judaism within Hellenism, and hence, a reading beyond the Judaism/Hellenism divide.

Both points emerge when one recognizes that ideas of knowledge like those found in philosophical idealism, and as distinct from ideas of temporal eschatology, play a formative role both in the apocalypses and in Paul's hierarchy of ideas.

In what follows, I shall discuss the interrelationship between Paul's ideas of knowledge, cosmology, eschatology, and human nature in the Corinthian correspondence. For reasons of space I shall confine myself to 1 Corinthians 1–2, 12, and 15, but bring in 2 Corinthians 4–5 and 12 as well. The argument will be that Paul's idea of knowledge, as developed in the first two chapters of 1 Corinthians, not only constitutes the basic content of his message to the Corinthians, but also informs what he has to say in terms of the three other ideas. For instance, certain inconsistencies and unclear details in the anthropology of his mythological account in 1 Corinthians 15 of the eventual eschatological transformation may be explained in terms of such a hierarchy in his ideas. In particular, his view of the two bodies may be seen to be molded by his idea of a cognitive transformation.

In order to place Paul in context, I shall bring in some non-Pauline texts in which ideas of a transcendent mode of perception play a formative role: Philo and the apocalypses of the Enoch tradition. At one end of the spectrum, I bring in a Jewish position which is undisputably thoroughly Hellenistic on the point that is central to this study: Even among scholars who presuppose the traditional Judaism/Hellenism divide, it is widely agreed that Philo's ideas of knowledge represent a heavily Hellenized Jewish position; they are taken over directly from Hellenistic philosophy; Philo's work is Middle Platonism at its best.[4] In this respect, therefore, comparing Paul with Philo's epistemology is at the same time comparing him with Hellenistic philosophy in a Jewish context.

Traditionally, the apocalypses and Philo have been placed at opposite poles of a supposed dichotomy between Jewish and Hellenistic. Yet, M. Hengel[5] and more recently among others M. Himmelfarb[6] and L. Hartman[7] have pointed to Hellenistic counterparts to several individual motifs in the Jewish apocalyptic works. I shall push that point much further, in the direction of the system of ideas as a whole. I shall point to pervasive structural similarities between the respective thought worlds of Philo and the Jewish apocalypses. I shall argue that the crucial ideas of the latter are molded by certain structures that we also find in the epistemology of Hellenistic philosophical idealism. Due to the close structural similarities between a position like Philo's and that of apocalypticism, the basically apocalyptic conceptual world of Paul's letters to Corinth comes out as floating smoothly between apocalyptic and philosophical ideas.

Finally, let me make a few introductory remarks on certain dichotomies that are traditionally linked to the supposed Judaism/Hellenism dualism and often presupposed in interpretations of Paul.

The first is the cognitive contrast between religion, faith, and revelation on the one hand and philosophy, knowledge, and reason on the other—a dichotomy that lies deep in the Western consciousness. This dichotomy cannot be maintained. That holds for both Philo and the apocalypses and Paul. Paul's ideas of faith, revelation, and the soteriological state of being united with Christ refer to a mode of perception with a particular rationality that is linked to a certain idea of cosmology.

A second dichotomy is of an even more fundamental nature: space versus time, cosmos versus history. Traditionally this dichotomy has played a major role in the construction of a dualism between Hellenistic and Jewish/Christian worldviews, and it has often been closely linked to the other presupposition of a dichotomy between (Hellenistic) philosophy and (Jewish/Christian) faith. This was done, for instance, by Th. Boman,[8] O. Cullmann,[9] and R. Bultmann.[10]

Here the cultural situation of postmodernism may help us out, for the priority of time and history over spatial categories seems to be partly due to certain presuppositions of modernism. As argued, for instance, by D. Harvey, the change from a modern to a postmodern way of thinking involves a change from time to space as the basic conceptual categories in the construction of meaning.[11] This change of perspective might open for a critical evaluation of the traditional heavy emphasis on temporal categories in the reading of Paul's theology and its context. I shall bring in the spatial perspective here and argue against a traditional reading that it is no less foundational in Paul and the apocalypses than in the Middle Platonism of Philo.

Ideas of Knowledge and Mythological Construction in Philo

A good starting point for seeing the structural and logical connections between Philo's ideas of knowledge and his mythological construction of the world is his idea of Logos.[12] In Philo, Logos is the transcendent rationality of the entire creation, the rational unity and conceptual structure of reality; Logos is the sum total of ideas.[13] Furthermore, Philo gives the rational activity of Logos both an objective, cosmological aspect and a cognitive one. Thus Logos is an extensive semantic structure in which world and cognition are fused.

Cosmology

The idea that creation is arranged by Logos as an all-embracing hierarchy of being is of crucial importance in Philo's cosmology. In *Her.* 130ff., he develops a cosmology and ontology that are directly based on ideas taken over from philosophical idealism, namely the interpretive method of *diairesis* ("division").[14] This method is an important part of Plato's logic (the rational deduction in his theory of ideas), and in the Hellenistic period it was continued by Middle Platonism in particular.[15] The method is an interpretive way of unveiling the conceptual and transcendent substance of empirical phenomena and their mutual conceptual and logical relations and order. This is done by intellectually grasping some kind of superior and general idea which embraces all the different phenomena that are to be interpreted, a purely abstract idea that is common to the phenomena in question. This idea is then made the object of a continuous intellectual process of deductive, logical division (*diairesis*) into still more specific ideas with a still smaller extension (usually into two subordinate ideas at each level down through the hierarchy of divisions). The result is a comprehensive, diairetical pyramid of ideas consisting of a hierarchy of ontological levels, a hierarchy of being. At the end of this logical process of division, the interpreter reaches the most specific ideas of the particular phenomena in question. Thus, the real conceptual being and true meaning of the particular, empirical phenomena in question can be appropriately defined in light of their true conceptual and logical relations in the world of ideas.[16]

According to *Her.* 130ff., God's creation has the form of a *diairesis* due to Logos's activity in the process of creation, which is diairetical. This creative activity encompasses the conceptual aspect of creation (the ideal world, *kosmos noētos*) as well as the empirical aspect of creation (*kosmos aisthētos*).[17] As Logos is the diairetically arranged sum total of ideas, the empirical world of phenomena is thereby arranged according to the ideal structure of *diairesis* that constitutes the order of creation. The diairetical conceptual structure of Logos is stamped into the material world by God's making the "universal being, which before was without form or quality,"[18] the object of his diairetically dividing Logos; in this way he turns chaotic matter into an ordered, rational cosmos. Philo thus depicts the ontological process of creation in distinctly interpretive categories: God makes the chaotic, formless, nonrational and meaningless state of empirical matter the object of the activity of his Logos, that is, of his *thoughts,* and by means of *diairesis,* which is an *interpretive* process, he turns it into a rationally ordered world, the cosmos.

This fusion of cosmology and interpretation is reflected in Philo's cosmological terms themselves. The two levels of his cosmology are throughout depicted as objects of two different modes of cognition: *kosmos noētos,* the object of the transcending, conceptual apprehension, and *kosmos aisthētos,* the object of the empirical approach. Thus, the cosmos is essentially depicted as a space of an interpretive activity (cf. below).

After creation, the cosmological activity of Logos has the function of maintaining the world's diairetical order. Logos *connects* the particular, empirical phenomena with their transcendent order. Logos functions as the link between the empirical and the conceptual levels.[19] Logos is "the glue and tie"[20] that keeps reality together in a rational unity.

Thus, as has been pointed out by U. Früchtel, Philo's cosmology results from objectifying the interpretive structure of the method of *diairesis.*[21] Further, Irmgard Christiansen has shown that the diairetical theory of ideas is also the basis for Philo's own allegorical approach. Thus, in a secondary way Philo's cosmology results from objectifying the semantic structures that goes into his own method of interpretation.

Epistemology

As is well known, Philo's theory of knowledge is deeply influenced by the dualistic categories originating in philosophical idealism. According to

Philo, the transcendent order of things is concealed from sense perception. While being of a purely conceptual nature, it is situated at an ontological level different from that of the empirical aspect of the phenomena.
Accordingly, a fundamental transformation of cognition is a precondition
of a true comprehension of the phenomena, from the immediate, natural,
human perception, that is, the merely empirical approach, to a transcending, intellectual mode of apprehension.[22]

According to Philo, that transformation takes place through *revelation,*
an inner ideal, conceptual vision.[23] That revelation is brought about by
the transcendent Logos.[24] Logos opens "the eye of the soul"[25] and raises
cognition to the transcendent level of reality, thereby enabling the interpreter to behold the ideal order and conceptual substance of the phenomena, their conceptual unity and mutual relations.[26]

The process of interpretation within that mode of comprehension is
shaped by Logos, too. Logos becomes the interpretive principle and leads
cognition in an intellectual process of *diairesis.* In that mode of cognition,
the interpretive process corresponds to the cosmological structure of the
world.[27] Thus, the connection of the interpreter with the transcendent
world is basically an interpretive event brought about through a transformation of cognition due to the revelatory activity of Logos. In this way
Logos links cognition with a level of the world that is, according to Philo,
substantively identical with the transformed cognition itself.[28] The
world's transcendent nature is recognized as a reflected image of cognition's own nature and rationality. In terms of ontological categories, this
is where cognition truly belongs, its homeland.[29]

To reach the transcendent mode of interpretation is, according to
Philo, to experience the supreme good and fulfillment of meaning. A
transformation of the value of particular phenomena is taking place
through the cognitive transformation itself. The world now shows up differently. In the merely empirical mode of approach, cognition confronts
a world that is chaotic and contingent, without meaning. In Philo's
words, the phenomena appear to be "deadly," "foreign," and "hostile"
when they are approached empirically.[30] By contrast, when cognition is
transformed into being linked with the transcendent level of reality, the
phenomena become "goods" and "blessings" for the interpreter since
their true substance is now seen to be related to the interpreter's own
rational being and true self.[31] It is this kind of interpretive event that
Philo objectifies in his account of God's creation of the world as an interpretive process of revaluation: God made chaotic matter the object of his
Logos (interpretation) and transformed it into a world shaped by Logos,
a rationally ordered world.

As a consequence, the transformation of cognition surmounts the initial experience of the world as foreign. That experience is replaced by a transcending experience of meaning. The acquisition of the blessed and happy life is thus basically an interpretive event.[32] Although Philo's interpretations are obviously of a distinctly rational character, nevertheless he often depicts this mode of perception by expressions that we would nowadays understand as having a distinctly religious character: revelation, visions of the divine light, a soteriological state of liberation and fulfillment, a kind of ecstasy depicted in terms relating to mysticism.[33] In Philo's case, the modern dichotomy between religious experience and philosophy is wholly inadequate.

We may conclude that the transcendent world is an imaginary, conceptual world of order and rationality *from where* the phenomena may be interpreted as meaningful *in spite of* the fundamental empirical experience of their foreignness. The basis of this interpretive process, the precondition of its logic, is the notion of transcendence, as developed in the epistemology of philosophical idealism, and its basic idea of a dichotomy (ontological dualism) as well as an interconnection between the empirical and the conceptual (ideal) aspects of the phenomena. Through this semantic structure, true meaning can be rationally defined as a *contrast* to the immediate empirical experience and thus be placed outside what may be grasped empirically and at the same time be claimed to be the meaning *of* the empirical phenomena themselves. By means of this idea of transcendence, an interpretive strategy is created for the rational handling of the empirical experience. Philo's "vertical" cosmological construct operates as a space for an interpretive activity, a mode of perception, in the approach to the world of experience—a semantic space that encapsulates the world of experience and transforms it into a context of meaning.

The Notion of Transcendence

Before turning to the apocalypses and 1 Corinthians, we should specify the precise character of Philo's notion of transcendence. As we have seen, the basic conceptual structure in Philo's cosmology and epistemology is a "vertical," timeless one. In that sense it is a spatially conceived structure of meaning. But reading *Her.* 130ff. as well as several passages in *Migr.*,[34] one quickly realizes that for Philo the transcendent world is not separated from the world of phenomena in any concrete spatial sense. On the contrary, it consists of the organizing structures in those phenomena; it is, in a modern terminology, a conceptual aspect of the phenomena. But it is an aspect that is situated on a different level from the aspect that may be grasped empirically. In that sense it is situated "outside" the phenomena and has to be revealed by Logos "from the outside," in a "vertical" structure. In terms of concrete spatial location, however, it really does not exist at any particular place.[35] What we find in Philo's version of the notion of transcendence (as well as in the method of *diairesis* of philosophical idealism) is thus a vertical, ontological dualism of *conceptually* separated levels, not a dualism of spatially separated levels. In spatial terms, as it were, the ideal world is situated in the same "place" as the empirical world; spatially, the two are inseparable from one another.

Of course Philo knows of a concrete heavenly world "up there"—the geographical region of the cosmos where the astral bodies, stars, angels, etc., are situated. But this heavenly world is not the transcendent, ideal world (*kosmos noētos*) that is the object of the transcending, conceptual vision. In ontological terms the heavenly world belongs to the empirical world of phenomena, the *kosmos aisthētos*; the relationship between the heavenly and the earthly parts of the world is a hierarchy of "stuff" *within* the *kosmos aisthētos,* reaching from "light stuff" (the heavenly region) down to "heavy stuff" (earth). The transcendent world, by contrast, consists of the structures, of a purely formal and conceptual character, that embrace and organize this whole world in its entirety.

Thus, as noted above, Philo constantly emphasizes the link between the transcendent, conceptual realm and the empirical realm. Logos embraces the empirical phenomena. True cognition—that is, the transcending, conceptual vision of the rational structures—always involves and brings in the empirical perception as well since it is a vision of the organizing structures *in* the empirical phenomena, which are perceived in sense perception; the conceptual apprehension involves a certain (true) mode of empirical perception as well;[36] the empirical perception *joins* the conceptual apprehension, thereby grasping the true meaning of the empirical world.

The same idea is emphasized by Philo in his account of the relationship between the conceptual vision and words and speech. Since it consists of structures of a purely formal character, or logical relations, the object of the conceptual vision cannot be directly grasped or communicated in words and speech, for words by nature refer to concrete phenomena or particular concepts. The transcendent world of structural and logical connections must therefore be communicated through vision; it must be "beheld" by the eye of the soul in an inner, conceptual all-embracing vision of the whole system of conceptual relations (a *synopsis*). Thus the transcending mode of apprehension involves a fundamental transformation from the categories of speech and hearing into the categories of (conceptual) sight and vision[37]—in accordance with the shift in its objects, from the empirical aspect to the formal and structural aspect.

But the sage does not have to be silent. Just as the transcendent world consists of structures situated in the empirical phenomena, so the conceptual vision can be communicated in speech in an indirect manner by describing the phenomena "in accordance with" the conceptual vision of their transcendent substance and order. In that description the transcendent structures form an implicit structure in the designations and words chosen. This is the true mode in which Logos may express itself in speech.[38]

That mode is seen in the words of scripture. Based on an all-embracing vision of the transcendent world brought about by the revelatory activity of Logos, Moses describes the concrete world of phenomena in perfect accordance with a transcending vision of its conceptual, rationally organizing structures, thereby indirectly communicating its transcendent meaning. (This, incidentally, is what makes the allegorical interpretation of scripture possible.)

As with the cosmological and cognitive activity of Logos, so also as speech Logos connects the transcendent structures with the concrete phenomena of the world in what is essentially an interpretive process.

Ideas of Knowledge and Mythological Construction in the Apocalypses

The cultural change from modernism to postmodernism with its change from temporal to spatial categories seems to have influenced recent studies of the apocalypses. In older studies it was argued that the temporal axis, a certain "linear" concept of history and eschatology, was the basic thought form of the apocalypses. Accordingly, Old Testament prophecy was considered the historical origin of apocalypticism and the book of Daniel held the position of the apocalypse *par excellence*. Compare, for instance, the studies of H. H. Rowley,[39] O. Plöger,[40] and D. S. Russell.[41]

During the last two decades, however, the spatial axis of the apocalyptic worldview, heaven and earth, and the accounts of heavenly ascents and otherworldly journeys have moved to the center of attention in a number of influential studies, for instance by Chr. Rowland,[42] J. J. Collins,[43] and M. Himmelfarb.[44] The apocalypses of the Enoch tradition, and not just the historical apocalypses of the Daniel tradition, are now considered genuine and original expressions of the apocalyptic outlook. But the question of the relationship between the two axes in the apocalyptic worldview, logically as well as historically, still confronts scholars with serious problems.[45] By reading the apocalypses in a Hellenistic context, the following remarks may contribute to solving these problems.

Cosmology and Revelation

In the worldview of the Enoch apocalypses, one finds a connection between cosmos and cognition that is similar to the one in Philo. The description of how the cosmos is organized is always given in connection with a revelation and interpretation. The various parts and levels of the cosmos are throughout presented as an object of certain visions. Further, the cosmic space is itself presented as essentially a framework for a cognitive transformation. It is while he is obtaining a certain transcendent perception of the world that the human recipient moves in this space, and the spatial structure itself constitutes the perspective from which he beholds the world.

Thus, for instance, 1 Enoch tells of several visions of a concealed, heavenly world that Enoch had experienced during his heavenly journeys. As in Philo, the basic theme is knowledge through revelation: Enoch's eyes were opened and he was lifted to the heavenly regions. The issue of interpretation is crucial: An *angelus interpres* attends Enoch on his journeys. The angel shows Enoch the things concealed in the heavenly world, but Enoch is not able to grasp their meaning. Then the angel develops an interpretation of Enoch's vision, thereby unveiling its meaning. Most of the objects of Enoch's visions are matters of the heavenly, eschatological community and the order of natural phenomena (mainly astronomy and meteorology).

Enoch's transformation into the transcendent mode of perception is literally a movement in space. His vertical movements to the heavenly region is of exactly the same kind as the horizontal movement across the surface of the earth. The transcending cognitive movement takes place within a concrete, empirical, and physical space.[46] In comparison with Philo, the transcendent and concealed nature of the superior level of reality is not due to its being of a different ontological kind, which renders it inaccessible to human perception. Rather, it is due to the fact that it is inaccessible in physical and spatial terms.

Accordingly, the transcending vision is not of a different epistemological nature than sense perception. Throughout the book, Enoch approaches the things of the heavenly world by means of the five senses.[47] When the guiding angel shows Enoch the heavenly objects, Enoch uses ordinary sight. Likewise, when the angel explains the meaning of his vision, Enoch listens by ordinary hearing.

Thus, there is no ontological or conceptual dualism in 1 Enoch, neither in the idea of cosmology nor in that of knowledge. Just as there is only empirical perception, so there is only one ontological level in his cosmology, the empirical and physical one. But the absence of an ontological dualism does not, of course, imply the absence of any dualism at all. On the contrary, there is a radical dualism between the earthly and the transcendent, heavenly world. Only, it is conceived of in spatial and physical categories.

In comparison with Philo, then, the basic dualistic structure of the transcendent mode of perception has been spatialized. Still, Philo and 1 Enoch may be seen as giving only two different versions of what is basically the same idea of transcendent cognition. To bring this out, I shall discuss the interpretive function of the *angelus interpres* in 1 Enoch in comparison with Philo's idea of Logos.

The Interpreting Angel

As with Logos in Philo, 1 Enoch attributes to the interpreting angel the function of showing the transcendent objects through revelation; he brings about the transcending vision. This vision is then followed by Enoch's question concerning the meaning of what he beholds.[48] The second phase of the angel's interpretive activity is thus an explanation. Here, too, we find some structural similarities with the interpretive activity of Philo's Logos. In his explanation the interpreting angel connects the heavenly objects of the vision with certain objects in the earthly world. The former are now seen to contain the transcendent meaning of the latter. Thus the angel's explanation is expressive of an interpretive movement from the revealed transcendent objects down to the well-known earthly objects.

Compare with this Philo's idea of Logos as speech. The explanation—that is, the angel's verbal expression (speech)—consists in depicting the well-known, concrete earthly phenomena in accordance with their revealed, heavenly counterparts. Thus the verbal expression, speech, of the interpreting angel provides the true description of the perceived objects in the earthly world. Only, in 1 Enoch the vision itself and the understanding of it are separated, due to the spatialized separation of the two dualistically related levels of the interpretive process. Understanding the vision presupposes the consequent establishment of a connection across the spatial separation.

What is the nature of the interpretive connection established by the angel between the two levels of the dualistically divided cosmos? The vision is not simply one of a heavenly world on its own. Rather, it is a vision of the well-known, earthly world as it appears in the heavenly world when seen through the lens of the spatial, cosmic dualism. What Enoch beholds in the heavenly world is the rationally arranged counterparts to the known earthly objects with which the angel connects them in his explanation. It is the transcendent order of the earthly world of ordinary experience, a transcendent order that is situated outside that world. When Enoch sees the heavenly, eschatological community, he sees the earthly society as being in order, though in a transcendent, concealed way:[49] the acts of people have been weighed; the wicked have been punished and spatially separated from the righteous.[50] Likewise, when Enoch sees the spatial structure and the chambers and portals of heaven, he sees the transcendent, concealed, rational order and rules of astronomical and meteorological phenomena.[51]

Further, 1 Enoch attributes to the interpreting angels the same twofold activity that Philo attributes to Logos. For instance, the angel Uriel leads the astronomical phenomena on their course in the cosmos, thus upholding their objective order (the objective activity). At the same time he is the one who reveals and explains that order to Enoch (the interpretive activity).[52]

It is noteworthy that Philo himself reflects on an allegorical relationship between Logos and angels. According to *Migr.* 173–175, the angels who escorted Abraham on his journey (Gen 18:16) stand for God's Logos that transforms human cognition into a transcendent mode of perception. Abraham himself obtains the nature of angels, that is, the transcendent nature of Logos. Compare a widespread motif in the later apocalypses, including 2 Enoch: at the end of his heavenly ascent, when he acquires knowledge of the whole world at the top of the heavenly hierarchy (compare Logos at the top of the diairetical hierarchy of being), the human recipient, for instance Enoch, is transformed into an angel.[53] In line with the interpretation given above of the interpreting angel, this mythological idea represents a cognitive claim. At the end of the heavenly ascent, which is essentially a cognitive transformation, the cognizing person is finally transformed into the same nature as the angel who is essentially a figure of interpretation.

In conclusion, both Logos and the interpreting angel are mythological figures which objectify a process of interpretation that goes into the construction of meaning for the ordinary world of experience. Likewise, the mythological cosmology that constitutes the framework for the movement of those figures results from objectifying the semantic structures of the same interpretive activity. The basic mold of the mythological ideas is interpretive processes and modes of perception. Only, the specific versions of what is essentially the same "vertical" and timeless semantic structure of interpretation differ.

Eschatology

How, then, about the idea of eschatological transformation that is so important in the apocalypses, but seems almost completely absent in Philo's world of ideas? How does that difference fit into the similarities and differences that I have delineated?

To answer this question we must take note of the spatial structure in which Enoch's perception of the eschatological, heavenly community takes place. There is no difference with regard to where or how Enoch sees the order of nature and the order of the heavenly community; he sees them in the same place and by means of the same sight,[54] that is, in the same space and by means of the same vertical movement. The transcendent order of the natural phenomena exists simultaneously with the natural phenomena of which it is the meaning. Likewise, the transcendent, heavenly community exists simultaneously with the earthly community of which it is the meaning.[55] It is a basically vertical, timeless, spatial relation between two levels of the dualistically divided cosmic space.

The temporal perspective that is also attached to this idea is to be explained as a logically secondary consequence of the spatialization itself of the basic, vertical interpretive structure. It results from the idea that the world of transcendence is spatially separated from the earthly, empirical world. Man in the earthly world may be cognitively connected with the transcendent world of order in so far as he learns about this world through the writings of Enoch. In this way he cognitively grasps the true meaning of his world of experience by using the dualistic spatial cosmology that was outlined in Enoch's heavenly ascent as his lens. But due to the idea of spatial separation, he is not fully united with the transcendent world of meaning and fulfillment simply by knowing about it and using the spatial dualism as his lens. In this he is unlike Philo, who simply by crossing an ontological gap that is conceptual in kind is united with the transcendent world of meaning and fulfillment through the mode of interpretation itself. Due to 1 Enoch's spatialized notion of transcendence, in his case a spatial gap has to be overcome; a repositioning in terms of empirical surroundings, a change in concrete space, has to take place. Such an event cannot, of course, occur at the time of the transcendent interpretation itself; it belongs to the future and is therefore an eschatological event.

Why, then, this spatialization of the notion of transcendence, which logically entails the eschatological postponement of fulfillment and salvation? Why this heavy emphasis on spatial distance and separation between the two interconnected dualistic levels of interpretation?

To reach an answer one should realize that the notion of spatial separation is not itself constitutive of the problem, as might seem at first glance; rather, it is constitutive of the cognitive *solution* to a problem. For the point of the apocalyptic outlook is to use the spatial structure as a lens for the interpretation of the social values and hierarchies of status and power in society. The spatial dualism and distance between the two levels that go into the act of interpretation, namely, the earthly social experience and its transcendent meaning, constitute the logic itself of a radical revaluation by which all status hierarchies are turned upside down.[56] The actual social experience of low status is turned into a confirmation of belonging to the transcendent world of fulfillment, salvation, and high status.[57] Thus it is due to the spatialized character of their notion of transcendence that the apocalypses are able to apply the essentially same kind of interpretive logic as philosophical idealism but in a much more radical way. For Philo, the actual world of the phenomena is basically in order, here and now. Although this is concealed to sense perception, the empirical world is a stamped image of the well-ordered transcendent one. According to the apocalypses, the rational order that the world does have at a transcendent level is to be found not here (but "up there" in the heavenly world) and consequently not now. The earthly world of experience is a *counter*-image of the well-ordered transcendent world. And the dualistic, spatial relation is the logical precondition for this interpretation.

Thus it is no surprise that it is the eschatological transformation that forms the counterpart to the present interpretive activity. What is now cognitively grasped by connecting the two cosmological levels of Enoch's journey will be physically grasped in the future when the interpreter is physically connected with the transcendent world and the spatial distance is overcome in the empirical, social surroundings. The reversal of status hierarchies which at present takes place cognitively by means of an interpretive movement within a cosmological dualism that serves as a perceptual lens will occur in physical, empirical, and social terms at the eschatological, cosmological reversal. The rich and powerful will be brought down, and the righteous of low status will be raised to a position of high status as they become angels in the heavenly hierarchy.[58] Thus the cosmic, eschatological event derives its meaning from the cognitive role of its present heavenly counterpart. That is manifest in the description of the eschatological transformation of the individual, too. It is cast in the mold of the essentially cognitive transformation of Enoch in the heavenly ascent: The righteous ones shall then arise from their sleep, have their eyes opened, and drink from the heavenly fountains of wisdom and become angels in heaven.[59] Once again we find an extensive use of cognitive categories.

Conclusion

The eschatological dimension in the apocalypses is derived from the cognitive dimension of the apocalyptic mode of perception, as evidenced in the relationship between Enoch and the interpreting angel, together with the spatialization of the notion of transcendence that forms part of this perception.

In view of the logical relationship between the spatial and temporal categories in the apocalypses that I have sketched, the traditional reference to the (quite different) prophetic outlook in order to explain the eschatology of the apocalypses becomes unnecessary. Although the apocalypses make use of some individual motifs from the prophetic tradition, the specifically eschatological dimension of the apocalypses may have evolved from within the apocalyptic cosmology itself and its particular version of a basically timeless, vertical mode of perception. Space and time, cosmology and eschatology, are not in tension (as suggested by scholars, cf. above), but belong intrinsically together. They are kept together within a particular version of an idea of interpretation which is structurally identical with that of philosophical idealism.

Thus, I suggest that the precondition for the rationality of the apocalyptic world of ideas that we find in the Enoch tradition lies in the development of particular ideas of transcendence and knowledge in the Hellenistic period that we find reflected in the epistemology of Hellenistic philosophical idealism as well: the philosophical invention of the idea of a conceptual dichotomy (ontological dualism) between the empirical and the conceptual (ideal) aspects of the perceived phenomena, that is, a mode of perception and rationality from where the experienced phenomena may be interpreted as meaningful in spite of the fundamental empirical experience of their foreignness. The rationality lies in the peculiar interconnection between the two levels of the dichotomy.

Although persecutions and oppression have taken place since the beginning of time, we do not find the characteristic, apocalyptic responses to those experiences prior to the rise of this concept of transcendence in the Hellenistic period. Some sociological explanations of the rise of apocalypticism may thus be too simplistic. The apocalytic worldview is not to be explained simply as caused by a political or economic crisis. It may be an answer to such circumstances, but the particular character of the answer is due to the rationality that had been developed in the history of *epistemology* during the Hellenistic period.

Although I am proposing a historical thesis of common origin, it should be emphasized that for the following reading of the Corinthian correspondence the point lies in the structural similarities alone. What concerns me in this essay is the possible relationship between the apocalyptic worldview and philosophical idealism in the first century C.E. Due to the structural similarities I have sketched, we may well find a mixture of apocalyptic and philosophical ideas in the mind of a first-century apocalyptic thinker like Paul even if my thesis of a common historical origin should prove wrong.

To strengthen this point I shall briefly bring in 2 Enoch. According to a widespread view among scholars, 2 Enoch was written in first-century Alexandria, at the time and place of Philo.[60] Second Enoch resembles 1 Enoch in its account of Enoch's heavenly journey. He travels through the hierarchy of heavens, is attended to by the interpreting angels, and acquires an extensive understanding of nature, history, and eschatology. At the summit of his cognitive movement he reaches the seventh heaven and is himself transformed into an angel.[61] At this moment he receives a revelation of the creation of the whole world.[62]

Although only in a tentative way, M. Himmelfarb has pointed to "broad similarities" between 2 Enoch's account of creation and Philo's. The cosmology of 2 Enoch is a "blend of biblical creation and popular Platonism," only the author of 2 Enoch is less "sophisticated" than Philo. Himmelfarb concludes that the account in 2 Enoch is "the effort of someone without technical philosophical education to make sense of the biblical account in light of the assumptions of the culture he lived in," "a literate but by no means philosophically learned Jew."[63]

A closer look than Himmelfarb's shows, however, that 2 Enoch's version of the popular Platonic categories is evidence of the kind of transformation that I pointed to above. Second Enoch 24ff. brings in the Platonic distinction between the "invisible" and the "visible" in the account of creation and also the idea of creation as the result of a process of divisions, solidification, and mixing, in a manner that is structurally similar to Philo's idea of the creation as a process of *diairesis*. But the author of 2 Enoch obviously does not entertain the idea of the invisible as a purely conceptual world of ideas and logical structures. On the contrary, 2 Enoch provides a concrete version of those ideas, and the distinction between the invisible and the visible is not genuinely incorporated into the account, but is replaced by the concrete spatial dualism between the heavenly and the earthly world.[64] Nevertheless, the author of 2 Enoch himself makes contemporary philosophical ideas of Platonic origin an integral part of his account of the transcendent mode of perception, the spatial, heavenly ascent. He is floating smoothly between distinctly apocalyptic ideas and ideas that are philosophical, though also of a very simplistic kind.

Ideas of Knowledge and Mythological Construction in the Corinthian Correspondence

At the very beginning of 1 Corinthians, Paul confronts the divisions in the community (1:10f.) and the connected problem of his own position as an apostle of the whole community (1:12). Paul's confrontation has a distinctly cognitive content. He urges the Corinthians to be united in the same knowledge (1:10). The extensive passage that follows, 1:18–2:16, is an elaboration of the content and nature of this mode of perception. In the next section, 3:1ff., Paul once again connects the social and cognitive nature of the community. Here, too, this issue is fused with the question of Paul's position as an apostle. This passage is followed by an argument for his appearance as God's apostle that likewise draws heavily on the mode of perception developed in 1:18–2:16. The whole argument that constitutes Paul's social intervention in the Corinthian situation, then, turns around the idea of knowledge.

Cosmology and Revelation

According to 1:18–2:16, the saving union with Christ is itself of a distinctly cognitive nature. Christ is depicted in cognitive terms: he is God's wisdom. The community's state of being "in Christ" means that Christ has become the wisdom of the community (1:30), a condition that is brought about by the heavenly Spirit. Accordingly, Paul attributes to the Spirit a cognitive activity that effects a transformation of cognition into a transcendent mode of perception. At the end of the section, he describes this as a union with Christ's "mind" (2:16).

As in Philo and the books of Enoch, the idea of a cognitive dualism is of crucial importance to Paul in this passage. He develops the idea of a dichotomy between two "wisdoms," the "wisdom of the World" versus the "wisdom of God" (1:19–21; 1:24; 1:30; 2:5). In 2:6–16 it becomes manifest that the framework of this dualism is the cosmological dualism adopted from the apocalyptic tradition. The principal interpretive structure behind Paul's idea of knowledge is that of the apocalyptic, spatial dualism. In 2:6–7 he explicitly links his epistemological dualism with the apocalyptic cosmology. He imagines two "spirits" that are placed in either part of the dualistically divided cosmic space: "the spirit of the World" as contrasted with "the spirit of God." These spirits constitute two substantively different modes of perception: a "psychic" or "carnal" one (*psychikos / sarkikos*) over against a "spiritual" one (*pneumatikos*). To the psychic person, who possesses the Spirit of the World, the transcendent, heavenly world is concealed and inaccessible (2:11f.; 2:14). The psychic mode of perception is able to comprehend neither the substance or meaning of the spiritual objects (*ta pneumatika*) that the Spirit brings forth from the transcendent world (2:14) nor the true, concealed nature of the heavenly wisdom and the Lord of Glory when these are manifested in the earthly world in Christ (2:8). To the psychic mode of perception all this appears as foolishness (2:14; 1:18; 1:21; 1:23). Grasping those spiritual objects and the manifestations of the transcendent world presupposes a transformation of cognition from the earthly into the heavenly realm.

This transformation, from "psychic" to "spiritual," takes place through revelation—just as in Philo and the apocalypses. And this revelation is brought about by the heavenly Spirit (2:10). Neither the historical Christ event nor the cross are in themselves the place of revelation; they reveal nothing. Their transcendent meaning and link with the transcendent, heavenly "power," "glory," and "wisdom" of God remain concealed to the merely human, psychic perception. Revelation occurs through a transformation into a heavenly mode of perception (2:10–12). To the spiritual person the Spirit has become an instrument of perception and interpretation (cf. Logos in Philo) that generates a transcendent comprehension of the heavenly world, "the depths of God," the spiritual objects, and the connection between the earthly Christ event, the cross, and its transcendent, heavenly counterparts and meaning.

Thus it is by the Spirit's revelatory activity, which is cognitive in nature, that the believer becomes connected with the transcendent world (cf. Logos in Philo). From there, cognition obtains a comprehensive grasp of the entire world (2:10; 2:15). In that mode of perception, the nature of cognition is reflected in the nature of the objects and vice versa. As "spiritually" interpreting (*pneumatikōs syg-/anakrinōn*) the "spiritual" person (*ho pneumatikos*) relates to "spiritual" objects (*ta pneumatika; ta tou pneumatos*), 2:13f. (cf. Philo). This is where the transcending perception truly belongs; the objects are a context of meaning while being a reflected image of the interpreter's own cognitive nature.

In conclusion, the transcendent linking of the believer with the heavenly, spiritual world and the heavenly Christ is of a distinctly cognitive nature. Being "spiritual" (*pneumatikos*) is explicitly seen as a cognitive matter—all the defining verbs in 2:10–16 have a distinctly cognitive meaning. The contrast itself between the believer and "this World" is also defined in distinctly cognitive categories. Even the liberation out of "this World" is a cognitive event: the state of being saved—through being linked with the heavenly world and united with the heavenly Christ— and the experience itself of salvation and fulfillment come about through the transcendent mode of perception.

Although Paul uses terms in this passage that sound anthropological (like flesh, soul, and spirit), he is not really concerned with different parts of the human constitution. The point of his argument lies in ideas of knowledge. "Carnal" (*sarkikos*), "psychic" (*psychikos*), and "spiritual" (*pneumatikos*) explicitly refer to cognitive categories and different modes of perception. It is not possible, therefore, to reconstruct a fully developed and consistent anthropology on the basis of 2:6–16. "Psychic" and "spiritual" refer to modes of perception that are both accounted for by (two different) "spirits."

Reversal of Values

What kind of interpretation is it then that underlies Paul's idea of the transcendent mode of perception as developed in 2:6–16? The answer may be seen from the context, 1:18–2:5 (and chapters 3–4): an interpretation that turns the traditional system of social values and status hierarchies upside down (as in the apocalypses). The church is essentially a community of interpretation that stands in direct opposition to the World and its mode of perception.

In 1:18ff., Paul identifies the World and its two different ethnic groups in cognitive categories. Jews are identified as people who "ask for signs" and Greeks as people who "seek wisdom," 1:22. Thus they are communities of a certain interpretive nature. The contrast between the World and the community of believers is drawn in the same categories: the church is essentially a community of a transcendent evaluative mode of interpretation compared with the World's mode of perception.

This revaluation of course takes place paradigmatically in relation to the cross. What is perceived by the World as foolishness and a scandal in terms of the system of value that goes with this mode of perception is comprehended by the community of believers as an earthly phenomenon that is connected and correlative with "God's power" and "God's Wisdom" in the heavenly world (in perfect accordance with 2:10–15; compare, too, the description of the "psychic" cognition in 2:14).

But the cross is not the sole object of this revaluation. It is of great importance to Paul's argument that the same interpretation takes place in relation to the social status hierarchy involved in the World's mode of perception, 1:26–30. What is perceived by the World as weak, base, despised, and worth nothing is comprehended by the transcendent mode of perception as being really correlative with belonging to God (being elected) and the heavenly world. In his idea of interpretation, Paul brings in the apocalyptic, cosmological dualism in order to turn the traditional status hierarchy in the worldly society upside down.[65] And God's election of people of low status, who make up the church, consists in bestowing upon them Christ as their "wisdom," that is, giving them the transcendent, evaluative mode of perception which essentially constitutes them as the community of the elect vis-à-vis the world of the condemned (1:30). Demythologizing this, we might say that God's act of election is itself of an interpretive nature. God makes people of low status the object of His "wisdom" (that is, his thoughts, interpretation), thereby turning the social system of values, the status hierarchy, upside down. The interpretive activity of the revaluation is objectified into a mythological idea of God's act of election, as in Philo's account of God's act of creation.

Finally, the same kind of interpretation is involved in Paul's empirical appearance as an apostle of God (2:1–5 and chapters 3–4). His low status appearance as well as his apparently negative experiences of suffering, persecution, expulsion, etc., are interpreted as being correlative with the heavenly world, thereby confirming that he belongs to God, that he is truly God's apostle.

As has become clear from our study of Philo and the apocalypses, this kind of interpretation is not paradoxical in the sense of "non-rational" or "non-logical," as some have claimed due to the presupposition of a dichotomy between faith and reason. On the contrary, the intrinsic rationality of the reinterpretation proposed in 1:18–2:5 lies in the structure of interpretation that is reflected in the mythological construction of 2:6–16. As in the apocalypses, the two levels of the structure of interpretation that accounts for the revaluation have been spatialized.

Thus, if we allow ourselves to demythologize Paul's mythological ideas, we (not Paul, of course) may conclude that Paul's description of the heavenly Spirit's movement within the dualistically divided cosmic space is a mythological projection of the interpretive movement that takes place within the semantic structures of a revaluation of phenomena in the social world. That also holds of Paul's construction of a christology in 2:6–16 as well as in 1:18–2:5. In his cosmological movement down through the dualistically divided cosmos, from heaven to earth, Christ connects the position and status of "glory," "power," and "wisdom" at the heavenly level, with the radically negative empirical position and social status of the cross and suffering at the earthly level and turns them into correlative entities. Thus the cosmological movement of the Christ figure ("wisdom") too is understood as standing for the interpretive activity of revaluation.

As in Philo and the apocalypses, so in Paul the transcending, evaluative mode of perception constitutes the intrinsic content of the religious experience of revelation, meaning, fulfillment, and salvation. It is this experience of meaning that Paul brings to expression when he describes how, through the Spirit's revelatory activity, the Christian is connected and united with the heavenly Christ.

The fact that Paul brings into his development of knowledge in 1:18–2:16 the issue of social status (1:26–31) as well as that of his own appearance as an apostle (2:1–5) shows that his account of the transcendent mode of perception forms part of his social intervention. As we saw, those two issues are directly related to the two main problems in the social situation of the community that Paul addresses at the very beginning of the letter (1:10–17). Thus, his social intervention consists precisely in urging the Corinthians to take over his own strategy of interpretation, that is, the radical revaluation that results from an interpretive use of the spatially conceived cosmological dualism. Since the community of Christ believers is essentially a community of interpretation, both problems would be solved as soon as the Corinthians took over the mode of perception that Paul advocates. The revaluation of the traditional social status hierarchy would make the division along lines of social status disappear and so unite the community. Likewise, the same mode of perception would lead to an acceptance and recognition of Paul's own low status appearance as being expressive of his status as God's apostle. For according to Paul, the social external situation and the social internal structuring of the community directly resulted from the nature of its interpretive activity. The social structure and situation of the community correlate with its interpretive structure.

The Body of Christ, I

Elsewhere[66] I have pointed to a mythological reflection of this idea on the body of Christ in 1 Corinthians 12. Here Paul depicts the ideal social arrangement and unity of the community by attributing to the heavenly Spirit a socially arranging activity (the very same Spirit as the one to which he attributes the interpretive activity in 2:6–16). Note then that this activity is explicitly described as being a *diairetical* one (12:4–11), that is, an activity of a distinctly interpretive nature (cf. above on Philo). Paul's idea of the social arrangement of the community, the body of Christ, derives from the notion of *diairesis*. Thus, in Paul's construction of the community, the ideal social structure is an interpretive one. It fits in with this that Paul goes immediately on to develop a revaluation of the traditional status hierarchy by means of the society-as-body metaphor that was widespread in the *homonoia* speeches of his time.[67] Like the interpretive structure of *diairesis,* the body of Christ is hierarchical in nature. But Paul opposes the traditional status hierarchy of body and society by turning it upside down in the body of Christ (12:22–26 and 12:28).[68] Thus he brings together the Philonic and Platonic interpretive structure of *diairesis* and the interpretive structure of the apocalyptic cosmological dualism. In conclusion, the structure of Christ's body as a social metaphor is essentially an interpretive one. We shall see that the same holds for Paul's idea of the future transformation into the heavenly, eschatological body of Christ.

The Heavenly Ascent

First, I want to bring in Paul's description of his heavenly ascent in 2 Cor 12:1–10. Whereas the cosmology itself and the revaluation of social hierarchies that we have considered are closely related to the apocalypses, Paul's description of the cognitive transformation through the work of the Spirit seems more closely related to Philo's idea of Logos than to the apocalyptic idea of heavenly ascent. However, since there is heavenly ascent in Paul, too, one may ask how Paul's description of the cognitive transformation and revaluation given in 1 Cor 1:18–2:16 relates to his description of his own heavenly ascent given in 2 Cor 12:1–10.

We can at least say that the basic issue is the same in either context: the question of social status hierarchies. In 2 Corinthians 10–12 Paul confronts opponents who criticize him for a lack of credentials and low-status appearance. As just before (2 Cor 11:21b-33), Paul again feels compelled to boast, this time of visions and revelations granted by the Lord. His account is made up of two revelations or rather two closely connected parts of a single revelation. The first one is a heavenly ascent; Paul was caught up into the third heaven, into Paradise. In 12:7 the story continues: in order not to be overly exalted, he was given a "thorn in the flesh." Paul appealed to the Lord, and the second part of the revelation follows, now in the form af an utterance from the Lord: "My grace is enough for you; for power is made fully present in weakness" (12:9). Paul's own conclusion follows in 12:10: the interconnection between God's power and Paul's appearance in weakness.

What is Paul talking about here? In addressing this question, A. F. Segal emphazises that Paul's account is a *construction* of experience, but he nevertheless claims that 12:1–10 is a report of two different mystical experiences of an ecstatic nature.[69] Segal compares Paul's account with the numerous accounts of heavenly journeys found in the apocalypses, which he likewise considers to be reports of actual mystical, ecstatic experiences. M. Himmelfarb,[70] among others, has argued against such an interpretation: the heavenly ascent is a literary form, and accounts of it are the results of careful intellectual and rational interpretation that make use of a wide range of literary conventions and traditional ideas.

I suggest that the understanding we have reached of the heavenly ascent in 1 and 2 Enoch fits 2 Corinthians 12 as well. I am not denying that Paul may have had ecstatic experiences. But the account in 2 Cor 12:1–10 is evidence of rational, intellectual work; it is a carefully composed literary construction. And just as was the case with 1 Cor 2:6–16, so this passage, too, is essentially Paul's development, in mytological, apocalyptic form, of a certain mode of perception. Though the form of the two accounts differ slightly, their purpose is exactly the same.

It has often been emphazised that Paul's account is really a parody of a heavenly ascent. The Corinthians are given no information at all about how Paul was caught up, what he saw or what he heard (cf. 1 Cor 3:1–4!). In other words, they are given no information about the cognitive content of the movement, only the form and structure of the movement. That feature has a specific point with reference to the connection between the two parts of the course of the revelation: the Corinthians are referred to the second part, when Paul is back on earth, for information about the cognitive content of the whole revelation; that content once more turns out to be the revaluation of status hierarchies that results from combining the power at the heavenly level of the interpretive, revelatory movement with weakness at its earthly level. Paul has carefully composed his account so that all the revelations turn into a single revelation *to the Corinthians,* the outcome of which is the revaluation of social status.

Once more, Paul's procedure is the same as in 1 Cor 2:6–16, though the form is slightly different. The account of the heavenly ascent itself shows the reader that this interpretive activity takes place in a "vertical," spatial cosmological structure—as in 1 Cor 2:6–16 where the Spirit transforms the cognition into the heavenly world. Paul's movement in cosmic space in 2 Corinthians 12 is once more a projection of the interpretive activity of revaluation—just as Christ's cosmic movement was in 1 Corinthians 2. And the aim of Paul's argument is once more social intervention: to make the Corinthians take over his own mode of perception in order to enable them to understand Paul's earthly, low-status appearance as a revelation of God's power. In 2 Cor 12:1–10 the cosmic space is literally a space of an interpretive movement.

Thus, 1 Corinthians 1–2 and 2 Corinthians 12 display how Paul is able to bring together ideas of cognitive transformation that derive from both a philosophical and an apocalyptical worldview in order to bring out the very same point. Once again, Paul floats smoothly between philosophical and apocalyptic ideas, though the basic framework of his understanding of interpretation is apocalyptic.

Eschatology: The Body of Christ, II

Since Paul's idea of the transcendent mode of perception relies on a spatialized understanding of the world (as in apocalypticism), one expects him to develop an eschatological counterpart to the interpretive movement itself that makes use of spatial and physical terms, too—an eschatological counterpart by means of which one may cross the spatial distance between the two semantic levels that serve to generate meaning by offering the rationality for radical revaluation.

That is what we find in 1 Corinthians 15. Contrary to a widespread interpretation of that chapter, I shall argue that Paul is not concerned to develop an anthropology or some concept of the nature of bodies. Rather, he is reinforcing the idea of knowledge that is so important to his social intervention.

In 1 Corinthians 15, Paul confronts some Corinthians who claim that there is no resurrection of the dead (15:12). I cannot go into the extensive scholarly discussion of the position of Paul's opponents (the "Strong"); the question is of minor importance to my point. I shall only give my own opinion. As in the case of Philo, the term "realized eschatology" would not have made much sense; Paul's opponents did not change some genuinely Christian "future eschatology" by claiming it for the present. Rather, they did not concern themselves with any idea of eschatology at all; eschatology was simply absent.[71] For like Philo, they experienced fulfillment and salvation and the state of being united with the transcendent world of meaning already in the present cognitive state of transcendent apprehension ("wisdom"). That is due to the peculiar character of their notion of transcendence, which operated through the interpretive activity ("wisdom") of conceptual structures of a hierarchy of being (and a corresponding hierarchy of status) *within* the surrounding world itself, though at levels that were *conceptually* separated. Although they probably had some conception of an afterlife, probably—as in the case of Philo and many others—as a separation of the soul from the body, they did not need any eschatological transformation in order to be fully united with the transcendent conceptual world of order and meaning. By contrast, Paul needed some sort of eschatological transformation due to *his* notion of transcendence in the interpretive activity of revaluation; Paul therefore spoke for a "postponed fulfillment" of the apocalyptic kind.

Scholars usually attempt to reconstruct the ideas of anthropology and the nature of bodies which they take to be the focal point of Paul's development of the eschatological transformation. Apparently this is in line with the question that Paul sets out to answer: "How are the dead raised? With what kind of body do they come?" (15:35). However, even a cursory look at the literature makes it abundantly clear that such an attempt at reconstruction meets with serious problems. The text is a poor basis for the information that is needed for even a vague reconstruction. Viewed from the angle of anthropology and the substantive nature of bodies, the text contains a lot of foggy details and raises questions that are not answered—questions that one would expect to be of importance had those issues been upmost in Paul's mind as part of his argument against the opponents.

Here I will mention only three questions that are intensively discussed by scholars who attempt to reconstruct the anthropology and Paul's idea of the nature of bodies, but are apparently of no importance to Paul himself.

Paul answers his question from 15:35 by referring to the existence of two different bodies: "A psychic body (*sōma psychikon*) is sown, a spiritual body (*sōma pneumatikon*) is raised up" (15:44).

1. What kind of matter, "stuff," is the *sōma pneumatikon* made of? Some scholars claim that it is made of spirit (*pneuma*).[72] Others reject this while pointing out that the *sōma psychikon* is obviously not a *sōma* made of soul (*psychē*), but a *sōma* made of dust and flesh and blood (cf. 15:47 and 15:50).[73] Either Paul's use of terminology is inconsistent (with *pneuma* really being the stuff of the *sōma pneumatikon*), or else *pneuma* is, like the *psychē* of the *sōma psychikon*, the lifegiving principle of the *sōma pneumatikon* (cf. 15:45). But in that case Paul has simply left the (supposedly important) question of the matter of the *sōma pneumatikon* without an answer in the subsequent discussion.[74] In contrast with his interpreters, Paul does not seem to care, apparently because the question is of no importance to his argument nor to the point of his construction of the terms themselves of a *sōma* that is either *psychikon* or *pneumatikon*.

2. Another problem concerns the *sōma psychikon*. Does the term reflect an anthropology that views man in his entirety? Or does the term reflect

distinctive parts of man? In the latter case, do we have to do with a dipartite or tripartite division of the human being? In other words, does the *sōma psychikon* possess a *pneuma*? The contrast with *sōma pneumatikon,* especially as developed in 15:45, seems to suggest that it does not. But that would be in conflict with 1 Corinthians 1–2 and a lot of other Pauline passages: man does possess a *pneuma,* either the *pneuma* of this Age or God's *pneuma.* The text simply does not provide an answer. Once more, these problems seem to indicate that Paul has not coined his terms with reference to any anthropological ideas, but for a different purpose. He seems not to care about the question of a dipartite or tripartite anthropology, and his use of terms might not even *implicitly* entail or presuppose any anthropological ideas of that kind.

3. Another problem of anthropology that scholars often point to concerns the question of possible elements of continuity and discontinuity between the two states of existence in the eschatological transformation from one body into the other. Does Paul imagine that the *sōma pneumatikon* is somehow a part of—and released from—the present *sōma psychikon* (by an implicit tripartite anthropology) as claimed by some scholars?[75] However, other elements in the text might point in the opposite direction, as has been claimed by others: the opposition of the *sōma pneumatikon* with the *sōma psychikon* in its entirety; the idea of being "dressed over" (15:53f.) etc. Again, Paul does not seem to care about the question; he does not develop any anthropological idea of a continuing element within the eschatological process of transformation as one would expect had anthropology been upmost in his mind and the pivot of his discussion.[76]

Before suggesting a solution, let us consider the importance of spatial, cosmological categories in Paul's argument.

In 15:46 Paul makes the crucial assertion: one can only possess the *sōma pneumatikon after* one has possessed the present *sōma psychikon,* and the change is only possible at the eschatological event. This point does not automatically follow from the argument in 15:45 ("first" [*prōtos*]—"last" [*eschatos*] in 15:45 are Paul's own additions). Why should it not be possible to possess—and be united with—the *sōma pneumatikon* while still being in the present *sōma psychikon?* That would present no problem if, for instance, the spiritual body was conceived of as the transcendent, *conceptual* counterpart to the present empirical body, that is, the ideal aspect that is logically and substantively prior in the process of creation to man's empirical body (cf. Philo), cf. 15:46a.

Paul's argument for his contention is given in 15:47–49. The starting point of the argument is Adam and Christ. And the point of the argument lies in the spatial separation between the two and, accordingly, between the two different bodies; they are situated in either part of the dualistically divided cosmic space, heaven and earth. Thus, the spatial definition of the two bodies and their relationship runs through the whole of the argument; the substantive, contradictory definitions of the two men (*anthrōpoi*) and the two bodies (*sōmata*), as "earthly" (*choïkos*) and "heavenly" (*epouranios*), are not concerned with the "matter" of the bodies but relate directly to the spatial location within the cosmological dualism. In 15:47f. any definitions in categories of time are missing and the categories of the spatially conceived cosmological dualism are all-pervasive. As is confirmed by 2 Cor 5:1–10, the heavenly bodies (which are "images" of Christ's heavenly body, 1 Cor 15:48f.) already exist in the heavenly world (a present reality "up there") and are spatially separated from the earthly Adamic bodies that human beings carry at present. The basic structure is the apocalyptic one of the spatial, vertical relation between two simultaneously existing levels. The crucial distinction between present and future, the eschatological reservation, does not show up until the very last verse of the argument, in 15:49: "And as we have borne the image of the earthly man, we shall bear the image of the heavenly man." Thus, Paul explicitly derives the eschatological reservation from the spatial separation between the two levels of the cosmos. The eschatological event overcomes the present spatial separation from the transcendent world. Thus, as in the "logical" connection between philosophical idealism and apocalypticism, the necessity of an eschatological event is due to the spatial structure that results from the spatialized notion of transcendence as part of the idea of a transcendent mode of perception. In other words, the spatial structure is logically prior to the temporal structure.

The connection between Paul's mythological construction in 1 Corinthians 15 and his ideas of knowledge in 1 Corinthians 2 is quite manifest.

a) Most importantly, the basic dichotomy is the same in the two chapters, that of *psychikos* versus *pneumatikos*. In 1 Corinthians 15 the future, *somatic* transformation is from a *sōma psychikon* into a *sōma pneumatikon*. In 1 Corinthians 2 the present, *cognitive* transformation is from a mode of *perception* which is *psychikos* into one that is *pneumatikos*.

b) According to 15:50, the future, somatic transformation is a transformation away from "flesh and blood." Thus, within the somatic transformation *sōma psychikon* and *sarx* (*kai haima*) are connected and opposed to the *sōma pneumatikon*. In 3:1–3 the same is true of the cognitive transformation. The *psychikos* mode of perception (2:14) is described as *sarkikos* and opposed to the *pneumatikos* mode. There is no second term opposed to *sarkikos* in Paul's elaboration of the cognitive transformation; *pneumatikos* is in opposition to both *psychikos* and *sarkikos*. Likewise, in 1 Corinthians 15 there is no second term opposed to *sarx kai haima,* only the term *pneumatikon.*

c) According to 1 Corinthians 15, the believers are not yet "in Christ" but "in Adam," namely in terms of spatial and somatic categories. The future transformation into the state of being "in Christ" occurs through a movement in the spatially conceived, dual cosmos into a union with the bodily "image" of the heavenly Christ's spiritual *sōma*. According to Paul's description in 1 Corinthians 2 of the cognitive transformation, believers are at present "in Christ," namely as regards their cognitive state. And that is described as the believer's cognitive movement within the very same cosmological dualism; thereby the believer is united with the "mind" of the heavenly Christ.

d) In the future transformation, believers will *become* the spiritual body of the heavenly Christ by means of a somatic, spatial transformation that moves within the cosmological dualism and overcomes the spatial separation. At present, by contrast, they *are* the spiritual body of the heavenly Christ through a cognitive transformation into a community of interpretation (Christ as "wisdom") that has been brought about by the heavenly Spirit operating within the same cosmological dualism and connecting the two separated levels of the cosmos. The spiritual body of Christ is basically an interpretive one (and through that a social one, too) and the eschatological transformation is its physical counterpart. Thus in both aspects of the body metaphor—the social as well as the eschatological one—the body of Christ is basically an interpretive entity.

As indicated by a–d, Paul's mythological construction of an eschatology in 1 Corinthians 15 directly reflects his idea of knowledge as he has developed that at the beginning of the letter; his idea of the eschatological transformation derives from the cognitive movement within the semantic structure of revaluation.

In conclusion, it seems to be the idea of knowledge that generates Paul's understanding of eschatology, including his construction of the two bodies; the idea of a certain mode of perception is foremost in Paul's mind during his mythological construction of an eschatology. It is therefore also the spatial location and separation of those bodies and not their substantive nature or "matter" that are of prime interest in Paul's definition of the two bodies. In other words, in the construction of Paul's terminology, *pneumatikos* and *psychikos* are not added to the two *sōmata* to provide more definite descriptions of them; rather, *sōma* seems to have been added to the *pneumatikon / psychikon* dichotomy in order to give it a more definite, descriptive character. Consequently, Paul probably created the two terms without having any *precise* idea of the nature, "matter," or other anthropological dimensions of the two bodies.

Thus a comparison of the internal coherence of Paul's development of the idea of knowledge in 1 Corinthians 1–2 and of human nature and bodies in 1 Corinthians 15 reveals the generative hierarchy between the two ideas in the process of Paul's mythological construction.

Further, as already indicated, the connection between 1 Corinthians 2 and 15 leads to some important insights concerning the relationship between theology and social intervention. First Corinthians 15 is not simply a dogmatic dispute about theological ideas of eschatology and human nature. Rather, the aim of the chapter is to reinforce a certain mode of perception that Paul urges the Corinthians to adopt in their approach to the traditional values and status hierarchy in society. If they do this, the current social problems in the Corinthian community will disappear. Likewise, the denial of Paul's apostolic authority due to his low-status appearance will be replaced by a recognition of Paul's authority as the apostle of God.

D. B. Martin has pointed to the importance of status categories in Paul's construction of the two bodies in 1 Corinthians 15.[77] That feature is due, I think, to the generative relation between the ideas of knowledge and eschatology in Paul's theological construction. It is the structural and logical link of 1 Corinthians 15 back to the issue of knowledge in 1 Corinthians 1–2 (in itself connected with the issue of the social situation in the Corinthian community, 1:10–17; 3:1ff.) that makes the theological construction of an eschatology in 1 Corinthians 15 directly operative in Paul's social intervention. Paul offers his readers a *space* for interpretation—and at the same stroke a transcendent, heavenly social space of values, the body of Christ.

The connections pointed to in this study are reflected in 2 Corinthians 4f. as well. Paul's construction of the idea of two separated bodies and of the eschatological transformation, 2 Cor 5:1–10, is directly connected with the issue of interpretation developed in the surrounding passages, 4:1–18 and 5:16f. The point again lies in the revaluation of status. And the aim of *that* point is to make the Corinthians understand that Paul's low-status appearance, his sufferings, expulsion, etc., should be seen as the empirical manifestation of his status as an apostle of God who is linked with the heavenly world. In fact, the section 5:1–10 on the two bodies and the eschatological transformation is stated by Paul to provide a reason (cf. *gar* in 5:1) for the mode of perception he has just advocated in 4:16–18. It supports the idea of revaluation of status that is so important for the relationship between the community and Paul as their apostle. Thus, we find the same basic structure in 2 Cor 5:1–10 and 1 Corinthians 15: the idea of two different bodies that exist simultaneously but are spatially separated at either level of the cosmological dualism; and the idea of the eschatological transformation as overcoming the spatial distance between those two levels. These are precisely the elements that support the revaluation, and the eschatological idea, again, results from objectifying the semantic structures and interpretive movement of this mode of perception. But notice that the terms themselves for those bodies (2 Cor 5:1) are different from those used in 1 Corinthians 15. Once more, as noted by Aune, the reconstruction of the supposed ideas of human nature in this passage is difficult.[78] And once more I think this difficulty is due to the same hierarchy of ideas as in Paul's theological construction in 1 Corinthians 15. Paul's major aim seems to be to underscore the spatial separation (compare "earthly," *epigeios,* versus "in the heavens," *en tois ouranois,* 2 Cor 5:1). Paul uses his terms in an *ad hoc* manner. He does not seem to have had any precise idea concerning the nature of these bodies. Just as in 1 Corinthians 15, it is the idea of knowledge which is foremost in his mind and which generates the eschatological construction. However, this relation between the idea of knowledge and the idea of the eschatological somatic transformation is more manifest in 1 Corinthians 15. The basic picture derived from the idea of knowledge is thus the same in 1 Corinthians 15 and 2 Corinthians 4–5, but the anthropological terms vary—in accordance with the place of ideas concerning the nature of bodies in comparison with ideas of knowledge in the hierarchy of ideas in Paul's theological construction.

In conclusion, the attempt to make the anthropological terms in Paul's letters the basis for placing him in context is an exercise that meets with serious problems. In an *ad hoc* manner Paul may use or create terms that are not internally consistent and may point in different directions for the question of Paul's Hellenistic context. Moreover, the terms probably do not even reflect any precise anthropological ideas at all.

Therefore, bringing in the whole system of ideas, including the hierarchy among those ideas, may provide a firmer basis for placing Paul in context. As regards the basic semantic structures of interpretation and mythological construction, we may conclude as follows. At a high level of generalization, the positions of Philo, the apocalypses, and Paul are all based on a certain structure of interpretation that had been developed in Hellenistic epistemology. At a lower level of generalization, certain important differences between those systems of ideas, for instance regarding cosmology and eschatology, are due to these authors having adopted different *versions* of the shared structure of interpretation (for instance, with regard to conceptual or spatial separation between the two levels of the interpretive structure). Thus, the Corinthian correspondence may be placed "somewhere between" a position like Philo's and that of the apocalypses. As we have seen, this does not mean "between Judaism and Hellenism." For Philo as well as the apocalypses are themselves part and parcel of Hellenism since they are both rooted in a structure of interpretation developed in the Hellenistic world of ideas. It is for this reason that Paul may float smoothly between apocalyptic and philosophical ideas, even though his basic interpretive framework is a distinctly apocalyptic one.

Chapter 9

Pauline Accommodation and "Condescension" (συγκατάβασις): 1 Cor 9:19–23 and the History of Influence

Margaret M. Mitchell

When thinking about Paul's relationship to Hellenism and Judaism, one naturally turns to 1 Cor 9:19–23. In these verses the apostle gives an extreme self-characterization as "all things to all people," including his becoming a Jew to Jews, a law abider to law abiders, a lawless one to the lawless, and a weak man to the weak. This was all to "gain" each of those groups, and to be a partner with the gospel. Thus, in terms of the topic of this volume, the passage represents Paul as to say the least ambivalently positioned with respect to Judaism and Hellenism—claiming to be both Jew and ἄνομος ("Torah-bereft"), and yet not essentially identified with either since the one who is a true chameleon never can be, for he assimilates to each group in its turn.

Recent Scholarship on 1 Cor 9:19–23 along the Judaism/Hellenism Divide

Scholarship on these essential and tantalizing verses has in the last twenty years witnessed a sea change that provides a valuable snapshot of current research on Paul and the Judaism/Hellenism divide. Whereas the commentaries of the last generation, such as those of Conzelmann and Barrett, had to address the work of David Daube, who claimed that Paul's missionary strategy was entirely consonant with what we see in later rabbinic materials,[1] more recent interpretation has produced very little engagement with Daube's suggested parallels, nor have any further analogues to these verses in Jewish writings been proposed.[2] Instead, the Hellenistic background (broadly speaking) and influence on these verses have been the major focus of a flurry of scholarly work.[3] Indeed, the most recent scholarship has not only been thoroughly convinced of the Hellenistic provenance of these sayings,[4] but it has also produced multiple attempts to refine even more narrowly within and among Hellenistic or Greco-Roman traditions, literature, or lore the precise strand that may have influenced Paul in calling himself "all things to all people." The most significant proposals for the major influence upon Paul as he writes these words are:

1) the epic legends of Odysseus and ongoing debate about his character (Malherbe);[5]
2) Greco-Roman friendship conventions, in particular that of the κόλαξ, the servile flatterer (Marshall);[6]
3) Cynic-Stoic arguments about true freedom (Vollenweider, Jones, Malherbe);[7]
4) the Proteus legends (Vollenweider);[8]
5) the enslaved leader *topos* (Martin);[9]
6) political commonplaces about the factionalist and the nonpartisan (Mitchell);[10]
7) Epicurean psychagogic theory and techniques (Glad).[11]

Clearly, contemporary New Testament scholarship is predominantly seeking to understand these Pauline verses as in some sense quintessentially Hellenistic, even as the words themselves constitute a Pauline self-declaration as a polycultural man.

Although my purpose here is not to evaluate each of these proposals singly, I shall at the outset make a few methodological observations applicable to them as a group, especially in relation to the theme of this volume.

Initially, the plausibility of each of these proposals as a historical argument for direct influence on Paul's self-depiction depends upon a cluster of pre-suppositions of a general character about Paul's educational background, his spectrum of cosmopolitan experiences, and assumptions about the level of Hellenistic popular culture generally in relation to the largely literary milieu of the extant remains commonly studied. In other words, we are speaking here of expectations for "cultural literacy" of a Greek-speaking Diaspora Jew in the first century. In that regard all of the schol-ars listed above would agree with one another more than they would with those who deny that Paul had such contact and first-hand acquaintance with higher Greek culture and literature at all.[12] But that very agreement makes it difficult to decide between and among the seven equally feasible Hellenistic lines of influence on Paul. One way to go at this is to pose some specific historical questions about influence and direct dependence. For instance, is it likely that Paul had read the *Odyssey*?[13] That he was aware of debates about Odysseus's variability and adaptability?[14] That he had ever encountered an Epicurean community of philosophers?[15] That he was well-acquainted with general and local political lore about leaders, politicians, and factionalists in the πόλις?[16] That he would deliberately apply Proteus descriptions to himself?[17]

While each of the proposals entails its own set of such particular ques-tions, it can be reasonably said that each of them is at least intrinsically feasible, for Paul as a citizen of the larger Greco-Roman world would probably have encountered and engaged—to some degree—all of these traditions.[18] But precisely that last phrase is problematic, for it is difficult, if not impossible, with present evidence to select from among these seven options a singular, discrete line of influence upon Paul. One may legiti-mately question whether each of these options represents an individual and independent "tradition" separable from the others, which Paul would have singularly encountered and adapted in 1 Corinthians 9 in some direct way. It is at this point that the word "tradition" appears problem-atic, since it reifies and puts boundaries around what may be much more diffuse and disparate reflections on a related theme or cluster of themes. While one may doubt whether there was "*a tradition* of Greco-Roman society which underlines the importance of adaptability and versatile approach," as Clarence Glad has phrased it,[19] his important and thorough work has demonstrated quite convincingly the pervasiveness of language and discussion about adaptability across different periods, genres, styles, and schools. His construct, "a tradition about variability," which recog-nizes both positive and negative evaluations of adaptability, becomes a snowball that takes in all the materials drawn upon by previous scholars, to which he adds further sources, with his special contribution of the Epicurean materials.[20] Indeed, the parallels to Paul's language in Greco-Roman literature thus amassed are impressive and extensive.[21] The great value of Glad's work is to have collected all this material and shown how much a general cultural preoccupation in Greco-Roman Hellenism the topic of variability was, and to have described various recurrent applications of such notions to pedagogy and psychagogy in particular. Further, by naming the overall topic more broadly as adaptability, rather than demagoguery or flattery, he has accented the inherent ambiguity in such appropriations, and thus given a richer context for understanding the Corinthian situation in which this was a contested depiction precisely because it was open to more than one interpretation.[22]

The other major methodological question posed by such research is the relationship (and the distinction) between the possible *background* of a given argument or Pauline allusion, and the *application* of such an argument to the task that Paul has at hand (rhetorical, theological, pastoral). This question is crucial, because the two are not necessarily identical. Daube's work is a prime example, for he seeks only "missionary" parallels to Paul's statements in rabbinic literature (even when he sometimes has to argue for such a connection where it is lacking in the present form of the saying). This is because he assumes that the Pauline disquisition in 1 Cor 9:19–23, which he takes to be presenting a missionary manifesto, must have come from prior missionary teachings. Glad, on the other hand, appears to read one particular background, of philosophical psychagogy, onto Paul's actual argument in 1 Corinthians 9 more heavily than that text can bear. Though Glad's reading is illuminating, it is not clear that Paul employs the variability *topos* in 1 Cor 9:19–23 *per se* to provide what Glad himself seeks: a full-scale description of Paul's psychagogical program of recruitment and guidance. Hence in his interpretation (and that of Martin, which applies the demagoguery *topos* to Paul) it is perhaps the case that what is gained from the wider historical context is at the cost of a loss in engagement with the immediate literary and rhetorical context of the argument.[23] At any rate, the methodological point about the relationship between "background" and "application" must be attended to in assessing this scholarship.

Does one approach the question of Paul's "cultural literacy" primarily from the side of the general (what a reasonably well-educated Hellenistic Jew might be expected to know), or from the particular, working backwards from Paul's own letters to a reconstructed background? Scholars starting at each of these places have come to divergent views, with present scholarship admittedly divided in its assessment of Paul's Hellenism.

Those who regard a Hellenistic Paul with suspicion insist that the "Jewish traditions" are the primary locus for Paul's teaching and interaction with others. Others (including myself) have a higher estimation of Paul's ease of familiarity with Hellenistic culture. But rather than fight this battle by lobbing parallel texts from opposing trenches, it seems to me best to wade into the murky middle and ask about the complex admixtures of Hellenism and Judaism present in Paul's thinking. Surely even if Paul is incorporating Hellenistic traditions or *topoi* in 1 Cor 9:19–23, they are integrated with other elements of his thought, training, experience, and personality. Thus we can move beyond parallels to inquire about the syntheses that Paul builds upon and creates. How might the specifically Greco-Roman commonplaces that are so abundantly attested have been adapted, recast, and recombined in Hellenistic Jewish discourse? It is the aim of this essay to address this question through finding another way of looking at the question of influence upon Paul as he wrote the words, "I have been all things to all people."

"All Things to All People" in Early Christian Interpretation

The different perspective I would like to offer is that provided by the early church fathers who deftly treated Paul's self-description in these verses. I suggest this approach because my own understanding of these lines has been altered by reading from John Chrysostom back through the history of interpretation of the passage, which has helped me to see aspects of Paul's thought that I had largely overlooked before. My specific task here is to ask, if Paul were self-consciously making reference to well-defined and discrete Hellenistic traditions or commonplaces in 1 Cor 9:19–23, is there any trace of recognition of this in the writings of the early Christian interpreters who commented on those verses? Do these writers give any hint, by allusion or by diversion, that Paul is here drawing upon Hellenistic lore, political realism, or philosophical traditions? The general answer to this question is that while early Christian interpreters give, not surprisingly, no attention to this issue directly (for instance, I have found no early interpreter who mentions Proteus or Odysseus directly in relation to Paul,[24] or refers to his language as "demagogic"),[25] their own engagement with the text suggests familiarity with general commonplaces about variability, and their assumption that that is the theme the text evokes. That early patristic exegetes often remark upon this language about variability and respond with customary *topoi* may constitute a tacit approval of the recent line of research into the Hellenistic provenance of the sayings by showing it to be not just a modern invention or importation, but an observation already well recognized by writers much closer to the cultural milieu of Paul than we are. Yet the early interpreters also have a distinct take on Paul's strategy here that illuminates the complex Hellenistic Jewish/Greco-Roman provenance of these sayings. In particular, I shall argue that the predominant patristic interpretation of these verses, which connects them with the concept of divine condescension, or accommodation, deserves consideration as an influence upon Paul himself, as he presents himself as an imitator of Christ via this self-characterization. The concept of divine condescension, as we shall see, is itself a complex mixture and fusion of Hellenistic and Jewish concepts.

Tertullian (c. 160–225) refers to 1 Cor 9:19–23 several times in order to defend Peter against the charge of hypocrisy leveled against him by Paul in Gal 2:13, an accusation that has been picked up by the Marcionites. Here he uses Paul's own words in 1 Corinthians to rehabilitate Peter and put him in conformity with a general apostolic principle: "it was according to times and persons and causes that they used to censure certain practices which they would not hesitate themselves to pursue, in like conformity to times and persons and causes" (*praescr.* 24).[26] To bring the scales back into balance against those who elevate Paul over Peter, Tertullian mentions Paul's circumcision of Timothy (Acts 16:3) as a like instance of apparent inconsistency. Tertullian recognizes what Paul did there as "giving way" or "conceding" for the sake of the weak, in accordance with his statement in 1 Cor 9:20.[27] He defends all the apostles (and therefore the Gospels that depend upon their authority) against Marcion's condemnation of their inconsistencies by an appeal to proper "consideration for the weak":

> They therefore gave way (in a partial concession), because there were persons whose weak faith required consideration. For their rudimentary belief, which was still in suspense about the observance of the law, deserved this concessive treatment (*Ergo cesserunt, quia fuerunt propter quos cederetur, hoc enim rudi fidei et adhuc de legis observatione suspensae competebat*) . . . [Paul] therefore made some concession, as was necessary, for a time (*Necessario igitur cessit ad tempus*); and this was the reason why he had Timothy circumcized, and the Nazarites introduced into the temple. . . . Their truth may be inferred from their agreement with the apostle's own profession, how "to the Jews he became as a Jew, that he might gain the Jews. . . ." (*Marc.* 5.3)[28]

Because of Tertullian's context, which is defined by Marcion's unquestioned and single-minded esteem for Paul, he does not have to defend Paul against a possible charge of hypocrisy, but can instead use his example to redeem Peter as being in conformity with Paul's standard mode of accommodation to the weak. Because Paul's authority is not in question, Tertullian can even build a *reductio ad absurdum* argument on the literal meaning of these words, which (clearly, in his eyes) the apostle did not intend:

> But elsewhere the same apostle commends us to endeavor to please all "just as I please everybody in everything." Would you assert that he used to please men by observing the Saturnalia and New Year's Day? Was it not by modesty and patience? Was it not by dignity, humanity and integrity? Likewise when he says, "I have become everything to everybody in order to win everybody," did he perhaps mean to the idolaters an idolater, to the heathens a heathen, to the worldly a man of the world (*numquid idololatris idololatres, numquid ethnicis ethnicus, numquid saecularibus saecularis*)? (*idol.* 14)[29]

Tertullian's treatment of these verses here only hints at a possible negative reading of Paul's expression as justifying censorious pagan behavior, but he unhesitatingly assumes that the apostolic example renders such extremes patently absurd. We shall see that other interpreters, because they could not presume such an unequivocal allegiance to Paul, had to reckon even more directly with a possible negative appraisal of these words.

Most noteworthy in this regard are the interpretations of 1 Cor 9:19–23 in the writings of Clement of Alexandria (c. 150–215), especially because of his wide acquaintance with and appropriation of Greek philosophy and literature. In fact, the first allusion to our passage occurs in the preface to his *Stromateis,* in which he defends his own incorporation of "the best of philosophy and other preparatory instruction" by appeal to the Pauline precedent, which he paraphrases as: "not only is it reasonable to become a Jew for the sake of Hebrews and those under the law (according to the apostle), but also for the sake of the Greeks to become a Greek, so that we might gain all" (οὐ γὰρ μόνον δι' Ἑβραίους καὶ τοὺς ὑπὸ νόμον κατὰ τὸν ἀπόστολον εὔλογον Ἰουδαῖον γενέσθαι, ἀλλὰ καὶ διὰ τοὺς Ἕλληνας Ἕλληνα, ἵνα πάντας κερδάνωμεν).[30]

1 Cor 9:19–23 figures prominently in Clement's writings when he is discussing what constitutes a lie. In *strom.* 7.9, a part of the description of the "true gnostic," Clement brings up the example of Paul's circumcision of Timothy (Acts 16:3) despite his arguments against the practice in the letters (Gal 5:2–6; Phil 3:2–11) to demonstrate that the apostle was "all

things to all people" in commendable conformity, not as an act of deceit. In so doing, Clement exhibits a clear understanding of Hellenistic reflections on adaptability.

> For [the true gnostic] thinks the truth and says the truth at once, except if at some time, taking the healing role, like a doctor for the sake of the health of the afflicted, he will lie or tell an untruth to those who are sick, according to the sophists. For example, the noble apostle circumcized Timothy, though he had cried out and written that the circumcision done by hand is of no benefit.

Clement explains Paul's behavior by reference to our passage:

> [Paul], accommodating (συμπεριφερόμενος) himself to Jews, "became a Jew that he might gain all." He, then, condescending (συγκαταβαίνων) to the point of accommodation (συμπεριφορά) for the sake of the salvation of his neighbors (that is, only for the sake of the salvation of those on account of whom he accommodates himself [συμπεριφέρεσθαι]), not partaking in any hypocrisy (οὐδεμιᾶς ὑποκρίσεως μετέχων) because of the danger hanging over the just from those who are jealous, was in no way being forced to do this. But he will do certain things for the sole benefit of his neighbors which would not have been done by him at first, if he didn't do them for their sake. . . . This man is unenslaved to fear, truthful in word, devoted to labor, not willing ever to lie by a proferred word even if by it he might correct the sin, since a very lie, inasmuch as it is spoken with deceit, is not an idle word, but works for evil.[31]

This fascinating passage highlights several themes. First, like Tertullian, Clement recognizes Paul's circumcising of Timothy in Acts as a prototypical instance of the kind of variability of which Paul spoke in 1 Cor 9:19–23.[32] But more than Tertullian Clement addresses directly the danger of Paul's words about accommodation and the Pauline behavioral record when seen together: that it sounds like an outright admission of deceit and hypocrisy. Here Clement plays on that charge nicely through the customary Greco-Roman adaptability *topos* of the physician,[33] though focused here not on the variability of treatment needed, but on the need for the physician to prevaricate at times for the protection of the patient[34]—and this with Paul as the *exemplum*! Central to the logic of this example is the claim that the physician is motivated solely by the advantage (ὠφέλεια) of his hearers, which is of course the point of Paul's own passage (as seen in the repeated ἵνα clauses). Clement explains this by recourse to the language of "condescension," literally "coming down to the level of" (συγκαταβαίνειν) and "accommodation" (συμπεριφορά / συμπεριφέρειν). In this passage we have the first instance of technical language that will be widely employed in early Christian interpretation of 1 Cor 9:19–23, in coordination with these terms' other significant theological senses. Here Clement is drawing upon terminology to describe Pauline variability which has a multifaceted connection with Hellenism and Judaism,[35] in particular as applied to God. This is demonstrated by *strom.* 2.16, where Clement takes up the topic of how to explain scriptural passages that attribute human emotions to the deity:

> But to the extent that it was possible for us who are fettered by the flesh to understand, the prophets thus spoke to us, as the Lord accommodated himself to the weakness of human beings in a saving manner (συμπεριφερομένου σωτηρίως τῇ τῶν ἀνθρώπων ἀσθενείᾳ τοῦ Κυρίου).[36]

Before we move on to the continuation and embellishment of this line of interpretation in the later commentators Origen and John Chrysostom, we must look more deeply into the concept of divine "condescension."

Συγκατάβασις, The Language of "Condescension"

The doctrine of divine condescension or accommodation has been a central preoccupation of both Christian and Jewish thought from antiquity to the present.[37] Essentially the doctrine holds that, because of human finitude and weakness, God has throughout history used different modes of communication and revelation that are suitably accommodating of his human correspondents. Just as Paul straddles Judaism and Hellenism, so also do the roots of the term and concept of συγκατάβασις, "condescension."[38] The exact term, though not terribly common, was apparently at home in the wide-ranging Greco-Roman discussions of rhetorical adaptability,[39] as used by Philodemus, for instance, to mean "condescension to the level of an audience."[40] Athenaeus preserves a Polybius fragment about Antiochus Epiphanes slipping out of his palace in order to consort with common people by joining their pursuits and condescending to speak their language.[41] Epictetus also used συγκαταβαίνειν when warning his students about being careful not to "stoop down to the level of" someone lower than themselves.[42] But the term is employed with a precise etymological focus in Philo of Alexandria, who uses it to respond to a theological difficulty posed by his Septuagintal biblical text: multiple instances of the God of Israel καταβαίνειν, "coming down" to meet his people.[43] Given Philo's Platonism, this anthropomorphism was patently unacceptable. One of the ways he explained it was by reference to "divine condescension," that God "came down" in mode of communication, but not in body. Philo's discomfort with the texts about God's "coming down" can be seen in his treatment of Gen 11:5 in *Conf.*

> The words, "the Lord came down (κατέβη κύριος) to see the city and the tower" (Gen 11:5), must certainly be understood in a figurative sense (τροπικώτερον). For to suppose that the Deity approaches or departs, goes down or, the opposite, goes up (κατιέναι ἢ τοὐναντίον ἀνέρχεσθαι), or in general remains stationary or puts Himself in motion, as particular living creatures do, is an impiety which may be said to transcend the bounds of the ocean or of the universe itself. No, as I have often said elsewhere, the lawgiver is applying human terms to the superhuman God, to help us, his pupils, to learn our lesson.[44]

Characteristic of Philonic thought is the way in which he deals with the different manifestations of the unchangeable and unseeable God via divine intermediaries such as the Λόγος, λόγοι, αἱ δυνάμεις, and οἱ ἄγγελοι.[45] In *Somn.* 1.147 Philo uses our exact terminology with reference to the λόγοι:

> Up and down throughout its whole extent are moving incessantly the "words" of God (οἱ τοῦ θεοῦ λόγοι),[46] drawing it up with them when they ascend and disconnecting it with what is mortal, and exhibiting to it the spectacle of the only objects worthy of our gaze; and when they descend not casting it down (ὁπότε δὲ κατέρχοιντο οὐ καταβάλλοντες), for neither does God nor does a divine Word cause harm, but condescending out of love for man and compassion for our race (ἀλλὰ συγκαταβαίνοντες διὰ φιλανθρωπίαν καὶ ἔλεον τοῦ γένους ἡμῶν), to be helpers and comrades.[47]

The emphasis here is on the need for condescension to the weak, in order to benefit them rather than cause them harm. Such thinking, and its expression in the term συγκαταβαίνειν, becomes very important for early Christian incarnational christology, which applies this logic to the Logos, Christ. The roots for this christological reflection are clearly manifest in Philo's theology, which is itself (as are so many of his creations) a curious admixture of Jewish theological presuppositions and Greek philosophical and literary notions. The basis of the idea of divine "accommodation" is the variable appearance of the deity, as manifested in a host of biblical theophanies, such as the appearance to Abraham in the form of three men at the Oaks of Mamre (Genesis 18). But the complexity of combinations of traditions at work is shown by the fact that Philo can appeal to none other than Homer as the authority for this notion of divine variability:

> Seeing the vision before his eyes, which was not constant, being at one time that of God, and another time that of strangers, [Abraham] decided to show piety as toward God, and equal oneness and love of man toward the strangers. Some, taking this as a point of departure, have gone astray in their beliefs, for they have been struck by the notion that there are measures and weights of proportion and structure [in God?]. As the clever and considerably learned Homer with beauty of sound describes the conduct of life, it is not right to be harmfully arrogant, for he says that the Deity in the likeness of a beautiful human form is believed to appear many times, (in this) not diverging from the belief of a polytheist. His verses are as follows: "And yet the gods in the likeness of strangers from other lands, in all kinds of form go about unknown, seeing and beholding the many enmities of men and their lawlessness and also their good laws." (*Quaest. Gen.* 4.2)[48]

Philo's commitment to this idea is shown again in *Somn.* 1.232–233, which makes allusion to this same Homeric passage, and demonstrates that the need for divine accommodation arises from the weak disposition of the listener:

> To the souls indeed which are incorporeal and are occupied in His worship it is likely that He should reveal Himself as He is, conversing with them as friend with friends (διαλεγόμενον ὡς φίλον φίλαις); but to souls which are still in a body, giving Himself the likeness of angels, not altering his own nature, for He is unchangeable, but conveying to those which receive the impression of his presence a semblance in a different form (ἑτερόμορφος),[49] such that they take the image to be not a copy, but that original form itself. Indeed an old saying is still current that the deity goes the round of the cities, in the likeness now of this man now of that man (τὸ θεῖον ἀνθρώποις εἰκαζόμενον ἄλλοτε ἄλλοις περινοστεῖ τὰς πόλεις ἐν κύκλῳ), taking note of wrongs and transgressions. The current story may not be a true one, but it is at all events good and profitable for us that it should be current.[50]

Thus in Philo we see a conflation of Old Testament legend, Homeric epic, and Greco-Roman moralistic and rhetorical commonplaces about adaptability, which serve to adjudicate the tension between his Platonic philosophical assumptions about the unchangeable nature of the divine and the variable activity predicated of the God of Israel in the scriptures. From this complex mix is born the idea that God, though unchanging, appears in multiform manifestions in order to accommodate to the weakness of humanity.[51] The Alexandrines Clement and especially Origen learned from Philo this concept of the "condescension" of the Logos,[52] and were easily able to translate it into the incarnation. What is also interesting—and what is of course our focus in this essay—is that they were likewise able to apply it to Pauline variability. As we shall see, they regarded Paul's adaptability as an instance of imitation of Christ's condescension in the incarnation.[53]

Many of the themes that are central to Clement of Alexandria's interpretation are found, and enlarged upon, by the great Alexandrine Origen (c. 185–254), to whom we turn next. In the fragments of his commentary on 1 Corinthians which have been preserved in the catenae, Origen, like Clement of Alexandria, denies that Paul was hypocritical in his behavior, by discussing 1 Cor 9:20 as an instance of Pauline "condescension":

> For Paul used to condescend (συγκατέβαινεν) to the synagogues of the Jews, he used to go in before them, he used to act according to their customs, without harm, not acting hypocritically (or "playing a part") with them (οὐ συνυποκρι–νόμενος), but hunting down some of them.[54]

When Origen turns to 9:21, "to the lawless I have become like a lawless one," he refers to the example of Paul in Athens in Acts 17, and describes his appropriate adaptability of speech to that audience of Greek philosophers, so that "he did not use either prophetic or halachic terms, but if he had a memory of some Greek learning (μάθημα Ἑλληνικόν) from his preparatory instruction he spoke about it to the Athenians."[55] But Origen reiterates Paul's own concern that he not be thought guilty by association. Thus he insists that "when condescending (συγκαταβαίνειν) to them he did not do any lawlessness, but 'I was keeping myself in the law of Christ.'" In *comm. in Joh.* 10.29–30, Origen goes through each of the four self-descriptions of 1 Cor 9:20–22 and presents corresponding examples from Paul's letters or from Acts: he was weak when he made a concession in 1 Cor 7:6;[56] as a Jew when circumcising Timothy and when he shaved and gave an offering (Acts 16:3; 21:24–26);[57] and as one without law in Acts 17:23 and 28.[58] Origen understands Paul's self-description as comprising a quintessential set of examples of appropriate and necessary condescension, and denies any hypocrisy.

This interpretation is especially noteworthy because the theme of divine "condescension" or "accommodation" appears often in Origen's writings, and is of crucial importance to his theology. Origen's familiarity with Hellenistic adaptability *topoi* is manifested in his use of the common examples of the teacher, the father, and the doctor.[59] A fragment on Deut 1:31 preserved in the catenae refers to a homily of Origen's on Jeremiah to explain the phrase "as a man gives nourishment" in regard to the deity:

> He was accommodated (συμπεριηνέχθη) and condescended (συγκατέβη) to us, identifying himself (οἰκειούμενος) with our weakness, like a teacher babbling with the children, like a father fostering his own children, putting on (ὑποδυόμενος)[60] their ways and leading them in a manner suitable to their smallness to the more perfect and higher things.[61]

This commonplace of the child needing to be "talked down to" is given a full and graphic amplification in another of Origen's homilies on Jeremiah, in which he has to try to explain why God would ever "repent":

> "God is not like a human being."[62] But when the divine providence (οἰκονομία)[63] has dealings with human matters, he bears the human mind, and ways, and speech. And this is just as we do, if we are speaking to a two-year-old: we babble (ψελ–λίζειν)[64] for the child's sake. For how could the children possibly understand, if we keep to language worthy of an adult of older age, and speak that way to the children, not condescending (συγκαταβαίνειν) to their way of speaking? Such a thing I presume is also the case with God, when he accommodates (οἰκονομεῖν) to the human race and especially those who are still children. See how we adults change the names of things for children. We call bread a unique word for the children and we call drinking another term, not using the grown up language which we employ toward adults our own age, but a childlike, babyish talk. And if we speak of clothes to children, but we give them other names, it is as if we are fashioning a children's glossary. Then, therefore, are we not full grown? And if someone hears us talking to children will they say, "this old man has become foolish, this man has forgotten his beard, his adult age?" Or is it allowed, for the sake of accommodation (κατὰ συμπεριφοράν), when one is speaking to a child, to speak not in an old or mature person's speech, but that of a child? And God surely speaks to children![65]

In these examples Origen is completely in line with Philo, whose writings he knew well.[66] Indeed in *contra Celsum,* when Origen was challenged by that opponent to explain the scriptural language of divine "descent," he sounds completely Philonic,[67] while simultaneously acknowledging the commonplace nature of his argument:

> For God "comes down" (καταβαίνειν) from his own great-ness and height when he takes charge of (οἰκονομεῖν) human affairs, and especially those of the weak. And as we customar-ily say (ὥσπερ ἡ συνήθεια φησί) that teachers "condescend" (συγκαταβαίνειν) to children, and wise men or advanced pupils condescend to youths who have just now been per-suaded to study philosophy, but not that they "come down" (καταβαίνειν) bodily, thus in the same way, if it is said in places in the divine scriptures that God "came down" (καταβαίνειν), it is to be understood as conforming to this customary use of the term, and likewise also with "going up" (ἀναβαίνειν).[68]

Where Origen's use of the language of condescension has a uniquely Christian cast is of course in his treatment of the incarnation. He inter-prets the hymn in Philippians as the supreme example of "coming down" to the level of human beings, condescending to their constricted ability to gaze upon the divine glory.[69] Origen often interprets the incarnation as such "condescension" of the Logos.[70] What is of prime importance for our topic is that he likewise describes this in Pauline language, as in his commentary on John:

> Therefore the savior, in a more divine fashion than Paul, has become "all things to all people," so that he might either "gain" or perfect "all things," and clearly he has become a human being to human beings and an angel to angels.[71]

All of these themes—condescension, the benefit of the weak, the exam-ple of children, and the *kenōsis* of the Christ in the Philippians hymn—are part of a single complex for Origen, all of which unite in his interpretation of 1 Cor 9:19–23, as can be seen in this final quotation from his Matthew commentary, treating the passage 19:13–15 on "allow-ing the children to come to me":

> Then to exhort his disciples always, though they are adults, to condescend for the benefit of the children (συγκαταβαίνειν τῇ ὠφελείᾳ τῶν παιδίων) (so that they might become as chil-dren to the children so that they might gain the children [ὅπως γένωνται τοῖς παιδίοις ὡς παιδία, ἵνα τὰ παιδία κερδήσωσι]), let the savior say: "the kingdom of the heavens belongs to such as these."[72]

The last patristic author whom we shall examine in this limited survey[73] is John Chrysostom (c. 349–407), the most prolific user of "condescension" language in the early church.[74] Chrysostom's description of συγκατάβασις in his treatise *De incomprehensibili dei natura* served as the definition of the term in the Suidas lexicon.[75]

> And what is condescension (συγκατάβασις)?[76] When God appears, not as he is, but he shows himself in just the manner in which it is possible for one to look upon him, measuring out the manifestation of his outward appearance in proportion to the weakness of the onlookers (τῇ τῶν ὁρώντων ἀσθενείᾳ).[77]

Although we could cite hundreds of instances of Chrysostom's utilization, like Clement and Origen before him, of the language of condescension for the God of Israel and for the incarnation,[78] here we shall focus on his application of this language to Paul. In his homilies on 1 Corinthians, when he reaches our passage, Chrysostom recognizes the need to defend Paul against the charges of hypocrisy and instability: ἦν δὲ ταῦτα οὐχ ὑπόκρισις ἀλλὰ συγκατάβασις καὶ οἰκονομία.[79] In this he was probably responding not only to an anticipated criticism, but to a real one from detractors of Christianity.[80] The defense Chrysostom constructs relies upon the complex of themes related to condescension as we have seen them above. His summary assessment of 1 Cor 9:19–23 is that it is an instance of "extreme condescension" (συγκαταβάσεως ὑπερβολή). Chrysostom urges his auditors likewise to be willing to sink low for the sake of others:

> For this is not to fall down (καταπίπτειν) but to descend (καταβαίνειν). For the one who fell down lies there scarcely able to rise back up. But the one who descended will also rise up, with great gain, just as also Paul descended alone, but rose up with the world, not just play acting (οὐχ ὑποκρινόμενος). For he would not have sought the gain of those who were being saved if he were just playing a role (ὑπεκρίνετο). For the hypocrite (ὑποκριτής) seeks destruction, and he plays a role (ὑποκρίνεται) in order to take, not give. But Paul was not like this. But just like a doctor, like a teacher, like a father, the one to a sick patient, the other to a student and the latter to a child, condescends (συγκαταβαίνει) for correction, not for harm, thus did Paul, too, act.[81]

Clearly Chrysostom has an easy familiarity with the *topoi* of the doctor, teacher, and father for condescension,[82] which excuse what others might interpret as hypocrisy or deceit, by the appeal to the appropriateness of behavior toward the intended addressees. In particular he refers to the benefit for the other as a justification for what might appear to be unscrupulous variability. He also, we should note, registers his own amazement at the extent to which Paul takes his argument in 9:22b with the exclamation: "Do you see the hyperbole" (ὁρᾷς τὴν ὑπερβολήν;)? Perhaps in this we can perceive Chrysostom's awareness of the rhetorical danger of these words, especially in a Greco-Roman context.[83] On another occasion Chrysostom connects Pauline condescension with that of the divine when he says that Paul should not be condemned for variability, at one time being as a Jew, at another time as a lawless man, since "he was imitating his own master, God" in so doing (this follows a long catalogue of the diverse manifestations of the God of Israel in the scriptures).[84] Elsewhere Chrysostom carries this one step further, to indicate that Paul's condescension as described in 1 Cor 9:19–23 was in imitation of Christ's:

> "I became to those under the law as though under the law, so that I might gain those under the law, and being free from all, I enslaved myself to all." Paul was doing these things in imitation of his own master (μιμούμενος τὸν ἑαυτοῦ Δεσπότην). For just as he "being in the form of God did not consider being equal to God a thing to be grasped, but emptied himself, taking the form of a slave, and being free became a slave" (Phil 2:6–7), thus also he, being free from all things, enslaved himself to all so that he might gain all. The Lord became a slave by taking up our nature, so that he might make the slaves free. "He inclined the heavens and came down (κατέβη)" (Ps 17:10), so that he might lead those remaining below into heaven. He did not say, "he left (κατέλιπεν) the heavens and came down," but "he inclined" (ἔκλινεν), making the entrance easier for you into the heavens. This too Paul imitated as was in his power; therefore he also said, "Be imitators of me, as also I am of Christ."[85]

Chrysostom was sure that Christ's example was foremost in Paul's mind as he wrote these words. Could he have been right? Finally we shall return to the question of the provenance of the Pauline sayings themselves.

"Divine Condescension"—An Influence on Paul?

Having established that early Christian interpretation of 1 Cor 9:19–23 regarded Paul as appropriately mirroring the long-standing and well-documented divine technique of condescension, we can now ask if this could have been operative in Paul's own self-understanding. Although the patristic interpreters do not necessarily preserve Paul's own intention, because they are closer to his cultural milieu than we are, their readings are significant, and propose a promising hypothesis that deserves to be tested for Paul himself. I would suggest four supporting arguments for the possibility that Paul was influenced by the theologoumenon of divine condescension as he wrote 1 Cor 9:19–23.[86]

The strongest arguments for this interpretation are internal and exegetical, and were remarked upon by John Chrysostom in what we have just read. The logic of condescension depends upon the concept of "weakness," for a person or a god only needs to "come down" to the level of those others who are in a lower state. The emphasis on weakness in this pericope, with "to the weak I became weak" (ἐγενόμην τοῖς ἀσθενέσιν ἀσθενής) as its crescendo (9:22a), is unarguable. And elsewhere in his Corinthian correspondence Paul will stress Christ's own weakness and affiliation with weakness (2 Cor 12:9–10; 13:4). Like divine variability, the apostolic variability of which Paul speaks is suited to the finitude and capacities of each recipient in the four groups he names, and likewise it has the goal of the benefit, the salvation, of his auditors. Second, with Chrysostom we note the obvious connection of the "Christ-hymn" which Paul quotes in Phil 2:6–11 with 1 Cor 9:19 on the theme of slavery voluntarily undertaken by one who is by nature above that status. And Paul himself makes the connection with Christ in 10:33–11:1, where, after quoting a synonym of "I have been all things to all people," "pleasing all people in all things" (κἀγὼ πάντα πᾶσιν ἀρέσκω) Paul calls on the Corinthians to imitate him, as he does Christ (μιμηταί μου γίνεσθε καθὼς κἀγὼ Χριστοῦ). Third, elsewhere in his correspondence Paul himself uses the customary examples of praiseworthy condescension, most conspicuously in this letter in 3:1–4 and 4:14–15, and he reckons with divine condescension to Jews and Gentiles in Romans 11,[87] and urges a human form of it in imitation of Christ in Rom 15:1–6.[88] Fourth, we have established that the concept of divine condescension was already attested in Hellenistic Judaism (as represented by Philo and Josephus, and rooted in the Septuagint),[89] and that it had been infused with Hellenistic variability *topoi* from Homer and other general lore. As such Paul very likely encountered the concept, and would have been able, as we have demonstrated exegetically, to apply it within his christological framework to this argument on renunciation of specific freedoms for the sake of the weak. The condescension motif may have been a conduit for the variability *topoi* from a range of Hellenistic sources into Pauline thinking.

This is not to minimize those Hellenistic influences in the least, but to reckon with the complex interpenetration of influences on Paul.

Conclusion

The hypothesis I have defended embodies the very dilemmas under discussion in this volume—that also in this case one cannot separate out "Jewish" from "Hellenistic" when evaluating influences on the single person, Paul (or any other Hellenistic Jew)—by suggesting that, even at his most "Hellenistic"-sounding, Paul may still be reading and incorporating Hellenistic lore with a complex mix of Hellenistic Jewish assumptions and reappropriations. And it is this "mix" which should claim our attention. In particular I regard it as significant that Clement of Alexandria, Origen, and John Chrysostom, while never mentioning Odysseus or other Hellenistic figures in connection with Paul's self-characterization, all regard these verses as instances of συγκατάβασις, a technical term for "condescension" or "accommodation for the weaker," an activity characteristic of the God of Israel and his Logos which, these writers easily contended, found human expression also in the work and life of the apostle to the Gentiles. In doing so they stand in a tradition of interpretation that is strongly Philonic (though not confined to him), in an instance where Philo was himself bringing together biblical stories, Platonic philosophical theology, Homeric epic, and Hellenistic moralizing commonplaces. Via this multifaceted appeal to condescension, early interpreters of Paul were able to defuse the negative side of Paul's self-characterization in 1 Cor 9:19–23, of which they were clearly and somewhat anxiously aware, and to make virtue of necessity by transforming the possible embarrassment into a mimetic exemplification of divine goodness and considerate accommodation to human weakness. Such a view is entirely consonant with Paul's own theological perspective and self-understanding.

Chapter 10

Anthropological Duality in the Eschatology of 2 Cor 4:16–5:10

David E. Aune

Introduction

Paul's understanding of the human person and the extent to which his anthropological perspectives were influenced by Jewish or Hellenistic models continues to be debated.[1] His eschatological or apocalyptic thought, on the other hand, while not free of problems, is generally accepted as firmly rooted in Judaism. There are a few places in the Pauline letters where anthropological and eschatological issues converge (1 Cor 15:50–57; 1 Thess 4:13–18; Phil 3:20–21). An additional instance is 2 Cor 5:17, where Paul has used the apocalyptic two-age model as a pattern for understanding the juxtaposition of the old and the new in the "eschatological existence"[2] of the Christian person: "If a person is in Christ, there is a new creation; the old has come to an end, behold the new has come into being."[3] In another such passage, one which is extremely problematic and which is also the focus of this paper, 2 Cor 4:16–5:10, Paul uses a medley of anthropological and eschatological motifs from Hellenism,[4] early Judaism and early Christianity to propose an eschatological resolution to the tension between the internal and external aspects of daily Christian experience.[5] In an immediately preceding section of text (4:7–11), Paul has contrasted the "treasure" (= the "life of Jesus") that Christians carry about within fragile earthen vessels (= their physical bodies). Paradoxically, suffering and persecution is the daily means whereby the presence of Jesus is revealed alive and at work within them.

Second Corinthians 4:16–5:10 uses a number of antitheses to contrast the present condition of Christians with the future realization of eschatological salvation, most of which appear to be of Hellenistic origin: (1) ὁ ἔξω ἄνθρωπος vs. ὁ ἔσω (ἄνθρωπος), "the outer person" vs. "the inner (person)" (4:16), (2) τὰ βλεπόμενα vs. τὰ μὴ βλεπόμενα, "the visible" vs. "the invisible" (4:18a), (3) πρόσκαιρος vs. αἰώνιος, "temporal vs. eternal" (4:18b), (4) ἡ ἐπίγειος οἰκία vs. οἰκία αἰώνιος ἐν τοῖς οὐρα–νοῖς, "an earthly house" vs. "an eternal house in heaven" (5:1), (5) γυμ–νοί and ἐκδύσασθαι vs. ἐνδυσάμενοι and ἐπενδύσασθαι "naked" and "unclothed" (i.e., "disembodied") vs. "clothed" and "put on an additional garment" (5:3–4). On the other hand, the brief reference to Christians appearing before "the judgment seat of Christ" to be rewarded or punished in accordance with their works (2 Cor 5:10), just as clearly originated in a Christian adaptation of a common eschatological theme from Jewish apocalypticism. Some features of this passage, however, rest comfortably neither with typical Hellenistic nor early Jewish conceptions, such as Paul's emphasis on the individual believer's postmortem dwelling in a heavenly residence (2 Cor 5:1).

The diverse cultural backgrounds of the anthropological and eschatological motifs that are concentrated in 2 Cor 4:16–5:10 make this a promising passage for testing the limitations of investing too heavily in understanding Pauline thought as largely explicable in terms of a conscious or unconscious debt to either early Jewish or Hellenistic influences. Hellenism and early Judaism are hardly mutually exclusive contexts for understanding Paul's letters, nor should the creative genius of Paul as a religious thinker be underestimated. In this essay, therefore, I propose a reading of 2 Cor 4:16–5:10 that attempts to understand the intersection of the anthropological and eschatological ideas found in this passage against whatever linguistic or conceptual background seems appropriate. Exploring the meaning and significance of these ideas in this passage will have priority, though it will also be appropriate to clarify some of the ways in which this text coheres with select themes in other eschatological scenarios in the Pauline corpus.

Apocalyptic and Hellenistic Eschatologies

In early Judaism and early Christianity, "apocalyptic eschatology" refers to the belief systems reflected in, but not limited to, early Jewish apocalypses (e.g., 1 Enoch, 2 Enoch, 4 Ezra, 2 Baruch, the Apocalypse of Abraham) and the earliest Christian apocalypse (Apocalypse of John).[6] "Apocalyptic eschatology" refers to a belief in the imminent end of an evil and oppressive world system that will occur through the decisive intervention of God, often thought to involve a decisive conflict between the people of God (with God or the Messiah as their champion) and the ungodly. The transition to God's rule in the world will be preceded by the judgment of the wicked and the reward of the righteous, following the resurrection of the righteous or of both the righteous and wicked. The ultimate defeat and judgment of evil (Satan, his demonic allies, and those humans they have led astray) will usher in a new age of righteousness in a renewed world. In apocalyptic eschatology, the primary dualism is temporal, involving a distinction between "this age" and "the age to come," though a spatial dualism of heaven and earth forms a traditional part of the basic apocalyptic perception of reality.

"Hellenistic eschatology," which exhibits great variety, refers to the spectrum of beliefs in the Hellenistic world involving death and the afterlife on the one hand, and cosmic destruction and renewal on the other, gathered from a variety of Greek sources beginning with Homer and Hesiod (which continued to be read through late antiquity),[7] and including Greek underworld mythology reflected in literary sources and epitaphs (including accounts of descents to the underworld and ascents to the realm of the planet and stars),[8] as well as the philosophical speculation of Plato (particularly in the *Timaeus*)[9] and Hellenistic philosophical traditions.[10] Hellenistic eschatology includes beliefs about the fate of the individual both in this world and the next, including death (as the separation of the soul from the body), and varied conceptions of the afterlife, optionally including some form of postmortem judgment, the possibility in some traditions of metempsychosis, and the eternal state of existence of the inner person, normally designated as the ψυχή ("soul") or νοῦς ("mind").[11] The primary form of dualism in Hellenistic eschatology is the distinction between mortality (characteristic of humans) and immortality (characteristic of the gods), though through time a happy afterlife became an increasingly common possibility for the ordinary dead.[12]

In these ideal formulations, it is obvious that few features are shared by both apocalyptic eschatology and Hellenistic eschatology, giving the

mistaken impression that there was some sort of invisible cultural boundary separating one system from the other. In reality, apocalyptic eschatology is a relatively narrow construct with a heyday of about three
centuries in some but by no means all segments of early Judaism (250
B.C.E. to 150 C.E.). In early Christianity, apocalyptic eschatology is
reflected in the Pauline letters, the Synoptic Gospels, and the Apocalypse
of John, but had all but disappeared or been transformed by the end of
the first century C.E., so that it is hardly a significant factor at all in those
early second-century Christian writings collectively designated as the
Apostolic Fathers. The matrix for the specific content of apocalyptic
eschatology was traditional Israelite-Jewish concerns about the death and
the afterlife of the individual found reflected in the Old Testament (which
exerted a perennial influence on Jewish beliefs) and the considerable body
of the non-eschatologically focused literature of early Judaism, which
provides occasional glimpses of funerary customs and beliefs.[13] Quite
apart from the issue of Hellenistic influence, the death and afterlife of the
individual were enduring concerns of early Judaism and its offshoot, early
Christianity.

One of the main reasons for the dissimilarity between apocalyptic and
Hellenistic eschatology is that in apocalyptic eschatology (in both its
early Jewish and early Christian forms), the individual is embedded in
the community, and the focal eschatological events (e.g., the great tribu-
lation, the parousia, the resurrection, the last judgment) involve not so
much the particular experience of isolated individuals as the community
to which those individuals belong (whether Israel, the remnant, the righteous, the "sons of light," or the followers of Jesus). Communal embed-
dedness is largely absent from Hellenistic eschatologies, however, and the
focal eschatological events are those that involve the death and postmortem experiences of the individual person. Hellenistic eschatology
was never culturally walled-off from either early Judaism or early Christianity, and the eschatologies of both were inexorably subject to subtly
modulated syncretistic pressures that led to the increasing assimilation of
Hellenistic eschatological conceptions.[14] The apocalypse genre inherited
from early Judaism essentially disappeared by the early second century
in early Christianity after the Revelation of John and the Shepherd of
Hermas, and was superseded by a different form of apocalypse that centered on narrations of tours of Hades (such as the Apocalypse of Peter),
which closely resembled pagan Greek narratives of descents to the underworld, in which visionary accounts of the postmortem sufferings of the
wicked served to reinforce the importance of ethical living in this
world.[15]

Approaches to 2 Cor 4:16–5:10

Second Corinthians 4:16–5:10 is one of the more problematic texts in the Pauline corpus and consequently has engendered an extensive discussion among New Testament scholars,[16] often motivated by the problem of reconciling Paul's eschatological perspective here with apparently different perspectives elsewhere in his letters (particularly 1 Cor 15:50–57; 1 Thess 4:13–18; Phil 3:20–21).[17] The differences between 2 Cor 4:16–5:10 and these other Pauline texts have been explained in a number of ways: (1) For some, the differences are primarily due to a change in perspective, either a change in Paul's own outlook (e.g., the development of his eschatological thought, between the composition of 1 and 2 Corinthians),[18] or to the changed situation of the Corinthian congregation (e.g., the appearance in Corinth, between the composition of 1 Corinthians and the letter fragments comprising 2 Corinthians, of anti-Pauline Christian missionaries).[19] (2) Another interpretive strategy has been to regard the passage as a dialogical section in which Paul engages his opponents in Corinth (whether identified as Gnostics, adherents to a form of Platonism, or Jewish Christians enamored with apocalyptic) in a conversation in which he has incorporated some of their language into the discussion (such as the Platonic antithesis ὁ ἔξω ἄνθρωπος – ὁ ἔσω ἄνθρωπος in 2 Cor 4:16), though introducing modifications, and using such language in his own distinctive way.[20] (3) Yet another interpretive strategy, though one which has found little acceptance, has been to construe the apparently eschatological language of 2 Cor 4:16–5:10 as referring exclusively to the present experience of Paul and other Christians.[21]

Specific features of 2 Cor 4:16–5:10 have also been subject to a number of conflicting interpretations. For some, Paul no longer expects the parousia to occur imminently, but regards the death of the individual believer as the norm.[22] For others, death results in an intermediate state of "nakedness," which will be resolved when the dead in Christ are clothed with the resurrection body at the parousia.[23] Yet others hold that those who through death are separated from their earthly body immediately receive a heavenly or resurrection body.[24] Further, both positive and negative reactions to the number of ostensibly Hellenistic conceptions that are clustered together in this brief passage and its immediate context has also sparked discussion. Although terms like "parousia," "resurrection," and "spiritual (resurrection) body" do not actually appear in 2 Cor 4:16–5:10, it is nevertheless not uncommon for interpreters to import these conceptions from other eschatological passages in the Pauline letters, often with the understandable concern of trying to discern the consistency in Paul's eschatological thought. In fact, however, the only motif drawn from Christian apocalyptic eschatology in this passage is the reference to the final judgment in v. 10 mentioned above: "For we must all appear before the judgment seat of Christ, so that each one may receive good or evil, according to what he has done in the body."

Interpreting Selected Themes in 2 Cor 4:16–5:10

Though many discussions focus on 2 Cor 5:1–10 as a textual subunit, it is important to ignore the inappropriate chapter division and recognize the coherence of the larger textual unit in 2 Cor 4:16–5:10,[25] and the even more comprehensive textual unit in 2 Cor 4:1–6:10. The antithetical style, which begins in 4:16 and continues through 5:10, links the core of this subunit together stylistically and rhetorically. Second Corinthians 4:1–6:10 is in turn part of the larger apologetic section consisting of 2 Cor 2:14–7:4 (excluding 6:14–7:1).[26] Second Corinthians 4:16–5:10 itself consists of three closely related subunits, 4:16–18 (introduced with the inferential conjunction διό, pointing back to 4:7–15), 5:1–5 (introduced with γάρ, which provides a basis for the statement in 4:18, and with the καὶ γάρ of vv. 2 and 4 used to introduce further support for 4:18), and 5:6–10 (introduced by οὖν in v. 6). In what follows, I will try to provide an explanation of the meaning of some of the major problems and issues in 2 Cor 4:16–5:10.

The Outer Person and the Inner Person (4:16)

The central interpretive problem in this verse is the meaning of the complementary phrases ὁ ἔξω ἄνθρωπος and ὁ ἔσω (ἄνθρωπος). The antithesis ὁ ἔξω ἄνθρωπος and ὁ ἔσω (ἄνθρωπος), "the outer person" and "the inner (person)" in 2 Cor 4:16, clearly expresses an anthropological *duality* (here I avoid the terms *dualistic* or *dualism* because they are often understood to connote opposition or conflict),[27] widely thought to allude to a philosophical theme that first appears in Plato *Republic* 9.588a–589b.[28] There Plato proposed a symbolic or mythical image of the tripartite soul (εἰ κὼν τῆς ψυχῆς, 588b) that took account of the experience of inner conflict. While the external container (τὸ ἔξω ἔλυτρον) of the human person is visible to others, the soul within is tripartite, including a πολυκέφαλον θηρίον or πολυκέφαλον θρέμμα, "a many-headed beast" (= the ἐπιθυμητικόν, the desiring part of the soul), a lion (= the θυμοειδές, the courageous part of the soul) and τοῦ ἀνθρ–

ὥπου ὁ ἐντὸς ἄνθρωπος, "the inner person" (= the λογιστικόν, the reasoning part of the soul). In the just individual, the inner person tames the inner beast and trains the lion to serve with him. The phrase ὁ ἐντὸς ἄνθρωπος occurs nowhere else in Plato's writings, though he does say elsewhere that ἡ ψυχή ἐστιν ἄνθρωπος, "the soul is the person," and that the soul should rule the body rather than the reverse (*Alc.* 1.130c).[29] The dichotomy between the inner and outer person was expressed in a variety of ways throughout Greco-Roman antiquity,[30] and the phrase ὁ ἐντὸς ἄνθρωπος never became a technical term for the inner person or νοῦς ("mind") until it was adopted by the church fathers and Neoplatonist philosophers in late antiquity.[31]

Both members of this "Platonic" antithesis occur in 2 Cor 4:16, where ὁ ἔξω ἄνθρωπος is described as "wasting away" (διαφθείρεται), while ὁ ἔσω (ἄνθρωπος) is said to be "renewed" (ἀνακαινοῦται) day by day. The ἔξω ἄνθρωπος is identified in the context as ὀστράκινον σκεῦος, an "earthen vessel" (4:7),[32] as σῶμα, "body" (4:10), as θνητὴ σάρξ, "mortal flesh" (4:11), ἡ ἐπίγειος ἡμῶν οἰκία τοῦ σκήνους, "our earthly dwelling or body" (5:1) and τὸ σκῆνος, "this (ephemeral) body" and τὸ θνητόν, "the mortal element" (5:4).[33] Together, these designations indicate that ὁ ἔξω ἄνθρωπος is a metaphor for the physical body, which is subject to weakness, disease, aging, and death. However, it is not described either as inherently evil or as in opposition to ὁ ἔσω ἄνθρωπος, though the outer person and the inner person are clearly in tension, for the latter is "sighing under a burden,"[34] i.e., desiring release from the drawbacks of physical existence.[35] It must also be made clear that while ὁ ἔσω ἄνθρωπος is not described as the soul or mind in typical Greek conceptual categories, it is certainly described as that part of the Christian person which survives physical death and lives on in a superior and transformed state of existence in heaven. When Paul uses the phrase ὁ ἔσω ἄνθρωπος again a few years later in Rom 7:22, he equates it with the νοῦς in vv. 23 and 25, an equation frequently made by Philo. Even though "the inner person" in Rom 7:22 refers to what the individual ought to be in contrast to what he or she actually is,[36] Paul's use of ὁ ἔσω ἄνθρωπος in both passages is basically similar. Perhaps I can conclude that while Paul may not have regarded the body as a tomb (the famous Orphic motto appropriated by Plato), it appears that, on the whole, he would rather be elsewhere (to paraphrase Paul in 5:8 as well as W. C. Fields).

What is Paul's source for this "outer person"/"inner person" dichotomy? While the concept of the "inner person" occurs for the first time in Plato

Republic 9.588a–589b (where the antithetical expression "the outer person" is missing), discussed briefly above, it is not at all obvious how this concept was transmitted to Paul.[37] He probably had not read Plato's *Republic*, and even if he did, he did not follow Plato in construing the "inner person" as the dominating rational faculty in a tripartite division of the soul. The difference in meaning and function between ὁ ἔσω ἄνθρωπος in Paul and τοῦ ἀνθρώπου ὁ ἐντὸς ἄνθρωπος in Plato suggests that at best he was only *indirectly* dependent on Plato, perhaps through popular forms of Platonism. Philo, an earlier contemporary of Paul, had read Plato and was certainly familiar with the relevant passage in the *Republic* (9.588a–589b).[38] He refers to the "inner person" using a variety of synonymous phrases, including τὸν ἐν ἡμῖν πρὸς ἀλήθειαν ἄνθρωπον, τουτέστι τὸν νοῦν, "the real person within us, that is, the mind" (*Plant.* 42), ὁ ἀληθινὸς ἄνθρωπος, "the true person" (*Det.* 10) and ἄνθρωπος ἐν ἀνθρώπῳ, "the person within the person," again a metaphor for the νοῦς, which is further characterized as "the better part within the worse, the immortal within the mortal" (*Congr.* 97). The slim evidence for the use of the concept between Plato and Philo makes the hypothesis of Paul's dependence on popular forms of Platonism which mediated the ὁ ἔσω ἄνθρωπος conception precarious though not impossible. Earlier, Jewett had proposed that in 2 Cor 4:16–5:10, Paul had co-opted the language of his Gnostic opponents in Corinth,[39] while more recently Heckel has argued that Paul had taken up the language of his opponents, the religious Platonists in Corinth, in order to provide a radical reinterpretation of that language.[40] In view of the fact that the notion of "the inner person" is not expressed in stereotypical language until late antiquity, Markschiess is probably correct in proposing that Paul himself coined the specific antithesis ὁ ἔξω ἄνθρωπος and ὁ ἔσω (ἄνθρωπος) to express a conception of Platonic origin that had been current for a very long time.[41]

In summary, ὁ ἔξω ἄνθρωπος is a metaphor for the transient physical body, which is in tension though not conflict with ὁ ἔσω ἄνθρωπος, and could appropriately be described as the vessel or container of ὁ ἔσω ἄνθρωπος. Indeed, another metaphor for ὁ ἔσω ἄνθρωπος in this context is οἰκία, a house whose occupant must leave when it is destroyed (2 Cor 5:1). While in 2 Cor 4:16, Paul does not describe ὁ ἔσω ἄνθρωπος as the soul or mind in typical Greek conceptual categories (though in 1 Thess 5:23, Paul is not averse to using the phrase "spirit and soul and body" to refer to the human person), when he uses the same phrase in Rom 7:22, he equates it with his νοῦς in Rom 7:23, 25. ὁ ἔσω ἄνθρωπος is (as we will learn from 2 Cor 5:1), the enduring inner reality that survives physical death to enjoy a more preferred state of existence in heaven.

From an Earthly House to a Heavenly House (5:1)

Second Corinthians 5:1 consists of a conditional sentence introduced by a phrase that seems to indicate that what follows is common knowledge: "For we know that if our earthly house, or body, is destroyed, we have a habitation from God, a house not man-made, eternal in the heavens." In v. 1a, the verb οἴδαμεν introduces an objective ὅτι-clause, which consists of the protasis and apodosis of a conditional sentence which makes up the remainder of v. 1. While Paul's use of the first-person plural is complex,[42] it is likely that οἴδαμεν here is not an simply an epistolary formula (the editorial "we" which really means "I"). Since Paul frequently used the phrase οἴδαμεν ὅτι to emphasize knowledge that he shared with his audience,[43] it is likely that it is used that way here.[44] If he is appealing to common knowledge, he is unlikely to be in dialogue with Corinthian opponents, unless agreement with his audience is a way of opposing the contrary position of a third party.

The phrase "if our earthly house, or body, is destroyed," is the protasis of a conditional sentence consisting of ἐάν + aorist subjunctive. ἐάν + subjunctive in any tense is an ambiguous construction in Hellenistic Greek, which often conveys the semantic meaning that it is uncertain of fulfillment but still likely. But it can also indicate, depending on the context, certainty of fulfillment, probability of fulfillment, improbability of fulfillment or no indication of fulfillment. I have translated ἐάν as "when" (implying increased probability) rather than "if" (suggesting reduced probability) because in this context the semantic meaning of ἐάν refers to a point of time (defined by the aorist subjunctive καταλυθῇ in the protasis) which is somewhat conditional and simultaneous with another point of time (defined by the verb ἔχομεν in the apodosis).[45] The pattern involved is: when A occurs, then (immediately) B occurs.

The aorist passive verb καταλυθῆναι means "to be destroyed" (frequently used of the literal demolition of buildings)[46] and is therefore appropriately used with οἰκία for the destruction of a house as a metaphor referring to death as the destruction of the physical body (σκῆνος).[47] οἰκία is, after all, the grammatical subject of καταλυθῇ. The formulation of the protasis leaves no room for the possible occurrence of the parousia, which might interrupt the fate of physical death which awaits everyone.[48] Paul refers to death in two other ways in 2 Cor 4:16–5:10. In v. 8a, he expresses the desire that "we would rather be away from the body (ἐκδημῆσαι ἐκ τοῦ σώματος) and at home with the Lord." Here ἐκδημέω means literally "to leave home," and is used with ἐκ τοῦ σώματος as an idiom for death. In the phrase εἴτε ἐνδημοῦντες, εἴτε ἐκδημοῦντες in

v. 9, the second phrase should be construed as εἴτε ἐκδημοῦντες (ἐκ τοῦ σώματος), ("or away *from the body*"), parallel to the phrase ἐκδημῆσαι ἐκ τοῦ σώματος in v. 8,[49] a third way of alluding to physical death.

In the pleonastic phrase ἡ οἰκία τοῦ σκήνους, the genitive τοῦ σκήνους is appositional or epexegetical and the whole phrase can therefore be translated "the house, i.e., the body."[50] The genitive of apposition is Paul's way of explicitly interpreting the metaphor ἡ οἰκία ("house") as really referring to the σκῆνος ("body"). Paul chooses not to use the term σῶμα here, though it occurs four times in the immediate context (4:10; 5:6, 8, 10), perhaps because σκῆνος is a more vivid Hellenistic term for the ephemeral human body (see below), a denotation not found in σῶμα. In 1 Cor 15:35–44, Paul uses the antithetical phrases σῶμα ἐπουράνιον / σῶμα ἐπίγειον (1 Cor 15:40) and σῶμα ψυχικόν / σῶμα πνευματικόν (1 Cor 15:44) and in Phil 3:21 he anticipates that the τὸ σῶμα τῆς ταπεινώσεως of the Christian will be transformed on analogy with τὸ σῶμα τῆς δόξης, i.e., the resurrected body of Christ. In 2 Cor 4:7–5:10, however, he has reserved the term σῶμα for earthly, mortal existence, and relies on various other building and clothing metaphors to depict the future state of believers.

Why did Paul change his way of speaking about future resurrection existence or heavenly existence? Walter has suggested that Paul was not theologically satisfied with his earlier use of σῶμα in 1 Cor 15,[51] while Jewett argues that the use of σῶμα in 2 Cor 5:6–8 is thoroughly Gnostic, and is actually a quotation by Paul of a Gnostic argument in order to integrate their views into his own eschatology.[52] Neither of these suggestions is completely convincing. More likely Paul does not refer to the postmortem heavenly state of existence with the term σῶμα, because he reserves that term for the resurrection body and in 2 Cor 4:16–5:10 he is not dealing with that subject.

While σκῆνος (used again in v. 4) has the basic semantic meanings "tent" and "[ephemeral] body" (the latter is a figurative extension in meaning of the former), here and in v. 4 the meaning is clearly "[ephemeral] body"[53] (often used in Greek literature in contrast to the soul) with the denotation of the temporary nature of physical existence.[54] A close parallel is found in 2 Pet 1:13–14, where "Peter" says:

> I consider it right, as long as I am in this body (ἐν τούτῳ σκηνώματι), to arouse you by remembrance, knowing that the abandonment of my body (ἡ ἀπόθεσις τοῦ σκηνώματός μου; i.e., my death) will be soon, as our Lord Jesus Christ showed me.

Here σκήνωμα, a formation that is a cognate of σκῆνος, clearly means "[ephemeral] body" rather than "tent" and the negative connotation of ἀπόθεσις contributes a negative denotation to σκήνωμα.

The figurative meaning of σκῆνος for the human body, emphasizing both its temporary and insubstantial nature, was widespread throughout the Hellenistic world.[55] One of the earliest uses of σκῆνος with the meaning "body" is found in Democritus (frag. B 187), a passage in which σῶμα and σκῆνος are used as synonyms:[56]

> ἀνθρώποις ἁρμόδιον ψυχῆς μᾶλλον ἢ σώματος λόγον
> ποιεῖσθαι· ψυχῆς μὲν γὰρ τελεότης σκήνεος μοχθηρίην
> ὀρθοῖ, σκήνεος δὲ ἰσχὺς ἄνευ λογισμοῦ ψυχὴν οὐδέν τι
> ἀμείνω τίθησιν.

> It is right that people should value the soul rather than the
> body; for perfection of soul corrects the inferiority of the body,
> but strength of body without intelligence does nothing to
> improve the mind.

Though this meaning of σκῆνος has no counterpart in Hebrew or Aramaic words for "tent," it was occasionally adopted by Jews[57] and early Christians[58] who wrote in Greek. Wis 9:15 is a frequently cited parallel to 2 Cor 5:1:

> φθαρτὸν γὰρ σῶμα <u>βαρύνει</u> ψυχήν,
> καὶ βρίθει τὸ <u>γεῶδες σκῆνος</u> νοῦν πολυφρόντιδα.

> For a perishable body weighs down the soul,
> and this earthly body burdens the thoughtful mind.

The underlined words in this quotation indicate relatively close verbal parallels with 2 Cor 5:1–10: (1) βαρέω (v. 4), (2) ἐπίγειος (v. 1), and (3) σκῆνος (vv. 1, 4), which suggests Paul's familiarity with this Hellenistic Jewish mediation of Platonic tradition, if not with this passage itself.[59] σκῆνος is also used with the meaning "body" in *Par. Jer.* (or *4 Bar.*) 6:6, a Greco-Jewish writing composed early in the second century C.E.:

> ἑτοίμασον σεαυτήν, ἡ καρδία μου, εὐφραίνου, καὶ ἀγάλλου
> ἐν τῷ σκηνώματί σου λέγων τῷ σαρκικῷ οἴκῳ σου· τὸ πέν–
> θος σου μετεστράφη εἰς χαράν· ἔρχεται γὰρ ὁ ἱκανός, καὶ
> ἀρεῖ σε ἐν τῷ σκηνώματί σου, οὐ γὰρ γέγονέ σοι ἁμαρτία.

> Prepare yourself, my heart, and rejoice and be glad while you
> are in your body, saying to your fleshly house, "Your grief has

been changed to joy," for the Sufficient One is coming and
will deliver you in your body—for there is no sin in you.

One of the fragments appended to *Aphorisms* 7, the most popular section of the Hippocratic corpus, describes the moment of death in these
words: "And the soul, leaving the tent, i.e., the body (τὸ τοῦ σώματος
σκῆνος), gives up the cold and mortal image to bile, blood, phlegm, and
flesh."[60] Here σκῆνος is used with the literal meaning "tent," while τοῦ
σώματος is a genitive of apposition, explaining the metaphorical meaning of σκῆνος. These uses of σκῆνος confirm the fact that the word has
two basic meanings, "tent" and "[ephemeral] body," and that the latter
meaning is most appropriate in 2 Cor 5:1a.

Turning now to 2 Cor 5:1b, there are several exegetical problems in the
apodosis: (1) Does the verb ἔχομεν refer to the present or future? (2) Does
the οἰκοδομὴν ἐκ θεοῦ refer to the individual resurrection body of the
believer (either reserved in heaven or attainable at the parousia), to a corporate entity such as the Church, to the resurrected body of Christ,[61] or
to some other heavenly reality? (3) Is this eternal heavenly dwelling temporary (i.e., an "intermediate state") or permanent?

(1) The subject of the first-person plural verb ἔχομεν is that inner aspect
or part of the person that will not be destroyed by death, explicitly contrasted with the dwelling place, garment, or body where the inner person
resides, whether earthly or heavenly, but never completely identified with
either. An implicit anthropological duality is reflected here.[62] ἔχομεν functions as the main verb in the apodosis of a conditional sentence and as such
defines the action that will occur when the protasis is fulfilled. There is some
grammatical ambiguity, since ἔχομεν (translated "we have" or "we already
have"), can be construed as a present conveying certainty (i.e., the action
of ἔχομεν occurs *immediately* upon the fulfillment of the protasis, i.e.,
death),[63] or as a futuristic present (intrinsically unlikely), the equivalent of
ἕξομεν (i.e., the fulfillment of the action of ἔχομεν occurs *after an indeterminate interval of time*).[64] If the fulfillment is immediate, the one who dies
comes into possession of the οἰκοδομὴ ἐκ θεοῦ (a heavenly alternative to
the earthly outer person) instantaneously, whereas if the fulfillment occurs
only after an undetermined interval of time, e.g., until the parousia, then
the possession of the οἰκοδομὴ ἐκ θεοῦ is delayed. Construing ἔχομεν as
a future is a possible but labored attempt to insert an intermediate state
between the destruction of the earthly house and the possession of the heavenly habitation. It is a more natural reading of the text to construe ἔχομεν
to mean "we [already] have," indicating that the οἰκοδομὴ ἐκ θεοῦ is an
existing heavenly reality that Christians will inhabit when they die.

(2) With regard to the phrase οἰκοδομὴ ἐκ θεοῦ ("building of God"), it is striking that although terms like "parousia," "resurrection," and "spiritual body" do not actually occur in 2 Cor 4:16–5:10, they are frequently imported into the discussion in the attempt to understand this passage in the context of other eschatological scenarios found in Paul. The phrase that immediately follows, οἰκίαν ἀχειροποίητον αἰώνιον ἐν τοῖς οὐρανοῖς ("a house made without hands eternal in heaven") is used in apposition to οἰκοδομὴ ἐκ θεοῦ, indicating that οἰκοδομή and οἰκία are synonymous. The three dwelling metaphors (οἰκοδομή, οἰκία, and οἰκητήριον) are clearly ways of referring to the same basic heavenly reality.[65] The use of three different but etymologically related words may be due either to the fact that Paul has no fixed nomenclature for conceptualizing the heavenly mode of existence he wishes to describe or that he is simply not interested in a systematic presentation. Whatever the reason, he does not choose to use the antithetical phrases σῶμα ψυχικόν and σῶμα πνευματικόν for the heavenly mode of existence here as he did in 1 Cor 15:42–44,[66] perhaps because here he is focusing on the contrast between the less desirable *here*, but the more desirable *there*. As already noted, a number of scholars have proposed that οἰκοδομή, οἰκία, and οἰκητήριον should be understood, not as metaphors for the heavenly mode of existence of individual believers, but rather as corporate entities, i.e., either as metaphors for the church as the body of Christ,[67] or for the heavenly temple or city which will be revealed in the eschaton.[68] The main obstacle to both views is that if the phrase ἡ ἐπίγειος οἰκία τοῦ σκήνους in v. 1 is the body of the individual Christian, that with which it is replaced upon death whether called οἰκοδομή, οἰκία, or οἰκητήριον (vv. 1–2), must probably refer to the heavenly counterpart of the earthly body of the individual.[69] On the other hand, it is also possible that Paul is expressing himself asymmetrically, i.e., an individual dwelling *here* is contrasted with a corporate dwelling *there*.

(3) For whatever reason, most commentators fail to deal with what appears to be a central problem in 2 Cor 5:1, namely the postmortem presence *in heaven* of believers. This expectation is phrased differently in 5:8, where Paul observes that Christians "would rather be away from the body and at home with the Lord," a statement with a close parallel in Phil 1:23, where Paul expresses the desire "to depart and be with Christ, which is far better." From the perspective of the Old Testament, it is simply not possible for mortals to go to heaven after death.[70] The tradition of the translations of Enoch and Elijah are exceptions that prove the rule, just as only exceptional Greek heroes like Menelaus spent the afterlife in Elysion or the Islands of the Blessed rather than Hades, the postmortem

destination of most mortals.[71] The conception of the righteous dwelling in heaven can be roughly correlated with the adoption of the so-called "new cosmology," i.e., the geocentric view of the cosmos that emerged during the Hellenistic period which held that the earth was stationary at the lowest or innermost part of the cosmos and was surrounded by seven planetary spheres (which rotated west to east) enclosed by an eighth sphere consisting of the fixed stars (which rotated east to west); the gods were thought to dwell in the highest sphere. During the late Hellenistic period a number of Jewish apocalyptic writers adopted an analogous geocentric view of the universe in which the earth was surmounted by three or seven heavens, with God enthroned in the highest heaven.[72] Despite the obvious similarities, there appears to be no demonstrable genetic relationship between the seven heavens of Judaism (probably of Babylonian origin) and the seven planetary spheres of Hellenism.[73]

In the world of Roman Hellenism, the new cosmology was generally presupposed by Jews as well as by Greeks and Romans.[74] Under the archaic three-tiered cosmology, the dead were thought to reside in Hades under the earth. According to the new cosmology, upon death, the soul (which was considered weightless) was separated from the body (which was thought heavy) and ascended upward. In the myth of Thespius narrated by Plutarch, postmortem punishment and reward both take place in regions above the earth (*De sera numinis vindicta* 564E–566A). According to one view, the mind was produced by the sun, the soul by the moon, and the body by earth; upon death, each returned to the place of their origin (Plutarch, *De facie* 943A–B; 945B–C). A preference for a heavenly mode of existence is similarly expressed by the Roman Stoic Seneca (*Ep.* 102.22):[75]

> When the day comes to separate the heavenly from the earthly blend, I shall leave the body here where I found it and shall of my own volition betake myself to the gods. I am not apart from them now, but am merely detained in a heavy and earthly prison. These delays of mortal existence are a prelude to the larger and better life.

This coheres with the views of some later Stoics, when Stoicism had been combined with Platonism, that the soul originated in heaven or the stars, and would eventually return there (Seneca *Ep.* 92.30–34).

When Paul says that upon death "we [already] have a building from God, eternal in the heavens" (5:1b), he means that the inner person, upon the destruction of his earthly dwelling or body immediately takes up residence in an analogous heavenly dwelling. Paul's conception is clearly similar to the late Platonic and late Stoic conceptuality of Plutarch and Seneca, though neither has a counterpart to Paul's use of the terms οἰκοδομή, οἰκία, or οἰκητήριον for the heavenly dwelling of the inner person.

Though Unclothed, We Shall Not Be Found Naked (5:3)

Both γυμνός ("naked") and ἐκδύσασθαι ("to remove one's clothes") are metaphors based on activities involving clothing; both are common Greek metaphors for conceptualizing the relationship between the body and soul.[76] These references have been interpreted in one of at least three ways:[77] (1) Paul wishes to avoid the temporary loss of the body by believers before the parousia (when deceased believers will receive a resurrection body and living believers a transformed body). (2) Paul disagrees with the view (held by Gnostics,[78] among others) that the "naked" or "unclothed" self of believers returns to the heavenly realm for a final state of salvation unencumbered by any sort of body.[79] (3) "Nakedness" applies to the future state of unbelievers (cf. 4 Ezra 7:80).[80]

The conception of "nakedness" is a metaphor used with some frequency in Greek philosophical and quasi-philosophical literature for the state of the soul that has left the body at death.[81] In these contexts *the term is always understood in a positive sense*. In contrast, it has often been emphasized that the phrase "in the hope that we, being clothed, shall not be found naked" (v. 3),[82] does not contemplate the state of γυμνός as either inevitable or desirable. The same is true for the use of the verb ἐκ-δύ-σασθαι in v. 4, in the phrase "we do not wish to be unclothed (ἐκδύσασθαι)." That is, Paul appears to be implicitly arguing against the widespread view of Hellenistic eschatology that the postmortem freedom of the soul free from the body is a desirable and permanent form of future existence.[83] It is unnecessary to insist that Paul is rejecting a particular form of Hellenistic eschatology (such as Gnosticism) with this statement since the sentiment was so widely held.

The classical Greek view of death exhibited some variety, though in general it was regarded as the event that separated body from soul. The question of the immortality of the soul was more problematic.[84] "Most people," according to Plato, thought that the soul ceased to exist when separated from the body (*Phaedo* 69e–70a). This view is supported by a considerable body of evidence from epitaphs indicating that many ancients denied any kind of postmortem existence whatsoever.[85] For others, however, the soul (whether material or immaterial) was contained within the body, and upon death was released to travel to the underworld, a remote region, or the sky (Cicero, *Tusc. disp.* 1.24, 40, 42, 75), to join other similarly disembodied, strengthless images.[86] For Stoics, on the other hand, the soul was no less physical or material than the body, even though the soul was thought to be "finer" than the body;[87] therefore, they never used the clothing metaphor to speak of the "naked" or "unclothed" soul. For those in the Orphic tradition who believed in rebirth,[88] the ultimate object of the process of death and rebirth was not to be reborn at all.

A number of texts of Jewish origin are concerned with the postmortem location of the righteous and wicked dead. Though there are often inconsistencies, many of these texts locate the souls of the righteous in the heavenly realm, while the souls of the wicked are located in the underworld. Some Jewish texts from the second century C.E. and later envision the presence of the souls of the righteous dead under the throne of God in heaven (*'Abot R. Nat.* 12; *b. Shabb.* 152b).[89] According to the late Sepher ha-Razim 7.1–3 (trans. Morgan, 81):

> The seventh firmament, all of it is sevenfold light, and from
> its light all the (seven) heavens shine. Within it is the throne
> of glory, set on the four glorious *Hayot*. Also within it are the
> storehouses of lives, and the storehouses of souls.

This conception goes back at least to the late first century C.E., for in Rev 6:9–11, John sees the souls of the martyrs under the heavenly altar who, when they cry for vengeance against their murderers, are given white robes and told to wait a bit longer until the determined number of martyrs are killed. This use of clothing imagery to conceptualize the postmortem state should not be confused with the resurrection mode of existence, which is cryptically narrated elsewhere by the author (Rev 20:4–6, 11–15). A very close parallel to Rev 6:9–11 is found in 4 Ezra 4:35–36:

> Did not the souls of the righteous in their chambers (*in
> promptuariis suis*) ask about these matters, saying, "How long
> are we to remain here? And when will come the harvest of our
> reward?" And Jeremiel the archangel answered them and said,
> "When the number of those like yourselves is completed."

In the *Ascension of Isaiah* (the earliest Christian text to reflect the Jewish cosmology of seven heavens), "Isaiah" reports that in the seventh heaven he saw all the righteous ones from the time of Adam (9:7), stripped of "the garment of the flesh" and "in their higher garments" (9:9). The seventh heaven, in fact, contains a storehouse of garments awaiting the righteous (8:14–15, 26; 9:24–26). It would be inappropriate, however, to consider these garments as metaphors for resurrection bodies (as some have done), for nothing in the text suggests this. In the Similitudes of

Enoch (1 Enoch 37–71), probably written early in the first century C.E., "Enoch" saw in heaven the dwelling of the righteous and the resting places of the holy where they are protected by the heavenly presence of God (1 Enoch 39:4–7; 41:2; 61:12; 70:2–4). Similar, perhaps, is the view of Philo of Alexandria, who conceived of heaven as the paternal house (οἶκος) of the soul (*Somn.* 1.256), the place to which souls return like pilgrims returning to their homeland (*Conf.* 78; *Her.* 274; *Mos.* 2.288).

Several Jewish texts from the first century C.E. refer to "storehouses" or "treasuries" which serve as temporary repositories of the souls of the dead between death and resurrection.[90] The location of these storehouses is suitably vague, making it difficult to determine whether they are located in heaven or the underworld. 4 Ezra 7:75–115 (a late first-century C.E. composition) contains a revelatory dialogue between "Ezra" and God on the subject of the soul after death and in which the intermediate state (the interval between death and resurrection) is treated in some detail. According to 7:78, when a person dies "the soul (*inspiratio*) leaves the body to return again to him who gave it" (probably alluding to Qoh 12:7). The wicked are then separated from the righteous and the former undergo torment in seven phases or orders (7:79–87), while the latter enjoy rest in seven phases (7:88–99). More specifically, the souls of the righteous are said to enter storehouses (Latin *promptuaria*, perhaps reflecting the Greek term ταμιεῖον, "treasury"),[91] located in heaven and guarded by angels, while the wicked wander about in torment (4 Ezra 4:35, 41; 7:32, 85, 95).[92] Then in 7:100–101, it is said that after the souls of the righteous have been separated from their bodies they will have seven days before "they shall be gathered in their dwellings (*congregabuntur in habitaculis suis*)." According to 4 Ezra 7:95, "The fourth order, they understand the rest which they now enjoy, being gathered into their chambers and guarded by angels in profound quiet, and the glory which awaits them in the last days." A relatively lengthy eschatological scenario in 4 Ezra 7:26–44 begins with the appearance of the new Jerusalem and the appearance of the hidden land (v. 26), followed by the revelation of the Messiah who will prevail for four hundred years and then die along with all other humans (vv. 28–29). The world will then return to primeval silence for seven days (v. 30), after which the following events occur (vv. 32–33a):

> And the earth shall give up those who are asleep in it, and the dust those who dwell silently in it; and the chambers shall give up the souls which have been committed to them (*et promptuaria reddent, quae eis commendatae sunt animae*). And the Most High shall be revealed upon the seat of judgment.

The same conception is reflected in Ps.-Philo *Liber antiquitatum biblicarum* 32.13, which refers to "the fathers in the chambers of their souls (*in promptuariis animarum eorum*)," and in 2 Baruch (21:23; 30:1–2), both Jewish works which originated in the first century C.E. The brief eschatological scenario in 2 Bar. 30:1–2 places the conception of an intermediate state in a larger narrative context:

> And it shall come to pass after this, when the time of the presence of the Messiah on earth has run its course, that he will return in glory to the heavens: then all who have died and have set their hopes on him will rise again. And it shall come to pass at that time that the treasuries will be opened in which is preserved the number of the souls of the righteous, and they will come out, and the multitude of souls will appear together in one single assembly; and those who are first will rejoice, and those who are last will not be cast down.

In 4 Ezra and Ps.-Philo, the terms *promptuaria* ("residences"), *habitationes* ("residences"), and *habitacula* ("dwelling places") are Latin designations used for the postmortem location of souls, presumably corresponding to the Hebrew and Syriac term אוצרות ("storehouses, treasuries").[93]

These texts can be correlated very generally with three texts in the Pauline corpus, which indicate that Paul expected that following death he would find himself in heaven, in the divine presence. In Phil 1:23, Paul claims that it is his desire to depart, i.e., die, and be with Christ (who is presumably in heaven), and in 2 Cor 5:8 he says that "we would rather be away from the body and at home with the Lord" (again referring to heaven as v. 1 indicates). Finally, in 1 Thess 4:14, in a passage that describes the parousia of Christ and the resurrection, Paul says that "God will bring with him those who have fallen asleep," presumably the dead who are with the Lord. Further, it appears likely that when Paul referred to the heavenly οἰκοδομή, οἰκία, or οἰκητήριον, he was not necessarily referring to the *individual* postmortem dwelling place of believers (the final resurrection had not yet taken place and there is no suggestion in early Jewish or early Christian apocalyptic texts that resurrected believers will dwell in heaven), but rather to a temporary form of heavenly existence (an intermediate state) in anticipation of the transformed bodies that believers would receive at the final resurrection.

At Home or Away from Home (5:6–10)

In 5:6, Paul introduces the conclusion to 2 Cor 4:16–5:10 with another metaphor from domestic life using the antithetical verbs ἐνδημεῖν ("at home") and ἐκδημεῖν ("absent [from home]"): "We are therefore always full of courage knowing that while we are at home in the body (ἐνδημοῦντες ἐν τῷ σώματι) we are absent from the Lord (ἐκδημοῦμεν ἀπὸ τοῦ κυρίου)." The "home" implied in the verb ἐνδημεῖν is the σῶμα that is identical with the οἰκία of v. 1 and the σκῆνος of vv. 1, 4. Absence from the Lord means absence from the actual heavenly presence of Christ, for here he is not thinking of the inner spiritual presence of Christ that he emphasizes so often elsewhere in his letters (e.g., Rom 8:9–11).[94] In v. 6 he has stated the facts of the present situation; in v. 8 he states his preference: "We are full of courage, but we rather prefer to be absent from the body (ἐκδημῆσαι ἐκ τοῦ σώματος) and at home with the Lord (ἐνδημῆσαι πρὸς τὸν κύριον)." In v. 9 Paul begins by express-ing the importance of pleasing the Lord with the ambiguous phrases "whether at home (εἴτε ἐνδημοῦντες) or away from home (εἴτε ἐκδημοῦντες)." The ambiguity lies in the fact that εἴτε ἐνδημοῦντες can in principle be construed as εἴτε ἐνδημοῦντες [πρὸς τὸν κύριον] ("whether at home [with the Lord]"), and εἴτε ἐκδημοῦντες as εἴτε ἐκδημοῦντες [ἐκ τοῦ σώματος] ("or away [from the body]"). But this is tautological and does not present a real alternative. It is preferable, there-fore, to construe εἴτε ἐνδημοῦντες as εἴτε ἐνδημοῦντες [ἐν τῷ σώματι] ("whether at home [in the body]"), essentially repeating the phrase in v. 6a and εἴτε ἐκδημοῦντες as εἴτε ἐκδημοῦντες [ἐκ τοῦ σώματος] ("or away [from the body]"), which presents a real alternative.[95] The notion that the contrasting terms ἐνδημεῖν and ἐκδημεῖν are taken over from the vocabulary of Paul's opponents and used in a polemical way, even though widely assumed by interpreters,[96] is an unfounded assumption based largely on the antithetical formulation of Paul's propositions taken together with the fact that these terms occur nowhere else in the Pauline corpus.

The sanction for pleasing the Lord is a traditional formulation of the future event of the last judgment (presided over by Christ),[97] introduced in v. 10 with the inferential particle γάρ followed by the reason why one ought to please the Lord. According to v. 10 (leaving the difficult clause momentarily untranslated): "For we all must appear before the judgment seat of Christ, ἵνα κομίσηται ἕκαστος τὰ διὰ τοῦ σώματος πρὸς ἃ ἔπραξεν, whether good or evil." First of all, the verb κομίσηται is always transitive and means "to come into possession of something," "receive a recompense."[98] The clause τὰ [ἔπραξεν] διὰ τοῦ σώματος (with ἔπραξεν supplied) is the object of κομίσηται, while the preposi-tional phrase πρὸς ἃ ἔπραξεν is adverbial, modifying κομίσηται. The problematic clauses can then be translated "so that each might receive what [he did] while living, in proportion to what he did." While the phrase διὰ τοῦ σώματος can either be construed instrumentally ("through the body") or temporally ("during life in the body," i.e., "in life"), I have chosen the latter. However, regardless of whether διὰ τοῦ σώματος is understood instrumentally or temporally, the action of the aorist verb ἔπραξεν indicates that the reception of the recompense is a postmortem event, i.e., that physical life is a thing of the past.

When does this judgment before Christ occur? In Table 1 (p. 237), I have placed the motif of judgment as the last of a series of eschatological motifs in Column 6, situating it chronologically after the event of the postmortem reception of a heavenly dwelling by the believer. We can also inquire into the relationship between this event and those of the parousia and resurrection to which Paul clearly referred in 2 Cor 4:14. Paul apparently assumes that the parousia and the resurrection have already occurred before Christ judges all people, but simply chooses to omit explicit mention of those events, because when he mentions the importance of pleasing the Lord no matter where one is (v. 9), the theme of accountability suggests itself to him, which is based on the threat and promise of eschatological judgment, a motif he evokes in v. 10.

While Jewish and Christian apocalyptic eschatology generally, though not exclusively, understood the final judgment to be a collective event,[99] some traditions of Greek underworld mythology depicted the judgment of each individual immediately following death.[100] In Judaism the notion of the postmortem judgment of the individual in anticipation of a final judgment are explored in 4 Ezra and the Testament of Abraham,[101] while in early Christianity this motif is expressed in Heb 9:27 in the motto "It is appointed to a person once to die, but after this the judgment."[102] In 2 Cor 5:10, a collective emphasis is apparently expressed by the phrase "*we all* must appear," though that can easily be understood as a *pluralis sociativus* and hence as referring to something that each individual must experience, confirmed by ἕκαστος ("each one"), which is used as the subject of the verb κομίσηται in the following purpose clause: "so that each might receive what [he did] while living." Whether Paul is here entertaining the notion of a collective final scene of judgment,[103] therefore, or an immediate postmortem judgment of each person (as apparently in Heb 9:27) is not clear,[104] though many commentators fail to consider the possibility of the latter. The mention of appearing "before the judgment seat of Christ," a phrase found nowhere else in Paul or the New Testament (though it does occur in Polycarp, *Phil.* 6:2), seems to tip the scales in favor of a collective apocalyptic event.[105]

Concluding Arguments

In this study, I have focused on several anthropological and eschatological themes that converge in 2 Cor 4:16–5:10. Paul chose an antithetical style throughout this section, apparently because he found it a tool useful for contrasting two different aspects of reality, τὰ βλεπόμενα and τὰ μὴ βλε–πόμενα (4:18), πρόσκαιρος vs. αἰώνοις (4:18), τὸ θνητόν vs. ζωή (5:4), contrasts that Paul elsewhere comfortably expresses through such antitheses as τὸ φθαρτόν vs. ἀφθαρσία or τὸ θνητόν vs. ἀθανασία (1 Cor 15:53–54). For Paul these two aspects of reality are both simultaneous and sequential (frequently referred to with the terms "already—not yet"), that is, eschatological salvation is experienced in a preliminary way in the present in such a way that its complete future attainment is guaranteed.[106]

The complementary phrases ὁ ἔξω ἄνθρωπος and ὁ ἔσω (ἄνθρωπος), which Paul used at the beginning of 2 Cor 4:16–5:10, enabled him to emphasize and localize the tension between the juxtaposition of the natural (ὁ ἔξω ἄνθρωπος) and the supernatural (ὁ ἔσω ἄνθρωπος) in the believer (= human being), and to provide self-explanatory labels for the believer's experience of salvation in popular philosophical categories ultimately traceable to Plato. Throughout the entire passage, ὁ ἔξω ἄνθρω–πος and ὁ ἔσω ἄνθρωπος are the only explicit labels used to characterize the tension and conflict daily experienced by the believer. Throughout the rest of the passage the "core self" (ὁ ἔσω ἄνθρωπος, or "inner person" who survives physical death) is expressed through a series of first-person plural verbs and pronouns ("*we* have," "*we* groan," "*we* are not found," "*we* desire," "*our* heavenly dwelling," etc.), which really represent a *pluralis sociativus*, i.e., Paul speaking on behalf of those he is addressing, and so really represents the first-person singular "I" of each person Paul is addressing.[107] This "core self" is implicitly contrasted with the various clothing and building metaphors that provide it with a covering or place of habitation. Thus it is this "we" (= "I") who survives the destruction of the physical body and will receive an eternal dwelling in heaven (5:1). It is this "we" (= "I") who groans, longing to put on "our" (= "my") heavenly dwelling (5:2). It is this "we" (= "I") who groans while still in this body, not longing to be unclothed, but to put on a garment (5:4), and so forth. There is clearly an anthropological duality involved here. While tension exists between the "core self" and the earthly house or body where it is located (5:2, 4, 8), that tension is apparently resolved after death when the "core self" is invested in a heavenly habitation. Paul does not speak of the "inner person" or the implied occupant of the house or body as a "soul" (like the Jewish authors of 4 Ezra and 2 Baruch), though unlike many scholars I do not think the body-soul duality inimical to Paul's thought any more than it is to his Jewish apocalyptic contemporaries.

An important issue yet unresolved is how, if at all, the sequence of eschatological motifs in 2 Cor 4:16–5:10 corresponds to other Pauline eschatological scenarios (e.g., 1 Cor 15:50–57; 1 Thess 4:13–18; Phil 3:20–21). Though there is no mention of the parousia or the resurrection whatsoever in the passage, it cannot have been far from Paul's mind, for both are referred to in traditional formulations in the immediately preceding context in 2 Cor 4:14:[108] "Knowing that he who raised the Lord Jesus will raise us also with Jesus and bring us with you into his presence."

In Table 1, I have provided a categorization of the sequence of eschatological motifs found in 2 Cor 4:16–5:10, most (but not all) of which have been discussed in this essay. In that Table it will be seen that Column 3, "Intermediate State," contains four phrases or terms that one or another commentator has taken to refer to the so-called "intermediate state" between physical death and physical resurrection or physical death and the parousia (a state that some Pauline scholars characterize as "bodiless").[109] None of these are convincing (hence the category and its contents are bracketed). The phrase ἔχομεν οἰκοδομὴν ἐκ θεοῦ is included because some have attempted to construe ἔχομεν as a futuristic present as a strategy to allow for an intermediate state to intervene before the reception of an eternal heavenly dwelling from God (5:1), often understood as the resurrection body. Yet this understanding of ἔχομεν is strained, and the text certainly is silent about a resurrection body. The references to being ἐκδυσάμενοι or ἐκδύσασθαι, "unclothed" (5:3a, 4b), or γυμνοί, "naked" (5:3b), do not indicate what Paul anticipates will happen, but what he anticipates will *not* happen. I conclude that Paul makes no reference to an intermediate state between death (Column 2) and the transformation to a form of existence appropriate to heaven (Column 4).

Nevertheless, the text does accommodate an intermediate state. In Column 5, Paul uses three dwelling metaphors (οἰκοδομή, οἰκία, and οἰκητήριον) to refer to the same basic heavenly reality, a structure that serves as a postmortem repository for the "core self" of believers, analogous to the early Jewish conception of a heavenly "treasury of souls" referred to by several first-century C.E. Jewish texts including 4 Ezra, 2 Baruch, and Ps.-Philo. In 4 Ezra, these postmortem structures (*promptuaria, habitationes, habitacula*), which the author (who wrote in Hebrew) may have designated with the term אוצרות ("storehouses, treasuries"), were imagined as a *corporate* dwelling place for the "core selves" or souls

Table 1.
A Categorized Sequence
of Eschatological Motifs in 2 Cor 4:16–5:10.

1. Present Earthly Life (4:18: τὰ βλεπόμενα, πρόσκαιρα)	2. Death	[3. Intermediate State]	4. Transformation	5. Future Heavenly Life (4:18: τὰ μὴ βλεπόμενα αἰώνια)	6. Judgment
4:16a ὁ ἔξω ἄνθρωπος					
4:16b ὁ ἔσω (ἄνθρωπος)					
5:1a ἡ ἐπίγειος οἰκία	1α καταλυθῇ	1b [ἔχομεν]		1b οἰκοδομὴν ἐκ θεοῦ	
1a τοῦ σκήνους					
				1c οἰκίαν ἀχειροποίητον αἰώνιον ἐν τοῖς οὐρανοῖς	
2a ἐν τούτῳ [σκήνει]			2b ἐπενδύσασθαι	2b τὸ οἰκητήριον ἡμῶν τὸ ἐξ οὐρανοῦ	
		[3a ἐκδυσάμενοι]			
		[3b γυμνοί]			
4a ἐν τῷ σκήνει		[4b ἐκδύσασθαι]	4b ἐπενδύσασθαι		
4c τὸ θνητόν			4c καταποθῇ	4c ὑπὸ τῆς ζωῆς	
6a ἐνδημοῦντες ἐν τῷ σώματι					
6b ἐκδημοῦμεν ἀπὸ τοῦ κυρίου					
	8a ἐκδημῆσαι ἐκ τοῦ σώματος			8b ἐνδημῆσαι πρὸς τὸν κύριον	
9 ἐνδημοῦντες [ἐν τῷ σώματι]				9 ἐκδημοῦντες [ἐκ τοῦ σώματος]	
					10 τὸ βῆμα τοῦ Χριστοῦ

of the righteous until the day of resurrection. Since in these early Jewish sources, the "storehouses," are usually referred to in the plural, it is not certain whether the conception involved a "storehouse" for each soul or a plurality of "storehouses," each of which could accommodate a plurality of souls. Similarly in 2 Cor 4:16–5:10, Paul uses the three dwelling metaphors (οἰκοδομή, οἰκία, and οἰκητήριον) only in the singular. This could mean that each person has their own dwelling place or that a single dwelling place accommodates a plurality of persons. Afterlife mythology can hardly be expected to exhibit consistency in details. Further while the location of these "storehouses" is vague in 4 Ezra, 2 Baruch, and Ps.-Philo, they appear to be set in the underworld, so that the separation of body from soul at death relegates the former to the grave and the latter to the underworld; body and soul are expected to be reunited at the resurrection. In 2 Cor 4:16–5:10, however, Paul emphatically locates the postmortem dwelling in heaven, the place that pagan Greeks and Romans thought was the destination of the soul when separated from the body.

Finally, a few remarks on the central problematic of the volume of which this essay is a part, namely the importance of going beyond the traditional divide between Judaism and Hellenism in Paul's thought. It has become increasingly evident in recent years that the conventional dichotomy between Judaism and Hellenism is an artificial construction buttressed by theological utility rather than historical viability. The tacitly monolithic character of "early Judaism," belied by the increasing use of the term "Judaisms" in historical descriptions of this period, is matched by the obviously pluralistic character of "Hellenism." In this study, no attempt has been made to minimize the "Jewish" features of Paul's thought in the interest of subordinating them to a "Hellenistic" understanding, nor have "Hellenistic" features been manipulated to make them compatible with a "Jewish" construal. Further, no evidence has been found to support the notion that Paul developed a new conception of what constitutes a human being in response to a perception of the supposed incompatibility of the conventional Greek anthropological dualism of body and soul with the Christian gospel.[110] The emphasis on the psychosomatic unity of the human person in the teaching of Paul, which is such a widespread theological presupposition among Pauline scholars who are the heirs of Bultmann's influential work on Pauline anthropology, functions fairly well for understanding Romans 7 (for example), but founders when Paul turns to the subject of death. In 2 Cor 4:16–5:10, Paul has articulated an anthropology duality in response to the tension experienced in daily life between the reality of external suffering and physical mortality on the one hand, over against his faith in the indwelling presence of

God on the other. Working out from this anthropology, he understood death as the beginning of life as well as the resolution of the tension between experience and faith, a conception that has both Hellenistic and Jewish features, but which is ultimately at home in neither. But this anthropological duality is also the common ground between Hellenistic and Jewish conceptions of death, since throughout the ancient world the physical aspect of the human being was considered temporary and corruptible, while the permanent aspect of the person was thought to live on in another dimension of reality. In death, the "inner person" is separated from the "outer person," and whether these two aspects of the person are labeled "body" and "soul" (as the author of 4 Ezra chose to do) or something else, the conception is basically one of anthropological duality.

Chapter 11

Paul and Paradigm Shifts: Reconciliation and Its Linkage Group

John T. Fitzgerald

Introduction

Paul was born a Jew, became a Christian, and worked in cities of the Greco-Roman world as an apostle to the Gentiles. Each of these three contexts—Judaism, Christianity, and the pagan Mediterranean world—influenced his life and thought: Modern scholars agree that all three contexts are important for the study of his letters, yet differ in their assessments of the relative importance of each context for understanding his theology. They also disagree about the particular context that is the proximate or ultimate source for various words, concepts, and stylistic and literary devices in both his own letters and those penned in his name. Indeed, the history of modern Pauline scholarship is in large part a history of the attempt to identify the sources of the apostle's thought and manner of expression.[1]

One example of the debate about Paul's sources is the recent discussion of reconciliation or καταλλαγή.[2] The noun appears in Rom 5:11, 11:15, and 2 Cor 5:18–19, and the verb καταλλάσσειν in Rom 5:10, 1 Cor 7:11, and 2 Cor 5:18–19. While Paul is the only New Testament author to use these two terms, he is not alone in invoking the concept. Three closely related terms for reconciliation appear elsewhere in the New Testament. The deutero-Pauline authors of Colossians (1:20) and Ephesians (2:16) use the cognate term ἀποκαταλλάσσειν, the Gospel of Matthew (5:24) uses διαλλάσσειν, and the author of Acts uses συναλλάσσειν (7:26).[3] To explain the origin of Paul's use of the concept and terminology of reconciliation, scholars have sought to derive it from Jewish, Christian, and Greco-Roman sources, as well as his own conversion experience. Although debate about this issue is still ongoing, the most important contribution is that of Cilliers Breytenbach,[4] whose chief conclusions are briefly discussed in the first section of this essay.

Following my analysis of Breytenbach's work and its consequences for Pauline scholarship, I turn in the second section of the essay to a discussion of Paul's penchant for making paradigm shifts.[5] That is, when Paul makes use of an existing conceptual paradigm, he does not do so mechanically or uncritically. On the contrary, by changing key elements within a given paradigm, he creatively transforms it. The result is a paradigm shift, as is seen in his treatments of two traditional paradigms—one concerning freedom, slavery, and the Torah, and the other involving sacrifice for sin. In the third and fourth sections of the essay, I argue that Paul makes a similar shift in regard to reconciliation. The third section is devoted to a reconstruction of the standard paradigm of reconciliation, and the fourth is an examination of the changes that Paul makes to this paradigm. In the fifth and final section of the essay I examine the nexus of ideas traditionally associated with reconciliation and show how Paul's use of the concept of reconciliation in 2 Corinthians 5 coheres with other concepts in his Corinthian correspondence.

Breytenbach's Analysis

Breytenbach argues persuasively that Paul's idea of reconciliation does not derive from the Hebrew Bible or contemporary Judaism, whether Palestinian or Hellenistic. As Paul's use of the term "ambassador" (πρεσβεύομεν: 2 Cor 5:20) in conjunction with his terms for reconciliation already suggests, the primary background of the concept as he uses it in 2 Corinthians 5 is to be found in the diplomatic sphere of the Hellenistic world, where words for reconciliation are used to denote the making of peace between enemies.[6] Καταλλάσσειν and its cognates are, furthermore, essentially secular terms, not religious ones. As such, they must be sharply distinguished from words for atonement, especially (ἐξ) ἱλάσκεσθαι. The latter derive ultimately from the cultic tradition of the Hebrew Bible, where כפר (*kipper*: "to atone for") is the key term. In the biblical tradition, the "reconciliation" and "atonement" word-groups are used in ways that are entirely independent of one another.[7] As Breytenbach points out, "The Greek translations of the Old Testament do not translate *kpr* with *di-* or *katallassō ktl.* Where the Hebrew *kpr* (*pi'el*) is used in the sense of 'to atone,' it is translated by *exilaskesthai ktl.* In Greek, in fact, *di-* or *katallassō ktl.* are not hyponymous to *(ex)hilaskesthai ktl.*"[8] "There is," consequently, "no semantic or traditio-historical reason to link the origins of the Pauline notion of 'reconciliation' (or the scant use the Greek translations of the Hebrew Scriptures make of *katallassō*) with the Old Testament theology of atonement."[9] "Neither *kipper* nor its translation in the LXX (*[ex]ilaskesthai*) are sense-related to *katallassō*."[10] Given this fact, there is no way in Jewish tradition in which atonement can be viewed as making reconciliation possible.[11]

According to Breytenbach, it is Paul who first merges these two different semantic fields.[12] He takes the Greek secular concept of reconciliation and combines it with the Jewish religious notion of atonement, and he creatively interprets both in light of the early Christian tradition of Jesus' death "for us," a tradition that he also further develops. It is Paul, therefore, who "interprets the concept of reconciliation in such a way that reconciliation is made possible through the representative atoning death of Christ."[13]

This essay is not the place to enter into a full discussion of Breytenbach's impressive analysis. Suffice it to say that, while we differ on a number of important points, I find his arguments in favor of his main thesis—that the ideas of atonement and reconciliation are different in origin—to be thoroughly persuasive. These ideas in fact belong to two different conceptual paradigms, a point that I hope to demonstrate later in this essay. As a consequence of this important distinction, Breytenbach is able to show us an extraordinarily adroit apostle, one who not only draws on well-established Greek and Jewish concepts as well as on developing Christian traditions but also skillfully combines and develops them in theologically creative ways. Breytenbach's demonstration that "reconciliation" is not a key biblical term has several important consequences, four of which merit emphasis.[14]

First, in pointing to Hellenistic diplomacy as the source of Paul's idea of reconciliation, Breytenbach has placed New Testament scholarship in his debt by calling attention to the significance of this notion in ancient politics as a whole. The concept of reconciliation attained monumental importance for the Greeks during the time of the Peloponnesian War and henceforth became a fixture in Greek political life and thought. It is, for example, a crucial concept in the plays of Aristophanes, who wrote many of his works during the War (431–404 B.C.E.) and supported those who endeavored to bring the conflict to an end.[15] Indeed, the notion of reconciliation is so strong in his *Lysistrata* that one of the alternate titles for the play in antiquity was *Reconciliation* (Διαλλαγαί).[16]

Second, Breytenbach's thesis that Paul's concept of reconciliation in 2 Corinthians 5 is drawn from the world of Hellenistic diplomacy is in continuity with other scholars' contention that Paul already in 1 Corinthians made use of terms and concepts drawn from Hellenistic politics.[17] This means that Greco-Roman political life was an important source for Paul throughout his lengthy interaction with the Corinthians.

Third, inasmuch as his analysis demonstrates that a key term in Pauline soteriology—and thus in Pauline theology as a whole—derives from the secular Hellenistic world, he proves that the word "reconciliation" is quite ill suited to serve as the *leitmotif* of a biblical theology that embraces both testaments.[18] Thanks, however, to Paul's theological transformation of this Greek notion, the *reconciliatio inimicorum* can rightly claim a place alongside the *iustificatio impiorum* in the apostle's theology.[19]

Fourth, his analysis offers yet another proof that one can readily acknowledge Paul's genuine indebtedness to Hellenistic terms and traditions without undermining the apostle's theological integrity.[20] It is, after all, what Paul does with derived concepts that is theologically significant, not the sources themselves. The determination of the latter are nevertheless important for at least three reasons. First, they alert us to the intellectual, cultural, and social matrix in which various ideas appear. Second, they help us to identify the nexus of ideas within a given matrix, i.e., the "linkage group" to which they belong.[21] Third, they aid us in understanding how Paul selectively adopts and adapts those ideas (and others that belong to their linkage group) in service to his developing theology. In the remainder of this essay I shall discuss Paul's penchant for modifying traditional paradigms (section two), his adaptation of the paradigm concerning reconciliation (sections three and four), and the linkage group to which the concept of reconciliation belongs (section five).

Paul and Paradigm Shifts

One of the most remarkable characteristics of Paul as a theologian is his ability to take over an existing conceptual paradigm and transform it.

The result is a paradigm shift in which the elements of the old paradigm remain, but they appear in a revolutionary new configuration. This is what happens in Paul's adaptation of the standard paradigm concerning reconciliation, but what he does in this regard is not unique. To set his adaptation of the reconciliation paradigm within the overall context of his theological activity, I shall briefly discuss two other paradigm shifts in Paul.[22]

The first is the paradigm concerning freedom, slavery, and the Torah. This paradigm obviously comes from the Hebrew Bible, where slavery is connected with Egypt and freedom with the Torah. This alignment of concepts appears most conspicuously in the narrative found in Exodus. The book begins by depicting the enslavement of the Hebrews by a new Egyptian king, who oppresses them and makes their life as slaves exceedingly difficult (1:8–14). In response to the slaves' cries, Yahweh sends Moses to deliver the Hebrews from their harsh taskmasters (3:7–10). The Egyptians' grip on their slaves is finally broken by the last of the ten plagues, and the Hebrews leave Egyptian slavery in a great exodus (12:29–36). But just as soon as the Hebrews leave the place of their enslavement the Egyptian king has a change of heart and goes after them, intending to reduce them once again to slavery (14:5–9). This threat ends at the Sea of Reeds, in which the Egyptians drown and through which the Hebrews escape to freedom (14:10–15:21). The liberated Hebrews then journey to Mt. Sinai, where they enter into a covenant with Yahweh and receive the Torah (19:1–40:38).

As this brief rehearsal of the biblical narrative makes clear, slavery is conceptually aligned with Egypt and freedom with Mt. Sinai.[23] For ancient Israelite tradition, there is liberation *into* law. Freedom and Torah go hand-in-hand; they are corollaries, not antithetical concepts. The Torah is God's precious gift to the newly emancipated slaves, and it is intended to provide a framework for their new freedom. In short, the alignment of Torah with freedom reflects the ancient Hebrew conception that the only enduring freedom is one that is structured by law.

With Paul, of course, there is an almost incredible paradigm shift. By equating Mt. Sinai with slavery (Gal 4:22–25), Paul shifts the paradigm, so that freedom now entails liberation *from* the law (Gal 5:1; Rom 7:6). Paul's new paradigm reflects his conviction that liberty and love go hand-in-hand, and that the only enduring freedom is one that is guided by the Spirit.[24]

The second paradigm shift involves sacrifice for sin.[25] As just indicated, ancient Israelites believed that Yahweh, in giving the Torah, was providing a structure within which humans could flourish in relation to both

God and one another. At the same time, they recognized that humans did not always give heed to the Torah. On the contrary, humans violated the law and harmed their relations with both God and one another. But the Israelites also believed that Yahweh had foreseen these breaches of the covenant and in his mercy had made provision for them in the Torah. According to the ancient Israelite priestly paradigm, Yahweh had prescribed sacrifice as the means for repairing the harm and making things right. Sacrifice was thus viewed as the divinely appointed means for healing and repairing the ruptured relationship between Yahweh and his people.[26] Humans who had violated the Torah and committed offenses against God offered sacrifice to the Deity, using the very means that God had ordained, and God in response graciously accepted their sacrifices. The altar was thus the place of atonement, the place where God and humans interacted through sacrifice. Those who offered sacrifice to Yahweh formed a community centered theologically on the altar, a community of people who were religiously obliged to maintain a proper relationship with one another as well as with God.

The shedding of blood was essential to all cultic expiation, but the manner in which the priest manipulated the blood differed according to the sacrifice offered. In most cases, blood was applied to the place where the sacrifice was wholly or partly incinerated, viz., the altar of burnt offering, which was located in the courtyard of the tabernacle and temple. In the case of burnt offerings (Lev 1:5), offerings of well-being (Lev 3:2), and reparation (guilt) offerings (Lev 7:2), blood was dashed on all sides of the altar. With the purification offering, however, the place where the priest applied the blood depended on the seriousness of the offense against the sanctuary. Inadvertent offenses by individuals were purged by daubing blood on the horns of the courtyard altar (Lev 4:25, 30, 34). In the case of unintentional offenses committed by either the entire nation or the high priest as its representative, the blood was sprinkled seven times before the veil and daubed on the horns of the altar of burnt incense, located within the sanctuary itself (Lev 4:6–7, 17–18). In the case of presumptuous sins, blood was applied on Yom Kippur to the *kappōret* of the ark of the covenant (Lev 16:14–15), which was located in the sanctuary's adytum and understood as the place of the divine presence (Lev 16:2; see also Exod 25:22; Num 7:89). In short, as this progression shows, the more serious the offense, the greater was the pollution of the sanctuary and the more serious the rupture of the relationship with God.[27] Consequently, the most grievous of sins were connected with the *kappōret*.

The precise meaning of the ark's *kappōret* is disputed. The term may originally have been an Egyptian loanword that was appropriated by the

Hebrews to indicate the place where Yahweh's feet rested.[28] But whatever its origin or original significance, its connection with the Yom Kippur ritual ensured that it would be interpreted in conjunction with the verb *kipper* and understood as its feminine abstract noun. Viewed from that perspective it would indicate "'that which expiates.'"[29] And since it was connected with the presence of God, it would also designate "the source of expiation, par excellence."[30] The LXX's standard rendering of it by the Greek word ἱλαστήριον reflects this understanding of the word.[31]

According to this priestly paradigm of sacrifice, there is absolutely no reason for any human—including, or especially, the Messiah—to die in order to repair the ruptured relationship. In ordaining animal sacrifice, God had relieved humans of the burden, whether real or imagined, of offering either themselves or their children as a means of atonement. Moreover, the paradigm presupposes repentance on the part of the individual offering the sacrifice; an unrepentant person or someone who does not care about the ruptured relationship with God will not offer sacrifice. And even if someone should venture to do so, the sacrifice would be neither acceptable nor efficacious. The indispensability of repentance is a point not only made emphatic by various prophets (Isa 1:10–17; 29:13–14; Jer 6:20; 7:1–15; Amos 5:21–24; Mic 6:6–8) but also articulated by the priests. Unless or until there is regret and repentance by the offending human, that person will bring no sacrifice and the damaged relationship with God will remain unrepaired. Consequently, the purgation rites on Yom Kippur purify the sanctuary from the pollution caused by wanton unrepented acts (Lev 16:16) and expiate the most egregious of the people's sins (Lev 16:22), provided that they join in the penitence, fasting, and other acts of self-denial that mark the day (Lev 16:21, 29; 23:26–32; Num 29:7). But they do not expiate the sins of the person who is still in revolt against God and refuses to repent.[32]

Here, too, Paul assumes the paradigm but shifts it in several important ways. He assumes the validity and efficacy of sacrificial blood (Rom 3:25) in repairing humanity's relationship with God, but he shifts the paradigm by making God, the offended party, the one who offers the sacrifice. Thus it is not humans, making use of the divinely appointed means, but God himself who does so. Indeed, the sacrifice is offered by God both prior to and apart from any human repentance. The latter is not jettisoned by Paul but relocated within the paradigm. Rather than being the presupposition of sacrifice, repentance is now the appropriate response to the goodness that God has shown in his offering (Rom 2:4).

Furthermore, the sacrifice that God offers is human, none other than his own Son (Rom 8:32), the Messiah.[33] And in Romans 3:25, Paul likely makes use of an early Christian tradition in which God's offering of Jesus is depicted as a ἱλαστήριον. This Greek term occurs twenty-seven times in the LXX, and in the vast majority of these instances (twenty-one times) it is used of the mercy seat.[34] Debate has, of course, centered on whether the term in Rom 3:25 also indicates the place of atonement or whether it indicates its means (as, for example, in 4 Macc 17:22). Either is possible, but given the paradigm that Paul assumes, it is likely that the Greek term here indicates both, so that Jesus is understood to be both the means and the place of expiation. In any event, the use of traditional "mercy seat" imagery in connection with Jesus indicates that God, through the offering of Jesus, has made atonement for the most grievous of human offenses. The community that is formed in response to this offering will thus be centered on him as source and on his death as means of its restored relationship with God.[35]

The Standard Paradigm of Reconciliation

The third paradigm shift involves reconciliation. As we have seen, the Greek terms for reconciliation are primarily used in secular social settings and have to do with the ending of hostility between warring or estranged parties. Paul's use of the term in 2 Corinthians 5 derives, as we also have seen, from its use in ancient diplomacy, where reconciliation is the task of the envoy. But the terms for reconciliation are also used widely in regard to the repairing of various interpersonal relationships (especially those involving the household and friends), and Paul himself uses καταλλάσ–σειν in this way in 1 Cor 7:11. That fact alone suggests that there is not a single source for Paul's concept of reconciliation, but that his thinking on this topic is shaped by several different settings in which the term is used. For that reason, I shall neither restrict my discussion of the paradigm to the diplomatic realm nor use only pagan sources in depicting it.[36] Using a variety of ancient texts, I shall attempt to reconstruct the standard paradigm of reconciliation by identifying both the presuppositions and logic of those who refer to reconciliation.

Regardless of whether the particular social setting was public or private, the standard paradigm of reconciliation presupposed that one or more of the parties in the strained relationship had acted in such a way as to create the conflict. The rule of thumb was that those responsible for the strife were to take the initiative in ending it and restoring peace. According to the paradigm, it is the offending party's responsibility to seek reconciliation, the offended party's duty to show goodwill by accepting the offer of reconciliation.[37] To be implacable (ἄσπονδος) and unwilling to forgive was a vice (2 Tim 3:3); to be forgiving and easily reconciled was a virtue,[38] for it meant that one did not bear a grudge or exact vengeance for past grievances but rather was gentle and showed mercy.[39] As Aristotle notes, one wants as friends "those who bear no malice (μνησικάκους) and do not cherish the memory of their wrongs, but are easily reconciled" (εὐκαταλλάκτους).[40]

Pseudo-Libanius's example of a letter written in a repenting style shows what was expected of both parties:

> I know, since I failed, that I did the job badly. Having then repented, I ask your forgiveness for my failure. Do not hesitate to grant it to me, for it is right to forgive friends when they make mistakes, and especially when they ask for forgiveness.[41]

The story of Joseph and his brothers in Gen 50:15–21 is a clear example of this dynamic in Jewish tradition. Here the brothers, fearing that Joseph will bear a grudge and exact vengeance on them in the wake of Jacob's death (50:15), acknowledge their crime against Joseph and ask for forgiveness (50:17). In response, Joseph not only refuses to bear a grudge but promises to take care of them and comforts (παρεκάλεσεν) them. In short, he is the perfect model of how the offended party was to respond to those who had wronged him.[42]

Because it was the guilty party's obligation to seek reconciliation, this person's initiative usually took the form of an appeal. These appeals are typically introduced or accompanied by some word of entreaty (such as παρακαλῶ or δέομαι). For example, Alexander the tyrant of Pherae begs (δεόμενον) Pelopidas to reconcile him with the Thessalian cities with which he has been fighting (Plut., *Pel.* 26.2).[43] Again, in *PMich.* VIII.502, 7–8 (second century C.E.) a soldier by the name of Valerius Gemellus writes to his estranged brother, urging him, "In response to my entreaty, brother, be reconciled to me" (παρα]κληθείς, ἄδελφε, διαλ–λάγηθί μοι).[44] Similarly, Pseudo-Demetrius's example of a supplicatory type of letter presupposes a situation in which one friend has infuriated the other, and the guilty friend's letter is a petition for forgiveness and reconciliation:

> I have censured So-and-so for what you said he had done to you, and I inveighed against him more bitterly than was fitting—even more, I dare say, than you (would have done) on your own behalf. Please forgive me again, therefore, for that offense. For I know that you are good and gracious to your

> friends. "Gain mastery," then, as Homer says, "over your great
> anger; it is not at all necessary that you have a pitiless heart,
> for the gods themselves can be appeased." (*Iliad* 9.496f)[45]

Another example of an appeal for reconciliation is provided by a
papyrus letter from the second century C.E. (*BGU* III.846). The letter is
written by a man by the name of Antonius Longus, and it is addressed to
his estranged mother Nilous, who lives in Karanis, a village in the Fayum.
The relevant portion of the letter is as follows:

> Antoni(u)s Longus to Nilous his mother, very many greetings.
> Continually I pray for your health. Supplication on your behalf
> I direct each day to the lord Serapis. I wish you to know that I
> had no hope that you would come up to the metropolis [= Arsi-
> noe]. On this account neither did I enter into the city. But I was
> ashamed to come to Karanis because I am going about in filthy
> rags. I write[46] to you that I am naked. I beseech you, mother,
> be reconciled to me (παρακα[λ]ῶ σαι, μήτηρ, δ[ι]αλάγητί
> μοι). Furthermore, I know what I have brought upon myself. I
> have been taught a fitting lesson. I know that I have erred (οἶδα
> ὅτι ἡμάρτηκα). I heard from [. . .]umus who found you in the
> Arsinoite nome, and he unreservedly[47] related everything to
> you. Do you not know that I would rather be a cripple than be
> conscious that I am still owing any one an obolus?[48]

Antonius Longus's letter is an appeal to his mother for reconciliation,
occasioned by the fact that a third party has divulged everything to the
mother. In the letter he seeks not only to explain his actions, intentions,
and circumstances but also to assert his constant concern for his mother's
health. Most important for our purposes, he both confesses the error of
his ways and acknowledges his own responsibility for his current plight.
He emphasizes the latter in order to appeal to his mother's mercy, so that
she will grant her son the reconciliation that he so urgently desires.

As the preceding letter suggests, appeals for reconciliation are often
accompanied by some philophronetic indication of the guilty party's
affection and concern for the estranged person.[49] In keeping with this sentiment, the urgent desire for an immediate reconciliation and reunion is
sometimes articulated. These features are especially prominent in an
extraordinarily touching letter (*PGiss.* 17) written in the early second century, probably from the time of Hadrian (117–38).[50] In this letter an
Egyptian woman[51] by the name of Tays writes to a *strategos* whose name
is Apollonius. That Tays is Apollonius's slave is indicated by her use of
both δεσπότης (l. 2) and κύριος (ll. 1, 5, 8, 14) in addressing him.[52]
Although it is perhaps possible that Apollonius is away from home,[53] it is

much more likely that Tays is the one who is not at home, either having been banished by an angry Apollonius or having run away from his house.[54] In any case, she is now apart from him and has heard that he was seriously ill (ll. 5–6). His illness, which caused her great agony (l. 5: Ἠγωνίασα), provides the occasion for the letter, in which she expresses her thanks to all the gods for preserving his life (ll. 6–7). She uses παρακαλῶ to ask Apollonius to "send for us," explaining that "we are dying because we do not see you every day" (ll. 7–10).[55] After expressing the wish that "we were able to fly" to him and stating once again her distress (ll. 10–12), she makes her appeal for reconciliation and repeats her request to Apollonius to send for her: "So, be reconciled to us (Ὥστε διαλλάγηθι ἡμεῖν) and send for us." (ll. 13–14).[56]

In many cases, a simple plea for forgiveness was not sufficient to effect reconciliation. Reparations of various kinds were necessary in order to appease the estranged party, and these had to be made if reconciliation was to be obtained. Indeed, the word καταλλαγή is fundamentally a commercial term indicating a monetary "exchange," "settlement," or "payment."[57] Thus καταλλαγή as reparations "payment" is the "settlement" that makes καταλλαγή as "reconciliation" possible. The necessity of making reparations was a standard precondition in the reconciliation of warring nations,[58] and the severity of the demands made by the more powerful nation often prolonged the conflict.[59] Similarly, the offended party's demand for financial restitution could constitute a significant impediment to the reconciliation of individuals. The Theognidea, for example, demand double compensation from the friend who gives bad counsel (1089–90).[60] Within this context, any concessions made by the stronger party were viewed "as gifts and acts of grace" (χάριτι καὶ δωρεᾷ: Polyb. 1.31.6, trans. LCL).

If the desire for reconciliation was typically prompted by the needs (whether physical or emotional) of the guilty party,[61] the fact of reconciliation brought both benefits and responsibilities. One of the benefits was the knowledge that one could fulfill one's tasks in the full confidence of a restored relationship. In *PMich.* VIII.502, for example, the soldier Gemellus asks his brother Valerius for reconciliation "so that I may enjoy your confidence also while I am in service" (ll. 8–9). The appeal stems from his recognition that "there is no other hope like the candid intercourse (παρησία) of brothers and one's own people" (ll. 11–13). For that reason, he also enjoins his brother to "persuade mother" (l. 14), viz., to be reconciled to him.[62]

As far as responsibilities are concerned, the reconciled were expected to live in light of their renewed concord with one another and henceforth to live irreproachably. An example of this aspect of the paradigm occurs in Euripides' play *Iphigenia at Aulis*, which was produced posthumously in 406 or 405 B.C.E. In the play Clytemnestra speaks to her husband Agamemnon and rehearses the history of their relationship. She says that their relationship began in great conflict, that he had killed her husband Tantalus, violently torn her baby from her breasts, and dashed the child upon the ground (1150–52). Thereupon he had married her "by force" and "against her will" (1149). Her brothers had then made war on him, forcing Agamemnon to supplicate Clytemnestra's father Tyndareus, who rescued Agamemnon and allowed him to keep his daughter (1153–56). Thereupon, Clytemnestra says,

> So, reconciled (καταλλαχθεῖσα) to thee and to thine house,
> A blameless (ἄμεμπτος) wife was I,—be witness thou,—
> Chaste (σωφρονοῦσα) in desires, increasing in thine halls
> Thy substance still, so that thine enterings-in
> Were joy (χαίρειν), and thine outgoings happiness
> (1157–61; trans. LCL).[63]

In short, her virtuous life and the benefits that she has brought Agamemnon provide empirical proof that she was in fact fully reconciled to her husband and did not just simply coexist with him under one roof. Joy, happiness, and prosperity were benefits that Agamemnon enjoyed as a result of Clytemnestra's reconciliation.

Paul's Shift of the Reconciliation Paradigm

As with the two other paradigms that we have examined, Paul does not simply take over the paradigm but shifts some of its elements. To begin with, he takes what was largely a secular term used for interpersonal and international relations and applies it to the divine-human relationship (2 Cor 5:18–20; Rom 5:10–11). There was solid albeit limited precedent for doing this, both in Greek and in Jewish tradition.[64] In Sophocles' *Ajax*, the protagonist Ajax angers the gods, especially Athena, by arrogantly refusing her proffered assistance in battle (756–77; see also 127–33). He refuses because he thinks that it will eliminate his ground for boasting as a great warrior (764–69). Subsequently humbled by the indignities that he suffered, he goes, according to the chorus, "to be reconciled with the gods" (744). In the context of the play, that means concretely to escape Athena's wrath (ὀργήν: 777) and harsh fury (μῆνιν: 656, 757).[65] Similarly in Jewish tradition, reconciliation with God involves averting his anger, which has been caused by sin (2 Macc 5:17–20; 7:33). Hence the appeal for God to be reconciled takes the form of prayer (1:5) and supplication (8:29), and this appeal is made with the firm conviction that God is not implacable but easily reconciled (εὐκατάλλακτον: 3 Macc 5:13; εὐδιάλλακτον: Josephus, *J. W.* 5.415).[66] The belief that the divine is easily reconciled is by no means unique to Judaism; it is also found in Greco-Roman pagan culture.

Indeed, while Paul is the first Jewish (Christian) author to merge the concepts of atonement and reconciliation, he is not the first person to do so in the Greco-Roman world. The two key terms are merged already by Dionysius of Halicarnassus (born no later than 53 B.C.E.), who, in blending these concepts, is almost certainly following established tradition rather than innovating. The two ideas appear in a speech that Dionysius places in the mouth of Veturia, the mother of Marcius Coriolanus, who is attempting to persuade her son to be less vengeful and more placable toward his fellow Romans:

> For the gods themselves . . . are disposed to forgive the offenses of men and are easily reconciled (εὐδιάλλακτοι); and many have there been ere now who, though greatly sinning against them, have appeased (ἐξιλάσαντο) their anger by prayers and sacrifices. Unless you think it is fitting, Marcius, that the anger of the gods should be mortal, but that of men immortal! (*Ant. rom.* 8.50.4; trans. LCL)[67]

While Paul, therefore, is not the first to integrate these two concepts, he has a far different notion of what atonement and reconciliation entail than does Dionysius. Indeed, Paul does more than apply reconciliation language to the divine-human relationship. He shifts the paradigm by making God, the offended party, the one who takes the initiative in reconciliation. This initiative is taken, moreover, when humans are still sinners (Rom 5:8) and hostile (ἐχθροί) to God (Rom 5:10). The shift here is thus in continuity with the shift in the paradigm involving sacrifice, where God's action is taken both prior to and apart from human repentance. The shift in these two paradigms is of momentous import, for it suggests a radically new and unprecedented understanding of God. Because sinful humanity would not or could not take the steps necessary to bring about atonement and reconciliation—the very steps that God had ordained—God has done so and thereby assumed responsibility for both atonement and reconciliation. Changes to traditional paradigms inevitably reflect changes in conception, and Paul's paradigm shifts are no exception.

Paul's appearance as the envoy for Christ also involves an interesting shift that is in keeping with the one he has made about God undertaking the initiative for reconciliation. Envoys usually were sent by those who were in difficult and desperate circumstances, and who thus were anxious to end the conflict and resume friendly relations.[68] Therefore, according to the normal paradigm, Paul would have been *humanity's* envoy to God, anxious to avert the wrath of an angry Deity.[69] But Paul appears here instead as an ambassador for Christ, having been sent by God to proclaim the good news of God's act and offer of reconciliation.[70] And what compels this apostolic embassy is not the anger of an offended God, but the love of Christ (2 Cor 5:14). Consequently, the philophronetic elements that typically accompanied appeals for reconciliation are also shifted in Paul's new paradigm, so that they now belong to both God (who acts "for us": 5:21) and Christ (5:14).

What about the death of Christ? Within the context of the reconciliation paradigm, it is best interpreted in one of two ways. First, it may represent Paul's appropriation of the cultic concept of sacrifice as the appropriate means of repairing the divine-human relationship. Because "reconciliation" was primarily a secular concept, religious terms were rarely used in discussing it. But the potential for doing so is shown by a passage in Plato's *Menexenus*, where reconciliation following the war at Eleusis is discussed (243e–244b). The survivors of the war can be reconciled in the normal way, but what about the dead? For them to be reconciled, they must be treated *as though they were gods* and thus reconciled through prayers and sacrifices:

> And of those who fell in this war also it is meet to make mention and to reconcile (διαλλάττειν) them by such means as we can under present conditions,—by prayer, that is, and by sacrifice,—praying for them to those that have them in their keeping, seeing that we ourselves also have been reconciled (διηλλάγμεθα). (*Menex.* 241a, trans. LCL)

Therefore, the process of blending the concepts of sacrifice and reconciliation begins as early as Plato and appears fully formed in Dionysius of Halicarnassus. If Paul's reference to the death of Christ is sacrificial, it fits well within this established process of integrating the two conceptual paradigms when speaking of the divine.[71]

Second, the death of Christ may also be interpreted strictly within the standard reconciliation paradigm. In that case, it can be viewed as the "reparations" payment essential to the reconciliation of God and humanity. If so, Paul has once more (as with sacrifice) shifted the paradigm, this time by removing the reparations item from offending humanity and attributing it to God, who thus reconciles "through the death of his Son" (Rom 5:10). The idea that death can bring about reconciliation was an old notion, but it usually involved the death of one or more of the antagonists in the conflict.[72] For example, in Aeschylus' *Seven against Thebes* the two warring brothers, Eteocles and Polyneices, kill each other and thus "now at last are reconciled (διήλλαχθε)—by the sword" (884–85).[73] As the chorus remarks, the death of Oedipus's two sons was a "heavy reconciliation price" (βαρεῖαι καταλλαγαί: 767) that brought his curse to fulfillment.[74] But that hefty price pales in comparison with that which God pays to effect reconciliation and bring his promised blessings to fulfillment.

It may well be the case that both ways of viewing the death of Christ are legitimate. In any case, Paul's merging of the two originally different paradigms of reconciliation and atonement was prompted by certain elements common to each. As we have seen, repentance is common to both paradigms, and to a certain extent, the idea of making reparations is also connected with the ancient Israelite cultic tradition. One of the offerings specified in the Hebrew Bible is the "reparation offering" (Lev 5:14–26 [= 5:14–6:7 NRSV]; 7:1–7), which involved making financial restitution to the injured party (5:16, 23–24) as an essential prerequisite of atonement (5:16, 18, 26; 7:7). Indeed, since the root אשם (ʾšm) when used as a verb means "to incur liability" (e.g., 5:19), it is not surprising that the reparation offering is "the only sacrifice that is commutable into currency" (5:15, 18, 25).[75]

In addition, Israelites used the word *kōper* ("ransom," "redemption payment")[76]—a cognate of *kipper*—as a legal term to designate a "material gift that establishes an amicable settlement between an injured party and the offending party."[77] "[F]or the recipient," therefore, the *kōper* as a payment "represents compensation, reparation, indemnification; from the perspective of the offender, it represents a ransom . . . , a gift to propitiate the enraged injured party."[78] Furthermore, Deutero-Isaiah depicts Yahweh as the One who makes a *kōper* payment to secure the freedom of the exiled Judahites; to compensate Cyrus for releasing his people, God gives him Egypt, Ethiopia, and Seba in exchange (ἄλλαγμα: Isa 43:3 LXX). This Isaianic depiction of Yahweh as a Deity who willingly pays compensatory damages on behalf of his people may well have been the catalyst for Paul's dramatic paradigm shifts involving God.[79]

One final shift in the reconciliation paradigm may be noted. The idea of divine wrath is still present, but it is shifted in Rom 5:9 from the present (where it belongs in the reconciliation paradigm) to the future, where it applies to those who either reject the "message of reconciliation" (2 Cor

5:19) or do not allow their reconciliation to be effectual and thus receive the grace of God in vain (2 Cor 6:1). In terms of the paradigm, they have shown themselves to be people of ill will, rejecting all efforts at reconciliation. They are like the impenitent in the second paradigm, subject to the wrath of God on the day of judgment (Rom 2:5).

While there are thus important Pauline shifts in the traditional reconciliation paradigm, some features also remain intact. Four of these in 2 Corinthians 5–6 merit mention. First, in the paradigm the good will of the offended or stronger party is typically demonstrated in one or two ways. One way is by promising "to forget and forgive the past," i.e., by granting an amnesty in regard to all past injuries (see, e.g., Dion. Hal., *Ant. rom.* 3.8.4; 3.9.2–3; 7.27.1). The other way is by granting certain concessions to those seeking reconciliation. These concessions are viewed as gifts—acts of grace (χάριτι: Polyb. 1.31.6) and good will—that are intended to facilitate reconciliation. In keeping with the paradigm, God as the offended party demonstrates his good will in both of these ways. By "not counting their trespasses against them" (5:19), God is granting humans an amnesty in regard to everything that has ruptured the divine-human relationship. And as far as concessions are concerned, those granted by God are so sweeping in scope that the reparations needed to be made by humans are not just reduced; they are completely eliminated. Since God himself has assumed that obligation, the reconciliation that He offers humans is a free gift of pure grace, to be accepted or rejected. The only question is whether the Corinthians will now confirm their reconciliation or receive this gift in vain (6:1).[80]

Second, in keeping with the paradigm, "the message of reconciliation" is here cast in terms of a plea, "Be reconciled to God" (5:20). That it is an appeal is underscored by Paul's use of two words of entreaty, παρακαλῶ (5:20; 6:1) and δέομαι (5:20). He who, according to the paradigm, should be the recipient of the appeal, is emphatic in extending it.

Third, the note of urgency that accompanies many appeals for reconciliation appears in Paul's statement, "Behold, now is the acceptable time! Behold, now is the day of salvation!" (6:2). It is perhaps not insignificant that he introduces these expressions of urgent timeliness with a quotation from Isa 49:8 LXX, where the key phrase "at an acceptable time" (καιρῷ δεκτῷ = בעת רעון) occurs. The same Hebrew phrase occurs (without the ב-prefix) in Ps 69:14, where the LXX (68:14) renders it καιρὸς εὐδοκίας, but Symmachus renders it καιρὸς διαλλαγῆς. That is, the "acceptable time" is the time of Yahweh's favor, the "time of reconciliation." The appeal that began using the language and imagery of Hellenistic politics is thus concluded with a citation from the Greek version of the Hebrew Bible.

Fourth, Paul does not simply make an appeal to the Corinthians in regard to their reconciliation with God. He issues that appeal as one who himself has been reconciled by God (5:18). As such, he has been entrusted with a position of responsibility (5:19), and he proceeds by offering proof of the reality of his own reconciliation. Clytemnestra, as we have seen, did this by pointing to her blamelessness (ἄμεμπτος) as a wife, her virtuous self-control (σωφρονοῦσα), and the way in which she had enriched Agamemnon's estate and brought him both joy and happiness (Eur., *Iph. aul.* 1157–61). In a similar fashion, Paul points to the blamelessness (μὴ μωμηθῇ) of his ministry (6:3), gives a list of the virtues that he exhibits (6:4–7), and calls attention to both his own joy and the way in which he enriches others spiritually (6:10).[81] And just as Clytemnestra offered proof of her reconciliation in order to lay the foundation for her subsequent appeal on behalf of Iphigenia and to increase that appeal's effectiveness, so Paul in 2 Corinthians 6–7 proceeds to make other appeals to the Corinthians.

Reconciliation and Its Linkage Group

The first and foremost of these additional appeals in 2 Corinthians 6–7 is the call for a full reconciliation between himself and the Corinthians (6:11–13 + 7:2–4). Indeed, since there can be no reconciliation with God apart from a reconciliation with Paul as God's ambassador, this appeal constitutes the real point of the apostle's earlier exhortation to be reconciled to God (5:20). Like the heart of the God who entrusted him with the message of reconciliation, Paul's own heart stands wide open to the Corinthians (6:11); he has done nothing to harm them (7:2) or to present an obstacle (6:3) to their opening wide their hearts (6:13) and making room for him (7:2). There is thus no impediment to their reconciliation; there are no reparations that need to be made. And just as God had taken the initiative in reconciling Paul to himself, Paul now takes the initiative in trying fully to reconcile the Corinthians to himself.

That Paul calls attention to the frankness of his speech (6:11; 7:4) and says that the Corinthians are in his heart "to die together and to live together" (7:3) is significant. In the Greco-Roman world, candor is one of the most conspicuous marks of friendship,[82] and the language about dying and living together is a Christianized version of a traditional friendship formula.[83] The use of friendship language is appropriate in this context, for "reconciliation" language belongs to the friendship *topos*. That is, friendship and reconciliation belong to the same linkage group. Indeed, the basic meaning of both καταλλάσσειν and διαλλάσσειν is "to change from enmity to friendship."[84] And the widespread use of other friendship terms in diplomatic circles guaranteed that the language of "reconciliation" would be conceptually important in the political friendships of the Greek and Roman worlds.[85]

As Peter Marshall argued in his seminal work *Enmity in Corinth*, Greco-Roman conventions of friendship help illuminate several aspects of Paul's interaction with Corinth.[86] The relationship between them began in friendship but became strained, a phenomenon that was in fact a frequent occurrence among friends.[87] In calling for reconciliation, Paul is thus calling for a resumption of friendship between himself and the Corinthians.

In literary terms it is striking that Paul does not issue this call at the outset of the letter. His use of reconciliation language in regard to himself (5:18) and his call for full reconciliation with the Corinthians (6:11–13 + 7:2–4) are instead placed within the narrative framework of his painful, disastrous trip to Corinth and subsequent events (1:1–2:13 + 7:5–16).[88] This framework functions to provide the literary and historical context for his talk about reconciliation. His confidence (1:15) about their proud relationship with one another (1:14) had been shattered by that painful visit, and it is only Titus's report of their response to his severe letter and of their penitence (7:9–10) and renewed zeal for him (7:7, 11–12) that has restored his confidence in them (7:16). Paul's renewed confidence in the Corinthians is a corollary of their improved relationship and partial reconciliation.[89]

It is especially noteworthy from a literary perspective that Paul mentions his anxious search for Titus (2:12–13) but astutely delays the report of his joyful meeting with his coworker until 7:5. He thereby forces the Corinthians to read the whole of 2:14–7:4 in a state of suspense, to share his anxiety about Titus and the kind of news that he will bring. At this point Titus is, after all, as much their messenger to Paul as he is the apostle's envoy to Corinth. Until and unless Titus arrives and delivers his report, Paul and the Corinthians will remain deeply estranged. Theologically, this allows Paul to depict Titus's arrival as God's act (7:6), an act that comforts Paul and enables him in turn to comfort the Corinthians (1:3–7). Through Titus's arrival and report, God has acted to reconcile Paul and the Corinthians. In short, just as God acts to reconcile the world to himself (5:18–20), he also acts to bring about reconciliation between feuding friends.[90]

But God's action in this regard does not exhaust Paul's concern with reconciliation. In the renewed confidence of his friendship with the

Corinthians the apostle calls upon them to forgive and comfort the person who had caused him grief on his second visit to the city (2:5–7). In doing so, he is calling for the reconciliation of this person with the other Corinthian Christians and the resumption of their friendship with him. For Paul, reconciliation is thus the joyous result of a series of initiatives begun and sustained by God. Through Christ, God had taken the initiative in reconciling Paul to himself, and through Titus he has subsequently acted to reconcile Paul and the Corinthians. Paul, in turn, has taken the initiative in trying to bring about a full reconciliation with the Corinthians, and they are now to take the initiative in reconciling the offender to themselves. The reconciled church, for Paul, is a community of friends who are reconciled to both God and one another.

Finally, because "reconciliation" indicates the restoration of friendship, Paul's use of this term in conjunction with the divine-human relationship means that he is depicting God as the One who makes friends of his human adversaries. The friendship of the Christian community is thus grounded in its members' friendship with God. Theologically, this is highly significant, but the implications have been only rarely realized or emphasized in any commentary or translation.[91] A major exception in this regard is William Barclay, whose translation of 2 Cor 5:18–20 correctly captures the theological implications of Paul's thought:[92]

> And the whole process is due to the action of God, who through Christ turned our enmity to himself into friendship, and who gave us the task of helping others to accept that friendship. The fact is that God was acting in Christ to turn the world's enmity to himself into friendship, that he was not holding men's sins against them, and that he placed upon us the privilege of taking to men who are hostile to him the offer of his friendship. We are therefore Christ's ambassadors. It is as if God was making his appeal to you through us. As the representatives of Christ we appeal to you to accept the offer of friendship that God is making to you.[93]

In conclusion, in 2 Corinthians Paul not only shifts the paradigm of reconciliation but also draws on ideas traditionally associated with it. That is, he makes use of ideas that belong to reconciliation's linkage group, that nexus of interconnected ideas within which reconciliation has its conceptual home. Chief among these associated ideas is friendship. In view of Paul's deep concern that there be friendship between God and the Corinthians, between himself and the Corinthian church, and among the Corinthians themselves, it is not at all surprising that he should make use of the language of reconciliation. The surprise comes rather in the remarkable way in which Paul re-conceives reconciliation, shifts its paradigm, and uses that transformed paradigm in his dealings with the Corinthians. Such paradigm shifts are typical of Paul and provide insight into his extraordinary creativity as a theologian.

Appendix

The list of works on reconciliation is becoming quite extensive. Recent studies and older key contributions include the following: Gregory J. Allen, "Reconciliation in the Pauline Tradition: Its Occasions, Meanings, and Functions" (Th.D. Diss., Boston University School of Theology, 1995); G. K. Beale, "The Old Testament Background of Reconciliation in 2 Corinthians 5–7 and Its Bearing on the Literary Problem of 2 Corinthians 6.14–7.1," *NTS* 35 (1989): 550–81; Reimund Bieringer, "2 Korinther 5, 19a und die Versöhnung der Welt," *ETL* 63 (1987): 295–326, reprinted in R. Bieringer and J. Lambrecht, *Studies on 2 Corinthians,* BETL 112 (Leuven: University Press; Leuven: Peeters, 1994), 429–59; Günther Bornkamm, "The Revelation of Christ to Paul on the Damascus Road and Paul's Doctrine of Justification and Reconciliation," *Reconciliation and Hope: New Testament Essays on Atonement and Eschatology presented to L. L. Morris on his 60th Birthday,* ed. R. Banks (Grand Rapids: Eerdmans, 1974), 90–103; Friedrich Büchsel, "ἀλλάσσω, κτλ.," *TDNT* 1.251–9; Christoph Burger, *Schöpfung und Versöhnung: Studien zum liturgischen Gut im Kolosser- und Epheserbrief,* WMANT 46 (Neukirchen-Vluyn: Neukirchener, 1975); Jacques Dupont, *La réconciliation dans la théologie de Saint Paul,* ALBO 2.32 (Bruges and Paris: Desclée de Brouwer, 1953); Hans-Jürgen Findeis, *Versöhnung—Apostolat— Kirche: Eine exegetisch-theologische und rezeptionsgeschichtliche Studie zu den Versöhnungsaussagen des Neuen Testaments (2 Kor, Röm, Kol, Eph),* FB 40 (Würzburg: Echter, 1983); Joseph A. Fitzmyer, "Reconciliation in Pauline Theology," *No Famine in the Land: Studies in Honor of John L. McKenzie,* ed. J. W. Flanagan and A. W. Robinson (Missoula: Scholars, 1975), 155–77, and reprinted with a new bibliographical footnote in his *To Advance the Gospel: New Testament Studies,* 2d ed., The Biblical Resource Series (Grand Rapids: Eerdmans; Livonia: Dove, 1998), 162–85; N. S. L. Fryer, "Reconciliation in Paul's Epistle to the Romans," *Neot* 15 (1981): 34–68; Victor Paul Furnish, "The Ministry of Reconciliation," *CurTM* 4 (1977): 204–18; W. Hulitt Gloer, *An Exegetical and Theological Study of Paul's Understanding of New Creation and Reconciliation in 2 Cor. 5:14–21,* Mellen Biblical Press Series 42 (Lewiston:

Mellen, 1996); Leonhard Goppelt, "Versöhnung durch Christus," *Christologie und Ethik: Aufsätze zum Neuen Testament* (Göttingen: Vandenhoeck & Ruprecht, 1968), 147–64; Lars Hartman, "Universal Reconciliation (Col 1, 20)," SNTSU 10 (1985): 109–21; Paul Michael Hedquist, "The Pauline Understanding of Reconciliation in Romans 5 and II Corinthians 5: An Exegetical and Religio-Historical Study" (Th.D. Diss., Union Theological Seminary, Richmond, Virginia, 1979); Otfried Hofius, *Paulusstudien*, WUNT 51 (Tübingen: Mohr-Siebeck, 1989), which contains his "Erwägungen zur Gestalt und Herkunft des paulinischen Versöhnungsgedankens" (1–14), "'Gott hat unter uns aufgerichtet das Wort von der Versöhnung' (2 Kor 5, 19)" (15–32), and "Sühne und Versöhnung: Zum paulinischen Verständnis des Kreuzestodes Jesu" (33–49); Ernst Käsemann, "Erwägungen zum Stichwort 'Versöhnungslehre' im Neuen Testament," *Zeit und Geschichte*, ed. E. Dinkler (Tübingen: Mohr-Siebeck, 1964), 47–59, and published in English as "Some Thoughts on the Theme 'The Doctrine of Reconciliation in the New Testament,'" *The Future of Our Religious Past: Essays in Honour of Rudolf Bultmann*, ed. J. M. Robinson (New York: Harper & Row, 1971), 49–64; Seyoon Kim, "2 Cor 5:11–21 and the Origin of Paul's Concept of 'Reconciliation,'" *NovT* 39 (1997): 360–84; Jan Lambrecht, "'Reconcile yourselves . . .': A Reading of 2 Cor 5, 11–21," *The Diakonia of the Spirit (2 Co 4:7–7:4)*, ed. L. de Lorenzi, Monographic Series of "Benedictina," Biblical-Ecumenical Section, 10 (Rome: St. Paul's Abbey, 1989), 161–209, reprinted in R. Bieringer and J. Lambrecht, *Studies on 2 Corinthians*, BETL 112 (Leuven: University Press; Leuven: Peeters, 1994), 363–412; G. W. H. Lampe, *Reconciliation in Christ* (New York: Longmans, Green, 1956); Eduard Lohse, "Das Amt, das die Versöhnung predigt," *Rechtfertigung: Festschrift für Ernst Käsemann zum 70. Geburtstag*, ed. J. Friedrich, W. Pöhlmann, and P. Stuhlmacher (Tübingen: Mohr-Siebeck; Göttingen: Vandenhoeck & Ruprecht, 1976), 339–49; Dieter Lührmann, "Rechtfertigung und Versöhnung: Zur Geschichte der paulinischen Tradition," *ZTK* 67 (1970): 437–52; I. Howard Marshall, "The Meaning of 'Reconciliation,'" *Unity and Diversity in New Testament Theology: Essays in Honor of George E. Ladd*, ed. R. E. Guelich (Grand Rapids: Eerdmans, 1978), 117–32; Ralph P. Martin, "Reconciliation and Forgiveness in Colossians," *Reconciliation and Hope: New Testament Essays on Atonement and Eschatology presented to L. L. Morris on his 60th Birthday*, ed. R. Banks (Grand Rapids: Eerdmans, 1974), 104–24; idem, *Reconciliation: A Study of Paul's Theology*, New Foundations Theological Library (Atlanta: John Knox, 1981); idem, "Reconciliation: Romans 5:1–1," *Romans and the People of God: Essays in Honor of Gordon D. Fee on the Occasion of His 65th Birthday*, ed. S. K. Soderlund and N. T. Wright (Grand Rapids: Eerdmans, 1999), 36–48; H. Merkel, "καταλλάσσω, κτλ.," *EDNT* 2.261–3; Leon Morris, *The Apostolic Preaching of the Cross* (Grand Rapids: Eerdmans, 1955), 186–223; Peter T. O'Brien, "Colossians 1:20 and the Reconciliation of All Things," *RTR* 33 (1974): 45–53; Rudolf Pesch, "Reconciliation, New Testament," *Encyclopedia of Biblical Theology*, ed. J. B. Bauer, 3d ed., 3 vols. (London: Sheed and Ward, 1970), 2.735–8; Stanley E. Porter, *Καταλλάσσω in Ancient Greek Literature, with Reference to the Pauline Writings*, Estudios de filología neotestamentaria 5 (Cordoba and Madrid: Ediciones el Almendro, 1994); idem, "Reconciliation and 2 Cor 5, 18–21," *The Corinthian Correspondence*, ed. R. Bieringer, BETL 125 (Leuven: University Press; Leuven: Peeters, 1996), 693–705; John Reumann, "Reconciliation," *IDBSup* 728–9; Jens Schröter, *Der versöhnte Versöhner: Paulus als unentbehrlicher Mittler im Heilsvorgang zwischen Gott und Gemeinde nach 2 Kor 2, 14–7, 4*, TANZ 10 (Tübingen: Francke, 1993), 291–320; Eduard Schweizer, "Versöhnung des Alls: Kolosser 1, 20," *Jesus Christus in Historie und Theologie: Neutestamentliche Festschrift für Hans Conzelmann zum 60. Geburtstag*, ed. G. Strecker (Tübingen: Mohr-Siebeck, 1975), 487–501, repr. in his *Neues Testament und Christologie im Werden: Aufsätze* (Göttingen: Vandenhoeck & Ruprecht, 1982), 164–78; A. Stöger, "Die paulinische Versöhnungstheologie," *TPQ* 122 (1974): 118–31; Vincent Taylor, *Forgiveness and Reconciliation: A Study in New Testament Theology* (London: Macmillan, 1941), 83–129; and H. Vorländer and C. Brown, "καταλλάσσω," *NIDNTT* 3.166–76. Additional bibliography will be found in the works cited above.

Notes

Chapter 1: Judaism, Hellenism, and the Birth of Christianity

1. H. D. Betz, "Hellenism," *The Anchor Bible Dictionary,* ed. D. N. Freedman et al. (New York: Doubleday, 1992), 3: 129.

2. E. Bickerman, *Der Gott der Makkabäer: Untersuchungen über Sinn und Ursprung der makkabäischen Erhebung* (Berlin: Schocken, 1937). To mention only some of the most influential of the other works: V. Tcherikover, *Hellenistic Civilization and the Jews,* trans. S. Applebaum (Philadelphia: Jewish Publication Society, 1961); M. Hengel, *Judaism and Hellenism: Studies in Their Encounter in Palestine During the Early Hellenistic Period,* trans. J. Bowden (London: SCM, 1974); J. J. Collins, *Between Athens and Jerusalem: Jewish Identity in the Hellenistic Diaspora* (New York: Crossroad, 1983); E. Bickerman, *From Ezra to the Last of the Maccabees: Foundations of Postbiblical Judaism* (New York: Schocken, 1962).

3. The banner of the Tübingen School's evolutionary revision of early Christian history was first raised by F. C. Baur, "Die Christuspartei in der korinthischen Gemeinde, der Gegensatz des petrinischen und paulinischen Christenthums in der ältesten Kirche, der Apostel Petrus in Rom," *Tübinger Zeitschrift für Theologie* 4 (1831): 61–206. For a full account of the development, see P. C. Hodgson, *The Formation of Historical Theology: A Study of Ferdinand Christian Baur,* Makers of Modern Theology (New York: Harper and Row, 1966). A searching challenge to the basis of Baur's construct and its continuing influence: C. C. Hill, *Hellenists and Hebrews: Reappraising Division Within the Earliest Church* (Minneapolis: Augsburg Fortress, 1992).

4. F. C. Baur, *The Writing of Church History,* A Library of Protestant Thought, ed. and trans. P. C. Hodgson (New York: Oxford University Press, 1968).

5. The literature on the history of anti-Semitism in modern German scholarship is large and growing. It is difficult to choose a representative sample, but I call attention to a developing school of social-historical analysis of the roots and flowering of anti-Semitism. See, e.g., the essays collected in W. Jochmann, *Gesellschaftskrise und Judenfeindschaft in Deutschland 1870–1945,* Hamburger Beiträge Zur Sozial- und Zeitgeschichte (Hamburg: Christians, 1988). See also H.-U. Wehler, ed., *Scheidewege der deutschen Geschichte: Von der Reformation bis zur Wende, 1517–1989* (Munich: Beck, 1995); R. P. Ericksen, *Theologians Under Hitler: Gerhard Kittel, Paul Althaus, and Emanuel Hirsch* (New Haven

and London: Yale University Press, 1985); M. Weinreich, *Hitler's Professors: The Part of Scholarship in Germany's Crimes Against the Jewish People* (New York: Yiddish Scientific Institute—YIVO, 1946); J. A. Zabel, *Nazism and the Pastors: A Study of the Ideas of Three* Deutsche Christen *Groups*, AAR Dissertation Series (Missoula, Mont.: Scholars, 1976). Further bibliography: H.-U. Wehler, *Bibliographie zur neueren deutschen Sozialgeschichte* (Munich: Beck, 1993). I hope soon to publish a study of the specific hermeneutical elements in anti-Semitic NT scholarship.

6. W. W. Tarn, *Hellenistic Civilization,* 3d ed., rev. G. T. Griffith (Cleveland: World Publishing, Meridian, 1961), 2.

7. See J. Rüsen, *Begriffene Geschichte: Genesis und Begründung der Geschichtstheorie J. G. Droysens,* Sammlung Schöningh zur Geschichte und Gegenwart (Paderborn: Schöningh, 1969), esp. 28–37, 46–9, 133–41. Droysen's best known work is *Geschichte des Hellenismus,* ed. E. Bayer (Basel: Schwabe, 1952–3).

8. G. Lüdemann and M. Schröder, *Die religionsgeschichtliche Schule in Göttingen: eine Dokumentation* (Göttingen: Vandenhoeck & Ruprecht, 1987); Carsten Colpe, *Die religionsgeschichtliche Schule: Darstellung und Kritik ihres Bildes vom gnostischen Erlösermythus,* FRLANT 78 (Göttingen: Vandenhoeck & Ruprecht, 1961).

9. A few signposts: W. Heitmüller, "Zum Problem Paulus und Jesus," *ZNW* 13 (1912): 320–37; W. Bousset, *Kyrios Christos: Geschichte des Christusglaubens von den Anfängen des Christentums bis Irenaeus,* 5th ed. (Göttingen: Vandenhoeck & Ruprecht, 1965); R. Bultmann, *Das Urchristentum im Rahmen der antiken Religionen,* Erasmus-Bibliothek (Zurich: Artemis, 1949); R. Bultmann, *Theology of the New Testament,* Scribner Studies in Contemporary Theology, trans. K. Grobel (New York: Scribner's, 1951).

10. F. V. Filson, *The New Testament Against Its Environment: The Gospel of Christ, the Risen Lord,* Studies in Biblical Theology (London: SCM, 1950); G. E. Wright, *The Old Testament Against Its Environment,* Studies in Biblical Theology (London: SCM, 1950). One of the most influential voices of the anti-Hellenism reaction was that of Gerhard Kittel, who, after a period of close collaboration with Jewish scholars in the Weimar Republic, put his talents to the service of National Socialism from 1933 until the end of World War II. In lectures at Uppsala University in 1931, Kittel declared that "Pharisaic-Rabbinic" Judaism, despite visible influences of Hellenistic culture on all parts of Jewish life, even in Palestine, was able to remain a "non-syncretistic religion," being a "religion of the Word." That same resistance to syncretism was transmitted to the daughter faith, Christianity, which however "fulfilled" and superseded Judaism (G. Kittel, *Die Religionsgeschichte und das Urchristentum* [Gütersloh: Bertelsmann, 1931]). See also his *Urchristentum, Spätjudentum, Hellenismus: akademische Antrittsvorlesung gehalten am 28. Oktober 1926* (Stuttgart: Kohlhammer, 1926). The historical-apologetic schema was incorporated into the plan for Kittel's major legacy to scholarship, his *Theological Dictionary of the New Testament*; see his 1937 lectures at Cambridge, *Lexicographia Sacra: Two Lectures on the Making of the Theologisches Wörterbuch Zum Neuen Testament,* "Theology" Occasional Papers (London: SPCK, 1938). The older scholars Gustav Dalman and Adolf Schlatter (Kittel's predecessor in the NT chair at Tübingen) had also weighed in on the Jewish side of the "Judaism or Hellenism" debate, and the younger Joachim Jeremias carried on the fight.

11. Robert Henry Charles, *Religious Development Between the Old and the New Testaments* (1914; repr., London: Oxford University Press, 1948).

12. Charles, *Development,* 33.

13. G. F. Moore, *Judaism in the First Centuries of the Christian Era: The Age of the Tannaim* (Cambridge, Mass.: Harvard University Press, 1927), 1.129, referring to G. F. Moore, "Christian Writers on Judaism," *HTR* 14 (1921): 247–8.

14. Moore, *Judaism*, 1.126, 125.

15. E. R. Goodenough, *Jewish Symbols in the Greco-Roman Period*, Bollingen Series (New York: Pantheon; Princeton: Princeton University Press, 1953–68); C. Hopkins, *The Discovery of Dura-Europos*, ed. B. Goldman (New Haven and London: Yale University Press, 1979), 126–77. For a recent survey of evidence found in the land of Israel, see R. Hachlili, *Ancient Jewish Art and Archaeology in the Land of Israel*, Handbuch der Orientalistik, 7. Abteilung, 1. Band, 2. Abschnitt, B: Vorderasien, 4. Lieferung (Leiden: Brill, 1988).

16. An attempt to select representative works out of Neusner's monumental list of publications would be pointless here. His critical method was established—and the gauntlet flung down to traditional historiography—in J. Neusner, *The Rabbinic Traditions About the Pharisees Before 70* (Leiden: Brill, 1971), and the findings popularized in *From Politics to Piety: The Emergence of Pharisaic Judaism*, 2d ed. (New York: Ktav, 1979).

17. Despite recent challenges to the scholarly reconstruction of the Qumran settlement and the sect (whether Essene or a close relative) that was thought to have occupied it and to have used and, in part, produced the scrolls, of the nature of the documents, and of the dates and interrelationship of the archaeological sites, the weight of the evidence still seems to me to support the general picture outlined in this paragraph. A balanced general presentation is F. G. Martinez and J. T. Barrera, *The People of the Dead Sea Scrolls: Their Writings, Beliefs and Practices* (Leiden: Brill, 1995). Some of the controversy may be sampled in M. O. Wise, N. Golb, J. J. Collins and D. G. Pardee, eds., *Methods of Investigation of the Dead Sea Scrolls and the Khirbet Qumran Site: Present Realities and Future Prospects*, Annals of the New York Academy of Sciences (New York: New York Academy of Sciences, 1994).

18. Hengel, *Judaism and Hellenism*; see n. 2 above and other works cited there. M. Smith, "Palestinian Judaism in the First Century," in *Israel: Its Role in Civilization*, ed. M. Davis (New York: Jewish Theological Seminary, 1956), 71.

19. M. Rostovtzeff, *The Social and Economic History of the Roman Empire*, 2d ed., rev. P. M. Fraser (Oxford: Clarendon, 1957). The names of A. H. M. Jones, Moses Finley, P. R. C. Weaver, Keith Hopkins, G. Alföldi, Peter Brown, and Geoffrey de Ste Croix are prominent in the shaping of the discipline, and many others could be added. Particularly influential on my own work has been Ramsay MacMullen, e.g., R. MacMullen, *Roman Social Relations 50 B.C. to A.D. 284* (New Haven: Yale University Press, 1974); also his *Paganism in the Roman Empire* (New Haven and London: Yale University Press, 1981), and the essays collected in *Changes in the Roman Empire: Essays in the Ordinary* (Princeton: Princeton University Press, 1990).

Chapter 2: Paul and the Judaism/Hellenism Dichotomy

1. *Judentum und Hellenismus: Studien zu ihrer Begegnung unter besonderer Berücksichtigung Palästinas bis zur Mitte des 2. Jh. v. Chr.*, WUNT 10 (Tübingen: Mohr-Siebeck, 1969). I have used the English translation of the second, revised German edition, published in one volume (*Judaism and Hellenism* [Philadelphia: Fortress, 1981]); page numbers are to the English translation unless otherwise noted.

2. Repeatedly, New Testament scholars since World War II have tried to dislodge the Hellenistic/Jewish dualism. (See my highlighting below of remarks made

long ago by W. D. Davies.) In his book *Hebrews and Hellenists: Reappraising Division within the Earliest Church* (Minneapolis: Fortress, 1992), Craig Hill speaks even of "the *eclipse* of the dichotomy between Judaism and Hellenism" in contemporary New Testament scholarship (see 16, emphasis added; see also 21). I applaud the extent to which the dichotomy has been eclipsed, though I think Hill's comment may be overly optimistic given the ease with which many scholars still invoke the dualism.

3. This is the conclusion of a recent work addressing the issue: Timothy H. Lim, *Holy Scripture in the Qumran Commentaries and Pauline Letters* (Oxford: Clarendon, 1997), 161–4. I am not sure that Lim is correct in his confident assertions about Paul's grasp of Hebrew or Aramaic. Lim depends mainly on an acceptance of the accounts in Acts of Paul's "Jerusalem education," and that author's claim that Paul learned at the feet of Gamaliel. In my opinion, claims of what "must" have been the case given Paul's Jewish education and such a reliance on Acts for historical data are precarious. I would be more convinced by evidence drawn linguistically from Paul's own letters. This is, of course, not to deny that Paul understood Hebrew and Aramaic, just to point out our lack of clear historical evidence for it.

4. For example: Lev Shestov, *Athens and Jerusalem* (Athens, Ohio: Ohio University Press, 1966). Other books using "Athens and Jerusalem" in their titles thereby designate the relation between philosophy and theology; e.g., E. G. Weltin, *Athens and Jerusalem: An Interpretive Essay on Christianity and Classical Culture* (Atlanta: Scholars, 1987); Jack Arthur Bonsor, *Athens and Jerusalem: The Role of Philosophy in Theology* (New York: Paulist, 1993).

5. See also *Apology* 47; *Against Marcion* 1.13, 5.19; *On the Soul* 3, 23; the phrase "fathers of all heresy" occurs in *Prescription* 7 as well as in *Against Hermogenes* 8. Of course, this was all a highly rhetorical stance for Tertullian; he could, when he wished, make use of Greek philosophy for his own ends, as he does, to mention only one such case, when appropriating philosophical critiques of traditional myths (e.g., *Apology* 10–11).

6. Wayne A. Meeks, ed., *The Writings of St. Paul* (New York and London: Norton, 1972), 273.

7. Meeks, *Writings of St. Paul,* 274.

8. *Paul the Apostle of Jesus Christ,* 2d ed., rev. A. Menzies (London and Edinburgh: Williams and Norgate, 1876; first edition 1845 republication of articles that originally appeared in 1835 and 1836).

9. Baur, *Paul,* 58–60. The best recent critique of this thesis—and its long history and influence—is provided by Hill, *Hebrews and Hellenists.*

10. Baur, *Paul,* 5. Recall that Schweitzer had used the rhetoric of "either/or" to frame his book on the historical Jesus: the account had to be either purely historical or supernatural (the accomplishment of Strauss); it had to be based on either John or the Synoptics (the accomplishment of the Tübingen School); it had to be either eschatological or noneschatological (Schweitzer himself).

11. *Paul,* 60. What I mean by the phrase "gives form to his historical account" is that the dichotomy imposes a dualism where Baur's data have none. One might think that Baur has identified several different historical groups or forces that interact with one another in a complex web of connections: Hellenism, Hellenistic Jews, Pauline Christianity, Christianity, Judaism, the Mother Church of Jerusalem, Jewish Christianity, Paul, Jews, Greeks. But what could have been a web of connections among multiple entities becomes in Baur's system a simple dualistic opposition. I believe there is nothing in the historical material itself that mandates this distilling of multiplicity down to dualism. The dualism comes from Baur himself.

12. English trans. ed. Allan Menzies (London: Williams and Norgate, 1878–79; originally published in 1860).

13. See, e.g., Immanuel Kant, *Critique of Pure Reason*, II.ii.sec. 2: "The Ideal of the Highest Good, as a Determining Ground of the Ultimate End of Pure Reason" (New York: St. Martin's, 1965), 635–44. True religion must be universal, and Judaism is particular: beginning of Division 2, Book 3, *Religion Within the Limits of Reason Alone* (Chicago and London: Open Court, 1934), 116–17.

14. On Baur's Hegelianism, see John Riches, *A Century of New Testament Study* (Valley Forge, Pa.: Trinity, 1993), 31–2.

15. Note also the nineteenth-century romanticism of Baur's Paulinism in his description of Paul's "religious consciousness" (Baur, *Paul*, 65).

16. For an important Jewish reaction to the Tübingen School—that prompted in its turn still other Protestant reactions to itself—see Susannah Heschel, *Abraham Geiger and the Jewish Jesus* (Chicago: University of Chicago Press, 1998), esp. 112–19.

17. Adolf von Harnack, *What Is Christianity?* (Philadelphia: Fortress, 1986; original 1900), 177.

18. Albert Schweitzer, *Paul and His Interpreters: A Critical History* (London: Black, 1912), 63–4.

19. Schweitzer, *Paul and His Interpreters*, 30; see also Riches, *A Century*, 33–4.

20. W. D. Davies noted Schweitzer's tendency to isolate both Jesus and Paul from most of their environment. See his "Paul and Judaism," in *The Bible in Modern Scholarship*, ed. J. Philip Hyatt (Nashville and New York: Abingdon, 1965), 178–86, at 182; reprinted in the 4th edition of his *Paul and Rabbinic Judaism: Some Rabbinic Elements in Pauline Theology* (Philadelphia: Fortress, 1980; original 1948).

21. James S. Pasto, "Who Owns the Jewish Past? Judaism, Judaisms, and the Writing of Jewish History" (Ph.D. diss., Cornell University, 1999). Some of Pasto's research may be found in his articles "Islam's 'Strange Secret Sharer': Orientalism, Judaism, and the Jewish Question," *Comparative Studies in Society and History* 40 (1998): 437–74; and "When the End Is the Beginning? or When the Biblical Past Is the Political Present: Some Thoughts on Ancient Israel, 'Post-Exilic Judaism,' and the Politics of Biblical Scholarship," *Scandinavian Journal of the Old Testament* 12 (1998): 157–202.

22. Pasto, "Who Owns the Jewish Past?", 1–2.

23. For more general studies of Germany and Judaism of the period, see H. G. Adler, *The Jews in Germany: From the Enlightenment to National Socialism* (Notre Dame: University of Notre Dame Press, 1969); Uriel Tal, *Christians and Jews in Germany: Religion, Politics, and Ideology in the Second Reich, 1870–1914* (Ithaca: Cornell University Press, 1975); for a useful study of the presentation of Jews in scholarship: Christhard Hoffmann, *Juden und Judentum im Werk deutscher Althistoriker des 19. und 20. Jahrhunderts* (Leiden: Brill, 1988).

24. *Cosmopolis: The Hidden Agenda of Modernity* (Chicago: University of Chicago Press, 1990), 95.

25. See Pasto, "Who Owns the Jewish Past?", 138, 143, on which my narrative to a great extent depends.

26. Maurice Olender, *The Languages of Paradise: Race, Religion, and Philology in the Nineteenth Century* (Cambridge: Harvard University Press, 1992), 11, 31–3.

27. This is a paraphrase of Renan's own words, quoted in Olender, *Languages of Paradise*, 53. I have consulted the fifth edition of Renan's text: *Histoire générale et système comparé des langues sémitiques* (Paris: Michel Lévy Frères, 1878).

28. Olender, *Languages of Paradise*, 52; see Renan, *Histoire générale*, 16–18.

29. Olender, *Languages of Paradise*, 56.

30. See Martin Bernal, *Black Athena: The Afroasiatic Roots of Classical Civilization: Vol. 1, The Fabrication of Ancient Greece, 1785–1985* (New Brunswick, N.J.: Rutgers University Press, 1987), 290–1.

31. The classic treatment by E. M. Butler, *The Tyranny of Greece Over Germany*, is still entertaining and useful, though a bit romantic and now dated (Cambridge: Cambridge University Press, 1935).

32. Vassilis Lambropoulos, *The Rise of Eurocentrism: Anatomy of Interpretation* (Princeton: Princeton University Press, 1993), 57; Butler, *Tyranny*, 34–5, 59, 105, 109, 154.

33. See Jennifer Tolbert Roberts, *Athens on Trial: The Antidemocratic Tradition in Western Thought* (Princeton: Princeton University Press, 1994).

34. *Vorlesungen über die Altertumwissenschaft* (1831) 1.14 (*non vidi*), quoted in Ismar Schorsch, *From Text to Context: The Turn to History in Modern Judaism* (Hanover, N.H.: University of New England/Brandeis University Press, 1994), 346.

35. Lambropoulos, *Rise of Eurocentrism*, 69.

36. Olender, *Languages of Paradise*, 112.

37. See Tal, *Christians and Jews*, 40, 50, 63, et passim; Paul Lawrence Rose, *German Question/Jewish Question: Revolutionary Antisemitism from Kant to Wagner* (Princeton: Princeton University Press, 1990); Enzo Traverso, *The Marxists and the Jewish Question: The History of a Debate (1843–1943)* (Atlantic Highlands, N.J.: Humanities, 1993), esp. 2, 21–2.

38. John J. Collins, "Judaism as *Praeparatio Evangelica* in the work of Martin Hengel," *RelSRev* 15 (1989): 226–8.

39. See also Pasto, "Who Owns the Jewish Past?", 352–3.

40. I have depended much on the nicely balanced (i.e., non-Whiggish) history by David S. Katz, *The Jews in the History of England, 1485–1850* (Oxford: Clarendon, 1994).

41. See Steven N. Zwicker, "England, Israel, and the Triumph of Roman Virtue," *Millenarianism and Messianism in English Literature and Thought, 1650–1800*, ed. Richard H. Popkin (Leiden: Brill, 1988), 37–64, at 42. For some idea of the variety of representations of the Jews in Western Europe outside Germany, see the various essays in Richard H. Popkin and Gordon M. Weiner, eds., *Jewish Christians and Christian Jews: From the Renaissance to the Enlightenment* (Dordrecht: Kluwer, 1994).

42. My presentation of the rise of Hebrew studies in England is heavily dependent on G. Lloyd Jones, *The Discovery of Hebrew in Tudor England: A Third Language* (Manchester: Manchester University Press, 1983).

43. On the Hebraism of early Puritans, see e.g. Popkin, "Christian Jews and Jewish Christians in the 17th Century," in Popkin and Weiner, *Jewish Christians and Christian Jews*, 57–72, at 58; see also 63 for Hebraism in the millenial fervor in England in the 1640s and 50s.

44. See, for example, John Lightfoot, *Horae Hebraicae et Talmudicae: Hebrew and Talmudical Exercitations upon the Gospels, the Acts, Some Chapters of St. Paul's Epistle to the Romans, and the First Epistle to the Corinthians*, ed. Robert Gandell, 4 vols. (Oxford: Oxford University Press, 1859; published also in a two-volume edition of Lightfoot's works, eds. George Bright and John Strype, 1684). See the dedication in vol. 2, pp. 3–6 (originally written in Latin in 1658) in which Lightfoot argues for the use of Jewish texts to ascertain "the Jews' style, idiom, form, and rule of speaking," and "to inquire how, and in what sense, those phrases and manners of speech were understood, according to the vulgar and common dialect and opinion of that nation; and how they took them, by whom they were spoken, and by whom they were heard."

45. *The Whole Works of the Rev. John Lightfoot,* ed. John Rogers Pitman (London: Dove, 1822), 6.214. I am grateful to Matthew Bederman for drawing my attention to this sermon.

46. Bernal, *Black Athena*, 168, 192; Margaret C. Jacob, *The Radical Enlightenment: Pantheists, Freemasons, and Republicans* (London and Boston: Allen and Unwin, 1981); Frank E. Manuel, *The Religion of Isaac Newton* (Oxford: Clarendon, 1974), esp. 55–7, 85. On the "Israelite" character of true Christianity for Newton, see also Richard H. Popkin, "Polytheism, Deism, and Newton," *Essays on the Context, Nature, and Influence of Isaac Newton's Theology,* eds. James E. Force and Richard H. Popkin (Dordrecht: Kluwer, 1990), 27–42, at 31. For Newton, Greek literature and institutions were derivative of more ancient Hebrew culture: see the essay by Popkin in the same volume: "Newton as a Bible Scholar," 103–18, at 111. See also James E. Force, "Newton, the Lord God of Israel and Knowledge of Nature," in Popkin and Weiner, *Jewish Christians and Christian Jews,* 131–58.

47. John Locke, *A Paraphrase and Notes on the Epistles of St. Paul to the Galatians, Corinthians, Romans, and Ephesians to which is prefixed an Essay for the Understanding of St. Paul's Epistles by consulting St. Paul Himself* (London: Rivington, 1824; originally published posthumously in 1705).

48. Edward Synge, *St. Paul's Description of his own Religion Opened and Explained,* 5th (corrected) ed. (London: Rivington, 1779; original 1721).

49. *Lectures on the Sacred Poetry of the Hebrews,* trans. from the Latin by G. Gregory (London: Johnson, 1787), 1.311.

50. See Lightfoot, *Horae Hebraicae* (1859), 2.4–5.

51. See the examples given in Zwicker, "England, Israel," 38–9.

52. Frederic E. Faverty, *Matthew Arnold the Ethnologist* (Evanston, Ill.: Northwestern University Press, 1951), 42, 229–30, note 38; see also Heinrich Heine, *Works of Prose,* ed. Hermann Kesten (New York: Fischer, 1943), 130.

53. English trans. of French edition of German *Götter in Exil,* quoted in Heine, *Works of Prose,* 130.

54. Peter Gay, *The Enlightenment: The Rise of Modern Paganism* (New York: Knopf, 1966), 33. Pasto points out that Heine did not actually use the term *Hebrew* or *Hebraism* in opposition to "Hellene." The basic opposition of Judaism to Hellenism is, nonetheless, present in Heine.

55. Matthew Arnold's father, Thomas Arnold, had already been influential in the first half of the nineteenth century for his introduction of German scholarship on Greece, and along with it a passionate philhellenism and anti-Semitism, into English intellectual circles and educational institutions. Matthew Arnold's Hebraism/Hellenism dichotomy shows influences from his father, from Heine, and from the older English traditions of Christian Hebraism.

56. *Culture and Anarchy,* ed. Samuel Lipman (New Haven and London: Yale University Press, 1994), 87–8. The influence of Arnold's ideas here was enduring. Toward the end of the century, for example, Edwin Hatch gave the Hibbert Lectures (in 1888). Hatch died in 1889 and had provided no reference notes to his lectures; they were edited by A. M. Fairburn from notes and published soon after Hatch's death. So it is not clear whether Hatch knew he was borrowing from Arnold when he identified "conduct" with the Sermon on the Mount and the "Semitic" origins of Christianity and "belief" with the church creeds, which became possible only after Christianity had been "transferred" to "a Greek soil." To me, at any rate, the influence, either direct or indirect, of Arnold seems clear. See Edwin Hatch, *The Influence of Greek Ideas on Christianity* (Gloucester, Mass.: Smith, 1970), 2.

57. For Arnold's application of these ideas to Paul, see his *St. Paul and Protestantism,*

with an Essay on Puritanism and the Church of England, 3d ed. (New York: Macmillan, 1875), a book prompted by Arnold's attempt to rescue Paul from E. Renan's characterization of him as the main representative of Protestantism (3). In Arnold's treatment, Protestantism is found in Calvinism (predestination and election) and Methodism (justification by faith and moralism), but not the Church of England. Paul is of "the Semitic race"; he "Hebraizes," "Oriental-izes," and even "Judaizes," but for Arnold this refers mainly to Paul's "arbitrary and uncritical" use of Scripture (30, 33; see xviii for typical anti-Jewish state-ments). Puritans and Methodists take certain tendencies in Paul too far. Paul's own beliefs in justification and election were tempered by his reliance on "expe-rience," and his "Hebraism" was deeper and more truly Christian than the Puri-tans' and Methodists'.

58. Brevard S. Childs, *Biblical Theology in Crisis* (Philadelphia: Fortress, 1970).
59. Grand Rapids: Eerdmans, 1961. By using Ellis's work as the example of the Bib-lical Theology Movement, I do not mean to imply that he himself would have characterized his position as one of "neo-orthodoxy." Ellis, like many other con-servatives of the time, may well have seen neo-orthodoxy as betraying essentials of Christian faith or even as liberalism in disguise. (See, for example, the account of conservative reaction to neo-orthodoxy provided by Dennis Voskuil, "Neoorthodoxy," *Reformed Theology in America: A History of Its Modern Devel-opment,* ed. David F. Wells [Grand Rapids: Eerdmans, 1985], 247–62.) I do believe that, regardless of how Ellis would characterize his own position theo-logically, his views on Hellenism and Judaism are those shared by American scholars across a wide spectrum of theological opinion and that those views show the broad influence of neo-orthodoxy on the biblical theology movement in America. On a different note, it is ironic that in the same year (1961) that Ellis was announcing the stability of a consensus valuing Hebrew mentality over Greek as a way of understanding Paul, one of the first, and most devastating, criticisms of the entire enterprise of opposing "Greek" to "Hebrew" "mentali-ties" was published. I refer to James Barr, *The Semantics of Biblical Language* (Oxford: Oxford University Press, 1961). For an estimate of the importance of Barr's criticisms, note the remark of Childs: "Seldom has one book brought down so much superstructure with such effectiveness" (*Biblical Theology,* 72).
60. Davies insisted, more than once, that the dichotomy itself was misleading and should be jettisoned. See the preface added to the fourth edition of *Paul and Rabbinic Judaism,* reprinted from *The Bible in Modern Scholarship.* But Davies had already made this point on p. 1 of the first edition. Ellis took Davies's com-ments merely to be a claim that Paul was influenced by Hellenism *only via* rab-binic Judaism, which is not Davies's view.
61. Note Childs's attention to the importance of "revelation in history" for the *American* biblical theology movement: Childs, *Biblical Theology,* 39–44. Childs also emphasizes that one of the things that make the biblical theology move-ment particularly American—or different in its American manifestation as opposed to British or Continental relatives—is its reflection of the earlier Fun-damentalist/Modernist debates in the U.S. in the 1910s and 1920s: see, e.g., Childs, 19. But we should also take note of the influence on American schol-ars (even outside biblical scholarship) exercised by a non-American work that became known in the U.S. after the war. I refer to Erich Auerbach, *Mimesis: The Representation of Reality in Western Literature* (Princeton: Princeton Univer-sity Press, 1953; German original written between 1942 and 1945 in Istanbul and published in Switzerland in 1946). Lambropoulos's discussion (one-sided though it is) rightly emphasizes the influence exercised by the first chapter of *Mimesis* ("Odysseus' Scar") on later constructions of Hellenism and Judaism.

I realize that my statements in this section are sweeping and generalizing, but I believe they are nonetheless accurate for the most part—and that some attempt must be made to link the themes of the biblical theology movement to broader cultural issues. There is a real need for an in-depth sociological or social-historical study of neo-orthodoxy in the U.S. The only account that claims to be such that I know of is Toyamasa Fusé, "A Sociological Analysis of Neo-orthodoxy in American Protestantism" (Ph.D. diss., University of California at Berkeley, 1962). But Fusé's study focuses almost solely on Reinhold Niebuhr's writings and influence, and it is really a "history of ideas" rather than a sociological study. For a fascinating social-historical account of a similar American phenomenon of biblical scholarship, see Burke O. Long, *Planting and Reaping Albright: Politics, Ideology, and Interpreting the Bible* (University Park, Pa.: The Pennsylvania State University Press, 1997). Long uses archival research and social network analysis (among other methods) in his study.

62. Note that in H. Richard Niebuhr's influential formulation, "culture" in differentiation from "Christ" refers to the "social," to "human achievement," "values" that "are dominantly those of the good of man" (i.e., humanism), the "temporal and material realization of values," the "conservation of values," and "pluralism" (*Christ and Culture* [New York: Harper and Brothers, 1951], 32–9). This is not to imply that Niebuhr himself placed Judaism on the "Christ" side of the dichotomy. That is the implication, rather, of much biblical scholarship.

63. See Paul Ritterband and Harold S. Wechsler, *Jewish Learning in American Universities: The First Century* (Bloomington and Indianapolis: Indiana University Press, 1994).

64. See *Die letzten dreißig Jahre: Rückblicke* (Stuttgart: Klett, 1956); and H.-J. Schoeps, *"Bereit für Deutschland!": Der Patriotismus deutscher Juden und der Nationalsozialismus: Frühe Schriften 1930 bis 1939, Eine historische Dokumentation* (Berlin: Haude und Spenersche, 1970), esp. 17.

65. Philadelphia: Westminster, 1961. The German publication date was 1959. See also the discussion by Friedrich Wilhelm Kantzenbach, Introduction to vol. 1 of Schoeps's *Gesammelte Schriften,* ed. Julius J. Schoeps (Hildesheim: Olms, 1990), v–xx.

66. Note such phrases as "Jewish belief of all ages" (188); "the Jews have never" (193); "every child of the Jews . . . knows" (194); "has always been unintelligible to the Jewish thinker" (202). In each case, Schoeps presents Paul's thoughts as absolutely inconceivable by any Jew anywhere, anytime—thus making Paul not a Jew.

67. Note that Schoeps himself explicitly draws a parallel between Paul's day and modern Germany, with "assimilation" as the salient feature: 280–1. Schoeps's views, of course, arose out of liberal Jewish thought of the "Second Reich": compare Adler, *Jews in Germany*, 105–9; Heschel, *Abraham Geiger.*

68. Berkeley: University of California Press, 1994.

69. New Haven and London: Yale University Press, 1990.

70. See 136, for example, for Segal's insistence that mystical union and other aspects of the mysteries that previous scholars attributed to Hellenism need not be so clearly marked. As Segal presents the situation, Jewish tradition had already absorbed much that we associate with Hellenistic mysteries, in apocalypticism and elsewhere. The two cultures, by this time, had already been mutually influenced and joined.

71. Alfred A. Kroeber and Klyde Kluckhohn, *Culture: A Critical Review of Concepts and Definitions* (Cambridge, Mass.: Papers of the Peabody Museum of American Archaeology and Ethnology, Harvard University, 1952), 3, quoted in Kathryn Tanner, *Theories of Culture: A New Agenda for Theology*, Guides to

Theological Inquiry Series (Minneapolis: Fortress, 1997), ix. My treatment of the development and changes in the category of *culture* is here very dependent on Tanner's concise and helpful summary of recent scholarship.

72. Margaret Mead, Preface to Ruth Benedict, *Patterns of Culture* (Boston: Houghton and Mifflin, 1961), xi; see Tanner, *Theories of Culture*, x.

73. The critique by Bruno Latour is especially intriguing; see his *We Have Never Been Modern* (Cambridge: Harvard University Press, 1993).

Chapter 3: Hellenism and Hellenization as Problematic Historiographical Categories

1. A comprehensive, if somewhat controversial, account of the concept of Hellenism in the modern period is M. Bernal, *Black Athena: The Afroasiatic Roots of Classical Civilization*, vol. 1: *The Fabrication of Ancient Greece 1785–1985* (London: Free Press Association, 1987). Also useful for the modern period is M. Olender, *The Languages of Paradise: Race, Religion, and Philosophy in the Nineteenth Century*, trans. A. Goldhammer (Cambridge, Mass.: Harvard University Press, 1992).

2. Academic historians when they define Hellenism tend to concentrate on only two aspects of the history of the term, namely its use by the Greeks and its use by modern academic historians. There is a disturbing implication here that the academy is somehow divorced from political influence and that the ideological associations of the term in common parlance do not affect its use in academic discourse. Such an ivory-tower attitude scarcely needs refutation. See further Dale Martin's essay.

3. Pinchas E. Lapide, *Hebräisch in den Kirchen,* Forschungen zum jüdisch-christlichen Dialog 1 (Neukirchen-Vluyn: Neukirchener, 1976), English trans.: *Hebrew in the Church: The Foundations of Jewish-Christian Dialogue* (Grand Rapids, Mich.: Eerdmans, 1984) offers a useful survey of Christian Hebraism, but with inaccuracies, particularly in the English translation.

4. See my "The Song of Songs as Historical Allegory: Notes on the Development of an Exegetical Tradition," *Targumic and Cognate Studies: Essays in Honour of Martin McNamara,* eds. K. J. Cathcart and M. Maher (Sheffield: Sheffield Academic Press, 1996), 14–29.

5. The current situation of Hebraism in the Church is full of irony. Contemporary Christian Hebraists, by going behind the Masoretic text through appeal to the Dead Sea Scrolls, the early versions and comparative philology, have largely freed themselves from dependence on Jewish Hebraism (though Israeli biblical scholarship, thanks to its generally superior command of Hebrew, is exerting an increasing influence on the academic study of the Hebrew Bible), and their work now constitutes a serious theological challenge to the Synagogue. However, these new developments have not solved any of the original theological problems that Hebraism poses for the Church. In fact, they have exacerbated them.

6. See M. Müller, *The First Bible of the Church: A Plea for the Septuagint* (Sheffield: Sheffield Academic Press, 1996).

7. An obvious case in point is the rendering of עלמה in Isa 7:14 as "young woman" rather than as "virgin" (παρθένος), as in Matt 1:23.

8. Scaliger's most mature reflections on the Qaraites are found in the *Elenchus*: see A. T. Grafton, *Joseph Scaliger: A Study of Classical Scholarship*, vol. 2 (Oxford: Clarendon, 1993), 511–12 and passim.

9. See Johann Reuchlin, *On the Art of Kabbalah: De Arte Cabbalistica,* trans. M. and S. Goodman, with introductions by G. Lloyd-Jones and M. Idel (Lincoln,

Nebr. and London: University of Nebraska Press, 1993). The similarities between Christianity and certain aspects of the Qabbalah, which Reuchlin and other Christian Qabbalists perceived, were not all imaginary. In some cases they were due to a shared Neoplatonism, in others to direct borrowings by the Qabbalah of Christian ideas and motifs: see Yehuda Liebes, *Studies in the Zohar* (Albany, N.Y.: SUNY Press, 1992), 139–62.

10. There is no clear word for "Hellenism" in premodern Hebrew: the closest one gets is *hokhmat yevanit*, on which see note 40 below. In Modern Hebrew, apart from the loanword *hellenismos*, one can also use *yevanut* or *tarbut yevanit*.

11. All this has been documented and analyzed at length by Yaacov Shavit, *Athens in Jerusalem: Classical Antiquity and Hellenism in the Making of the Modern Secular Jew*, The Littman Library of Jewish Civilization (London: Vallentine Mitchell, 1997). The original Hebrew of this work, which appeared under the title *Ha-Yahadut bire'i ha-Yevanut ve-hofa'at ha-Yehudi ha-Hellenisti ha-Moderni*, contains quite a few errors that have been corrected in the English translation.

12. On the "Ways of the Amorites" see Giuseppe Veltri, *Magie und Halakhah,* Texte und Studien zum Antiken Judentum 62 (Tübingen: Mohr-Siebeck, 1997), 195–220. It can include cutting one's hair in the Roman fashion. See Bavli Bava Qamma 83a quoted below.

13. See my "Jerusalem as the *Omphalos* of the World: On the History of a Geographical Concept," *Jerusalem: Its Sanctity and Centrality to Judaism, Christianity and Islam,* ed. L. I. Levine (New York: Continuum, 1999), 104–19.

14. Shavit, *Athens in Jerusalem,* 355–480.

15. S. A. Handelman, *The Slayers of Moses: The Emergence of Rabbinic Interpretation in Modern Literary Theory* (New York: SUNY Press, 1982); J. Faur, *Golden Doves with Silver Dots: Semiotics and Textuality in Rabbinic Tradition* (Bloomington, Ind.: Indiana University Press, 1986).

16. Faur, *Golden Doves with Silver Dots,* xxix and passim.

17. See my "Quid Athenis et Hierosolymis? Rabbinic Midrash and Hermeneutics in the Graeco-Roman World," *A Tribute to Geza Vermes: Essays on Jewish and Christian Literature and History,* eds. P. R. Davies and R. T. White (Sheffield: Sheffield Academic Press, 1990), 101–24. Faur's analysis involves the same kind of breathtaking essentializing of Greek thought as opposed to Jewish thought which was earlier advocated by Thorleif Boman, *Hebrew Thought Compared with Greek* (London: SCM, 1960), and which one had thought had been terminally knocked on the head by James Barr in *The Semantics of Biblical Language* (London: Oxford University Press, 1961).

18. E. W. Said, *Orientalism* (Harmondsworth: Penguin, 1985).

19. H. S. Chamberlain, *Die Grundlagen des Neunzehnten Jahrhunderts* (Munich: Bruckmann, 1899).

20. John of Damascus, *The Fount of Knowledge: On Heresies,* §§4 and 101, trans. F. H. Chase Jr., *Saint John of Damascus: Writings,* The Fathers of the Church: A New Translation 37 (Washington, D.C.: Catholic University of America Press, 1958). A similar attitude is found in the decrees of the Fourth Lateran Council.

21. R. Ballard, "Islam and the Construction of Europe," *Muslims in the Margin: Political Responses to the Presence of Muslims in the West,* eds. W. A. R. Shadid and P. S. Koningsveld (Kampen: Kok Pharos, 1996), 1–50.

22. Theodor Herzl, *Der Judenstaat* (1896: repr. Osnabrück: Zeller, 1968), 29: "Für Europa würden wir dort ein Stück des Walles gegen Asien bilden, wir würden den Vorpostendienst der Cultur gegen die Barbarei besorgen."

23. Two volumes that were influential in defining Hellenism when I was a classics

student at school and university in the 1950s and 1960s were G. Lowes Dickinson, *The Greek View of Life* (1896; repr. London: Methuen, 1962) and C. M. Bowra, *The Greek Experience* (1957; repr. New York: Mentor Books, 1964). Rereading these today I am astonished at how idealizing and elitist they are, how confidently they identify the philosophical and the aesthetic traditions as the essence of Greek culture, and how little they seem to have to do with the historical Greeks. They are arguably conservative ideological constructs that were attempting to assert the continuing relevance of the Greeks, and hence of a classical education, in the face of the rise of modern science. E. R. Dodds, *The Greeks and the Irrational* (London: University of California Press, 1951) was one of the earliest and most successful attempts to challenge the historical accuracy of this view.

24. See W. Burkert, *The Orientalizing Revolution: Near Eastern Influences on Greek Culture in the Early Archaic Age,* trans. M. E. Pinder and W. Burkert (Cambridge, Mass.: Harvard University Press, 1992). Also useful is M. Bernal, *Black Athena,* vol. 2: *The Archaeological and Documentary Evidence* (New Brunswick, N.J.: Rutgers University Press, 1991).

25. M. L. West, *Hesiod: Theogony* (Oxford: Clarendon, 1966), passim; West, *Hesiod: Works and Days* (Oxford: Clarendon, 1978), 3–30; West, *Early Greek Philosophy and the Orient* (Oxford: Clarendon, 1971).

26. S. Dalley, *Myths from Mesopotamia* (Oxford: Oxford University Press, 1989), 47–9; Dalley, ed., *The Legacy of Mesopotamia* (Oxford: Oxford University Press, 1998).

27. A. Momigliano, *Alien Wisdom: The Limits of Hellenization* (Cambridge: Cambridge University Press, 1975).

28. Josephus, *J. W.* 2.119; *Ant.* 13.171; 18.23. It is revealing how quick some modern historians have been to dismiss Josephus's comparison as a mere accommodation to Greek ideas, which lacks any cultural validity.

29. See "Quid Athenis et Hierosolymis," (n. 17) 109–15.

30. For an overview of the site see S. Applebaum, "Gerasa," *Encyclopaedia of Archaeological Excavations in the Holy Land*, vol. 2, ed. M. Avi-Yonah (Jerusalem: Israel Exploration Society, 1976), 417–28.

31. For updates on the progress of deciphering these important texts, which date to the reigns of Justinian (527–65), Justin (565–78), and Tiberius the Second (578–82), see the *Newsletter* of the American Center of Oriental Research in Amman. Legal forms and terms provide an interesting test case of Hellenization. We now have in the Babata archive, and the various Nabataean and Greek texts, a significant corpus of legal documents from southern Jordan in late antiquity. My impression of this material is that what is striking is not so much its Hellenism as the persistence of native legal forms and practices.

32. See my essays "Quid Athenis et Hierosolymis" (n. 17) and "'Homer the Prophet of All' and 'Moses our Teacher': Late Antique Exegesis of the Homeric Epics and of the Torah of Moses," *The Use of Sacred Books in the Ancient World,* eds. L. V. Rutgers, P. W. van der Horst, H. W. Havelaar, and L. Teugels (Leuven: Peeters, 1998), 111–26.

33. This is implicit in the original Greek meaning of the term *hellenismos*: "*Hellenismos,* which is a noun from the verb *hellenizo* ('to speak Greek'), originally meant the correct use of the Greek language. The concept seems to have been first employed by the teachers of rhetoric. Theophrastus, who like his master Aristotle made rhetoric a part of his teaching in the Lyceum at Athens, built up his theory of the perfect style in five parts, which he called the 'virtues of diction' (*aretai*), the first and most basic of them being *Hellenismos,* i.e., a grammatically correct use of the Greek language, Greek free from barbarisms and solecisms. . . . This requirement was characteristic of the time, in fourth cen-

tury Greece, when foreigners of every social status had become so numerous that they exercised a deteriorating influence on the spoken idiom, even on the language of the Greeks themselves. The word *Hellenismos* thus did not originally have the meaning of adopting Greek manners or a Greek way of life that it later inevitably assumed, especially outside Hellas where Greek culture became fashionable" (W. Jaeger, *Early Christianity and Greek Paideia* [London: Oxford University Press, 1961], 107). An element of political conservatism, not to say chauvinism, may be inherent in the word right from the beginning.

34. J.-B. Frey, *Corpus Inscriptionum Iudaicarum*, vol. 2: *Asie-Afrique* (Città del Vaticano: Pontificio Istituto di Archeologia Cristiana, 1952). Frey is, of course, hopelessly out of date, and was not all that good to begin with. He will in due course be superseded by the *Corpus Inscriptionum Iudaeae/Palestina* (CIIP), which is being directed by Jonathan Price at the University of Tel Aviv, but that is still a long way from completion. Important inscriptions have, of course, been discovered and published since Frey (see, for example, note 36), but they do not seem significantly to alter the overall percentages. For a report on the CIIP, a valuable survey of the epigraphic evidence and a slightly different set of statistics, see P. W. van der Horst's forthcoming article, "Greek in Palestine in Light of Jewish Epigraphy."

35. I have not counted as mixed the many Greek inscriptions which end with the Hebrew שלום, on the grounds that the use of *Shalom* on its own was no more indicative in antiquity of a knowledge of Hebrew than it would be today.

36. None of these is in Frey. For the Beth Shearim texts see M. Schwabe and B. Lifshitz, *Beth She'arim*, vol. 2: *The Greek Inscriptions* (Jerusalem: Israel Exploration Society, 1967 [in Hebrew]), no. 127 (pp. 45–51) and no. 183 (pp. 76–81). Also rather interesting is no. 130 (pp. 53–4). For the Gophna inscription see M. Schwabe, "A Greek Epigram from Gofna," *Scripta Hierosolymitana* 1 (1954): 99–119. The authenticity of the Gophna inscription remains in some doubt, as does its Jewish origin.

37. S. Krauss, *Griechische und Lateinische Lehnwörter im Talmud, Midrasch und Targum*, I–II (1898–99; repr. Hildesheim: Olms, 1964). A substantial part of the material has been reworked by Saul Lieberman (in *Greek in Jewish Palestine* [New York: The Jewish Theological Seminary of America, 1942], *Hellenism in Jewish Palestine*, 2d ed. [New York: JTSA, 1962] and *Tosefta Kifshutah*, I–X [New York: JTSA, 1955–88]) and by Daniel Sperber ("Greek and Latin Words in Rabbinic Literature: Prolegomena to a New Dictionary of Classical Words in Rabbinic Literature," *Bar-Ilan* 14–15 [1977]: 9–60; 16–17 [1979]: 9–30; *Essays on Greek and Latin in the Mishna, Talmud and Midrashic Literature* [Ramat-Gan: Bar-Ilan University Press, 1984]; *A Dictionary of Greek and Latin Legal Terms in Rabbinic Literature* [Jerusalem: Magnes, 1984]; *Nautica Talmudica* [Ramat-Gan: Bar-Ilan University Press, 1986]). However, as with the inscriptions, our overall statistics are probably accurate enough. Greek loanwords, Greek formulae, and even whole Greek incantations are fairly common in Jewish magical and mystical texts in Hebrew and Aramaic from late antiquity (see D. Sperber, *Magic and Folklore in Rabbinic Literature* [Ramat-Gan: Bar-Ilan University Press, 1994], 92–8). However, this is no proof of a knowledge of Greek, since it may have been the very unintelligibility of these words and texts that made them attractive.

38. The text actually says שילמד אדם את בנו ספר יווני, "that a man should teach his son *a Greek book*" (ed. Zuckermandel 461, 29). The Greek book is most likely to have been a school edition of Homer, the staple of Greek education. See Alexander, "'Homer the Prophet of All' and 'Moses our Teacher,'" 136.

39. The standard editions read: בפולמוס של טיטוס גזרו על עטרות כלות ושלא ילמד אדם את בנו יוונית, but since the text has just mentioned "the war of Vespasian," a

reference to "the War of Titus" is redundant. We should, therefore, read בפולמוס שׁל קיטוס, with the Cambridge and Parma manuscripts.

40. However, it is possible that Bavli Menahot 99b is also referring to the study of the Greek *language*. The text strictly speaks of "the wisdom of Greek" (חוכמה יוונית), and not "Greek wisdom" (חוכמה יוונית), though Lieberman, presumably through a slip of the pen, reads the latter at the end of the quotation (*Hellenism in Jewish Palestine*, 100). "The wisdom of Greek" could be either "the wisdom comprising a knowledge of the Greek language" or "the wisdom written in the Greek language." The possible equivalence of חוכמה and φιλοσοφία is noteworthy. Wandering philosophers were a feature of the Greco-Roman world in the Rabbis' day, and occasionally the Rabbis met and argued with them. Note the famous story of Rabban Gamliel's encounter with a philosopher in the public baths at Acco in Mishnah 'Avodah Zarah 3:4. Note also Justin Martyr's portrait of Trypho as a Palestinian Jew with a taste for philosophy.

41. I find completely unconvincing Lieberman's argument that this and parallel texts do not actually amount to a ban on the study of Greek and Greek wisdom (*Hellenism in Jewish Palestine*, 100–1). They clearly do. The only points at issue are how widely supported by the authorities the ban was, and how widely it was observed.

42. So Lieberman correctly translates the verse: see *Hellenism in Jewish Palestine*, 104 n. 31.

43. *Greek in Jewish Palestine*, 1.

44. *Hellenism in Jewish Palestine*, 4–5.

45. The Shim'on ben Gamliel referred to is probably the second of that name, the father of Judah ha-Nasi. If, however, the reference is to Shim'on ben Gamliel I, then the situation envisaged is before 70 C.E., and the dispersal of the academy an outcome of the First Revolt.

46. See Lieberman, *Hellenism in Jewish Palestine*, 105, with reference to M. Schwabe, לתולדות טבריה, Jerusalem 1949, p. 36 and n. 91 [*non vidi*].

47. It is very probable that the ספרי המירס mentioned several times in Mishnah and Talmud (Mishnah Yadayim 4:6; Yerushalmi Sanhedrin X 1 [28a]) are the Books of Homer.

48. The most extreme view, found in Mekhilta deRabbi Ishmael, *Bahodesh* 6 (to Exod 20:4), forbids even images reflected in water. A more lenient view is found in Mishnah 'Avodah Zarah 3:1–4. Exegetically the issue was whether Exod 20:4 ("you shall not make a graven image") and 20:5 ("you shall not bow down to a graven image") are two separate commandments or one commandment. In other words, is "making" *per se* forbidden, or only "making in order to bow down"? The latter leaves open the possibility that making purely for ornamentation is permissible. Judging by the archaeological record the more lenient view seems to have prevailed, since Jewish art in the Talmudic period seems strikingly less worried by images than Jewish art of the Second Temple period.

49. The Gospel may be "foolishness" (μωρία) to the Greeks, but it is equally a "stumbling block" (σκάνδαλον) to the Jews. It is, therefore, divine in origin and comprehensible to humanity *as a whole* only through the enlightenment of the Spirit (1 Cor 1:23). But this is theology and rhetoric, rather than a sober statement about the cognitive powers of either Greeks or Jews to understand the Gospel.

Chapter 4: Does Pauline Christianity Resemble a Hellenistic Philosophy?

1. On the necessity of comparison and failures resulting from lack of comparison see Jonathan Z. Smith, *Drudgery Divine: On the Comparison of Early Chris-*

tianities and the Religions of Late Antiquity (Chicago: University of Chicago Press, 1990) and Luther H. Martin, "Comparison," *Guide to the Study of Religion,* eds. Willi Braun and Russell McCutcheon (London: Cassell, 2000), 45–56.

2. Richard S. Ascough, *What Are They Saying About the Formation of the Pauline Churches?* (New York: Paulist Press, 1998). Ascough's helpful book selects these models and reviews scholarship that has compared them with Pauline communities. I have not treated mystery religions as a separate topic in what follows because most of what I say about "voluntary cults" also applies to them. They were not distinct religions, but elaborations of polytheism. The modern concept of mystery religions places a highly heterogeneous collection of entities into a category shaped to match up with Christianity and nineteenth-century interests in religious experience. See Walter Burkert, *Ancient Mystery Cults* (Cambridge, Mass.: Harvard University Press, 1987).

3. Scholars mention many other points of comparison, but these seem to be the most frequent and broadest, i.e., divisible into all the models. For examples of these categories of comparison, see Robert L. Wilken, *The Christians as the Romans Saw Them* (New Haven, Conn.: Yale University Press, 1984), 44; S. G. Wilson, "Voluntary Associations: An Overview," *Voluntary Associations in the Graeco-Roman World,* eds. John S. Kloppenborg and Stephen G. Wilson (London: Routledge, 1996), 9–13. Wilson is more nuanced than most and is aware of some of the problems connected with the category of voluntary (especially pp. 1–2).

4. C. H. Roberts, T. C. Skeat, and A. D. Nock, "The Guild of Zeus Hypsistos," *HTR* 29 (1936): 75; Lloyd Gaston, "Pharisaic Problems," *Approaches to Ancient Judaism,* New Series 3, ed. Jacob Neusner (Atlanta: Scholars, 1993), 85. These are cited in Ascough, *Formation,* 74.

5. *Democracy in America,* trans. George Lawrence, ed. J. P. Mayer, 2 vols. (New York: Doubleday, 1969).

6. Note how, like many who have written on ancient associations in the Hellenistic age, de Tocqueville associates forming groups "to his taste" (i.e., choice) with individualism, e.g. (p. 506): "'Individualism' is a word recently coined to express a new idea. Our fathers only knew about egoism. . . . Individualism is a calm and considered feeling which disposes each citizen to isolate himself from the mass of his fellows and withdraw into a circle of family and friends; with this little society formed to his taste, he gladly leaves the greater society to look after itself."

7. *Voluntary Associations* (see n. 3 above). In spite of my critique of categories and mode of comparison, I nevertheless view this as a significant and pioneering volume on a long-neglected topic.

8. The approach is one broadly informed by theories of practice. I believe, however, that all of the current theories have major problems that hinder a more explicit theorization in such studies as this one. Bourdieu wants to make background understanding explicit, even though on his own theory and in philosophy in general, "the background" is by definition what cannot be articulated. He also collapses the organization of practices into practical understanding (Theodore Schatzki, *Social Practices: A Wittgensteinian Approach to Human Activity and the Social* [Cambridge: Cambridge University Press, 1996], 150–1). Anthony Giddens's theory also yields a similar collapse of organization into practical understanding to be described by the scholar/social scientist in terms of rule-following. I believe that Wittgenstein's critique of using rule-following to explain such regularities is persuasive. In my estimation, Schatzki's theory has many advantages over the others. I adopt, with some modifications to be noted, his conceptions of practice, sociality, expressions,

reactions, dispersed and integrative practices, nexuses, spaces, and signifying among others. Social formations are constituted of bundled practices. Unfortunately the benefits of Schatzki's theory is greatly limited because he follows the kind of use theory of meaning found in Wittgenstein, Heidegger, and Quine. I follow Robert Brandom (*Making It Explicit: Reasoning, Representation and Discursive Commitment* [Cambridge, Mass.: Harvard University Press, 1994]) in seeing inference (rather than "use" or representation) as central to discursive practice and discursive practice as making explicit what is implicit in our nondiscursive doings, e.g., asserting and changing commitments and entitlements. Thus I am still working on solving some quite basic problems in practice theory at this point, but have a definite orientation and some useful tools. For a helpful discussion of a key term, see Burton L. Mack, "Social Formation," in *Guide*, eds. Braun and McCutcheon, 283–96. I use social formation in the way that *soziales Gebilde* is commonly used by German social theorists. I call a practice or social formation religious if it involves (imagined) reciprocity with or reference to a god or objects and practices associated with gods.

9. Thus, in what follows, I will be drawing on Paul's representation of what life in Christ was and ought to be, and not making inferences about how members of the groups received and reacted to Paul's conceptions.

10. Ascough, *Formation*, 11–28.

11. *Ancient Synagogues: Historical Analysis and Archeological Discovery*, eds., Dan Urman and Paul Flesher, 2 vols. (Leiden: Brill, 1995); Ascough, *Formation*, 11–28.

12. L. Michael White, *The Social Origins of Christian Architecture*, vol. 1, Harvard Theological Studies 42 (Valley Forge, Pa.: Trinity, 1990), 60–101.

13. Jodi Magness, "The Question of the Synagogue: The Problem of Typology," *Judaism in Late Antiquity*, Vol. 3, *Where We Stand: Issues and Debates in Ancient Judaism*, Part 3, eds. J. Neusner and A. Avery-Peck (Leiden: Brill, 1999); "Synagogue Typology and Earthquake Chronology at Khirbet Shema', Israel," *Journal of Field Archeology* 24 (1997): 211–20; "Dating of the Black Ceramic Bowl with a Depiction of the Torah Shrine from Nabratein," *Levant* 26 (1994): 199–206; Howard Clark Kee, "The Transformation of the Synagogue After 70 C.E.: Its Import for Early Christianity," *NTS* 36 (1990): 1–24; "The Changing Meaning of Synagogue: A Response to Richard Oster," *NTS* 40 (1994): 281–3; "Defining the First Century C.E. Synagogue: Problems and Progress," *NTS* 41 (1995): 481–500. Note that my arguments about the links of synagogues or Jewish communities to the temple apply not only to synagogues in the Diaspora, but even to those in Palestine with some modifications for communities close to Jerusalem.

14. I do not mean to suggest that modern forms of Judaism do not to various degrees have an ethnic element, but that forms of modern Judaism are often conceived as religions in the modern sense, especially by Christians.

15. "Most important" does not mean that practices like circumcision, sabbath observance, and prayer, that were not necessarily tied to the temple, were unimportant, but Jews did not generally consider these either a substitute for the temple or the center of their interactions with divine. If I were to press my case, I would argue that the way that Philo and Josephus, for example, discuss the temple and cult makes this absolutely clear. Furthermore, those practices were not tied to an institution called "the synagogue."

16. For the evidence, see Margaret Williams, *The Jews Among the Greeks and Romans: A Diasporan Sourcebook* (Baltimore: Johns Hopkins University Press, 1998), 59–64.

17. I would expect this sense of the relationship between God and land/place/blessings to concretely shape the Diasporan Judean's life where he/she lived and not just to be an attitude toward a distant place.

18. Williams, *Diasporan Sourcebook,* 67–8.

19. Williams, *Diasporan Sourcebook,* 68–71.

20. Here one might note that gentile interference with and resentment toward these Diasporan offerings was a major source of violence between Jews and their neighbors. See Williams, *Diasporan Sourcebook,* 68–71.

21. E.g., for scriptural bases for these temple-oriented prayer practices see Dan 6:11; Ezra 9:4–5, 21; and compare Jdt 9:1; Luke 1:10; Acts 3:1.

22. E. P. Sanders, *Judaism: Practice and Belief 63 B.C.E.–66 C.E.* (Philadelphia: Trinity, 1992), 133–4.

23. This, of course, begins with the Mishnah.

24. Stanley K. Stowers, "Greeks Who Sacrifice and Those Who Do Not: Toward an Anthropology of Greek Religion," *The Social World of the First Christians: Essays in Honor of Wayne A. Meeks,* eds. L. Michael White and O. Larry Yarbrough (Minneapolis: Augsburg Fortress, 1995), 299–320; "Truth, Identity and Sacrifice in Classical Athens" (unpublished paper); "A Cult from Philadelphia: Oikos Religion or Cultic Association?" *The Early Church and Its Context,* eds. A. J. Malherbe, F. W. Norris and J. W. Thompson (Leiden: Brill, 1998), 287–301; "On the Comparison of Blood in Ancient Israelite and Greek Sacrifice," *HESED VE-EMET: Essays in Honor of Ernest Frerichs,* eds. Jodi Magness and Seymour Gitin (Atlanta: Scholars, 1998), 179–94; "Blood in Greek Cult," *Text, Artifact and Image,* eds. T. Lewis and G. Beckman (Philadelphia: University of Pennsylvania Press, forthcoming).

25. Thus, for instance, I would expect that Judeans living in the Diaspora before 70 widely recognized and dealt with birth and death pollution because they were Judeans who had contact with people who traveled to the temple, and more importantly, just because they in principle could sacrifice in the temple.

26. Animal sacrifice played an important part in Greek and Roman weddings.

27. David Fredrickson, "Passionless Sex in Paul's Epistles," paper read at the annual national meeting of the Society of Biblical Literature, San Francisco, 1997; Dale Martin, *The Corinthian Body* (New Haven, Conn.: Yale University Press, 1995), 214–17.

28. It is not a sufficient historical explanation to say that Paul gave such advice because he believed that the "eschaton" was imminent. First, although scholars talk about the end of the world, I think it more accurate to say that he looked for a changed world that would have substantial continuities as well as differences. Second, whatever Paul believed, he and his churches were still social groups both organizing themselves in ways that they understood and also being shaped by social forces that were beyond their awareness. Eschatology should not be used as a slogan to limit social analysis.

29. On this tendency among Weberians, see Stanley Greenberg, *Race and State in Capitalist Development* (New Haven, Conn.: Yale University Press, 1980), 13–16.

30. There is a long-standing tendency to treat these groups in isolation from the rest of Greek and Roman religion and to fail in seeing how intimately religious practices are tied to the economic and social productivity of the people involved. See my "A Cult from Philadelphia" for a domestic cult's relation to the order of the household.

31. In particular, for all of the great contributions of the so-called French structuralists and their followers elsewhere, they have the tendency to make beliefs and motifs in literature, myth, and rites into one great text in which they find a systematic order of fundamental ideas that lie behind everything in the culture.

32. For a useful discussion of some of the issues involved here, see G. E. M. Anscombe, *Intention* (Ithaca, N.Y.: Cornell University Press, 1957).

33. I am using the loose language of areas and features to indicate the possibility of the detailed description and complex comparison of practices and social formations. Features are thus roughly social practices and social formations. Areas are sites where dispersed and integrative social practices are "bundled" into social formations and social formations are linked to produce more complex formations.

34. With the kind of comparison (or perhaps taxonomic distinctions) that I advocate in this essay, one could compare such activities as meals—say, Judean, Christian, and pagan—in a way that would more adequately allow for the analysis of differences.

35. Jonathan Z. Smith, *Imagining Religion: From Babylon to Jonestown* (Chicago: University of Chicago Press, 1982), 1–18.

36. A. A. Long, "Hellenistic Ethics and Philosophical Power," *Hellenistic History and Culture,* ed. Peter Green (Berkeley: University of California Press, 1993), 138–56, esp. 138–42. When I speak of choice in connection with someone adopting a Hellenistic philosophy, I do not mean to imply the idea frequently found in modern thought that what is important about the choice is that it is "mine." On another point, one unfortunately still sometimes encounters the idea that the schools had by Paul's era melded into an eclectic or syncretistic Hellenistic philosophy in which the schools could hardly be distinguished. The last thirty years of intensive work on Hellenistic philosophy should have destroyed this myth that was promoted by Eduard Zeller and others near the turn of the century.

37. Long, "Hellenistic Ethics," 138.

38. Long, "Hellenistic Ethics," 152.

39. E.g., A. A. Long and D. N. Sedley, *The Hellenistic Philosophers,* vol. 1 (Cambridge: Cambridge University Press, 1987), 18–22, 154–7, 377–86.

40. There is now a vast literature on the topic of antifamily and ascetic tendencies in early Christianity. For a recent contribution with excellent bibliography, see Andrew S. Jacobs, "A Family Affair: Marriage, Class and Ethics in the Apocryphal Acts of the Apostles," *JECS* 7 (1999): 105–38.

41. Gentiles are not to become Judeans, i.e., keep the law, but the Gentile cultures are morally and religiously debased (e.g., Rom 1:18–32) and must be rejected.

42. Abraham J. Malherbe, "Conversion to Paul's Gospel," *The Early Church in Its Context,* 230–44. Malherbe does not speak of a "rhetoric of conversion," but I think that such language is necessary seeing that the philosophies had no theory of conversion and it never functioned as a normative conception. It is best to think of it as a literary and discursive tradition made possible by my characteristics 1, 2, and 4.

43. *Conversion: The Old and New in Religion from Alexander the Great to Augustine of Hippo* (Oxford: Oxford University Press, 1933).

44. Long and Sedley, *Hellenistic Philosophers,* 368 (virtue); 385–6 (the possibility of attaining virtue and instantaneous change).

45. E.g., Plutarch, *Comp. Argum. Stoic. Absurd,* 4.

46. E.g., Phil 2:10; 1 Cor 15:24–28. Even this difference should not be exaggerated in light of conceptions like those attributed to Demetrius in the prayer of Seneca, *De Prov.* 1.5.5 and Seneca's treatise in general.

47. Long, "Hellenistic Ethics," 142–5.

48. Martha Nussbaum, *The Therapy of Desire: Theory and Practice in Hellenistic Ethics* (Princeton, N.J.: Princeton University Press, 1994); Clarence E. Glad, *Paul and Philodemus: Adaptability in Epicurean and Early Christian Psychagogy,*

NovTSup 81 (Leiden: Brill, 1995). Note Glad's important corrections (152–60) of points on the nature of Epicurean communities in Nussbaum's excellent study.

49. Michel Foucault, *The Care of the Self* (New York: Vintage Books, 1986); Pierre Hadot, *Exercices spirituels et philosophie antique,* 2d rev. ed. (Paris: Etudes Augustiniennes, 1987); Catherine Edwards, "Self-Scrutiny and Self-Transformation in Seneca's Letters," *Greece and Rome* 44 (1997): 21–38.

50. Abraham J. Malherbe, *Paul and the Thessalonians* (Philadelphia: Fortress, 1987), 34–94; *Paul and the Popular Philosophers* (Minneapolis: Augsburg Fortress, 1989), 67–77; Glad, *Paul and Philodemus.*

51. Already noted by Nock, *Conversion,* 175–6; Abraham Malherbe, "Hellenistic Moralists and the New Testament," *ANRW* 2.26.1 (1992): 293–301.

52. On the figures of Zeno and Epicurus, see Fernanda Decleva Caizzi, "The Porch and the Garden: Early Hellenistic Images of the Philosophical Life," *Images and Ideologies: Self-definition in the Hellenistic World,* eds. A. Bulloch, E. Gruen, A. A. Long, and A. Stewart (Berkeley: University of California Press, 1993), 303–29. Zeno is one extreme among Stoics for whom the wiseman would generally lead a fairly conventional life unless circumstances arose where preferred indifferents like wealth conflicted with virtue. Seneca *Ep.* 14.14 is perhaps the other extreme that reflects the tenor of middle and Roman Stoicism. Thus, the degree of contrast between the wiseman and convention varied by school, historical period, and circumstances. The Cynic wiseman is certainly the most extreme.

53. Long, "Hellenistic Ethics," 153.

54. Long and Sedley, *Hellenistic Philosophers,* 133, 138–9.

55. John T. Fitzgerald, *Cracks in an Earthen Vessel: An Examination of the Catalogues of Hardships in the Corinthian Correspondence,* SBLDS 99 (Atlanta: Scholars, 1988).

56. Harlow G. Snyder, "Teachers, Texts and Students: Textual Performance and Patterns of Authority in Greco-Roman Schools" (Ph.D. diss., Yale University, 1998).

57. Dana Chyung is currently writing a dissertation at Brown University on Paul's presentation of himself as a producer of knowledge and a teacher in 1 and 2 Corinthians.

58. On animal sacrifice and for bibliography on this complex practice, see n. 24 above. Although myths were certainly associated with specific cults, thinking of sacrificial cults as the expression of myths or the representation of beliefs is misleading. For a discussion of this problem in the study of ritual, see Catherine Bell, *Ritual Theory, Ritual Practice* (Oxford: Oxford University Press, 1992). Telling and writing stories about the gods are practices themselves that can play a part in rituals, but rituals should not be reduced to representations of them. Animal sacrifice could take place without any reference to myth beyond the belief that the offering was being given to a deity.

59. *Saving the City: Philosopher-Kings and Other Classical Paradigms* (London: Routledge, 1999), 51–68. Also see his earlier *The Stoic Idea of the City* (Cambridge: Cambridge University Press, 1991).

60. Andrew Erskine, *The Hellenistic Stoa: Political Thought and Action* (Ithaca, N.Y.: Cornell University Press, 1990). Erskine provides much evidence for Stoic political and social activity as reformers. Schofield (*Stoic Idea,* 42 n. 37) doubts that Sphaerus's influence was as strong as Erskine thinks.

61. For Epiphanes and his work *On Justice,* see Morton Smith, *Clement of Alexandria and a Secret Gospel of Mark* (Cambridge, Mass.: Harvard University Press, 1973). On the similarities to Zeno, see Erskine, *Hellenistic Stoa,* 112–13.

62. On the latter, see Troels Engberg-Pedersen, "Philo's *DE VITA CONTEMPLA-TIVA* as a Philosopher's Dream," *JSJ* 20 (1999): 40–64.
63. I am, of course, also rejecting any fixed form/content scheme that implies essentialism. Form/content is a trope of our own analyses in virtue of specific contexts, purposes, and practices.
64. This essay was written before Engberg-Pedersen's *Paul and the Stoics* (Louisville, Ky.: Westminster John Knox, 2000) appeared. Otherwise the essay would have been in conversation with his important book. See also his earlier "Stoicism in Philippians," *Paul in His Hellenistic Context,* ed. Troels Engberg-Pedersen (Philadelphia: Augsburg Fortress, 1995), 256–90.
65. There is now a large bibliography on these similarities. On the similarities and bibliography on the subject, see Malherbe, *Paul and the Philosophers,* and Ascough, *Formation,* 29–49.
66. He also, of course, most emphasizes what Jesus' actions have objectively effected.
67. See my *A Rereading of Romans: Justice, Jews and Gentiles* (New Haven, Conn.: Yale University Press, 1994), 194–226.
68. In light of gross distortions of Greek conceptions of virtue or excellence in Christian apologetics going back to Augustine, I would emphasize that virtues and, of course, Pauline virtues are social virtues. Put in theological terms, character is thus to a large extent constitutive of ecclesiology, the community. For an example of the apologetic distortion of Greek conceptions of virtue, see Wolfgang Schrage, *The Ethics of the New Testament* (Philadelphia: Fortress, 1982), 217–18. Such misrepresentations seem to combine Augustine's and Luther's charge that pagan virtue was motivated by pride and the projection of a Kantian ethics and individualism onto the Greeks. On endurance and related virtues in Paul, Themistocles Adamopoulo, "Endurance, Greek and Early Christian: The Moral Transformation of the Greek Idea of Heroic Endurance from Homer to the Apostle Paul" (Ph.D. diss., Brown University, 1995).
69. This was made especially clear by the discovery of the Qumran literature. Philo and Josephus portray the Essenes as having an asceticism based on a limited good, whereas the scrolls show purity concerns that order life in certain ways, but do not necessarily require a limited good. The purity concerns are generated by the priestly community's obsession with the temple and not principles about the good being based on the soul or virtue rather than the body. In fact, their practices concern people, temple, and land. It is their specialization as intellectuals (textual interpretive experts) that gives them a focus and discipline.
70. One can certainly use them as sources for understanding ancient Judaism, but they must be read very critically in view of the biases of their cultural and social strata and power interests. Reading them only in light of their "Jewish apologetic" bias has often worked against a recognition of the extent to which they are unrepresentative. The philosophical bias connects with apologetic in the way they construct Jews, and especially Jewish heroes, as fanatically strict, preferring adherence to central principle and practice above all else. Unfortunately, scholars have often accepted this picture of "strict Judaism" uncritically.
71. Ronald Hock, *The Social Context of Paul's Ministry* (Philadelphia: Fortress, 1980), esp. 37–42.
72. I use "material" and "spiritual" in an ancient and not a Cartesian sense.
73. I do not think that calling this attitude eschatological changes anything. I say this with two points of view in mind. From the perspective of social formation, the actual human sociality is constituted as such whatever the beliefs. From the perspective internal to Paul's thought, I see no indication that the sole focus on Christ as a good would be lost in the age to come or that the ordinary human goods would be reintroduced.

74. See my *Rereading of Romans*.
75. On the character of Greek and Roman friendship with attention to philosophers and ancient Christianity, see David Konstan, *Friendship in the Classical World* (Cambridge: Cambridge University Press, 1997).
76. See the volumes edited by John T. Fitzgerald, *Friendship, Flattery and Frank Speech: Studies in Friendship in the New Testament World* (Leiden: Brill, 1996), and *Greco-Roman Perspectives on Friendship* (Leiden: Brill, 1996).
77. *Rereading of Romans*, 227–53; Caroline Johnson is currently writing a dissertation at Brown University entitled, "'If Children, Then Heirs': A Study of Kinship and Ethnicity in Galatians and Romans."
78. The language of fictive kinship may have been at home among later Platonists and Pythagoreans. This phenomenon also deserves study.
79. Glad, *Paul and Philodemus*, 8–9 and n. 14; Richard A. Wright, "Christians, Epicureans, and the Critique of Greco-Roman Religion" (Ph.D. diss., Brown University, 1994), 83–95.
80. I am following scholarly convention in not classifying Platonism and Pythagoreanism as Hellenistic philosophies since they began before the Hellenistic age.
81. For what follows, see my suggestions in "Meals, Mythmaking and Power in the World of Paul," a programmatic paper for the Consultation, Ancient Myths and Modern Theories of Christian Origins, annual national meeting of the Society of Biblical Literature, New Orleans, Louisiana, November 23, 1996; "Elusive Coherence: Ritual and Rhetoric in I Corinthians 10–11," *Reimagining Christian Origins: A Colloquium Honoring Burton L. Mack*, eds. E. Castelli and Hal Taussig (Valley Forge, Pa.: Trinity, 1996), esp. 78–9; *Rereading of Romans*, 328–9, especially in light of chapter 2; and now the important article by Andrew Wallace-Hadrill, *"Mutatio morum:* the idea of a cultural revolution," *The Roman Cultural Revolution*, eds. T. Habinek and A. Schiesaro (Cambridge: Cambridge University Press, 1997), 1–22.
82. I do not mean "new" here in the sense of unique, unrecognizable, or not fitting the social context. Rather, Pauline Christianity capitalized on tendencies that had been in formation for centuries by creating a religion dependent on specialized knowledge that claimed universal validity at the same time that it broke the links with land, ethnic people, and the landed aristocracy.

Chapter 5: *IPSE DIXIT*: Citation of Authority in Paul and in the Jewish and Hellenistic Schools

1. A. D. Nock, *Conversion: The Old and the New in Religion from Alexander the Great to Augustine of Hippo* (Oxford: Clarendon, 1933), 202–3. Wayne Meeks considered and dismissed the potential of the philosophical schools as a contemporary "model from the environment" in *The First Urban Christians* (New Haven, Conn.: Yale University Press, 1983), 74–84. However, interest in the school model has continued to develop, not least through the work of Abraham Malherbe on Paul and the popular philosophers (cf. n. 4 below), and through the continuing work of the Hellenistic Moral Philosophy group at the Society for Biblical Literature. For a full critical survey of scholarship in this field, see now Richard S. Ascough, *What Are They Saying About the Formation of the Pauline Churches?* (New York: Paulist Press, 1998), 29–49.
2. "Paul and the Hellenistic Schools: The Evidence of Galen," *Paul in His Hellenistic Context,* ed. T. Engberg-Pedersen (Minneapolis: Augsburg Fortress, 1995), 60–83.
3. Clarence E. Glad, *Paul and Philodemus: Adaptability in Epicurean and Early Christian Psychagogy,* NovT Sup 81 (Leiden: Brill, 1995), 8–9.

4. Glad, *Psychagogy*, 4, citing A. J. Malherbe, *Paul and the Popular Philosophers* (Minneapolis: Fortress, 1989), 8. Cf. also Malherbe's *Paul and the Thessalonians: The Philosophic Tradition of Pastoral Care* (Philadelphia: Fortress, 1987); and his "Hellenistic Moralists and the NT," *ANRW* II.26.2, ed. W. Haase (Berlin: de Gruyter, 1992), 267–333.

5. For full details of the texts, see Alexander, "Evidence of Galen," 64–5. They are studied in full in Richard Walzer, *Galen on Jews and Christians* (London: Oxford University Press, 1949). For reasons that will become clearer as we proceed, it is not easy to be sure whether Galen is referring here to Jewish and Christian groups as two separate entities, or to a single group that cites both "Moses" and "Christ" as authority.

6. Alexander, "Evidence of Galen," 67.

7. Dispassionate, that is, about the early church: Galen has many axes to grind, but none of them concern the internal debates of the Jewish and Christian groups he invokes. In this sense his observation is valuable to historians of early Christianity precisely because he does not have a theological agenda.

8. Cf. T. F. Carney, *The Shape of the Past: Models and Antiquity* (Lawrence, Kans.: Coronado, 1975), 15–17; P. F. Esler, "Models, Context and Kerygma in NT Interpretation," *Modelling Early Christianity*, ed. P. F. Esler (London: Routledge, 1995), 1–20.

9. Loveday Alexander, "Schools, Hellenistic," *The Anchor Bible Dictionary* (New York: Doubleday, 1992), 5.1005–11.

10. D. Goodblatt, *Rabbinic Instruction in Sasanian Babylonia* (Leiden: Brill, 1975), 267.

11. Richard Walzer, *Galen*, 15 (frag. of Εἰς τὸ πρῶτον κινοῦν ἀκίνητον, cited from the Arabic). Walzer also cites (p. 14) references to "the followers/school of Moses and Christ" from *De puls. diff.* 2.4, Kühn, 8.579; and from *De puls. diff.* 3.3, Kühn, 8.657.

12. Alexander, "Evidence of Galen."

13. *De puls. diff.* 2.4, Kühn, 8.579: Walzer, 14.

14. Alexander, "Evidence of Galen," 65–6.

15. Origen makes a similar point in *Contra Celsum* 1.10: "Our opponents, although they do not acknowledge it, yet practically do the same. For who is there that, on betaking himself to the study of philosophy, and throwing himself into the ranks of some sect, either by chance, or because he is provided with a teacher of that school, adopts such a course for any other reason, except that he *believes* his particular sect to be superior to any other?" (ANF 4.400)

16. John G. Gager, *Moses in Greco-Roman Paganism*, SBLMS 16 (Nashville: Abingdon, 1972), 25–79.

17. Cf. Philo, *Spec.* 1.59, "the most holy Moses . . . loves and teaches the truth which he desires to engrave and stamp upon all his disciples, dislodging and banishing false opinions to a distance from their understanding"; *Opif.* 8: "Moses, both because he had attained to the very summit of philosophy, and because he had been divinely instructed in the greater and most essential part of nature's law. . . ." For a contrast with Greek philosophy, cf., e.g., *Leg.* 2.14, *Opif.* 131: "Other philosophers say . . . But Moses. . . ."

18. P. S. Alexander, "The Bible in Qumran and Early Judaism," *Text in Context: Essays by Members of the Society for Old Testament Study*, ed. A. Mayes (Oxford: Clarendon, forthcoming).

19. On the importance of this theme in the early Church, cf. Samuel Byrskog, *Jesus the Only Teacher: Didactic Authority and Transmission in Ancient Israel, Ancient Judaism, and the Matthean Community*, ConBNT 24 (Stockholm: Almqvist & Wiksell, 1994). Further, Rainer Riesner, *Jesus als Lehrer: Eine Untersuchung zum*

Ursprung der Evangelien-Überlieferung, WUNT 2/7 (Tübingen: Mohr-Siebeck, 1984).

20. Lucretius, *De rerum natura* 5.8; and see the notes ad loc. in Cyril Bailey, *Titi Lucreti Cari De Rerum Natura Libri Sex* (Oxford: Clarendon, 1947), 3.1323–4.
21. H. Usener, *Epicurea* (Leipzig: Teubner, 1887), frag. 49.
22. David Sedley, "Philosophical Allegiance in the Greco-Roman World," *Philosophia Togata,* eds. M. Griffin and J. Barnes (Oxford: Clarendon, 1989), 97–119, esp. 97.
23. Sedley, "Philosophical Allegiance," 99; cf. Cicero, *De nat. deor.* 2.12.32: *audiamus enim Platonem quasi quendam deum philosophorum.* Cf. the terms in which Pliny describes Christian worship to Trajan (*Ep.* 10.96): *carmenque Christo quasi deo dicere.*
24. Sedley, "Philosophical Allegiance," 97–8.
25. Justin, *Dialogue* 2.2, cited from J. C. M. van Winden, *An Early Christian Philosopher: Justin Martyr's Dialogue with Trypho, Chapters One to Nine* (Leiden: Brill, 1971), 42.
26. Galen, *On Medical Experience* §135 (trans. Walzer; first publ. Richard Walzer, *Galen On Medical Experience* (Oxford: Clarendon, 1944); cited from R. Walzer and M. Frede, *Galen: Three Treatises on the Nature of Science* (Indianapolis: Hackett Publishing Co., 1985), 91); cf. *On the Passions of the Soul* §8.
27. Galen, *Outline of Empiricism* §1 (Latin text and Greek back-translation publ. by K. Deichgräber, *Die griechische Empirikerschule* [Berlin, 1930]; cited from Walzer & Frede, *Three Treatises,* 23).
28. H. von Staden, *Herophilus: The Art of Medicine in Early Alexandria* (Cambridge: Cambridge University Press, 1989), 427–9.
29. Goodblatt, *Rabbinic Instruction,* 267.
30. Diogenes Laertius cites wills for Plato (3.41–43), Arcesilaus (4.43), Aristotle (5.11–16), Theophrastus (5.51–57), and Epicurus (10.16–22).
31. Cf. David Weiss Halivni, *Revelation Restored* (Boulder, Colo.: Westview, 1997), 54–74, esp. 58. Further, P. S. Alexander, "The Bible."
32. Sedley, "Philosophical Allegiance," 98.
33. Sedley, "Philosophical Allegiance," 99; John Dillon, *The Middle Platonists: A Study of Platonism 80 B.C. to A.D. 220* (London: Duckworth, 1977), 10–11: "The inner-academic tradition, then, preserving as it did both accounts of the Unwritten Doctrines and the interpretation of such authorities as Speusippus and Xenocrates, continued to have a profound influence all through antiquity, an influence we can only dimly comprehend."
34. Sedley, "Philosophical Allegiance," 100. For a broader discussion on the fate of the Aristotelian library, cf. Felix Grayeff, *Aristotle and His School* (London: Duckworth, 1974), 69–85. Cf. also Marcello Gigante, *Philodemus in Italy,* trans. Dirk Obbink (Ann Arbor, Mich.: University of Michigan Press, 1995), 15–48, on the library of Philodemus.
35. Loveday Alexander, "The Living Voice: Scepticism Towards the Written Word in Early Christian and in Greco-Roman Texts," *The Bible in Three Dimensions,* eds. D. J. A. Clines, S. E. Fowl, S. E. Porter (Sheffield: Sheffield Academic Press, 1990), 221–47; eadem, "Ancient Book-Production and the Circulation of the Gospels," *The Gospels for All Christians: Rethinking the Gospel Audiences,* ed. R. J. Bauckham (Grand Rapids: Eerdmans, 1997), 71–111, esp. 94–7.
36. *On the Passions of the Soul* §8 (cited from *Galen on the Passions and Errors of the Soul,* trans. P. W. Harkins, ed. W. Riese [Columbus: Ohio State University Press, 1963]); and cf. *De libr. propr.* xi (Kühn 19.43/*Scripta Minora* 2.119.4).
37. von Staden, *Herophilus,* 429.
38. Sedley, "Philosophical Allegiance," 101.

39. Cf. Sedley, "Philosophical Allegiance," 98–100, on the philosophers, and von Staden, *Herophilus,* chap. 9, on Hippocratic exegesis in Alexandria.

40. Cf. *De sectis* §8 = Kühn 1.89f/*Scripta Minora* 3.208ff; and *De ord. libr. suor* §3 = Kühn 19.56ff/*Scripta Minora* 2.86ff.

41. von Staden, *Herophilus,* 445.

42. Sedley, "Philosophical Allegiance," 98 n. 3, 107ff.

43. See further Alexander, "Living Voice."

44. Sedley, "Philosophical Allegiance," 98.

45. Sedley, "Philosophical Allegiance," 105–7: Sedley notes the "obvious biblical parallel," 106. For an example of textual emendation in the medical tradition, cf. Galen, *Hipp. De officina medici comm.,* ed. M. Lyons (CMG Suppl. Or. I; Berlin: Akademie-Verlag, 1963), 23.19–26.

46. Pierre Hadot, *Philosophy as a Way of Life,* trans. A. I. Davidson (Oxford: Blackwell, 1995; English trans. of *Exercises spirituels et philosophie antique,* 2d ed. [Paris: Éd. Augustiniennes, 1987]), 73–4.

47. Cf. Diogenes Laertius 3.63: "Plato has employed a variety of terms in order to make his system less intelligible to the ignorant."

48. Cf. Galen's revealing remark, "In this way the remark of Hippocrates can be found to coincide with the correct method of treatment" (*In Hipp. De officina medici comm.* [cited in n. 45] p. 73.21–3).

49. E. Bikerman, *"La chaine de la tradition pharisienne"* (*RB* 59 [1952]: 44–54; cited from *Essays in Greco-Roman and Related Talmudic Literature,* ed. H. A. Fischel [New York: Ktav, 1977], 127–37).

50. Charles Talbert and Perry Stepp have given a wide-ranging survey of this material in "Succession in Mediterranean Antiquity. Part I: The Lukan Milieu," *Society of Biblical Literature 1998 Seminar Papers* (Atlanta: Scholars, 1998), 148–68.

51. Galen, *Introductio sive medicus* 4, Kühn 14.683: trans. von Staden, *Herophilus,* 50.

52. Apollonius of Citium, *Comm. in Hipp. De Articulis* I pref., my trans. (ed. J. Kollesch & F. Kudlien; CMG XI 1,1; Berlin: Akademie-Verlag, 1965). For further examples, cf. Loveday Alexander, *The Preface to Luke's Gospel,* SNTSMS 78 (Cambridge: Cambridge University Press, 1993), 82–4.

53. Sedley, "Philosophical Allegiance," 103.

54. Cf. Dillon, *Middle Platonists,* 338; Alexander, "Living Voice"; Wesley D. Smith, *The Hippocratic Tradition* (Ithaca, N.Y.: Cornell University Press, 1979), 72–3.

55. Alexander, "Living Voice."

56. Alexander, *The Preface,* 116–25.

57. For this view of Acts, cf. esp. Talbert and Stepp, "Succession in Mediterranean Antiquity: Part II: Luke-Acts," 169–79.

58. There is a useful survey of New Testament material in A. F. Zimmermann, *Die urchristlichen Lehrer,* WUNT 2/12 (Tübingen: Mohr-Siebeck, 1984). Cf. also Byrskog, *Jesus the Only Teacher.*

59. H.-I. Marrou, *History of Education in Antiquity,* trans. G. Lamb (New York: Sheed & Ward, 1956), 337–8 (English trans. of 3d ed. of *Histoire de l'Éducation dans l'Antiquité,* Paris: Éd. du Seuil). Cf. Philip S. Alexander, "'Homer the Prophet of All' and 'Moses our Teacher': Late Antique Exegesis of the Homeric Epics and the Torah of Moses," *The Use of Sacred Books in the Ancient World,* eds. L. V. Rutgers, P. W. van der Horst, H. W. Havelaar, L. Teugels (Leuven: Peeters, 1998), 127–42.

60. G. Glockmann, *Homer in der frühchristlichen Literatur,* TU 105 (Berlin: Akademie-Verlag, 1968). More recent attempts to find allusions and parallels

to Homer and other classical authors in the New Testament (as in e.g. *Ancient Fiction and Early Christian Narrative,* eds. R. F. Hock, J. B. Chance, J. Perkins; Society of Biblical Literature Symposium ser. 6 [Atlanta: Scholars, 1998]; M. P. Bonz, *The Past as Legacy: Luke-Acts and Ancient Epic* [Minneapolis: Fortress, 2000]) do not alter the point being made here: it is the lack of explicit citation of Greek authors that would strike the Greek reader.

61. H.Conzelmann, *I Corinthians,* Hermeneia (Philadelphia: Fortress, 1975), 278 n. 139; A. J. Malherbe, "The Beasts at Ephesus," *JBL* 87 (1968), 71–80.

62. Richard B. Hays, *Echoes of Scripture in Paul* (New Haven, Conn.: Yale University Press, 1989), 97.

63. See on this especially O. Cullmann, "The Tradition," in Cullmann, *The Early Church,* ed. A. J. B. Higgins (London: SCM, 1956; English trans. of *La Tradition* [Neuchatel: Delachaux et Niestlé, 1953]), 55–99.

64. We might wish to argue that it is implied in the *paidagōgos* metaphor of Galatians 3:24 (the *paidagōgos* was the slave who took the child to school); cf. also perhaps, the metaphor of learning letters in 1 Cor 4:6. It is also noteworthy on a broader front how the language used of the believer's relationship with Christ is cognitive as much as it is explicitly religious; and many of the less explicitly educational *motifs,* like the language of "imitation" (e.g., 1 Cor 11:1) are, as others have amply demonstrated, familiar school territory. See on this esp. S. K. Stowers, "Paul on the Use and Abuse of Reason," *Greeks, Romans, and Christians: Essays in Honor of Abraham J. Malherbe,* eds. D. L. Balch, E. Ferguson, W. A. Meeks (Minneapolis: Fortress, 1990), 253–86.

65. Well documented in B. W. Winter, *Philo and Paul among the Sophists,* SNTSMS 96 (Cambridge: Cambridge University Press, 1997), 126–44.

66. Paul's citations are studied in detail in C. D. Stanley, *Paul and the Language of Scripture: Citation Technique in the Pauline Epistles and Contemporary Literature,* SNTSMS 74 (Cambridge: Cambridge University Press, 1992). In fact, the study reveals that Paul's practice is more varied than first impressions might suggest. "As it is written" occurs in eighteen out of sixty-six explicit citations (27 percent); other expressions using a verb of writing are found in another fourteen places (21 percent), and expressions using "to say" occur in twenty-five passages (38 percent): 253 and nn. 3–4.

67. Paul uses this formula at 1 Cor 6:16 and elsewhere. Stanley (*Language*) found that the Greek authors he studied (who were not from the school tradition) were flexible and inventive in finding ways to introduce citations into a flowing text (290): but verbs of saying tend to predominate (273). A computer search for the formulation *gegraptai* might produce some interesting results. It occurs in Plutarch, *Adv. Col.* 1126E—but the context is polemical, and the reference to the *writings* of the Epicurean school may be pointed (cf. also 1126C). A random search of medical commentaries shows a similarly wide variety of verbs of saying (normally active): cf. on Apollonius of Citium Alexander, *Preface,* 101 n. 58. But Cajus Fabricius, *Galens Exzerpte aus älteren Pharmakologen* (Berlin: de Gruyter, 1972), notes a particular class of citations introduced with *gegrammena* (74–82).

68. "It is written": 4Q266, fr.11, 2.4–6, Vermes (G. Vermes, *The Complete Dead Sea Scrolls in English,* 5th ed. [Harmondsworth: Penguin, 1997], 152); "He said": CD X, Vermes, 139.17; "that which is said": 4Q266, fr.6, Vermes, 148.10. Further on Qumran, Stanley, *Language,* 296–306.

69. Cullmann, "Tradition," 63.

70. Philo of Byzantium, *Belopoeica* chap. 5, Diels-Schramm, 51.15–23, my trans.

71. Vitruvius, *De Architectura* 9.1.16, *uti a praeceptoribus accepi . . . uti traditum est nobis a maioribus.*

72. Hero, *Belopoeica,* chap. 2, Diels-Schramm, 73.29; Dioscorides, *Mat. Med.* 1 pref., Wellmann 1.1.11.
73. See further Alexander, *Preface,* 82–5, 98, 118–19; Alexander, "Living Voice."
74. Cicero, *De nat. deor.* 1.5.10 *Pythagorei respondere solebant, Ipse dixit*; cf. Quintilian 11.1.27 *quod Pythagoras inter discipulos potest: Ipse dixit.* Cf. also Diogenes Laertius 3.61 on the epistolary idiolects of Plato, Epicurus, and Cleon.
75. Seneca, *Ep.* 33, cited from *Seneca: Letters from a Stoic,* ed. and trans. R. Campbell (Harmondsworth: Penguin Books, 1969).
76. On Hippocrates, cf. Smith, *Hippocratic Tradition.* On Aristotle, cf. Felix Grayeff, *Aristotle,* chap. 4, esp. 72: "According to custom, these rolls were inscribed in the name of the founder of the school, Aristotle, or in the names of the two most famous scholarchs, Aristotle and Theophrastus, and perhaps even some in the name of Strato."
77. Saul Lieberman, *Hellenism in Jewish Palestine: Studies in the Literary Transmission, Beliefs and Manners of Palestine in the I Century B.C.E.–IV. Century C.E.,* 2d ed. (New York: Jewish Theological Seminary, 1962). Partially reprinted as "Rabbinic Interpretation of Scripture," chap. 17 of Fischel, *Essays,* 289–324.
78. E.g. Lieberman, *Hellenism,* 61–4 (= Fischel, *Essays,* 303–6); 78–9 (= Fischel 320–1).
79. Bikerman, "La chaîne," 49 = Fischel, *Essays,* 132. A similar point might be made in the ongoing debates about the "Cynic" Jesus.
80. Lieberman, *Hellenism,* 53 = Fischel, *Essays,* 295.
81. Lieberman, *Hellenism,* 75 = Fischel, *Essays,* 317.
82. Cf. M. L. West, *Early Greek Philosophy and the Orient* (Oxford: Clarendon, 1971).
83. Cf. Lieberman, *Hellenism,* 57 (= Fischel, *Essays,* 299): "It goes without saying that any thinking person who was acquainted with Greek logic and who heard something of the nature of rabbinical exegesis of the Bible would be inclined to associate it in some way with the former."
84. Josephus *Life* 10–12; cf. *J.W.* 2.119–166; *Ant.* 13.171; 18.11.
85. A. Momigliano, *Alien Wisdom* (Cambridge: Cambridge University Press, 1975); John Gager, *Moses.*
86. Cf. also Judah Goldin, "A Philosophical Session in a Tannaite Academy," *Traditio* 21 (New York: Fordham University Press, 1–21; repr. in Fischel, *Essays,* 366–86), esp. 375 on the careful way in which Josephus sets up the comparison.
87. Cf. G. E. Sterling, *Historiography and Self-Definition: Josephus, Luke-Acts and Apologetic Historiography,* NovT Sup 64 (Leiden: Brill, 1992), 382, 385–6. Sterling places Acts alongside Manetho, Berossos, and Josephus's *Antiquities* in a tradition that he labels "apologetic historiography." Despite the use of such well-known apologetic motifs as the antiquity and political innocence of the movement (he argues), the book is addressed to Christians, not to Romans, and offers "examples and precedents to Christians so that they can make their own *apologia.* Luke-Acts is like the Hellenistic Jewish historians who addressed their works to Jews in an effort to provide them with identity in the larger world." Philip Esler gives a sociological twist to this perspective: Philip F. Esler, *Community and Gospel in Luke-Acts,* SNTSMS 57 (Cambridge: Cambridge University Press, 1987), 222. See further Loveday Alexander, "The Acts of the Apostles as an Apologetic Text," *Jewish and Christian Apologetic in the Graeco-Roman World,* eds. M. J. Edwards, M. Goodman, S. Price, C. Rowland (Oxford: Oxford University Press, 1999), 15–44.

88. On Philo's audience, cf. E. R. Goodenough, "Philo's Exposition of the Law and his De Vita Mosis," *HTR* 27 (1933): 109–25; S. Sandmel, *Philo of Alexandria: An Introduction* (New York: Oxford University Press, 1979), 47–52: Philo was "appealing to half-assimilated Jews, arguing that since outsiders could have so high a regard of Judaism, there is reason for half-assimilated Jews to do the same."

89. W. D. Davies, "Reflections on Tradition: The 'Aboth Revisited," *Jewish and Pauline Studies* (London: SPCK, 1984), 27–48, esp. 39, referring to Goldin, "Session."

90. Goldin, "Session," 370–1. The case for real acquaintance with Epicureanism, at least for the Jerusalem Talmud, is argued now by Hans-Jürgen Becker, "'Epikureer' im Talmud Yerushalmi," *The Talmud Yerushalmi and Graeco-Roman Culture,* ed. Peter Schäfer; Texte und Studien zum Antiken Judentum 71 (Tübingen: Mohr-Siebeck, 1998), 1.397–421.

91. Goldin, "Session," 372–3.

92. *Pirke Aboth* 2.9; Goldin, "Session," 376–84.

93. Campaign launched by British Chief Rabbi Jonathan Sacks to counter assimilation by reminding the Jewish community of the riches of its own tradition.

94. Galen's rationalism was exceptional in his own time, and even—as he himself complains—among the Greek schools. Cf. further Alexander, "Evidence of Galen," 64–8.

95. See on this Nock, *Conversion,* chap. 11—and now esp. Hadot, *Philosophy as a Way of Life.*

96. Glad, *Psychagogy,* 9 and n. 16.

97. Goldin, "Session," 385.

98. Goldin, "Session," 385f. Goldin notes the parallel with Midrash Rabba on Lamentations 1:1, "where an Athenian, in other words, one universally reputed to be particularly clever, is outwitted by Jerusalemites, and even by youngsters of Jerusalem" (n. 93)—an interesting parallel to Acts 17!

99. Isa 29:14, 19:11f., 33:18, 44:25; Ps 33:10; Job 12:17.

100. Barnabas Lindars, *New Testament Apologetic* (London: SCM, 1961), 164–8.

101. Cf. Strack-Billerbeck ad loc., citing *Hag* 15b where the Isaiah reference is expounded as "the one who has counted every letter in the Torah."

102. Cf. Strack-Billerbeck ad loc.; Lieberman, *Hellenism,* 48 (= Fischel, *Essays,* 290), argues that the closest Greek equivalent to *midrash* is *ekzētēsis.*

103. The LXX (which Paul is clearly not quoting) has *grammatikoi* at Isa 33:18, a term that is equally applicable to the activity of the *sopherim* and to that of their Alexandrian counterparts (Lieberman, *Hellenism,* 4 = Fischel, *Essays,* 289). Is it merely an undesigned coincidence that Paul introduces into his citation of Isa 29:14 (v. 19) the non-LXX *athetēsō,* a word that is indelibly associated with the textual labors of the Alexandrian scholars?

104. LSJ s.v. cite Epicurus, *Sent. Vat.* 74, and three passages from Philodemus; the only other citation apart from Philo (twice) and Acts (15:7) is Cicero, *Ad Fam.* 16.21.4.

105. Norman W. deWitt, *Epicurus and His Philosophy* (Minneapolis: University of Minnesota Press, 1954), 98–100.

106. Some degree of anti-Epicurean polemic in 1 Corinthians is argued by an increasing number of scholars: cf. A. J. Malherbe, "The Beasts at Ephesus," *JBL* 87 (1968): 71–80; Stowers, "Use and Abuse"; B. Fiore, "Passion in Paul and Plutarch: I Corinthians 5–6 and the Polemic against Epicureans" (*Greeks, Romans, and Christians,* 135–43); G. Tolmin, "Christians and Epicureans in I Corinthians," *JSNT* 68 (1997): 51–72.

Chapter 6: Corinthian Christians as Artificial Aliens

1. See my "Judaism, Hellenism, and the Birth of Christianity," above, pp. 17–27.
2. I do not mean to imply that Ἰουδαῖ ος has always a geographical referent, as it sometimes does in New Testament texts and as some, following A. T. Kraabel's suggestion about one Smyrnan inscription, have assumed for inscriptions: an assumption refuted by M. H. Williams, "The Meaning and Function of Ioudaios in Graeco-Roman Inscriptions," *Zeitschrift für Papyrologie und Epigraphik* 116 (1997): 251–2. Kraabel's suggestion was in A. T. Kraabel, "The Roman Diaspora: Six Questionable Assumptions," *Journal of Jewish Studies* 33 (1982): 455, an essay otherwise filled with salutary observations and cautions.
3. Probably they were bilingual, Greek and Latin, for the official face of the colony, as revealed by inscriptions, in the first century was Latin. With the accession of Hadrian as emperor, the bulk of inscriptions quickly changed to Greek, suggesting that most of the residents had been Greek-speaking all along; see J. H. Kent, *Corinth: Results of Excavations Conducted by the American School of Classical Studies at Athens 8/3: Inscriptions 1926–1960,* American School of Classical Studies at Athens (Princeton: Princeton University Press, 1966), 19. The fact that the single, fragmentary Jewish inscription, of uncertain date, is in Greek tells us very little. On the return of people of Greek ancestry from Campania to eastern colonies under Augustus, see G. W. Bowersock, *Augustus and the Greek World* (Oxford: Clarendon, 1965), chap. 5.
4. The most comprehensive recent study of this range of issues is J. M. G. Barclay, *Jews in the Mediterranean Diaspora: From Alexander to Trajan (323 B.C.E.–117 C.E.)* (Edinburgh: Clark, 1996), which was not yet available to me when I wrote the version of this essay discussed at the Rolighed conference. Barclay recognizes that the categories so often used for sorting out the variety of Jewish responses to the Greco-Roman world, "orthodoxy" and "deviant" or "Palestinian" and "Hellenistic," are both inadequate and misleading. Instead, he adopts the sociological categories "assimilation," "acculturation," and "accommodation." The dominant picture that emerges is one of wide diversity among the Jews in each community and among the different communities. "The greater the precision in attention to detail, the more generalizations will appear impossible" (400). Nevertheless, Barclay rightly insists that "Diversity is not the only characteristic of the Diaspora, and some explanation is required for the way that Jewish communities survived *as coherent and enduring entities*" (400, emphasis original). To speak of different "Judaisms," as has become common in some circles, is wrong, he insists, for the great range of differences did not result in separation along ideological lines: "If Judaism is defined—as it should be—as a *social* and not just an *intellectual* phenomenon, it is hard to see how the plural 'Judaisms' could apply to the Diaspora" (401). All this seems to me quite right.
5. L. M. White, "The Delos Synagogue Revisited: Recent Fieldwork in the Graeco-Roman Diaspora," *HTR* 80 (1987): 133–60; P. Bruneau, *Recherches sur les cultes de Délos à l'époque hellénistique et à l'époque impériale,* Bibliotèque des Ecoles Françaises d'Athènes et de Rome (Paris: Boccard, 1970), with older literature cited there; on the immigrants from Beirut, see Bruneau, *Recherches,* 622–30.
6. B. Lifshitz, *Donateurs et fondateurs dans les synagogues juives: Répertoire des dédicaces grecques relatives à la construction et à la réfection des synagogues,* Cahiers de la Revue Biblique (Paris: Gabalda, 1967).
7. L. M. White, *The Social Origins of Christian Architecture,* Harvard Theological Studies (Valley Forge, Pa.: Trinity, 1996).
8. Edgar J. Goodspeed, "Gaius Titius Justus," *JBL* 69 (1950): 382–3.
9. G. Lüderitz, "What is the Politeuma?" *Studies in Early Jewish Epigraphy,*

Arbeiten zur Geschichte des Antiken Judentums und des Urchristentums, ed. J. W. v. Henten and P. W. v. d. Horst (Leiden: Brill, 1994), 183–225.

10. L. Feldman, *Jew and Gentile in the Ancient World: Attitudes and Interactions from Alexander to Justinian* (Princeton: Princeton University Press, 1993), 64.

11. This seems clear in the case of Alexandria, from the delegation to Rome in response to the events of 38 C.E. (see Philo, *Legat.* and *Flacc.*) and from Claudius's subsequent decree and letter. Inscriptional evidence from Ephesus attests corporate actions by "the Jews of Ephesus" (*IE* 6.1676 and 1677), and the several appeals from Sardis, Ephesus, and elsewhere to Rome, cited by Josephus (*Ant.* 14.235, 259–261, 262–264; compare the other decrees collected by Josephus in this section, *Ant.* 14.185–267) indicate some ability, at least in time of need, to speak with one voice.

12. P. W. v. d. Horst, ed., *Ancient Jewish Epigraphs: An Introductory Survey of a Millennium of Jewish Funerary Epigraphy (300 B.C.E.–700 C.E.)*, Contributions to Biblical Exegesis and Theology (Kampen: Kok Pharos, 1991).

13. The pioneer in studying women's leadership in synagogues was B. J. Brooten, *Women Leaders in the Ancient Synagogue* (Chico, Calif.: Scholars, 1982). For further evidence, see van der Horst (previous note).

14. M. Stern, *Greek and Latin Authors on Jews and Judaism* (Jerusalem: Israel Academy of Sciences and Humanities, 1974–1984).

15. That still seems probably the best solution, though it requires the assumption that the workman carving the inscription transposed καὶ and τῶν. For a rehearsal of the debate, see J. Reynolds and R. Tannenbaum, *Jews and Godfearers at Aphrodisias,* Supplementary Series (Cambridge: Cambridge University Press, 1987), 54. But if the inscription is read as it stands, "Place of the Jews who are also pious" (Why would the theater managers care whether the Jews were pious?), the argument above would not be affected.

16. W. A. Meeks, "'And Rose Up to Play': Midrash and Paraenesis in 1 Corinthians 10:1–22," *JSNT* 16 (1982): 64–78.

17. S. J. A. Cohen has explored this issue in a provocative and insightful series of essays, now collected in Shaye J. D. Cohen, *The Beginnings of Jewishness: Boundaries, Varieties, Uncertainties* (Berkeley, Los Angeles, and London: University of California Press, 1999).

18. On the tangled question of "god-fearers," see, for a start, Reynolds and Tannenbaum, *Jews and Godfearers at Aphrodisias,* 48–66. Jewish usage of "living God": M. Goodwin, *The Living God* (Ph.D. diss., Yale; 1992). Conversion experience presupposed in 1 Thessalonians: E. Pax, "Beobachtungen zur Konvertitensprache im ersten Thessalonicherbrief," *Studii Biblici Franciscani Analecta* 21 (1971): 220–61; A. J. Malherbe, *Paul and the Thessalonians: The Philosophic Tradition of Pastoral Care* (Philadelphia: Fortress, 1987), 34–52.

19. W. A. Meeks, "Breaking Away: Three New Testament Pictures of Christianity's Separation from the Jewish Communities," *"To See Ourselves as Others See Us": Christians, Jews, "Others" in Late Antiquity,* eds. J. Neusner and E. S. Frerichs, Scholars Press Studies in the Humanities (Chico, Calif.: Scholars, 1985), 93–116.

20. Here it is sufficient to refer to the work of A. J. Malherbe and H. D. Betz and their students.

21. M. M. Mitchell, *Paul and the Rhetoric of Reconciliation: An Exegetical Investigation of the Language and Composition of 1 Corinthians,* HUT (Tübingen: Mohr-Siebeck, 1992; Louisville: Westminster/John Knox, 1993).

22. Cf. the sage observations in Erich S. Gruen, *Heritage and Hellenism: The Reinvention of Jewish Tradition,* Hellenistic Culture and Society (Berkeley: University of California Press, 1998).

23. W. A. Meeks, *The Moral World of the First Christians,* Library of Early Christianity (Philadelphia: Westminster Press, 1986); W. A. Meeks, "The Polyphonic Ethics of the Apostle Paul," *Annual of the Society of Christian Ethics* (1988), 17–29; W. A. Meeks, "The Circle of Reference in Pauline Morality," *Greeks, Romans, and Christians: Essays in Honor of Abraham J. Malherbe,* eds. D. L. Balch, E. Ferguson, and W. A. Meeks (Minneapolis: Fortress, 1990), 305–17; W. A. Meeks, *The Origins of Christian Morality: The First Two Centuries* (New Haven and London: Yale University Press, 1993).

24. Alexandria: Philo, *Flacc., Legat.*; E. M. Smallwood, *The Jews Under Roman Rule from Pompey to Diocletian: A Study in Political Relations,* Studies in Judaism in Late Antiquity (Leiden: Brill, 1981), 235–55; Barclay, *Jews in the Mediterranean Diaspora,* 48–81; Antioch: Josephus, *J.W.* 7.47–61, 100–111.

Chapter 7: Matching Theory and Practice: Josephus's Constitutional Ideal and Paul's Strategy in Corinth

1. Examples include Cicero, *De legibus,* and Plutarch, *De tribus rei publicae generibus.* See T. A. Sinclair, *A History of Greek Political Thought* (London: Routledge & Kegan Paul, 1951).

2. The political aspects of Paul's church-formation have received only sporadic discussion; see, e.g., E. Judge, "Contemporary Political Models for the Inter-Relations of the New Testament Churches," *RTR* 22 (1963): 65–75; M. Mitchell, *Paul and the Rhetoric of Reconciliation* (Louisville, Ky.: Westminster/John Knox, 1991).

3. See C. Schäublin, "Josephus und die Griechen," *Hermes* 110 (1982): 316–41; C. Gerber, *Ein Bild des Judentums für Nichtjuden von Flavius Josephus. Untersuchungen zu seiner Schrift Contra Apionem* (Leiden: Brill, 1997), 226–43.

4. See D. R. Schwartz, "Josephus on the Jewish Constitutions and Community", *SCI* 7 (1983–84): 30–52.

5. On the relationship between this utopian depiction of the constitution and the emphases of Josephus's earlier works, see T. Rajak, "The *Against Apion* and the Continuities in Josephus's Political Thought," *Understanding Josephus. Seven Perspectives,* ed. S. Mason (Sheffield: Sheffield Academic Press 1998), 222–46.

6. Josephus appears to use the terms πολιτεία and πολίτευμα as synonyms; their usage is intertwined throughout the second half of Book 2 (πολιτεία: 2.188, 222, 226, 256, 264, 273, 287; πολίτευμα: 2.145, 164–165, 184, 250, 257).

7. As well as κατάστασις (2.145, 184), Josephus uses τρόπος (2.170) and τάξις (2.250) to refer to this "structure"; cf. *Ant.* 1.10: ἡ διάταξις τῆς πολιτείας.

8. On Josephus's coinage see Y. Amir, "Θεοκρατία as a Concept of Political Philosophy: Josephus' Presentation of Moses' *Politeia," SCI* 8–9 (1985–88): 83–105. The common but false assumption that Josephus refers primarily to the rule of priests is evidenced, for instance, in H. Cancik, "Theokratie und Priesterherrschaft: Die mosaische Verfassung bei Flavius Josephus, c. Apionem 2,157–198," *Religionstheorie und politische Theologie,* ed. J. Taubes (München/Paderborn/Wien/Zürich: Fink/Schöningh, 1987), 3.65–77.

9. All translations are my own.

10. ἅτε δὴ τὰ ἔργα παρέχων σύμφωνα τοῖς νόμοις. This is the text quoted in Eusebius, *Praep. evang.* 8.8.6, and adopted in the edition by S. A. Naber (Leipzig: Teubner, 1896); the editions by B. Niese (Berlin: Weidmann, 1889), H. St.J. Thackeray, LCL (Cambridge, Mass.: Harvard University Press, 1926), and T. Reinach, Budé (Paris: Les Belles Lettres, 1930) follow L and the sixth-century Latin translation in reading τοῖς λόγοις for τοῖς νόμοις.

11. It is not easy to decide between the textual variants at this point (between ἤθη and ἔθη), which in any case make little difference to the sense.

12. Philo praises Moses' character (though not precisely his constitution) for its harmony of λόγος and βίος, especially the way Moses exemplified his philosophical creed in his daily life (διὰ τῶν καθ᾽ ἑκάστην ἡμέραν ἔργων, *Mos.* 1.29); cf. Iamblichus, *Vita Pyth.* 170. At *Praem.* 80–84, Philo utilizes the threefold "mouth, heart, and hand" of Deut 30:14 (LXX) to extol the Jewish unity of word, thought, and action. On such as an ideal combination see Schäublin, "Josephus und die Griechen," 334–5.

13. βραχυλόγος, Plato, *Laws* 641e, etc.; the epithet λακωνικός is already proverbial in Plato. See the classic statements on this Spartan characteristic in Plutarch, *Lycurgus* 19–20.

14. "Uneducated" Spartans (Isocrates); disciplined obedience (Xenophon, Plutarch, and many others).

15. Josephus's skill in deploying these contrasts in this context is clear from the fact that elsewhere he can put them to rather different use. Thus at 2.292 he claims that Jews are unsophisticated in verbal tricks, while always supported by actions (ἀσόφιστοι λόγων παρασκευαῖς, τοῖς ἔργοις ἀεὶ βεβαιούμενοι); the latter, in fact, constitute clearer testimony than any document (τῶν γραμμάτων ἐναργέστερα).

16. See, e.g., Plato, *Republic* 376e–412b, *Laws* book 7 (788a–824c), Aristotle, *Politics* books 7–8 (1323a–1342b). Josephus himself notes the importance of this topic to Plato (*Ag. Ap.* 2.257).

17. On the significance of this theme in Josephus, see B. Schröder, *Die 'väterlichen Gesetze'. Flavius Josephus als Vermittler von Halachah an Griechen und Römer* (Tübingen: Mohr-Siebeck, 1996).

18. In *Antiquities* Book 4, Josephus had not attributed this custom to Moses. There mention is made only of the septennial reading of the law (4.209–211; based on Deut 31:10–13), though its effect is described in similar terms as an engraving on souls (ταῖς ψυχαῖς ἐγγραφέντας, 4.210). For Josephus's pride in the Sabbath readings cf. *Ant.* 16.43.

19. K.-W. Niebuhr thus rightly characterizes the Sabbath gatherings for instruction in the law: "Sie bilden den Kristallisationskern für die Bewahrung jüdischer Identität unter den Alltagsbedingungen der Diaspora" ("Identität und Interaktion. Zur Situation paulinischer Gemeinden im Ausstrahlungsfeld des Diasporajudentums," *Pluralismus und Identität*, ed. J. Mehlhausen [Gütersloh: Kaiser Gütersloher Verlaghaus, 1995], 339–59, esp. 346). See further, J. M. G. Barclay, *Jews in the Mediterranean Diaspora from Alexander to Trajan (323 B.C.E.–117 C.E.)* (Edinburgh: Clark, 1996), 412–13, 416–17.

20. The same three recur, alongside others, in a later list of customs that Josephus regards as especially demanding (signaling that the Jews' capacity for endurance was even greater than that of the Spartans!): there he highlights simplicity of diet, restraint of greed and extravagance, care in matters of food and drink, restrictions in sexual relations, and the Sabbath rest (2.234–235).

21. See Barclay, *Jews in the Mediterranean Disapora*, 411–12, 434–42.

22. See W. C. van Unnik, "Josephus' Account of the Story of Israel's Sin with Alien Women in the Country of Midian (Num. 25.1ff.)," *Travels in the World of the Old Testament,* ed. M. S. H. G. Heerma von Voss (Assen: Van Gorcum, 1974), 241–61.

23. M. Mitchell, *Paul and the Rhetoric of Reconciliation* (Louisville, Ky.: Westminster/John Knox, 1991).

24. M. Wolter, "Ethos und Identität in paulinischen Gemeinden," *NTS* 43 (1997): 430–44.
25. "Von entscheidender Bedeutung ist in diesem Zusammenhang zunächst, dass Paulus die Abgrenzungsfunktion des Ethos von der Ebene des Handelns ablöst und auf das πιστεύειν überträgt" ("Ethos und Identität," 439).
26. "Weil die exklusive Identität der christlichen Gemeinden ihren Ausdruck allein im Ethos des Glaubens findet, kann deren Lebensführung davon entlastet werden, sich—mit Ausnahme des Verzichts auf πορνεία und εἰδωλολατρία—durch habitualisierte Handlungen nach außen abgrenzen zu müssen" ("Ethos und Identität," 444).
27. See W. A. Meeks, "Breaking Away: Three New Testament Pictures of Christianity's Separation from the Jewish Communities," *"To See Ourselves as Others See Us": Christians, Jews, "Others" in Late Antiquity,* eds. J. Neusner and E. S. Frerichs (Chico, Calif.: Scholars, 1985), 93–115.
28. Among recent discussions of this complex passage see especially R. Hays, *Echoes of Scripture in the Letters of Paul* (New Haven/London: Yale University Press, 1989), 122–53, and S. J. Hafemann, *Paul, Moses and the History of Israel* (Tübingen: Mohr-Siebeck, 1995).
29. See further J. M. G. Barclay, "The Family as the Bearer of Religion in Judaism and Early Christianity," *Constructing Early Christian Families,* ed. H. Moxnes (London: Routledge, 1997), 66–80.
30. I have suggested elsewhere that some of Paul's converts may have practiced only "segmental" participation in the community, regarding certain spheres of life (e.g., their legal business) as beyond its purview (J. M. G. Barclay, "Thessalonica and Corinth: Social Contrasts in Pauline Christianity," *JSNT* 47 [1992]: 49–74, esp. 70–1); by contrast, it is Paul's specific contention that the Christian ethos is fully comprehensive.
31. In many circumstances it was difficult enough for Jews in the Diaspora to gain permission to abstain from work on the Sabbath, and it is difficult to see on what grounds Gentile Christians could gain this right. It is this dramatic change in routine which made such an impact on Jewish life and social reputation.
32. See W. A. Meeks, *The First Urban Christians* (New Haven: Yale University Press, 1983), 140–63.
33. See the discussion of this topic by A. J. Malherbe, "Determinism and Free Will in Paul: The Argument of 1 Corinthians 8 and 9," *Paul in His Hellenistic Context,* ed. T. Engberg-Pedersen (Edinburgh: Clark, 1994), 231–55.
34. W. A. Meeks, "The Polyphonic Ethics of the Apostle Paul," *Annual of the Society of Christian Ethics,* 1988, 17–29. See further the important reflections on Paul's pattern of instruction and exhortation in T. Engberg-Pedersen, "The Gospel and Social Practice According to 1 Corinthians," *NTS* 33 (1987): 557–84; idem, "1 Corinthians 11:16 and the Character of Pauline Exhortation", *JBL* 110 (1991): 679–89.
35. The double-edged character of Paul's strategy is rightly noted by Wolter, "Ethos und Identität," 443–4.
36. For a discussion of 1 Corinthians that points in this same direction see J. T. Sanders, "Paul between Jews and Gentiles in Corinth," *JSNT* 65 (1997): 67–83.

Chapter 8: The Corinthian Correspondence between Philosophical Idealism and Apocalypticism

1. David E. Aune, "Human Nature and Ethics in Hellenistic Philosophical Traditions and Paul: Some Issues and Problems," *Paul in His Hellenistic Context,* ed. T. Engberg-Pedersen (Minneapolis: Fortress, 1995), 291–312.

2. Ibid., 299.
3. Ibid., 305.
4. J. Dillon, *The Middle Platonists. A Study of Platonism 80 B.C. to A.D. 220* (London: Duckworth, 1977), 139ff.
5. M. Hengel, *Judentum und Hellenismus,* WUNT 10, 2d ed. (Tübingen: Mohr-Siebeck, 1973).
6. M. Himmelfarb, *Ascent to Heaven in Jewish and Christian Apocalypses* (New York and Oxford: Oxford University Press, 1993).
7. L. Hartman, "Hellenistic Elements in Apocalyptic Texts," *The New Testament in Its Hellenistic Context,* eds. G. A. Jónsson, E. Sigurbjörnsson, and P. Pétursson; Studia theologica islandica 10 (Reykjavík: Gudfrædistofnun, 1996), 113–33.
8. Th. Boman, *Das hebräische Denken im Vergleich mit dem Griechischen* (Göttingen: Vandenhoeck & Ruprecht, 1952; English trans. *Hebrew Thought Compared with Greek* [London: SCM, 1960]).
9. O. Cullmann, *Christus und die Zeit. Die urchristliche Zeit- und Geschichtsauffassung* (Zürich: Evangelischer, 1946).
10. R. Bultmann, *History and Eschatology* (Edinburgh: Edinburgh University Press, 1957).
11. D. Harvey, *The Condition of Postmodernity* (Oxford: Blackwell, 1989).
12. The following section is a rewritten version of my sketch of Philo's position in H. Tronier, "Hellenistic Hermeneutics and Paul's Idea of the Spirit in First Corinthians," *The New Testament in Its Hellenistic Context,* eds. G. A. Jónsson, E. Sigurbjörnsson, and P. Pétursson; Studia theologica islandica 10 (Reykjavík: Gudfrædistofnun, 1996), 37–55.
13. Dillon, 159: "the intelligible cosmos is simply the Ideas taken as a whole. The Logos, the divine reason-principle, is the active element of God's creative thought, and is often spoken of as the 'place' of the Ideas. . . . the Logos is only the sum-total of the Ideas in activity, as the intelligible cosmos was only their sum-total viewed as being at rest."
14. The importance of the method of *diairesis* in Philo's cosmology as well as the connection between that cosmology and cognition was brought out by U. Früchtel, *Die kosmologischen Vorstellungen bei Philo von Alexandrien,* Arbeiten zur Literatur und Geschichte des hellenistischen Judentums 2 (Leiden: Brill, 1968), 41–52. The importance of the method of *diairesis* for Philo's allegorical hermeneutics was brought out by I. Christiansen, *Die Technik der allegorischen Auslegungswissenschaft bei Philon von Alexandrien,* Beiträge zur Geschichte der biblischen Hermeneutik 7 (Tübingen: Mohr-Siebeck, 1969).
15. See the expositions by Früchtel, 43ff. and Christiansen, 29ff.
16. Compare Plato's definition in *Soph.* 253d-e, trans. H. N. Fowler, *Plato in twelve volumes,* vol. VII; LCL 123 (London: Heinemann/Cambridge, Mass.: Harvard University Press, 1967):

    - Shall we not say that the division of things by classes (*to kata genē diaireisthai*) and the avoidance of the belief that the same class is another and another the same belongs to the science of dialectic?

    - Yes we shall.

    - Then he who is able to do this has a clear perception of one form or idea extending entirely through many individuals each of which lies apart, and of many forms differing from one another but included in one greater form, and again of one form evolved by the union of many wholes, and of many forms entirely apart and separate. This is the knowledge and ability to distinguish by classes how individual things can or cannot be associated with one another.

17. Cf. *Her.* 130f. Cf., too, 233–236.
18. Ibid., 140.
19. Ibid., 130. Cf., too, *Migr.* 102ff.; 181.
20. *Her.* 188; cf. *Migr.* 102ff. and 181.
21. Cf. Früchtel, 45 and 52.
22. This is the very issue of *Migr.* as well as of *Her.*
23. *Migr.* 5; 35f.; 38–40; 42; 46; 47ff.; 52; 53f.; 77.
24. Ibid., 5f., cf. 73; 75.
25. Ibid., 38f.; 48 and 191.
26. Cf. ibid., 5–13; 14; 18; 36; 38.
27. *Her.* 130f.; 234–236. Cf. 109ff. and *Migr.* 4–6.
28. *Migr.* 209. Cf. *Her.* 130ff.
29. Cf., too, *Her.* 280.
30. *Migr.* 9–13.
31. Ibid., 13; 209; 36ff.; 185f. Cf. *Her.* 110f.
32. *Migr.* 11; cf. *Her.* 110f. and *Migr.* 36ff.; 59–63; 67; 70.
33. Compare the description of his own experience in *Migr.* 35 with his description of the cognitive transformation that leads to conceptual apprehension in *Migr.* 2.
34. For instance *Migr.* 102ff.; 180ff.
35. Cf. *Opif.* 17. Früchtel, 28, n. 5.
36. Among other passages see *Her.* 110f.
37. *Migr.* 38f.; 47–49; 52; 103. See Früchtel, 111; 167, and Christiansen, 153.
38. *Migr.* 71ff.; 78–81. See Christiansen, 162f. and 170.
39. H. H. Rowley, *The Relevance of Apocalyptic* (London: Lutterworth, 1944).
40. O. Plöger, *Theokratie und Eschatologie* (Neukirchen: Kreis Moers, 1959).
41. D. S. Russell, *The Method and Message of Jewish Apocalyptic 200 B.C.–A.D. 100* (Philadelphia: Westminster, 1964).
42. Chr. Rowland, *The Open Heaven: A Study of Apocalyptic in Judaism and Early Christianity* (New York: Crossroad, 1982).
43. J. J. Collins, *The Apocalyptic Imagination* (New York: Crossroad, 1984).
44. M. Himmelfarb, *Ascent to Heaven.*
45. For a summary of the discussion cf. J. J. Collins, ed., *Apocalypse: The Morphology of a Genre, Semeia* 14 (1979): 16f. and 21ff.
46. Cf. 14:8; 17:4; 18:6; 39:3; 52:1f.; 60:10–12; 93:11–14.
47. Cf. G. W. E. Nickelsburg, "The Apocalyptic Construction of Reality in 1 Enoch," *Mysteries and Revelations: Apocalyptic Studies since the Uppsala Colloquium,* eds. J. J. Collins and J. H. Charlesworth, JSPSup 9 (Sheffield, 1991), 51–64, esp. 54: "What is obvious in 1 Enoch, once one sees it, is the author's preoccupation with a world that is described in spatial and material terms, a world that can be experienced, at least in principle, by the five senses." See also Nickelsburg, 56.
48. Cf. 18:13ff.; 21:4ff.; 22:2f.; 23:1–4; 26:6–27:2; 40:2; 40:8f.; 43:3f.; 46:2; 52:1–5; 53:1–5; 54:4ff.; 61:1; 108:5f.
49. Cf. 41:1; 60f.; 90:41.
50. Cf. 41:1ff. and 22; 26; 53f.; 39:4ff. Cf., too, 18:11ff.; 19; 21; 56:3. See Nickelsburg, 56.
51. Cf. 33–36; 41:1ff.; 72ff. Cf., too, 18:1ff.; 60:11ff. See Nickelsburg, 55f.
52. 72:1; 74:2; 75:3; 79:6. Cf. 60:17, 19, 21, 22, and 82:7ff.
53. For references see Himmelfarb, 47ff., although Himmelfarb's interpretation of the motif differs from mine (cf. Himmelfarb, 69–71).
54. Cf. 39ff.; 71:3ff. and the connection between 72–79 and 80ff. Cf., too, 22ff.; 58f.; 60.

55. Cf. 38:1; 39:1.4ff.; 41:1f.; 52:1f.; 53:6.
56. Cf., for instance, 1 Enoch 46ff. and 91–104.
57. Cf., for instance, 108:8–10; 103:4.
58. Cf., for instance, 1 Enoch 46:4–6; 48:8–10; 50:1f.; 103:5–12; 104:6.
59. Cf., for instance, 1 Enoch 5:8; 48:1; 49:1; 51:1–5; 90:35; 91:10; 91:16; 93:10.
60. Himmelfarb, 85f.
61. 2 Enoch 21f.
62. 2 Enoch 24ff.
63. Himmelfarb, 85f.
64. 2 Enoch 25f.
65. Cf. D. B. Martin, *The Corinthian Body* (New Haven and London: Yale University Press, 1995), 60 on 1 Cor 1:18–31: "The apocalyptic world is not one in which hierarchies are dissolved into equality but one in which the values of the Greco-Roman world are acknowledged but then turned on their heads."
66. H. Tronier, "Hellenistic Hermeneutics."
67. See M. M. Mitchell, *Paul and the Rhetoric of Reconciliation: An Exegetical Investigation of the Language and Composition of 1 Corinthians* (Tübingen: Mohr-Siebeck, 1992). See also Martin, 38ff.
68. Cf. Martin, 92–6 and 38ff.
69. A. F. Segal, *Paul the Convert: The Apostolate and Apostasy of Saul the Pharisee* (New Haven and London: Yale University Press, 1990), 34ff.
70. Himmelfarb, 95ff.
71. Martin, 105f. makes the same point, although he refers to the character of their ideas of anthropology and the nature of bodies, not their ideas of cognition and notions of transcendence.
72. So Martin, 126f. with reference to contemporary ideas of astral bodies as being made up of *pneuma*.
73. So, among others, K. G. Sandelin, *Die Auseinandersetzung mit der Weisheit in 1. Korinther 15* (Åbo: Åbo Akademi, 1976), 132; P. W. Gooch, *Partial Knowledge: Philosophical Studies in Paul* (Notre Dame, Ind.: University of Notre Dame Press, 1987), 68f.
74. Cf. Sandelin, 133: "Der Mensch besteht sowohl hinsichtlich seines Körpers als auch hinsichtlich seiner Seele aus Erde. Hier muss man wohl von Substanz sprechen. Im Hinblick auf der Auferstehungsleib ist Paulus dagegen sehr zurückhaltend. Er bezeichnet die Substanz weder als *doxa* noch als *pneuma*. Aus dem Zusammenhang (VV. 47–49, cf. V. 40) geht hervor, dass der Auferstehungsleib himmlisch ist. Zweifellos setzt Paulus voraus, dass der himmlische Leib aus irgendetwas besteht. Er spekuliert aber nicht darüber."
75. Martin, 126 and 128.
76. Sandelin, 128f. On the one hand: "Paulus sagt nicht, dass der 'eine Leib' 'eine neue Bestimmtheit' bekommt. Das vergängliche *sôma* geht nicht in ein unvergängliches über, sondern wird von einem unvergänglichen überkleidet. Die Kontinuität liegt somit nicht im *sôma*" (128). On the other hand: "Wir, die wir verwandelt werden, sind auch diejenigen, welche das Abbild des himmlischen Menschen tragen werden (V. 49). Wir werden nicht von anderen abgelöst. Paulus setzt also einerseits voraus, dass diejenigen, welche auferstehen, dieselben sind, die gestorben waren. Andererseits hat Paulus keinen anthropologischen 'Begriff für das überdauernde, die Kontinuität Bildende.' Die Frage der Kontinuität bzw. Identität scheint darum nicht von besonderem Interesse für Paulus in 1. Kor. 15,35ff. zu sein" (129).
77. Martin, 127.
78. Aune, 301–3: "2 Cor 5.1–10 is an important passage for understanding Paul's views of human nature. (1) The use of the image of the house (*oikia*) or tent (*skênos*) as a metaphor for the physical aspect of human existence (the *sôma*, cf.

vv. 6–8) occurs frequently in Hellenistic tradition from Plato on, but rarely in early Judaism. (2) Paul distinguishes the real person from the purely physical dimension of human existence, so that this is essentially a pluralistic or dualistic appraisal of human nature reflecting neither common Hellenistic nor common early Jewish conceptions, but rather appears to be Paul's own theological construct. . . . (5) The *oikodomê ek theou* (v. 1) or the *oikêtêrion ex ouranou,* is a way of referring to the glorified body of the Christian—a form of corporeality in which the dualistic conflict between flesh and spirit is transcended by a monistic form of existence. He does not explicitly label the part of human nature that will be separated from the body upon death. If pressed, however, Paul probably would have preferred the term *pneuma* to *psychê*."

Chapter 9: Pauline Accommodation and "Condescension" (συγκατάβασις): 1 Cor 9:19–23 and the History of Influence

1. *The New Testament and Rabbinic Judaism,* Jordan Lecture, 1952 (London: Athlone, 1956), 336–49. His general conclusion is expressed on p. 341: "Paul, when he wrote the passage from I Corinthians [9:20–23] . . . was drawing on a living element in Jewish religion," and p. 349: "Paul drew on a rabbinic tradition." Daube refers principally to passages in the Talmud, Mishnah, and Tosefta about Rabbi Hillel's accommodation of would-be proselytes, and two passages in Derek Eretz Zuta and Derek Eretz Rabbah, the most relevant being the latter, 7.7: "A man should not be joyful among the weeping, nor weep among the joyful, nor wake among the sleeping, nor sleep among the waking, nor stand among the sitting, nor sit among the standing—the principle of the matter is this: a man should not make different his mind from that of his fellows and the sons of men" [Daube's translation, 339]). The Hebrew of this negatively phrased principle reads:

לא ישׂמח אדם בין הבוכים ולא יבכה בין השׂמחים. ולא יהא ער בין הישׁנים ולא ישׁן בין הערים. ולא עומד בין היושׁבים ולא יושׁב בין העומדים. כללו שׁל דבר אל ישׁנה אדם דעתו מדעת חביריו ובני אדם (*Soncino Talmud,* vol. 39, p. 47). But Daube also cites the (highly hellenized) *Epistle of Aristeas* 257, a question-and-answer about how a king may find a good welcome when he travels. The reply is: "by becoming equal to all" [πᾶσιν ἴσος γινόμενος]. Compare also *Ep. Arist.* 267: "'In view of the heterogeneous multitudes in the kingdom, how can one be in harmony with them?' 'By adopting the role appropriate to each one (Τὸ πρέπον ἑκάστῳ συνυποκρινόμενος), with justice as your guiding principle' " (text H. St. J. Thackeray, in H. B. Swete, *Introduction to the Old Testament in Greek* [Cambridge: Cambridge University Press, 1914; repr. Peabody, Mass.: Hendrikson, 1989]; trans. R. J. H. Shutt, *OTP* 2.30, a text not mentioned by Daube, for he is looking for explicitly "missionary" parallels). He also refers to Athenaeus, *Deipnosophistae* 7.317A and 12.513B on commonplaces about travelers needing to accommodate to their surroundings. Daube's scholarship of course was notable for its accent on the Hellenistic influences on rabbinic Judaism, as, for instance, in Hillel's hermeneutical rules, so even here Judaism and Hellenism cannot simply be opposed.

2. Although not taking up exactly that challenge, Peter J. Tomson has produced an interpretation of these verses that presents Paul as a thoroughly and consistently law-observant Jew (*Paul and the Jewish Law,* CRINT 3/1 [Assen: Van Gorcum; Minneapolis: Fortress, 1990], 274–81). But this reading seems imposed on the text by the governing assumptions of his study, and depends upon some strained text-critical and translation moves, and wide-ranging con-

textual pleas (from Galatians and Pauline behavior in Acts). For instance, the argument that v. 20a should be translated "I was born a Jew," but the other parallel verses in which the same elided verb ἐγενόμην is to be understood are rendered "I became" (20b-21), whereas v. 22 means, "I was born a delicate," is weak because there are no grounds for such a significant shift in semantic meaning of the elided verb (in this particular case or in Greek generally). It also relies upon the exclusion of the phrase μὴ ὢν αὐτὸς ὑπὸ νόμον, a textual reading that is poorly attested and can be easily explained as a classic instance of deletion by homoioteleuton. Even Barclay, who generally takes Paul to have been only minimally influenced by Hellenism, regards these verses as outlining "tactical adaptability (or 'inconsistency,' cf. Gal. 1.10) [which] enabled Paul to justify a degree of assimilation which brought him into continuous controversy with fellow Jews" (John M. G. Barclay, *Jews in the Mediterranean Diaspora from Alexander to Trajan [323 B.C.E.–117C.E.]* [Edinburgh: Clark, 1996], 384).

3. There have of course been general studies on the flow of the passage itself, and what it says about Pauline missionary practice (e.g., Günther Bornkamm, "The Missionary Stance of Paul in I Corinthians 9 and in Acts," *Studies in Luke-Acts,* eds. Leander E. Keck and J. Louis Martyn [Nashville: Abingdon, 1966], 194–207; W. Willis, "An Apostolic Apologia? The Form and Function of 1 Cor 9," *JSNT* 24 [1985]: 33–48; Peter Richardson, "Pauline Inconsistency: I Corinthians 9:19–23 and Galatians 2:11–14," *NTS* 26 [1980]: 347–62), but my concern here is with research into the background or cultural milieu of these sayings.

4. Already in 1897 Johannes Weiss regarded the Greek style of the passage as proof of Paul's rhetorical training: "Dies eine Beispiel würde genügen zum Beweise, dass Paulus rhetorische Uebung erworben und dass er mit grosser Sorgfalt und Feile an seinen Briefen gearbeitet hat" ("Beiträge zur Paulinischen Rhetorik," *Theologische Studien für Professor D. Bernhard Weiss an seinem 70. Geburtstag dargebracht,* eds. C. R. Gregory, A. Harnack, et al. [Göttingen: Vandenhoeck & Ruprecht, 1897], 165–247, esp. 194–5). I would like to thank Prof. Lars Rydbeck for reminding me of the central role of 1 Cor 9:19–23 in Weiss's extremely important study.

5. Abraham J. Malherbe, "Antisthenes and Odysseus, and Paul at War," *HTR* 76 (1983): 143–73; repr. in *Paul and the Popular Philosophers* (Minneapolis: Fortress, 1989), 91–119 (I cite this pagination). See also the study by Clarence E. Glad, *Paul and Philodemus. Adaptability in Epicurean and Early Christian Psychagogy,* NovTSup 81 (Leiden: Brill, 1995), esp. 1–20, but also 272, where he does not want to align "Paul too closely with the Antisthenic tradition." Malherbe also refers to the older work of Hermann Funke, "Antisthenes bei Paulus," *Hermes* 98 (1970): 459–71, which focuses on Odyssean themes in the next pericope, 9:24–27.

6. Peter Marshall, *Enmity in Corinth: Social Conventions in Paul's Social Relations with the Corinthians,* WUNT 2/23 (Tübingen: Mohr-Siebeck, 1987), 70–90, 306–17.

7. Samuel Vollenweider, *Freiheit als neue Schöpfung: Eine Untersuchung zur Eleutheria bei Paulus und in seiner Umwelt,* FRLANT 147 (Göttingen: Vandenhoeck & Ruprecht, 1989), 199–232; F. Stanley Jones, *"Freiheit" in den Briefen des Apostels Paulus. Eine historische, exegetische und religionsgeschichtliche Studie,* GTA 34 (Göttingen: Vandenhoeck & Ruprecht, 1987); Abraham J. Malherbe, "Determinism and Free Will in Paul: The Argument of 1 Corinthians 8 and 9," *Paul in His Hellenistic Context,* ed. Troels Engberg-Pedersen (Minneapolis: Fortress, 1995), 231–55 (he combines this reading with his incorporation of the Odyssean example).

8. Vollenweider, *Freiheit,* 216–20, in relation to 22b, especially, and only suggestively. He treats 9:19–21a in connection with Greek philosophical arguments about freedom.
9. Dale B. Martin, *Slavery as Salvation: The Metaphor of Slavery in Pauline Christianity* (New Haven: Yale University Press, 1990), esp. 86–116.
10. Margaret M. Mitchell, *Paul and the Rhetoric of Reconciliation. An Exegetical Investigation of the Language and Composition of 1 Corinthians,* HUT 28 (Tübingen: Mohr-Siebeck, 1991; Louisville: Westminster/John Knox, 1993), 133–6.
11. This comparative work is the central task of Glad's fine study. It should be acknowledged that Glad at the outset of his study overtly eschews the task of making an argument about influence: "My purpose then is not to demonstrate either a pattern of influence and cultural borrowing or direct influence or reaction, but to highlight a widespread and shared communal practice among Epicureans and early Christians" (p. 9). However, this stated qualification appears to go against the grain of the fundamental assumption from which Glad proceeds: "This book agrees though with the presentation of Paul in Malherbe's studies, a Paul who is at once *Paulus christianus* and *Paulus hellenisticus,* one who is thoroughly familiar with the traditions of his philosophic contemporaries and who knows these traditions first-hand" (p. 4). Thus the overall force of Glad's study is to suggest more than coincidental or parallel similarities: "Paul is then not promoting a new type of community education for adults but conforms to a widespread pedagogical pattern witnessed in contemporary Epicurean schools. Such a socio-cultural perspective on the contemporary pedagogical models *available to and appropriated by Paul* helps us to appreciate the special affinities that Paul's nurture of the proto-Christian communities, and the participatory psychagogy he attempts to implement in these communities, have with the psychagogic practices of contemporary Epicureans in Athens, Naples, and Herculanaeum" (p. 336, emphasis added). Because of this tension in the book, I think it is justifiable to include Glad's hypothesis among the other lines of influence. At the very least, even if Glad himself does not want to stake that claim overtly, others may take the argument of his book in that direction.
12. The most recent and detailed proposal in this line is that of Barclay, *Jews in the Mediterranean Diaspora,* whose arguments present a direct challenge to the assumptions and conclusions of each of the seven positions we have noted: "[Paul] does not give the impression of one who has undergone the literary and rhetorical training which was characteristic of the gymnasium. It seems he had no more than a rudimentary knowledge of Greek literature (contrast Ezekiel and Aristobulus, not to mention Philo): the occasional literary tag (Menander in 1 Cor 15:33) reflects only popular parlance. . . . At no point does Paul prize the Greek *paideia* which was valued so highly by Jews like Aristeas and Philo" (p. 383). It seems to me that Barclay's judgment is based upon some assumptions that one might profitably debate: 1) the firm distinction between "popular parlance" and Greek literature; 2) assumptions about what type and frequency of allusions to classical literature would be required to demonstrate knowledge of or familiarity with them; 3) a reconstruction of Paul's formal education positing Pharisaism as the "filter" of Hellenism into Paul's mind ("Thus the evidence points to a Greek-medium Jewish education, in which the broad spectrum of Hellenism entered Paul's mind *only* through the filter of his conservative Pharisaic environment" [p. 384, emphasis added]), which, even leaving aside the plausibility of Luke's reference to Paul's schooling in Jerusalem, does not seem adequately to incorporate other arenas of cultural influence; 4) an assumption about the region where Paul's Hellenism should be manifested,

if it is to "count": "Yet Paul makes little attempt to express his new commitments in the terms or categories of Hellenistic culture. Despite years of association with Gentiles, Paul's letters show little acculturation *in the core of his theology,* and he rarely attempts to effect any cultural synthesis with the Graeco-Roman world he sought to evangelize" (p. 387, emphasis added). Barclay's important book has nicely set the table for these discussions.

13. Opinions on this vary. Günther Glockmann, *Homer in der frühchristlichen Literatur bis Justinus,* TU 105 (Berlin: Akademie-Verlag, 1968), 57, finds no reference, conscious or unconscious, to Homer in the New Testament. However, he is appropriately cautious (p. 65) about drawing conclusions from this about the Homeric knowledge of individual NT authors. Glockmann also notes that all three explicit classical citations in the NT (1 Cor 15:33; Tit 1:12; Acts 17:28) are associated with Paul (p. 64). Hellenistic Jewish acquaintance with Homer generally through the παιδεία is argued for by Martin Hengel, on the basis of Homeric references in Aristobulus, the Sibylline Oracles, Josephus, and Philo (*Judaism and Hellenism. Studies in their Encounter in Palestine during the Early Hellenistic Period,* trans. John Bowden [Philadelphia: Fortress, 1974], 1.75, 103). See also Dennis R. MacDonald, *Christianizing Homer. The Odyssey, Plato, and The Acts of Andrew* (Oxford: Oxford University Press, 1994), 17–34 ("Homer in the Early Church"), and idem, *The Homeric Epics and the Gospel of Mark* (New Haven: Yale University Press, 2000), esp. 1–14, with further bibliography. Philo of Alexandria of course referred to Homer frequently, by both direct reference and allusion, and was likewise au courant with contemporary allegorizing techniques for the Homeric writings (see Robert Lamberton, *Homer the Theologian: Neoplatonist Allegorical Reading and the Growth of the Epic Tradition* [Berkeley: University of California Press, 1986], 44–54). For skepticism about Paul's knowledge of Greek classics, see also the previous note.

14. Malherbe argues for direct influence: "It is therefore likely that it is Paul who in some respect thought of himself along the lines of the Antisthenic ideal" (*Paul and the Popular Philosophers,* 119; he also suggests on 118 the possibility that the first to introduce the Odyssean parallels were Paul's Corinthian opponents). Another possibility worth investigating further is whether the influence of Odyssean epithets and characteristics has come through their application to Old Testament figures in Hellenistic Jewish literature. There may have been less direct and more complicated forms of mediation of Odyssean lore, by which they were filtered into early Christian writings, thus accounting for the presence of the *topoi,* but, rather understandably, not the name of Odysseus. Particularly relevant here is Joseph, an ambiguous figure in his own right, whose variable and clever behavior Philo, as is well known, evaluates sometimes negatively and sometimes positively (see Martin, *Slavery,* 93–4; Glad, *Paul and Philodemus,* 38–40; Earle Hilgert, "The Dual Image of Joseph in Hebrew and Early Jewish Literature," *Papers of the Chicago Society of Biblical Research* 30 [1985]: 5–21). To cite just one point of possible comparison, in *De Josepho* 32–34, Philo treats him as the quintessentially variable politician, because of his χιτὼν ποικίλος, and employs language familiar from depictions of Odysseus: καὶ τὸν πολιτικὸν ἀναγκαῖον εἶναί τινα πολυειδῆ καὶ πολύμορφον (see Glad, *Paul and Philodemus,* 18). Philo himself insists that this reading of Joseph is traditional, not just his own (*Migr.* 159).

15. See the overt assumption of Glad and Malherbe (n. 11 above).

16. It seems to me that the strength and weakness of my own proposal (*Paul*), and that of Martin, *Slavery,* is that they appeal to "what is in the air," rather than to specialized Pauline knowledge. But how can one move beyond such contentions to nail down the influence further? My argument sought to demonstrate the

influence of the commonplaces about factionalists and nonfactionalists in Hellenistic Judaism, as evidenced by Philo and Josephus. It was based upon the methodological assumption that if the influence can be found in the writings of roughly contemporary persons inhabiting largely the same cultural milieu or mix, it is a reasonable judgment that this particular person, Paul, might also have "caught" that which was "in the air." The other body of evidence in this regard is the speeches of Dio Chrysostom, a wandering preacher in Asia Minor, who makes abundant use of such commonplaces, without explanation (thus documenting his presumption that a good proportion of his audience would comprehend them). My sense was that Paul and his congregations would fit comfortably within such audiences. Is this line of argument convincing?

17. For the parallels, see Vollenweider, *Freiheit,* 216–17 nn. 86–7.

18. With all such arguments, moving from the universal to the particular is fraught with difficulty. As today, the level of direct or accurate knowledge of cultural phenomena contemporary to oneself depends largely upon individual circumstances, happenstance, initiative, and attitude toward the surrounding world. If we were to try to analyze our own use of cultural "traditions" or commonplaces we would probably be unable to discern the precise lineage from which we learned and appropriated them. One doesn't need to know who originally said "when in Rome do as the Romans" to employ the maxim, or comprehend it when hearing it (the contemporary maxim apparently arose from Ambrose's description of his fasting customs to Augustine [*Ep. to Januarius* 54], which was given its now-memorable phrasing by Jeremy Taylor, a seventeenth-century British divine [*The Oxford Dictionary of Quotations,* ed. Angela Partington, 4th ed. (Oxford: Oxford University Press, 1992), 10, 679]). This same dynamic figures in scholarly debate about the significance of Paul's citation of Menander in 1 Cor 15:33. Does it demonstrate direct Pauline knowledge of Greek drama, or more general acquaintance with a free-floating proverb (see Glockmann, *Homer,* 61–2)?

19. Glad, *Paul and Philodemus,* 334, emphasis added.

20. See, for example, Glad, *Paul and Philodemus,* 273, for the combination: "I have shown that the form of 1 Cor 9:19–23 viewed against discussions of the flatterer, the friend of many, the political man, and defences of versatility in the social matrix of patronage, throws light on its function."

21. The material is much too vast to list here, but see, e.g., Plutarch, *Mor.* 96F-97; *Alcib.* 23.3–5; Lucian, *Peregr.* 1 (ἅπαντα γὰρ . . . γενόμενος) and 11 (πάντα μόνος αὐτὸς ὤν); and Philostr. *VA* 3.43, a text I would like to add to the discussion (Ἕλλην ὑπ' αὐτοῦ γενόμενος).

22. This is where the models of Martin and Marshall are less effective, in my view, for they catch only one side of a caricature.

23. On the other hand, my own proposal (Mitchell, *Paul,* 133–6) emphasizes the application of the variability language to the specific problem of factionalism that Paul faces throughout 1 Corinthians, thus tying in with one specific manifestation of the wider complex on adaptability. This remains an argument in its favor, I think, though some may object that it suffers the same fault in another way, as not doing enough justice to the more immediate literary context of chapter 9 in the argument on idol meat (which I regard as, for Paul, one manifestation of the larger problem of dissension).

24. But there is one very important exception: Proteus is mentioned in one of Gregory of Nazianzus's poems, not mentioning Paul, *per se,* but with language which clearly echoes 1 Cor 9:22: Πρωτεὺς σοφιστὴς εἰς κλοπὰς μορφωμάτων, ἢ καὶ Μελάμπους, ἤ τις ἄλλος ἄστατος, πᾶσιν τὰ πάντα ῥᾳδίως τυπούμενος, "Proteus, a sophist for thefts of forms, or even Melampus, or someone else unstable,

being formed as all things to all with ease" (*carm.* 2.728–30 [PG 37.1219], my trans., as with all Greek patristic passages in this essay; the passage is also cited by Vollenweider, *Freiheit,* 216 n. 86). Near the climax of the hymn is the summation: Τοιοῦτός ἐστι πᾶς ἀνὴρ πολύτροπος, "such is every man of many turns" (line 746), an epithet widely associated with Odysseus, from the first line of the *Odyssey* (on which see W. B. Stanford, *The Ulysses Theme. A Study in the Adaptability of a Traditional Hero,* 2d ed. [Oxford: Blackwell, 1963], 90–101; Glad, *Paul and Philodemus,* 17–23). Gregory's keen appreciation of the doublesidedness of being "all things to all people" can be seen by comparing his *or.* 43.81 [SC 384.304, ed. Jean Bernardi], where he praises Basil as ὁ πάντα πᾶσι γενόμενος ἵνα κερδάνῃ τοὺς πάντας ἢ πλείονας ("the one who was all things to all so that he might gain all or the majority"), and his famous farewell oration in which he rebukes the crowds for seeking not priests but orators, though he offers the concession that the clerics are partly responsible, for οὕτως ἡμεῖς αὐτοὺς ἐπαιδεύσαμεν, οἳ πᾶσι πάντα γινόμεθα, οὐκ οἶδα πότερον ἵνα σώσωμεν πάντας ἢ ἀπολέσωμεν ("for thus we have trained them, we who are all things to all—though whether it is so that we might save all, or destroy them I do not know") (*or.* 42.24 [SC 384.106]).

25. As we shall see, patristic exegetes were at pains to show that Paul is not being a hypocrite here, but did not so much mention flattery in this connection as they did on 1 Cor 10:33 (see, e.g., Thdt., *interpr.,* on 1 Cor 10:33 [PG 82.309], quoted in Mitchell, *Paul,* 148 n. 491).

26. Trans. Peter Holmes, ANF 3.254. See also *Marc.* 1.20, for the same argument.

27. See also *monog.* 14.

28. Trans. Holmes, ANF 3.433 (PL 2.505). See also *Marc.* 4.3.

29. Text and translation J. H. Waszink and J. C. M. van Winden, *Tertullianus De Idololatria. Critical Text, Translation and Commentary,* Supplements to Vigiliae Christianae 1 (Leiden: Brill, 1987), 48–51.

30. *Strom.* 1.1 (GCS, *Clemens Alexandrinus* 2.11, ed. Otto Stählin).

31. *Strom.* 7.9 (GCS, *Clemens Alexandrinus* 3.39, ed. Otto Stählin and L. Früchtel). In the continuation of the text Paul is praised as "an example for those who are able to receive the highest accommodation of the human-loving and God-loving instructor (ἡ ἄκρα οἰκονομία τοῦ φιλανθρώπου καὶ φιλοθέου παιδευτοῦ)." On the technical term οἰκονομία and its place in the discussion about adaptability, where it functions as largely a synonym of συγκατάβασις, see R. P. C. Hanson, *Allegory and Event. A Study of the Sources and Significance of Origen's Interpretation of Scripture* (London: SCM, 1959), 225; Stephen D. Benin, *The Footprints of God. Divine Accommodation in Jewish and Christian Thought* (Albany: SUNY Press, 1993), 29–30, 35–7; John Reumann, "*Oikonomia* as 'Ethical Accommodation' in the Fathers, and its Pagan Backgrounds," *Studia Patristica* 3 (1961): 370–9.

32. See also *strom.* 6.15 (GCS, *Clemens Alexandrinus* 2.494) for the same example. By doing this Paul "confessed 'to being all things to all people,' by way of accommodation [συμπεριφορά], but saving the most important of the dogmas 'so that he might gain all.'"

33. This has been well documented by Glad, *Paul and Philodemus,* 20, 72–7, and index under "Physician[s]."

34. The same example of the physician's lie is used by Philo, *Deus* 65–67, and Origen, *hom. in Jer.* 20.3 (PG 13.476). For other examples, see Jean Daniélou, *Origen,* trans. W. Mitchell (New York: Sheed and Ward, 1955), 94, and Hanson, *Allegory,* 229–31.

35. As is characteristic of the hodgepodge of the *Stromateis,* elsewhere Clement can refer to these verses in the context of analogues from the Old Testament, such

as Prov 10:14: "answer a fool according to his folly," and New Testament passages, such as Matt 5:45 and Rom 3:29–30 on God's impartiality, in order to demonstrate his theme that "suitable things (τὰ οἰκεῖα) should be presented to those who seek the wisdom we possess, so that they might with the most ease through their own ways arrive with probability at the true faith" (*strom.* 5.3 [GCS, *Clemens Alexandrinus* 2.337–8]).

36. GCS, *Clemens Alexandrinus* 2.151.

37. The best treatments are K. Duchatelez, "La 'condescendance' divine et l'histoire du salut," *NRT* 95 (1973): 593–621, and Benin, *The Footprints of God: Divine Accommodation in Jewish and Christian Thought,* who begins his study with Justin Martyr and extends it through the eighteenth century (further bibliography may also be found there). Though he mentions the roots of the theme in Philo (p. 10), unfortunately Benin does not trace its history prior to Christian sources. Duchatelez, "La 'condescendance,'" 594–8, helpfully catalogues some pre-Christian uses of the terms συγκαταβαίνειν and συγκατάβασις, but stresses the uniqueness of the Christian usage. On the concept in the writings of John Chrysostom in particular, see Robert C. Hill, "On Looking Again at *Sunkatabasis,*" *Prudentia* 13 (1981): 3–11, and idem, *Saint John Chrysostom: Homilies on Genesis 1–17,* FC 74 (Washington: Catholic University of America Press, 1986), 17–18.

38. See Duchatelez, "La 'condescendance,'" 593–8; Benin, *Footprints,* xv; and Hanson, *Allegory,* 210–31.

39. For the subject in general, for which many different terms were used, Glad, *Paul and Philodemus,* is now the standard treatment. He does not, however, place particular emphasis on the term or concept of "condescension," with which we are dealing here.

40. LSJ, 1662, citing *Rh.* 2.25 (*Philodemi Volumina Rhetorica,* ed. Siegfried Sudhaus, 2 vols. [Leipzig: Teubner, 1892], 2.25 [col. 31]). The text itself, however, is rather difficult to decipher, given its fragmentary state and limited context. The phrase is ὡς δ' ἐκείν[ω]ι πολλή [τί]ς ἐστι δ[υ]σχέ[ρει]α [τῶι] βια[ζ]ομέν[ωι] οὐ[θὲ]ν εἰς τὴν [συ]γκατάβασ[ιν ο]ὔτ' ἴδιον τῆς πατρίδος ἢ τῶν προσι . . . , which means something like: "As there is some great difficulty for that person who suffers no wrong for the condescension, not even to what belongs to his homeland, or those. . . ." More comprehensible is *Rh.* 1.383 (Sudhaus), o[ὐδὲ σ]υγκαταβαίνειν [ἐν πλ]ή[θεσι]ν εἰς λοιδορ[ία]ν, "not to condescend into abuse among the crowds" (my translations).

41. *Deipnosophistae* 5.193D: "He would sometimes slip out of the palace without the knowledge of his attendants, and would appear wandering about in some quarter of the city with one or two companions; usually he was found near the shops of the silversmiths and goldsmiths talking glibly, and airing his views on art before the workmen engaged in making reliefs, as well as before other artisans. Then he would condescend to men of the common people [μετὰ δημοτῶν ἀνθρώπων συγκαταβαίνων] and converse with anybody, no matter whom, and he used to drink with travellers of the meanest sort who came to town" (text and trans. C. B. Gulick, LCL; cf. 10.439A). See also the use of the verb by Chrysippus (H. von Arnim, *Stoicorum Veterum Fragmenta,* BT [Stuttgart: Teubner, 1979], 2.883).

42. 3.16.9 (συμβουλεύω ὑμῖν εὐλαβῶς τοῖς ἰδιώταις συγκαταβαίνειν); 4.2.1 (μή ποτε ἄρα τῶν προτέρων συνήθων ἢ φίλων ἀνακραθῆς τινι οὕτως, ὥστ' εἰς τὰ αὐτὰ συγκαταβῆναι αὐτῷ).

43. E.g., Gen 11:5; 18:21; Exod 3:8; 19:20; Num 11:25; 2 Sam 22:10=Ps 17:10 (Benin, *Footprints,* xiii and 217 n. 1).

44. *Conf.* 134–135; text and trans. F. H. Colson, LCL.

45. See John Dillon, *The Middle Platonists: A Study of Platonism 80 B.C. to A.D. 220* (London: Duckworth, 1977), 158–74.

46. Many other things besides the λόγοι also "descend" from heaven to earth, such as the principle of the number seven (*Opif.* 117) and joy (*Abr.* 205).

47. Text and trans. F. H. Colson and G. H. Whitaker, LCL.

48. Text and trans. R. Marcus, LCL. The Homeric citation is from *Od.* 17.485–88: καί τε θεοὶ ξείνοισιν ἐοικότες ἀλλοδαποῖσι, παντοῖοι τελέθοντες, ἐπι–στρωφῶσι πόληας, ἀνθρώπων ὕβριν τε καὶ εὐνομίην ἐφορῶντες. (I thank Prof. Earle Hilgert for advice on Philo.)

49. For the concept of the variability of the God of Israel see also Josephus, *Ant.* 10.14: "how varied and manifold is the nature of God" (ποικίλη τέ ἐστι καὶ πολύτροπος). Compare Eph 3:10, in the Pauline school: ἡ πολυποίκιλος σοφία τοῦ θεοῦ ("the manifold wisdom of God").

50. Text and trans. F. H. Colson and G. H. Whitaker, LCL. This text nicely testifies to the role of oral transmission of Homeric lore in the cultural dissemination of the epic tradition.

51. Interestingly the same concept of divine condescension was also used later by Julian in reference to the pagan gods, Attis in particular: "For by their nature the gods dwell in a higher world, and the higher powers do not desire to drag them hence down to our world: rather through the condescension of the higher (ἡ τῶν κρειττόνων συγκατάβασις) they desire to lead the things of our earth upwards to a higher plane more favoured by the gods . . . though [the Mother of the Gods] is no longer angry, she was angry at the time on account of his condescension (διὰ τὴν συγκατάβασιν), in that (Attis) as a higher being and a god had given himself to that which was inferior (ὅτι κρείττων ὢν καὶ θεὸς ἔδωκεν ἑαυτὸν τῷ καταδεεστέρῳ)" (*or.* 5.171B–C; text and trans. W. C. Wright, LCL).

52. "Supported by the wealth of an intellectual tradition embracing Jewish, Hellenistic, and Christian elements, Alexandrian exegetes would justify accommodation's use in Christian thought" (Benin, *Footprints,* 10). See also Hanson, *Allegory,* 224, on Philo's influence on the later Alexandrines. But even on this issue there is debate among scholars, because of the syncretistic nature of this theologoumenon as known to us in extant texts. For example, Daniélou, *Origen,* 92–4, suggests that perhaps Maximus of Tyre was a direct influence on Origen at this point. And Hanson himself makes the following concession (*Allegory,* 225): "It is even possible that Philo (and Clement and Origen through him) ultimately derived this thought from Rabbinic exegesis" (though the one example he gives is rather inconclusive). Scholarly uncertainty about the precise lineage of these ideas demonstrates once again the complex interpenetration of these concepts and voices.

53. The linkage of early church interpretation of Paul's accommodating behavior with Philo's concept of divine variability has, as far as I know, been suggested previously only by Vollenweider, *Freiheit,* 217–20, who briefly sketches out much the same line of influence that I do here, though without discussion of συγκατάβασις in particular. See his plea for consideration of this suggestion on p. 218: "Im Blick auf das jüdische Theologumenon der Selbsterniedrigung Gottes einerseits, auf hellenistiche kosmologische Formeln andrerseits wäre diese Möglichkeit immerhin zu erwägen. Jedenfalls hat die altkirchliche Theologie in 1 Kor 9,22 eine fundamentale christologische Dimension wahrgenommen und gibt dazu Anlass, sich die Aufmerksamkeit für die christologiefähige Sprache, zu welcher sich der Apostel in seiner Rechenschaft über sein missionarisches Verhalten aufschwingt, schärfen zu lassen." Duchatelez, "La 'condenscendance,'" 618–19, did, however, remark on the application of the language

of condescension to Paul's circumcision of Timothy (Acts 16:3), a recurrent theme in this larger complex of ideas.

54. *Comm. in 1 Cor.* 3.43, ed. C. Jenkins ("Origen on 1 Corinthians," *JTS* 9 [1907–08]: 231–47, 353–72, 500–14), 513.

55. ἀλλ' εἴ που ἦν ἐκ προπαιδεύσεως μάθημα Ἑλληνικὸν τοῦτο ὑπομνηθεὶς ἔλεγεν πρὸς Ἀθηναίους (*comm. in 1 Cor.* 3.43 [Jenkins, "Origen," 513]). This is how Origen accounts for the quotation from Aratus in Acts 17:28.

56. Origen regards many of the statements in 1 Corinthians 7 as an act of condescension to the weak Corinthians [τῇ ἀσθενείᾳ συγκαταβαίνειν τῶν ἀσθεν-εστέρων] (*comm. in 1 Cor.* 3.33 [Jenkins, "Origen," 500]; see also 3.34 [Jenkins, "Origen," 502]).

57. For these same examples in illustration of 1 Cor 9:20, see *comm. in Joh.* 1.42 (SC 120.42, ed. Cécile Blanc); *comm. in Mt.* 11.8 (GCS, *Origenes Werke,* 10.46, ed. Erich Klostermann).

58. SC 157.400–2, ed. Cécile Blanc. Origen cannot put his hand on an example of where Paul was as though one under the Law to those who though non-Jews placed themselves under the Law (as he understands τοῖς ἀνόμοις ὡς ἄνομος), but he insists that there undoubtedly was such a case.

59. Duchatelez, "La 'condescendance,'" 618.

60. For the nuance see LSJ, 1880–81: "metaph., put on a character (because the actor's face was put under a mask)."

61. *Adnot. in Dt. 1:31* (PG 17.24).

62. Num 23:19. On Origen's knowledge of Philo's exegesis of this passage, see David T. Runia, *Philo in Early Christian Literature: A Survey,* CRINT 3/3 (Minneapolis: Fortress, 1993), 162, 176.

63. As documented above (n. 31), this term often carries the meaning "accommodation" in patristic texts.

64. Or "stammer, stutter."

65. *Hom. in Jer. 18* 6 (PG 13.476). Cf. also the next column (13.477), where Origen says God "plays the part of a child" (ὑποκρινόμενος τὸ βρέφος) when in propounding prophetic oracles he pretends not to know the future.

66. Hanson, *Allegory,* 224, 229, 230; Runia, *Philo,* 157–83, who also reminds us that Origen took a complete set of Philo scrolls with him to Caesarea (pp. 22–4), where Philo's writings were preserved for posterity.

67. Note also his rebuttal to Celsus's charge that the incarnation necessitates a change in the nature of the unchangeable deity, which takes recourse to condescension (μένων γὰρ τῇ οὐσίᾳ ἄτρεπος συγκαταβαίνει τῇ προνοίᾳ καὶ οἰκονομίᾳ τοῖς ἀνθρωπίνοις πράγμασιν) (*Cels.* 4.14 [SC 136.216], ed. Marcel Borret). This sounds exactly like Philo, *Deus* 22, and throughout that treatise. On the general question of influence, see Benin, *Footprints,* xv: "Like so much else in the patristic garden, accommodation benefitted immensely from the animating influence of Philo, and while it is discernible in the philonic corpus, perhaps its most luxuriant patristic examples are displayed in the works of Philo's great student, Origen."

68. *Cels.* 4.12 (SC 136.212).

69. *Cels.* 4.15 (SC 136.218–20); 7.41 (SC 150.110): Jesus condescended to the level of commoners, simple women, and household slaves.

70. E.g., *or.* 23.2 (PG 11.488), note the emphasis on ταπεινούμενος; *comm. in Mt.* 15.32 (GCS, *Origenes Werke,* 10.447).

71. Ὁ τοίνυν σωτὴρ θειότερον πολλῷ ἢ Παῦλος γέγονε τοῖς πᾶσι πάντα, ἵνα πάντα ἢ κερδήσῃ ἢ τελειώσῃ, καὶ σαφῶς γέγονεν ἀνθρώποις ἄνθρωπος καὶ ἀγγέλοις ἄγγελος (*comm. in Joh.* 1.217 [SC 120.166]). For other places where Origen puts Jesus in conformity with the Pauline example, see *comm. in Mt.*

12.4 (GCS, *Origenes Werke*, 10.74), on Jesus becoming ὑπὸ νόμον διὰ τοὺς ὑπὸ νόμον ἵνα τοὺς ὑπὸ νόμον κερδήσῃ, and 11.8 (GCS, *Origenes Werke*, 10.46), where Jesus' "becoming a curse on our behalf" (Gal 3:13) is just like Paul appropriately becoming a Jew to Jews (. . . γενόμενος ὑπὲρ ἡμῶν κατάρα ἀλλ' ὡσπερεὶ καθηκόντως καὶ Παῦλος τοῖς Ἰουδαίοις Ἰουδαῖος ἐγένετο, ἵνα Ἰουδαίους κερδήσῃ). Later patristic writers will often refer to Jesus as "all things to all people" (see, e.g., Greg. Naz. *or.* 37.1 [SC 318.270, ed. Paul Gallay]; Cyr. H. *catech.* 10.5 [PG 33.665]).

72. *Comm. in Mt.* 15.7 (GCS, *Origenes Werke*, 10.368).

73. Space precludes anything like a thorough treatment, which should include at the very least Athanasius, Didymus the Blind, and the Cappadocians (for which see Duchatelez, "La 'condescendance,'" 600–8; Benin, *Footprints*, 13–58).

74. Henry Pinard ("Les infiltrations païennes dans l'ancienne loi d'après les pères de l'église," RSR 9 [1919]): 197–221, 209) said Chrysostom deserved the title "le docteur de la condescendance." The terms συγκατάβασις and συγκατ– αβαίνειν appear over four hundred times in Chrysostom's corpus of writings. See also now the valuable treatment of Rudolf Brändle, "Συγκατάβασις als hermeneutisches und ethisches Prinzip in der Paulusauslegung des Johannes Chrysostomus," in idem, *Studien zur Alten Kirche*, ed. Martin Heimgartner, et al. (Stuttgart: Kohlhammer, 1999), 134–48 (which appeared after this essay was completed).

75. *Suidae Lexicon*, ed. Ada Adler, BT (Stuttgart: Teubner, 1989), 4.450; Benin, *Footprints*, 229 n. 15.

76. The passage begins with a reference to the temple vision of Isaiah and his companions (Isaiah 6), in which, Chrysostom avers, they did not gaze upon the pure light itself or its essence, but what they saw was "condescension" (συγκατάβα– σις).

77. *Incomprehens.* 3.160–166 (SC 28.200, ed. Anne-Marie Malingrey).

78. See in general, Hill, FC 74.17–18 (with reference also to Chrysostom's application of the concept to scripture), and his *St. John Chrysostom, Commentary on the Psalms*, vol. 1 (Brookline, Mass.: Holy Cross Orthodox Press, 1998), 21–41; Fabio Fabbi, "La 'condiscendenza' divina nell'ispirazione biblica secondo S. Giovanni Crisostomo," *Biblica* 14 (1933): 330–47; and Benin, *Footprints*, 57–71 (whose treatment is limited to only four treatises, among which are no exegetical works).

79. *Hom. in 1 Cor.* 12.1 (PG 61.96), in commenting upon 1 Cor 4:6.

80. See, for example, the denigrations of Paul by a Greek philosopher, probably Porphyry, which are preserved in Macarius Magnes, *apocrit.*, who claimed that if Paul were lawless to the lawless and a Jew to the Jews and comported himself equally with all, he would have been truly "a slave of variegated forms of evil" (πολυτρόπου κακίας ἀνδράποδος) (3.30 [Adolf Harnack, *Kritik des Neuen Testaments von einem griechischen Philosophen des 3. Jahrhunderts (Die im Apocriticus des Macarius Magnes enthaltene Streitschrift)*, TU 37/4 (Leipzig: Hinrichs, 1911), 58–60]). Citing the now-familiar example of Paul's circumcision of Timothy, this opponent wonders if it were some "stage trick" (παραπαίγνιον), and later goes on to say that such variability is not the product of a healthy soul, nor the narration of free thoughts, but the wordy proposal of one who is feverishly sick in mind and reasoning. In claiming the identity of a Jew at one time (Acts 22:3), a Roman elsewhere (Acts 22:25–27), and at other times a lawless man or a Greek, he was "play acting" or being a hypocrite (ὑποκρινόμενος). In this he was a liar, a cheat, a vacillator, a user of magical crafts, engaging in flattery (θωπεία), and, in general, an evil-doer carrying on a rotten way of life (3.31 [Harnack, 60–2]).

81. *Hom. in 1 Cor.* 22.3 (PG 61.185). See also *hom. in Eph.* 6.3 (PG 62.46), where Chrysostom explicitly offers the behavior of being to the Jews as a Jew, to those without law as one lawless, etc., as proof of Paul's οἰκονομία.

82. For other passages in which Chrysostom employs these images, see *hom. in Gen.* 2.3 (PG 53.29); *hom. in Gal. 2:11* 3 (PG 51.374); *hom. in 1 Cor.* 12.1 (PG 61.96); *hom. in Tit.* 3.1–2 (PG 6.677–678), using the same example of fathers using baby-talk and babbling or stammering [ψελλίζειν] as used by Origen, quoted above.

83. There is a hint of Odyssean language applied to Paul in Chrysostom's homilies, especially *laud. Paul.* 5.4, 5 (SC 300.238, 242, ed. Auguste Piédagnel), where he calls Paul ποικίλος τις . . . καὶ παντοδαπός, "a variable and many-sorted man" (for these terms applied to Odysseus see Stanford, *Ulysses Theme*, 90–101, and Glad, *Paul and Philodemus*, 17–23). I have discussed this text in depth in my article, "'A Variable and Many-sorted Man': John Chrysostom's Treatment of Pauline Inconsistency," *JECS* 6 (1998): 93–111.

84. *laud. Paul.* 5.6 (SC 300.240): Οὕτω καὶ Παῦλος τὸν ἑαυτοῦ μιμούμενος Δεσπότην οὐκ ἂν κατεγνώθη, νῦν μὲν ὡς Ἰουδαῖος γινόμενος, νῦν δὲ ὡς ἄνομος. See also *hom. in Tit.* 3.2 (PG 62.678) on God as one who πανταχοῦ συγκαταβαίνει, as do also the scriptures, in both word and deed (πανταχοῦ συγκατάβασίς ἐστι τὰ ἐν ταῖς Γραφαῖς, καὶ ῥήματα καὶ πράγματα).

85. *hom. in Ac. princ.* 4.4 (PG 51.102–3).

86. Cf. Vollenweider, *Freiheit,* 217–18. Recently Stanley K. Stowers has argued for the centrality of the theme of adaptability (of Christ, Paul, and the believer) in the argument of Romans, and, indeed, in Paul's theology generally (*A Rereading of Romans: Justice, Jews, and Gentiles* [New Haven: Yale University Press, 1994], 213–26, 317–23).

87. See the suggestion of Peter Richardson, which is buttressed from another direction by the present study: "When, in Romans 11, Paul attempts to understand what God is doing in his missionary activity, he speaks in terms reminiscent of 1 Corinthians 9. God too adapts himself to the realities of the Jew/Gentile dichotomy. . . . This is a kind of divine accommodation which bears on Paul's understanding both of his own task as a missionary to the Gentiles and of his view of the relation of Jew and Gentile. . . . *The notion of divine accommodation may be one of the roots of Paul's view of apostolic accommodation*" ("Pauline Inconsistency," 357–8, emphasis added).

88. As argued by Stowers, *Rereading Romans,* 213–26.

89. In a communication after I presented this paper (letter of September 3, 1997), Peter Tomson argues that this is a Hasidic wisdom tradition, attested also in rabbinic writings about "condescension" and the ten "descents" of the deity (e.g., *Lev. Rab.* 1, 5), which is reflected also in some general ethical teachings (such as *S. Eli. Zut.* 15 and *S. Eli. Rab.* 18). Most important here is the material about the descents of the deity, which reflects some of the same commonplaces about divine accommodation in the Sinai theophany that we find in Greek Jewish writings. In general Tomson's parallels seem to me demonstrative of the ubiquity of a range of ideas converging on the theme of adaptability, but I am less convinced that they establish a unified "wisdom tradition" at work here. An even better parallel is provided by *Pesiq. Rab Kah.* 12.24–25: "Because the Holy One appeared to Israel at the Red Sea as a mighty man waging war, and appeared to them at Sinai as a pedagogue who teaches the day's lesson and then again and again goes over with his pupils what they have been taught, and appeared to them in the days of Daniel as an elder teaching Torah, and in the days of Solomon appeared to them as a young man, the Holy One said to Israel: Come to no false conclusions because you see Me in many guises (אמ' להן)

(הקב״ה לא בשביל שאתם רואים אותי בדמויות הרבה), for I am He who was with you at the Red Sea and I am He who is with you at Sinai: *I am the Lord thy God.* The fact is, R. Hiyya bar Abba said, that He appeared to them in a guise appropriate to each and every place and time (לפי כל עסק ועסק וכל דבר ודבר היה נראה להם). . . . Moreover, said R. Jose bar R. Hanina, the Divine Word spoke to each and every person according to his particular capacity" (לפי כחון של כל אחד) (text פסקתא דראב כהנה, ואחד היה הדיבר מדבר עמו), ed. Bernard Mandelbaum [New York: Rabbinical School of America, 1962], 223–4; trans. William G. Braude and Israel J. Kapstein, *Pesikta de-Rab Kahana* [Philadelphia: Jewish Publication Society of America, 1975], 248). This and other rabbinic passages are discussed by Benin, *Footprints,* 127–38, who infers an influence on Origen from some rabbis contemporary with him at Caesarea (p. 133), but, given the broad attestation of the concept of accommodation among Alexandrines, again, I would caution that no single tradition can be posited.

Chapter 10: Anthropological Duality in the Eschatology of 2 Cor 4:16–5:10

1. Among the more recent studies, see Jörg Frey, "Die paulinische Antithese von 'Fleisch' und 'Geist' und die palästinisch-jüdische Weisheitstradition," *ZNW* 90 (1999), 45–77, and Hans Dieter Betz, "The Concept of the 'Inner Human Being' (ὁ ἔσω ἄνθρωπος) in the Anthropology of Paul," *NTS* 46 (2000): 315–41.
2. Rudolf Bultmann, *Der zweite Brief an die Korinther,* MeyerK (Göttingen: Vandenhoeck & Ruprecht, 1976), 128; Victor Paul Furnish, *II Corinthians,* AB 32A (New York: Doubleday, 1984), 332.
3. David E. Aune, "Zwei Modelle der menschlichen Natur bei Paulus," *TQ* 176 (1996): 28–39, esp. 36–38. This article exists in an expanded form: "Two Pauline Models of the Person," *The Whole and the Divided Self,* eds. D. E. Aune and J. McCarthy (New York: Crossroad, 1997), 89–114.
4. In the judgment of Nikolaus Walter, this passage goes the further in the direction of "Hellenistic eschatology" than any other Pauline text ("Hellenistische Eschatologie bei Paulus? Zur 2 Kor 5,1–10," *TQ* 176 [1996]: 56).
5. This is the theme of Jan A. du Rand, "Paulus se vernuftige vervlegting van antropologie en eskatologie in 2 Korintiërs 4:7–5:10," *Skrif en Kerk* 20 (1999): 340–53, who argues that Paul's anthropology and eschatology are mutually illuminating.
6. See the appropriate sections of J. J. Collins, ed., *The Origins of Apocalypticism in Judaism and Christianity,* vol. 1 of *The Encyclopedia of Apocalypticism,* 3 vols. (New York: Continuum, 1998).
7. C. Sourvinou-Inwood, *"Reading" Greek Death to the End of the Classical Period* (Oxford: Clarendon, 1995).
8. M. Herfort-Koch, *Tod, Totenfürsorge und Jenseitsvorstellungen in der griechischen Antike: eine Bibliographie,* Quellen und Forschungen zur antiken Welt 9 (München: Tuduv, 1992); G. Binder and B. Effe, eds., *Tod und Jenseits im Altertum* (Trier: Wissenschaftler, 1991); I. P. Culianu, *Psychanodia: A Survey of the Evidence concerning the Ascension of the Soul and Its Relevance,* EPRO 99 (Leiden: Brill, 1983).
9. P. M. Steiner, *Psyche bei Platon,* Neue Studien zur Philosophie 3 (Göttingen: Vandenhoeck & Ruprecht, 1992).
10. W. Deuse, *Untersuchungen zur mittelplatonischen und neuplatonischen Seelenlehre* (Mainz: Akademie der Wissenschaften und der Literatur, 1983).

11. D. Sigel, "Eschatologie," *Der neue Pauly: Enzyclopädie der Antike* (Stuttgart and Weimar: Metzler, 1996), 4.123–8; Hubert Cancik, "The End of the World, of History, and of the Individual in Greek and Roman Antiquity," *The Origins of Apocalypticism in Judaism and Christianity,* vol. 1 of The *Encyclopedia of Apocalypticism,* ed. John J. Collins, 3 vols. (New York: Continuum, 1998), 1.84–125. Cancik defines eschatology as "a collective term for the ideas that Greeks and Romans developed concerning the death and life to come of individuals, the world, people and states" (87). Since these four topics are not in fact as closely related as they are in early Judaism and early Christianity, I have focused on the first topic in the definition formulated above.

12. Sourvinou-Inwood, *"Reading" Greek Death,* 205–7.

13. See the still valuable synthesis of Israelite beliefs in the soul in J. Pedersen, *Israel: Its Life and Culture,* 4 vols. (London: Cumberlege; Copenhagen: Branner og Korch, 1926), 1.99–181.

14. Early Jewish conceptions of the soul/body dichotomy and of immortality are surveyed by H. Cavallin, *Life after Death: Paul's Argument for the Resurrection of the Dead in 1 Cor. 15,* ConBNT 7 (Lund: Gleerup, 1974).

15. Martha Himmelfarb, *Tours of Hell: An Apocalyptic Form in Jewish and Christian Literature* (Philadelphia: University of Pennsylvania Press, 1983); H. D. Betz, "The Problem of Apocalyptic Genre in Greek and Hellenistic Literature: The Case of the Oracle of Trophonius," *Apocalypticism in the Mediterranean World and the Near East,* ed. David Hellholm (Tübingen: Mohr-Siebeck, 1983), 577–97.

16. F. G. Lang, *2. Korinther 5,1–10 in der neueren Forschung* (Tübingen: Mohr-Siebeck, 1973).

17. John Gillman, "A Thematic Comparison: 1 Cor 15:50–57 and 2 Cor 5:1–10," *JBL* 107 (1988): 439–54; A. C. Perriman, "Paul and the Parousia: 1 Corinthians 15:50–57 and 2 Corinthians 5:1–5," *NTS* 35 (1989): 512–21.

18. C. H. Dodd, "The Mind of Paul: Change and Development," *BJRL* 18 (1934): 69–110; W. Wiefel, "Die Hauptrichtung des Wandels im eschatologischen Denken des Paulus," *TZ* 30 (1974): 65–81; Udo Schnelle, *Wandlungen im paulinischen Denken,* SBS 137 (Stuttgart: Katholisches Bibelwerk, 1989).

19. Andreas Lindemann, "Paulus und die korinthische Eschatologie: Zur These von einer 'Entwicklung' im paulinischen Denken," *NTS* 37 (1991): 204–20. While Lindemann claims that the basic apocalyptic-eschatological perspective of 2 Cor 4:7–6:2 is essentially the same as 1 Cor 15 (apart from the mention of the parousia and a definite future occurrence of the resurrection of the dead, motifs that would have no real function in 2 Cor 4:7–6:2), he provides no convincing exegesis of the many cruces in 2 Cor 4:16–5:10.

20. Gnostic opponents are proposed by Bultmann, *Der zweite Brief an die Korinther,* 132; Walter Schmithals, *Gnosticism in Corinth: An Investigation of the Letters to the Corinthians,* trans. John E. Steely (Nashville and New York: Abingdon, 1971), 259–75; Robert Jewett, *Paul's Anthropological Terms: A Study of Their Use in Conflict Settings* (Leiden: Brill, 1971), 274–7; Jerome Murphy-O'Connor, "'Being at Home in the Body we are in Exile from the Lord' (2 Cor. 5:6b)," *RB* 93 (1986): 214–21. A religious form of Platonism is proposed by T. K. Heckel, *Der Innere Mensch: Die paulinische Verarbeitung eines platonischen Motivs,* WUNT 2/53 (Tübingen: Mohr-Siebeck, 1993): 98–101.

21. Norbert Baumert, *Täglich Sterben und Auferstehen: Der Literalsinn von 2 Kor 4,12–5, 10,* SANT 34 (München: Kösel, 1973).

22. C. H. Dodd, "The Mind of Paul: Change and Development," *BJRL* 18 (1934): 69–110.

23. C. K. Barrett, *A Commentary on the Second Epistle to the Corinthians* (New York: Harper & Row, 1973), 151.

24. F. F. Bruce, "Paul on Immortality," *SJT* 24 (1971): 457–72; M. J. Harris, "2 Corinthians 5:1–10: Watershed in Paul's Eschatology," *Tyndale Bulletin* 22 (1971): 32–57; "Paul's View of Death in 2 Corinthians 5:1–10," *New Dimensions in New Testament Study*, ed. R. N. Longenecker and M. C. Tenney (Grand Rapids: Eerdmans, 1974), 317–28.

25. Victor P. Furnish, *II Corinthians*, AB 32A (Garden City: Doubleday, 1984), 288.

26. While the composition history of 2 Corinthians is very complex, there is strong support among critical scholars that it is a compilation consisting of six elements put together in the following chronological order: (1) 2 Cor 2:14–7:4 (excluding 6:14–7:1) constitutes a textual unit which functions as a "first apology" crafted by Paul in defense of his apostleship. (2) 10:1–13:10, the so-called "letter of tears," which functions as a second apology. (3) The third unit is the "letter of reconciliation" (1:1–2:13; 7:5–16; 13:11–13). (4) and (5) 2 Corinthians 8 and 9 constitute originally separate administrative letters, and (6) 6:14–7:1 is a later interpolation. This analysis of 2 Corinthians was proposed by G. Bornkamm, *Die Vorgeschichte des sogenannten zweiten Korintherbriefes* (Heidelberg: Winter, 1961), followed by Dieter Georgi, *The Opponents of Paul in Second Corinthians* (Philadelphia: Fortress, 1986), 9–14. On 2 Corinthians 8–9, see H. D. Betz, *2 Corinthians 8 and 9,* Hermeneia (Philadelphia: Fortress, 1985), 3–36. On the more general history of research, see Lars Aejmelaeus, *Streit und Versöhnung: Das Problem der Zusammensetzung des 2. Korintherbriefes* (Helsinki: Kirjapaino Raamattutalo, 1987).

27. A. Sand, *EDNT* 1.102, regards Paul's use of the phrases ὁ ἔξω ἄνθρωπος and ὁ ἔσω ἄνθρωπος in 2 Cor 4:16 as dichotomous but not anthropologically dualistic, and Hans Dieter Betz claims that Paul's anthropology changed and developed "as he formulated a Christian alternative to the predominant religio-philosophical dualistic anthropology of body and soul" ("Paul's Anthropology," 316).

28. T. K. Heckel, *Der Innere Mensch: Die paulinische Verarbeitung eines platonischen Motivs*, WUNT 2/53 (Tübingen: Mohr-Siebeck, 1993).

29. Essentially the same view is attributed to the Stoic Cleanthes by Epiphanius of Salamis (*SVF* 1.538), though the judgment of Epiphanius in this case is problematic.

30. Walter Burkert, "Towards Plato and Paul: The 'Inner' Human Being," *Ancient and Modern Perspectives on the Bible and Culture: Essays in Honor of Hans Dieter Betz*, ed. Adela Yarbro Collins (Atlanta: Scholars, 1998), 59–82.

31. Christoph Markschiess, "Die platonische Metapher vom 'inneren Menschen'," *ZKG* 105 (1994): 5–7; idem, "Innerer Mensch," *RAC* 18 (1997), 266.

32. The metaphor of the body as the *container* or *vessel* of the soul, particularly common among Epicureans, conveyed the notion that the body contains or holds the soul together, so that when the body is destroyed upon death, the soul is dispersed, just as liquid would splash out of a smashed jar (Epicurus, *Ep. Herod.*, 63–66; Lucretius, 3.425–444, 555). The Epicurean metaphor of the body as the container or vessel of the soul is in tension with the Epicurean view that the body and soul are mutually interdependent; see Julia E. Annas, *Hellenistic Philosophy of Mind* (Berkeley and Los Angeles: University of California Press, 1992), 147–51. Seneca, a Roman Stoic, refers to the body as a *receptaculum* (*Ep.* 92.34). Paul uses the term σκεῦος in this sense in 2 Cor 4:7 and Rom 9:21–23 (1 Thess 4:4 is a disputed usage).

33. Furnish is wrong, I think, when he claims that "In accord with his Jewish heritage, the apostle regards the body, mortal as it is, not as the receptacle of the soul but as a constituent part of the total human being" (*II Corinthians*, 279). The "constitutent part of the total human being" language works only with

descriptions of the living person, as in Romans 7, for how can the human being still be a human being when one of the constituent parts is missing?

34. The apt translation of Furnish, *II Corinthians*, 269.
35. Death as a gain for those whose life is burdensome is a commonplace in Greek and Latin literature; see D. W. Palmer, "'To Die is Gain' (Philippians i 21)," *NovT* 17 (1975): 203–18.
36. N. Walter, *EDNT* 1.65.
37. This is one of the concerns of Betz, "Anthropology of Paul," 315–41.
38. Heckel, *Der Innere Mensch*, 42–76; Markschiess, "Innerer Mensch," 276–8.
39. Jewett, *Anthropological Terms*, 396–9, 460.
40. Heckel, *Der Innere Mensch*, 102–47.
41. Markschiess, "Die platonische Metapher," 4; idem, "Innerer Mensch," 279–80.
42. Samuel Byrskog, "Co-Senders, Co-Authors and Paul's Use of the First Person Plural," *ZNW* 87 (1996): 230–50.
43. Rom 2:2; 3:19; 7:14; 8:22, 28; 1 Cor 8:4; cf. 1 Tim 1:8. The functionally parallel plural participle εἰδότες + ὅτι in 5:6 similarly conveys shared knowledge and also occurs several times in the Pauline letters (Rom 5:3; 6:9; 13:11; 1 Cor 15:58; 2 Cor 1:7; 4:14; 5:11; Gal 2:16; Phil 1:16; cf. Eph 6:8, 9; Col 3:24; 4:1; cf. Polycarp, *Phil.* 1:3; 4:1; 5:1; 6:1).
44. J.-F. Collange, *Énigmes de la Deuxième Épître de Paul aux Corinthiens: Étude exégétique de 2 Cor. 2:14–7:4*, SNTSMS 18 (Cambridge: Cambridge University Press, 1972) 181–5, pushes this to the extent that he supposes that a specific shared tradition is involved, namely the logion of Jesus preserved in Mark 14:58. Collange is followed by Andrew Lincoln, *Paradise Now and Not Yet: Studies in the Role of the Heavenly Dimension in Paul's Thought with Special Reference to His Eschatology*, SNTSMS 43 (Cambridge: Cambridge University Press, 1981), 62.
45. J. P. Louw and E. A. Nida (eds.), *Greek-English Lexicon of the New Testament Based on Semantic Domains*, 2 vols. (New York: United Bible Society, 1988), 1.633.
46. Mark 13:1 and par.; Mark 14:58.
47. The verb καταλύω can be used with σκῆνος (see Polybius 6.40.2).
48. Hans Windisch, *Der zweite Korintherbrief*, MeyerK 6 (Göttingen: Vandenhoeck & Ruprecht, 1924), 159, argues that the parousia (which Paul refers to elsewhere as a possibility eliminating physical death in 1 Thess 4:15; 1 Cor 15:51–53; Phil 3:21) is excluded by this formulation.
49. Hans Lietzmann and W. G. Kümmel, *An die Korinther I/II*, HNT 9 (Tübingen: Mohr-Siebeck, 1969), 121.
50. BDR ¶168.1.
51. Walter, "Hellenistische Eschatologie," 59.
52. Jewett, *Anthropological Terms*, 274–7. A related proposal is made by Jerome Murphy-O'Connor, "'Being at Home in the Body we are in Exile from the Lord' (2 Cor. 5:6b)," *RB* 93 (1986): 214–21, who regards only v. 6b as Paul's quotation of a Corinthian slogan of the *pneumatikoi* in Corinth because it contradicts Paul's own views.
53. W. Michaelis, *TDNT* 7.382; J.-A. Bühner, *EDNT* 3.252; Lang, *2. Korinther 5,1–10*, 178. Many commentators and lexicons still try to translate σκῆνος as "tent" or "dwelling" in all contexts; cf. Bauer-Aland, 1509.
54. J. P. Louw and E. A. Nida (eds.), *Greek-English Lexicon of the New Testament Based on Semantic Domains*, 2 vols. (New York: United Bible Societies, 1988), 1.¶8.5.
55. Plato, *Phaedo* 81c; Ps.-Plato, *Axiochus* 366a; *Corpus Hermeticum* 13.12, 15; frag. IIa.1 (A. D. Nock and A. J. Festugière, *Corpus Hermeticum*, 4 vols. [Paris:

Société d'Édition "Les Belles Lettres," 1954–60], 3.5); frag. V.4 (Nock and Festugiĉre 3.31); frag. XXIII.34, σκηνώματα (Nock and Festugiĉre 4.34); *Papyri
Graecae Magicae* I.319; IV.448, 1951, 1970, 2141; XIXa.49 (here in the line
"every member of this corpse and the spirit of this body" [πᾶν μέλος τοῦ νεκροῦ
τούτου καὶ τὸ πνεῦμα τούτου τοῦ σκηνώματος], the terms "corpse" and "tent"
are synonymous; cf. Eusebius, *Hist. eccl.* 7.16; *Vita Const.* 4.60).

56. Hermann Diels and Walther Kranz, *Die Fragmente der Vorsokratiker,* 2 vols.
    (Zürich and Hildesheim: Weidmann, 1951–52), 2.183.

57. Philo, *QG* 1.28 ("the human tent [loanword: σκηνή] is made of bones,
    flesh, arteries, veins, nerves, ligaments and the vessels of breathing and of the
    blood," trans. Marcus 1953: 17, reads much like a medical text); Wis 9:15; Par.
    Jer. 6:6 [2x], 7.

58. 2 Cor 5:2, 4; *Diogn.* 6:8; Tatian, *Oratio ad Graecos* 15.3; Clement Alex., *Strom.*
    4.25, 26; 5.14; Methodius, *Res.* 1.53; G. Kaibel, *Epigrammata Graeca* (Berlin,
    1878), 422.1; see *PGL* 1237a (s.v. σκηνή), 1237b (s.v. σκῆνος).

59. Alfred Plummer, *A Critical and Exegetical Commentary on the Second Epistle of
    St Paul to the Corinthians,* ICC (Edinburgh: Clark, 1915), 142. Wis 9:15 in
    turn appears to be literarily dependent on Plato, *Phaedo* 88c, where three sim-
    ilar words, rare in the Septuagint, appear in the same context: βρίθει, γεῶδες,
    and βαρύνει, an example of Platonic influence on Paul through the medium of
    Hellenistic Judaism.

60. ἀπολείπουσα δὲ ἡ ψυχὴ τὸ τοῦ σώματος σκῆνος τὸ ψυχρὸν καὶ τὸ θνητὸν
    εἴδωλον ἅμα καὶ αἵματι καὶ φλέγματι καὶ σαρκὶ παρέδωκεν.

61. This is the view of Collange, *Énigmes,* 190–1.

62. The term "duality" is used in place of "dualism" because of the unsatisfactory
    denotions of that term in the present context. According to Norbert Baumert
    (*Täglich Sterben und Auferstehen: Der Literalsinn von 2 Kor 4,12–5,10,* SANT
    34 [München: Kösel, 1972], 144), "Im Text fehlt jede Spur einer Entgegenset-
    zung von Körper und Seele." Baumert is correct, since there is no opposition
    between the inner and outer aspects of the person nor is the term ψυχή found
    in this passage.

63. C. K. Barrett, *A Commentary on the Second Epistle to the Corinthians* (New York:
    Harper & Row, 1973), 151.

64. Lietzmann and Kümmel, *An die Korinther,* 118.

65. Murray J. Harris, "Paul's View of Death in 2 Corinthians 5:1–10," *New Dimen-
    sions in New Testament Study,* eds. R. N. Longenecker and M. C. Tenney (Grand
    Rapids: Eerdmans, 1974), 321.

66. Walter, "Hellenistische Eschatologie," 59.

67. John A. T. Robinson, *The Body: A Study in Pauline Theology,* SBT 5 (London:
    SCM, 1952), 75–83; E. Earle Ellis, "II Corinthians v,1–10 in Pauline Escha-
    tology," *NTS* 6 (1960): 218. Robinson (*Body,* 76) points out that when
    οἰκοδομή is not used figuratively of "edification" in Paul's letters, it is used of
    the Church, the Body of Christ (1 Cor 3:9; Eph 2:21; 4:12, 16).

68. Karel Hanhart, "Paul's Hope in the Face of Death," *JBL* 88 (1969): 453–4.

69. Joseph Osei-Bonsu, "Does 2 Cor. 5.1–10 Teach the Reception of the Resur-
    rection Body at the Moment of Death?" *JSNT* 28 (1986): 83–5.

70. C. Houtman, *Der Himmel im Alten Testament: Israels Weltbild und Weltan-
    schauung,* OTS 30 (Leiden: Brill, 1993), 3–5. The view that Ps 49:15 refers to
    the righteous dead escaping Sheol and being taken to heaven (R. H. Charles,
    Eschatology: The Doctrine of a Future Life in Israel, Judaism and Christianity
    [New York: Schocken, 1963 (reprint of 1913)], 75–6), is based on a misinter-
    pretation of that passage.

71. Sourvinou-Inwood, 32–56.

72. A. Yarbro Collins, "The Seven Heavens in Jewish and Christian Apocalypses," *Cosmology and Eschatology in Jewish and Christian Apocalypticism* (Leiden: Brill, 1996), 21–54.

73. Ioan P. Culianu, *Psychanodia* (Leiden: Brill, 1983), 56.

74. However, there are striking exceptions in Judaism. None of the five apocalypses that comprise 1 Enoch reflects the new cosmology, which is also absent from the Apocalypse of John.

75. See also Seneca *Ep.* 71.16; *Moral Essays, Ad Marciam* 25.1.

76. Empedocles, frag. B 126; Diels and Kranz, *Die Fragmente der Vorsokratiker* 1.362; Plato, *Phaedo* 83e; G. Kaibel, *Epigrammata Graeca* 403.5; *Corpus Hermeticum* 1.26; 13.6; Plotinus, *Enneads* 1.6.7; *Asc. Isa.* 9:9 (trans. Schneemelcher): "And there [in the seventh heaven] I saw Enoch and all who were with him, stripped of the garment of the flesh, and I saw them in their higher garments, and they were like the angels who stand there in great glory" (see also 9:17; 10:1–31).

77. Oepke, *TDNT* 1.773–5; Weigelt, *NIDNTT* 1.313–14.

78. Bultmann, *Der zweite Brief an die Korinther*, 137–40.

79. Rudolf Bultmann, *Theology of the New Testament*, 2 vols., trans. Kendrick Grobel (New York: Scribner's, 1951–55), 1.202.

80. Oepke, *TDNT*, 1.774; 2.320.

81. Plato, *Cratylus* 403b; *Gorgias* 523d–e, 524d; *Phaedo* 67d–e; 81c; *Republic* 9.577b; *Corpus Hermeticum* 1.26; Philo, *Virt.* 76; *Leg.* 2.57, 59; Plutarch, *De sera numinis vindicta* 565A; Lucian, *Hermotimus* 7; *Dial. mort.* 20 (10); *Ver. hist.* 2.12 (in Lucian's utopian city, the citizens have no bodies, but their naked souls [γυμνή τις ἡ ψυχὴ αὐτῶν] go about in the semblance of their bodies. Cicero mocks this notion in *Tusc. disp.* 1.36–38); Aelian, *De natura animalium* 11.39; Maximus of Tyre 7.5a–e.

82. This reflects a preference for the reading ἐνδυσάμενοι, which has much stronger external attestation than does ἐκδυσάμενοι, which was adopted in the twenty-sixth and twenty-seventh editions of the Nestle-Aland edition of the Greek New Testament. A cogent defense of ἐνδυσάμενοι is found in Margaret Thrall, "'Putting On' or 'Stripping Off' in 2 Cor 5.3," *New Testament Textual Criticism: Its Significance for Exegesis*, eds. E. J. Epp and G. Fee (Oxford: Clarendon, 1981), 223–37.

83. T. F. Glasson, "2 Corinthians v. 1–10 *versus* Platonism," *SJT* 43 (1989): 150.

84. According to Richmond Lattimore, *Themes in Greek and Latin Epitaphs* (Urbana, Ill.: University of Illinois, 1962), 53–4: "No epitaph containing an unequivocal assertion of immortality is earlier than the fourth century B.C."

85. Lattimore, *Epitaphs*, 74–86.

86. Lattimore, *Epitaphs*, 22.

87. Annas, *Hellenistic Philosophy of Mind*, 37–70.

88. Empedocles, frag. B 117; Diels and Kranz, *Die Fragmente der Vorsokratiker*, 1.358–9.

89. Hermann L. Strack and Paul Billerbeck, *Kommentar zum Neuen Testament aus Talmud und Midrasch*, 3 vols. (München: C. H. Beck, 1965), 3.803.

90. G. F. Moore, *Judaism in the First Centuries of the Christian Era: The Age of the Tannaim*, 3 vols. (Cambridge, Mass.: Harvard University Press, 1927), 3.389–92; E. E. Urbach, *The Sages: Their Concepts and Beliefs* (Cambridge, Mass.: Harvard University Press, 1987), 238–42.

91. Michael Stone, *Fourth Ezra: A Commentary on the Book of Fourth Ezra*, Hermeneia (Minneapolis: Fortress, 1990), 96.

92. G. H. Box, *The Ezra-Apocalypse* (London: Pitman & Sons, 1912), 33–4; Michael Stone, *Features of the Eschatology of IV Ezra*, HSS (Atlanta: Scholars,

1989) 144–5. In Ps.-Philo, *Liber antiquitatum biblicarum* 19.12, Moses is addressed: "You will rest in it [an unknown sepulchre] until I visit the world. I will raise up you and your fathers from the earth in which you sleep and you will come together and dwell in the immortal dwelling place (*et habitabitis inhabitationem immortalem*) that is not subject to time." Nothing is said here about the location of this "immortal dwelling place," though an earlier eschatological passage claims that after the resurrection, "There will be another earth and another heaven, an everlasting dwelling place (*habitaculum sempiternum*)," apparently with the righteous dwelling on the renewed earth; see Howard Jacobson, *A Commentary on Pseudo-Philo's Liber Antiquitatum Biblicarum*, 2 vols., AGJU 21 (Leiden: Brill, 1996), 1.328.

93. Stone, *Fourth Ezra*, 96.

94. See J. D. G. Dunn, *The Theology of Paul the Apostle* (Grand Rapids: Eerdmans, 1998), 390–441.

95. Lietzmann and Kümmel, *An die Korinther*, 121; Windisch, *Der zweite Korintherbrief*, 169; Plummer, *Corinthians*, 154–5.

96. Furnish, *II Corinthians*, 302; R. P. Martin, *2 Corinthians*, WBC 40 (Waco: Word Books, 1986), 111.

97. Christian Wolff, *Der zweite Brief des Paulus an die Korinther* (Berlin: Evangelische Verlagsanstalt, 1989), 114.

98. BDAG, 557.

99. Matt 25:31–46; Rev 20:11–15; 4 Ezra 7:30–44; 2 Baruch 49–51; *Sib. Or.* 4.40–48, 179–192; *1 Enoch* 38:1–6; 62:2–16; 90:20–27.

100. Plato, *Gorgias* 526a–e; *Phaedrus* 249a–b; *Republic* 2.364e–365a; 10.614c; *Laws* 870d; Lucian, *Dial. mort.* 10.13; cf. Apollodorus 3.1.1; Plutarch *De facie quae in orbe lunae apparet* 943; *De sera numinis vindicta* 564E–565B; Diodorus Siculus 5.79.1–2; L. Ruhl, *De mortuorum iudicio* (Berlin: Töpelmann, 1903); T. F. Glasson, "The Last Judgment—in Rev. 20 and Related Writings," *NTS* 28 (1982): 536–8; M. Eugene Boring, Klaus Berger and Carsten Colpe, *Hellenistic Commentary to the New Testament* (Nashville: Abingdon, 1995), 454; Georg Strecker and Udo Schnelle, *Neuer Wettstein: Text zum Neuen Testament aus Griechentum und Hellenismus*, 2 vols. (Berlin and New York: de Gruyter, 1996), II/1.449. The popularity of the idea of postmortem judgment is suggested by Plutarch in *De superstitione* 166F–167A, where he ridicules popular beliefs in the terrors of the afterlife, including judgment after death on analogy with a trial in a Greek court, see Morton Smith, "De Supersitione (Moralia 164E–171F)," *Plutarch's Theological Writings and Early Christian Literature*, ed. Hans Dieter Betz (Leiden: Brill, 1975), 19. Denying the validity of the popular view of judgment and punishment in the underworld was also a theme in consolation literature; see Seneca *Moral Essays, Ad Marciam* 19.4. See also Frederick E. Brenk, *In Mist Apparelled: Religious Themes in Plutarch's Moralia and Lives* (Leiden: Brill, 1977), 21–7. Postmortem judgment, including rewards and punishments, is particularly associated with Orphism; see W. K. C. Guthrie, *Orpheus and Greek Religion* (London: Methuen, 1935; repr. Princeton: Princeton University, 1993), 156–87.

101. 4 Ezra 7:75–90; 8:38; 9:12; 14:35; *Test. Abr.* [Rec. A] 12–14.

102. According to *3 Baruch* 4:1–7, Hades is actually located in the third heaven, implying the immediate postmortem punishment of the wicked (Yarbro Collins, "Seven Heavens," 44–5).

103. Lietzmann and Kümmel, *An die Korinther*, 122–3; Wolff, *Korinther*, 114.

104. Glasson, "2 Corinthians v. 1–10," 152.

105. Rom 14:10 refers to the "judgment seat of God," while according to Acts 10:42, Christ has been designated by God as the judge of the living and the dead; cf. 2 Tim 2:9; see also Acts 17:31; Rom 2:16.

106. On Paul's view of the process of salvation, see Dunn, *The Theology of Paul*, 461–98.
107. M. Carrez, "Le 'Nous' en 2 Corinthiens," *NTS* 26 (1980): 477; see also Byr-skog, "Co-Senders," 230–50.
108. Windisch, *Der zweite Korintherbrief*, 149–50; Furnish, *II Corinthians*, 286–7.
109. Martin, *2 Corinthians*, 106.
110. Most recently, see Betz, "Anthropology of Paul," 316.

Chapter 11: Paul and Paradigm Shifts: Reconciliation and Its Linkage Group

1. Victor Paul Furnish correctly identifies the issue of Paul's presuppositions as one of "two absolutely fundamental issues" in the modern study of the apostle's letters. See his "Pauline Studies," *The New Testament and Its Modern Interpreters*, eds. E. J. Epp and G. W. MacRae, SBLBMI 3 (Philadelphia: Fortress; Atlanta: Scholars, 1989), 321–50, esp. 331–3.
2. For a list of recent studies and older key contributions on the topic of reconciliation, see the appendix to this essay. The present essay is written almost entirely on the basis of my own independent reading of texts relating to reconciliation. For that reason, I do not explicitly interact with the scholars listed in the appendix. My agreements and disagreements with them will be apparent to any reader who compares my own conclusions with theirs.
3. For other New Testament terms that may also belong to the semantic domain of reconciliation, see Johannes P. Louw and Eugene A. Nida, eds., *Greek-English Lexicon of the New Testament Based on Semantic Domains*, 2d ed., 2 vols. (New York: United Bible Societies, 1989), 1.502–3 (§ 40.1–7). For some other Greek terms that belong to the semantic domain of reconciliation, see S. C. Woodhouse, *English-Greek Dictionary: A Vocabulary of the Attic Language*, 2d ed. (London: Routledge & Kegan Paul, 1932), 680.
4. See esp. Cilliers Breytenbach, *Versöhnung: Eine Studie zur paulinischen Soteriologie*, WMANT 60 (Neukirchen-Vluyn: Neukirchener, 1989). See also his "Reconciliation: Shifts in Christian Soteriology," *Reconciliation and Construction: Creative Options for a Rapidly Changing South Africa*, ed. W. S. Vorster (Pretoria: University of South Africa, 1986), 1–25; "On Reconciliation: An Exegetical Response," *Journal of Theology for Southern Africa* 70 (1990): 64–8; and "Versöhnung, Stellvertretung und Sühne: Semantische und Traditionsgeschichtliche Bemerkungen am Beispiel der paulinischen Briefe," *NTS* 39 (1993): 59–79.
5. The concept of paradigm shifts was pioneered and popularized by Thomas S. Kuhn in his landmark study of scientific research and thought, *The Structure of Scientific Revolutions* (Chicago: University of Chicago Press, 1962), a work that is now in its third edition (1996). Its extension to other disciplines, such as political science and business management, has been widespread. Although frequently applied to various theological disciplines, its use among biblical scholars has been surprisingly limited.
6. Since Paul himself links his activity as an agent of reconciliation to his role as an ambassador for Christ (οὖν: 2 Cor 5:20), Breytenbach is exegetically on solid ground in calling attention to the involvement of ancient envoys in the work of reconciliation as the pertinent background for interpreting 2 Corinthians 5. For a discussion of ambassadors, especially in the Greek east, see now Anthony Bash, *Ambassadors for Christ: An Exploration of Ambassadorial Language in the New Testament*, WUNT 2.92 (Tübingen: Mohr-Siebeck, 1997), who, preferring the remote to what lies close at hand, unpersuasively seeks to minimize the

conciliatory work of ambassadors in order to establish the thesis that Paul's language of reconciliation derives from Hellenistic Jewish writings about Moses.

7. Breytenbach, *Versöhnung*, 100.

8. Breytenbach, "Reconciliation," 65. The terms "hyponymous" and "hyponymy" are drawn by Breytenbach from the field of modern linguistics and structural semantics, where they are used to indicate the relationship of a specific term to a more general one. "More specific terms subsumed under a more general term are described as its hyponyms: e.g. *rose*, *tulip*, etc. are hyponyms of *flower*." So John Lyons, ed., *New Horizons in Linguistics* (Harmondsworth: Penguin, 1970), 321. See Lyons's discussion of hyponymy in his *Introduction to Theoretical Linguistics* (Cambridge: Cambridge University Press, 1968), 453–5, and *Semantics*, 2 vols. (Cambridge: Cambridge University Press, 1977), 1.291–5.

9. Breytenbach, "Reconciliation," 66.

10. Ibid., 65.

11. Breytenbach, *Versöhnung*, 100.

12. Since Breytenbach, *Versöhnung*, 118–19, views 2 Cor. 5:19a–b as pre-Pauline, he does not claim that Paul was the first to use the term "reconciliation" of God's action in Christ.

13. Ibid., 221.

14. On reconciliation as a peripheral biblical term, see note 18 below. Certain strong affinities between the Israelite and the Greek traditions, however, should not be denied. For example, the Isaianic imagery of the wolf and the lamb living together in peace (11:6; 65:25) occurs in an even stronger form in Aristophanes' *Peace* (1076a), where the seer Hierocles speaks of a wolf "wedding" a sheep. With this image the seer objects to the pact of reconciliation (1049) that will end the war between the Greek states and bring peace, asserting that the time for this era has not yet come. Therefore, the imagery that the book of Isaiah uses to describe the age inaugurated by the righteous Davidic monarch (11:1–9) and to depict the new heavens and the new earth (65:17) occurs in Aristophanes in connection with the topic of peace and reconciliation. For other instances of this image in Greek and Latin literature, see S. Douglas Olson, *Aristophanes, Peace* (Oxford: Clarendon, 1998), 275. Finally, one should not overlook the fact that the imagery in both Isaiah and Aristophanes is employed in a highly political context. For the Josianic background of Isa 11:1–9, see Marvin A. Sweeney, *Isaiah 1–39 with An Introduction to Prophetic Literature*, Forms of the Old Testament Literature 16 (Grand Rapids: Eerdmans, 1996), 196–211.

15. See, for example, *Ach.* 989; *Av.* 1532, 1577, 1588, 1601, 1635, 1640, 1683; *Lys.* 900, 932, 984, 1009, 1091, 1101, 1104, 1114, 1161, 1175; *Pax* 1049; *Vesp.* 472, 1394–95. Aristophanes even personifies the concept and presents Reconciliation as a character in two of his plays (*Ach.* 989; *Lys.* 1114), though only in *Lysistrata* does she appear on stage (where her beauty makes the Athenians and Spartans lust for her).

16. Jeffrey Henderson, *Aristophanes, Lysistrata* (Oxford: Clarendon, 1987), 197.

17. See, for example, Margaret M. Mitchell, *Paul and the Rhetoric of Reconciliation: An Exegetical Investigation of the Language and Composition of 1 Corinthians* (Louisville, Ky.: Westminster/John Knox, 1993), and L. L. Welborn, *Politics and Rhetoric in the Corinthian Epistles* (Macon, Ga.: Mercer University Press, 1997). For Paul's use of political imagery (including reconciliation) in Romans, see Troels Engberg-Pedersen, *Paul and the Stoics* (Louisville, Ky.: Westminster John Knox, 2000), 360–1 n. 46.

18. The standard Greek terms for reconciliation are extremely rare in the books of the LXX that belong to the Hebrew Bible, and *none* of these texts involves the

divine-human relationship. The verb διαλλάσσειν occurs only six times in these books (Judg 19:3 [Codex A]; 1 Kgdms 29:4; Job 5:12; 12:20, 24; 36:28) and in only two of these instances does it mean "to reconcile" (Judg 19:3 [Codex A] and 1 Kgdms 29:4). Elsewhere in the LXX it occurs only once in the sense of "to reconcile" (1 Esd 4:31), and three other times (Wis 15:4; 19:18; and 2 Macc 6:27) with a different meaning. The noun διαλλαγή does not occur in books that belong to the Hebrew Bible and is found only twice in the remainder of the LXX, both times in the sense of "reconciliation" (Sir 22:22; 27:21). The verb καταλλάσσειν occurs in books of the Hebrew Bible only once, in Jer 31:39 (= 48:39 MT), where it is clearly corrupt; see Peter Walters (= Peter Katz), *The Text of the Septuagint: Its Corruptions and Their Emendation*, ed. D. W. Gooding (Cambridge: Cambridge University Press, 1973), 257, 293 n. 83. In the remainder of the LXX it occurs three other times, all in 2 Maccabees (1:5; 7:33; 8:29) and all in the sense of being "reconciled" to God. The noun καταλλαγή occurs in Hebrew Bible books of the LXX just once (Isa 9:5 = 9:4 MT), where it means "money" or "profit"; see I. L. Seeligmann, *The Septuagint Version of Isaiah: A Discussion of Its Problems*, Mededelingen en Verhandelingen 9 (Leiden: Brill, 1948), 50, and J. Lust, E. Eynikel, and K. Hauspie, *A Greek-English Lexicon of the Septuagint*, 2 vols. (Stuttgart: Deutsche Bibelgesellschaft, 1992–96), 2.238. Elsewhere in the LXX it occurs only once (2 Macc 5:20), where it is used of "reconciliation" with God. Therefore, the use of the terms for reconciliation in regard to the divine-human relationship is restricted to just one book (2 Maccabees) in the entire LXX, and that book is not part of the Hebrew Bible. A term that is appropriate for a biblical theology that encompasses both the Old Testament and the New Testament should be prominent in both testaments and have a firm basis in books of the Hebrew Bible.

19. For an attempt to use "reconciliation" as an overarching theological concept for the entire New Testament, see Peter Stuhlmacher, "The Gospel of Reconciliation in Christ: Basic Features and Issues of a Biblical Theology of the New Testament," *HBT* 1 (1979): 161–90. See also his "Jesus als Versöhner," *Jesus Christus in Historie und Theologie: Neutestamentliche Festschrift für H. Conzelmann zum 60. Geburtstag*, ed. G. Strecker (Tübingen: Mohr-Siebeck, 1975), 87–104, which is available in English as "Jesus as Reconciler: Reflections on the Problem of Portraying Jesus Within the Framework of a Biblical Theology of the New Testament," in his *Reconciliation, Law, and Righteousness: Essays in Biblical Theology* (Philadelphia: Fortress, 1986), 1–15.

20. Abraham J. Malherbe rightly notes the lamentable fact that "there is still a tendency on dogmatic grounds to deny any real Hellenistic influence on Paul and to speak rather of analogies and verbal borrowings. Paul's indebtedness to Jewish traditions, however, is accepted as somehow preserving his theological integrity." See his "Greco-Roman Religion and Philosophy and the New Testament," *The New Testament and Its Modern Interpreters*, eds. E. J. Epp and G. W. MacRae, SBLBMI 3 (Philadelphia: Fortress; Atlanta: Scholars, 1989), 3–26, esp. 7. Malherbe's own work, of course, provides numerous examples of Hellenistic influence on Paul.

21. I am adapting the term "linkage group" from the field of genetics, where it is used of the tendency of some genes to remain linked together and be inherited as a unit. Thus a linkage group is "a group of hereditary characteristics which remain associated with one another through a number of generations" (J. A. Simpson and E. S. C. Weiner, eds., *The Oxford English Dictionary*, 2d ed., 20 vols. [Oxford: Clarendon, 1989], 8.996 [s.v. linkage], citing *Chambers's Techn. Dict.*). See also David B. Guralnik, ed., *Webster's New World Dictionary of the American Language*, 2d College Edition (New York: Simon and Schuster, 1984),

823 (s.v. linkage). I use it here to indicate certain ideas and terms that remain associated with one another in a given culture through a number of generations.

22. In discussing paradigm shifts in Paul, I shall make no attempt to distinguish between the apostle himself and any pre-Pauline traditions and formulas that he may employ. Also, I wish to express my gratitude to Marvin A. Sweeney of the Claremont School of Theology for reading and commenting upon my presentation of the first two paradigms.

23. For the conceptual link between slavery and Egypt, see esp. Exod 2:23; 6:5–6; 13:3, 14; 20:2; Deut 5:6, 15; 6:12, 21; 7:8; 8:14; 13:5, 10; 15:15; 16:12; 24:18, 22; Josh 24:17; Judg 6:8–9; Neh 9:17; Jer 34:13; and Mic 6:4.

24. The first scholar to help me understand this point was Wayne A. Meeks. See his "Paul as Heretic: A Study of Opposition to the Apostle in Galatia," *Enquiry* 3 (Sept.-Nov., 1970): 21–48, esp. 41: "For the Jew, . . . the only durable freedom was freedom structured by law. For Paul all law, even God's own law, is for the Messianic community a barrier against the freedom and free responsibility given in Christ."

25. Both the impetus and the conceptual framework for my reflection on this topic was given in a lecture by Professor William Scott Green on "Levitical Religion." My understanding of sacrifice in ancient Israel derives chiefly from the work of Jacob Milgrom. See esp. his "Atonement in the OT," *IDBSup* 78–82; "Atonement, Day of," *IDBSup* 82–3; "Sacrifices and Offerings, OT," *IDBSup* 763–71; *Cult and Conscience: The Asham and the Priestly Doctrine of Repentance*, SJLA 18 (Leiden: Brill, 1976); *Studies in Cultic Theology and Terminology*, SJLA 36 (Leiden: Brill, 1983); and *Leviticus 1–16: A New Translation with Introduction and Commentary*, AB 3 (New York: Doubleday, 1991). The paragraphs that follow represent my attempt to integrate the insights of these two scholars and to supplement them with my own.

26. Sacrifice also played an indispensable role in maintaining the purity of the sanctuary itself. Indeed, Milgrom shows that the so-called "sin offering" was really a purgation offering that functioned to purify the sanctuary on behalf of the person or group that had polluted it. See esp. *Studies*, 67–95.

27. Sin not only damages the relationship with the Deity but also defiles both the sanctuary and the land, making it necessary for both to be purified. For the graded power of impurity, see the discussion and charts in Milgrom, "Sacrifices and Offerings," 767; *Studies*, 78–9; *Leviticus 1–16*, 254–8.

28. See esp. Manfred Görg, "Eine neue Deutung für *kappōret*," *ZAW* 89 (1977): 115–8, and "Nachtrag zu *kappōret*," *Biblische Notizen* 5 (1978): 12.

29. Milgrom, "Atonement," 80.

30. Ibid.

31. The understanding of the *kappōret* as a "covering" is reflected in the LXX of Exod. 25:17, where *kappōret* is first translated by ἱλαστήριον, then explained as a "lid" or "cover" (ἐπίθεμα) for the ark.

32. On the indispensability of repentance in priestly circles, see Milgrom, "Atonement," 80–1; *Cult and Conscience*, 117–24; "Sacrifices and Offerings," 767–9; *Studies*, 47–66; *Leviticus 1–16*, 373–8.

33. Rom 8:32 is an allusion to the binding of Isaac in Genesis 22. On this allusion, see the now classic study by Nils A. Dahl, "The Atonement—An Adequate Reward for the Akedah? (Ro 8:32)," *Neotestamentica et Semitica: Studies in Honour of Matthew Black*, eds. E. E. Ellis and M. Wilcox (Edinburgh: Clark, 1969), 15–29, reprinted in Dahl's *The Crucified Messiah and Other Essays* (Minneapolis: Augsburg, 1974), 146–89.

34. See C. E. B. Cranfield, *A Critical and Exegetical Commentary on the Epistle to the Romans*, 2 vols., ICC (Edinburgh: 1975–79), 1.215.

35. For a nonsacrificial interpretation of Rom 3:24–25, see Stanley K. Stowers, *A Rereading of Romans: Justice, Jews, and Gentiles* (New Haven: Yale University Press, 1994), 206–13.

36. In the discussion of the reconciliation paradigm, I shall make use of both καταλλάσσειν and διαλλάσσειν. The two terms are equivalent in meaning when used to indicate reconciliation.

37. This conviction is quite old, appearing already in Hesiòd *Op.* 707–14. On this passage, see J. T. Fitzgerald, "Friendship in the Greek World Prior to Aristotle," *Greco-Roman Perspectives on Friendship*, ed. J. T. Fitzgerald, SBLRBS 34 (Atlanta: Scholars, 1997), 32. For the idea in a Jewish text, note the saying of Rabbi Eleazer ben Azariah recorded in *m. Yoma* 8.9: "For transgressions between man and his fellow, the Day of Atonement atones, only if the man will regain the good will of his friend." The translation is that of Jacob Neusner, *The Mishnah: A New Translation* (New Haven: Yale University Press, 1988), 279.

38. See Plato, *Prot.* 346b; Arist., *Rhet.* 1.9.31; Marcus Aurelius, *Med.* 1.7; compare Plut., *Caes.* 54.1–2.

39. See Zech 7:9–10 LXX and Arist., *Eth. eud.* 2.5.9. For the contrary idea of remembering injuries and exacting vengeance, see Ezek 25:12 LXX and Joel 4:4 LXX.

40. Arist., *Rhet.* 2.4.17; the translation is a slightly modified version of that given in the LCL. See also Dion. Hal., *Ant. rom.* 3.8.4–5; 3.9.2–3; and Diodorus Siculus 14.34.6: "After the battle the Cyrenaeans negotiated with each other and agreed to be reconciled, and they immediately swore oaths not to remember past injuries and lived together as one body in the city" (trans. LCL).

41. Pseudo-Libanius, *Epistolary Styles* 63 (76, 8–11 Malherbe). The translation is that of A. J. Malherbe, *Ancient Epistolary Theorists*, SBLSBS 19 (Atlanta: Scholars, 1988), 77.

42. See also Antiphon, *Or.* 6.38–39. For an example of feigned repentance in an effort to obtain reconciliation, see Dion. Hal., *Ant. rom.* 4.38.1 (see also 3.73.1; Philo, *Flacc.* 18–19).

43. For reconciliation by means of petition, see also Josephus, *J.W.* 1.320; *Ant.* 6.143–145; 14.438.

44. Full text and translation are available in Herbert C. Youtie and John G. Winter, *Papyri and Ostraca from Karanis*, Second Series, Michigan Papyri 8 (Ann Arbor: University of Michigan Press; London: Cumberlege, Oxford University Press, 1951), 121–3. The aorist participle παρακληθείς may also be translated "I urge you," which is how C. Spicq, *TLNT*, 1.310, renders it.

45. Pseudo-Demetrius, *Epistolary Types* 12 (36, 30–35 Malherbe). The translation is that of Malherbe, *Ancient Epistolary Theorists*, 37.

46. Or "wrote." The translation depends on whether αἴγραψα is a true or an epistolary aorist.

47. The meaning of the papyrus' ἀκαιρέως is debated; some papyrologists construe it as ἀκαίρως ("unseasonably" or "at the wrong time"), whereas others take it as ἀκεραίως ("unreservedly" or "accurately").

48. My translation is based largely on the version offered by George Milligan, *Here and There among the Papyri* (London: Hodder & Stoughton, 1923), 108–9, though I have modified it in several places. The Greek text is available in Milligan's *The New Testament Documents: Their Origin and Early History* (London: Macmillan, 1913), 259–60. Both text and translation are available in George Milligan, *Selections from the Greek Papyri* (Cambridge: Cambridge University Press, 1910; repr. Chicago: Ares, 1980), 93–5 (Nr. 37); Adolf Deissmann, *Light from the Ancient East*, rev. ed. (London: Hodder & Stoughton, 1927), 186–92; A. S. Hunt and C. C. Edgar, *Select Papyri*, 2 vols., LCL (London: Heinemann;

New York: Putnam, 1932), 1.316–19 (Nr. 120); and John L. White, *Light from Ancient Letters*, Foundations and Facets (Philadelphia: Fortress, 1986), 181–2 (Nr. 114). For comments on the text, see Friedrich Preisigke, *Berichtigungsliste der Griechischen Papyrusurkunden aus Ägypten* (Berlin: de Gruyter, 1922), 72–3.

49. See, for example, Menander *Perik.* 1020, where Polemon says to his angry girl-friend Glykera ("Sweetie"), "Just be reconciled, darling."

50. The papyrus was first edited by Ernst Kornemann and published in Kornemann and Otto Eger, *Griechische Papyri im Museum des Oberhessischen Geschichtsvereins zu Giessen*, 3 vols. (Leipzig: Teubner, 1910–12), 1.56–7. It was repr., with a slight change, in L. Mitteis and U. Wilcken, *Grundzüge und Chrestomathie der Papyruskunde*, 2 vols. in 4 parts (Leipzig: Teubner, 1912; repr., Hildesheim: Olms, 1963), 1/2.566 (Nr. 481). George Milligan prints the text in his *New Testament Documents*, 258–9, and provides an English translation of it in his *Here and There among the Papyri*, 98. Text and translation are also available in Hunt and Edgar, *Select Papyri*, 1.308–11 (Nr. 115). The text is printed and discussed by Wilhelm Schubart in *Griechische Papyri: Urkunden und Briefe vom 4. Jahrh. v. Chr. bis ins 8. Jahrh. n. Chr.*, 2 vols., Sammlung lateinischer und griechischer Schulausgaben (Bielefeld and Leipzig: Velhagen & Klasung, 1927), 1.46 (Nr. 29), 2.36–7. Schubart gives a German translation of the text in his *Ein Jahrtausend am Nil: Briefe aus dem Altertum verdeutscht und erklärt*, 2d ed. (Berlin: Weidmann, 1923), 75 (Nr. 54).

51. Unfortunately, the writer of the letter is depicted as a male in the English translation of Ceslas Spicq's discussion of this papyrus (*TLNT* 1.310). The error lies with the (usually excellent) translator, not with Spicq, who clearly understands the writer as female. See his *Notes de lexicographie néo-testamentaire*, 3 vols., OBO 22.1–3 (Göttingen: Vandenhoeck & Ruprecht, 1978–82), 3.117: "une esclave fugitive."

52. The view that Tays is Apollonius's slave goes back to Kornemann, the first editor of the papyrus (*Griechische Papyri*, 1.56), and it is adopted by both Milligan (*New Testament Documents*, 258–9, and *Here and There among the Papyri*, 98) and Spicq (*TLNT* 1.310). Wilcken, moreover, thinks that the familiarity with which Tays writes may suggest that she is Apollonius's παιδίσκη; he concedes, however, that "that assumption is probably not absolutely necessary." See Mitteis and Wilcken, *Grundzüge und Chrestomathie der Papyruskunde*, 1/2.566. Alternatively, Tays could well be Apollonius's old nurse and guardian, a relationship that would also explain the familiar language that she uses. For this suggestion, see Schubart, *Griechische Papyri*, 2.36, and *Ein Jahrtausend*, 75.

53. This is the assumption of Kornemann, *Griechische Papyri*, 1.56, who thinks that Apollonius is far away from home and has been gone for an extended period of time.

54. The request for reconciliation makes clear that Tays and Apollonius are estranged, but I see no basis for deciding whether she is a runaway (so Spicq, *TLNT* 1.310) or has been banished by Apollonius. In either case, she knows that her return to his presence depends upon his willingness to receive her. Whether this letter is relevant to the discussion of Paul's letter to Philemon depends upon one's reconstruction of the historical situation reflected in the Pauline document.

55. There is an interesting shift in the letter from the first person singular, used in the first half, to the first person plural, used in the second half. The shift occurs in the first sentence of the παρακαλῶ-section of the letter, which begins with "I beseech" and ends with "send for (or 'to') us." It is unclear whether "us" refers to Tays's family (children?) or is an example of an epistolary plural, with no

difference in meaning between the singular and the plural. Milligan, *New Testament Documents*, 259, apparently views it as the latter, and Hunt and Edgar, *Select Papyri*, 1.309–11, use the first person singular for their translation of the whole letter. In any case, Tays's use of "we are dying" contrasts nicely with her thanksgiving to the gods for sparing Apollonius's life when he was ill and in a state of torpor: "Thanks (χάρις) be to all the gods because they are preserving you free from harm" (ll. 6–7).

56. Deissmann, *Light from the Ancient East*, 189 n. 15, translates "be no more angry with us." Hunt and Edgar, *Select Papyri*, 1.311, render it "be friends with me."

57. For these meanings of καταλλαγή, see LSJ 899 (s.v. καταλλαγή, 1–2); H. J. Rose, *A Commentary on the Surviving Plays of Aeschylus*, 2 vols. (Amsterdam: N. V. Noord-Hollandsche Uitgevers Maatschappij, 1957–58), 1.226; Christopher M. Dawson, *The Seven Against Thebes by Aeschylus*, Prentice-Hall Greek Drama Series (Englewood Cliffs: Prentice-Hall, 1970), 97; and esp. T. G. Tucker, *The Seven Against Thebes of Aeschylus* (Cambridge: Cambridge University Press, 1908), 157: "καταλλαγή is exactly the English 'settlement,' whether of a feud … or of an outstanding account." For καταλλαγή as a commercial term in the LXX, see Isa 9:5 (= 9:4 MT) and note 18 above.

58. The envoys (πρέσβεις) of Antiochus, for example, ask what they must do (τί δεῖ ποιήσαντας) in order to obtain peace and friendship with Rome (Polybius 21.16.9), and the requisite actions are specified in the treaty itself (21.17.1–8). See also 4.52.6–9 for another example of terms necessary for peace and friendship.

59. See, for example, Polybius 1.31.1–8, where the harshness of Rome's demands prolongs the war with Carthage.

60. See Fitzgerald, "Friendship in the Greek World Prior to Aristotle," 32.

61. Josephus, *J.W.* 3.496: "necessity will quickly reconcile them."

62. I have used the translation of Youtie and Winter, *Papyri and Ostraca from Karanis*, 123, who correctly note that Valerius is being asked to persuade the mother to be reconciled to her son Gemellus.

63. See also the more expansive rendering of Kenneth Cavander, *Iphigeneia at Aulis by Euripides*, Prentice-Hall Greek Drama Series (Englewood Cliffs: Prentice-Hall, 1973), 146. For more detailed comments on this passage, see esp. Walter Stockert, *Euripides, Iphigenie in Aulis*, 2 vols., Wiener Studien 16 (Vienna: Verlag der Österreichischen Akademie der Wissenschaften, 1992), 2.523–7, and Liana Giovannini, *Euripide, Ifigenia in Aulide* (Rome: Angelo Signorelli, 1967), 109–10.

64. The fact that formal reconciliation ceremonies were sometimes held in or near temples (e.g., Antiphon, *Or.* 6.39; Josephus, *J.W.* 1.122) doubtless facilitated the application of reconciliation language to the divine-human relationship.

65. See also the reference in *Aj.* 744 to "bitter anger" (χόλου). It is sharply debated whether this is a reference to the gods' anger that needs to be averted or to Ajax's own anger, which, in keeping with his "new counsels" (735–36), "new mood" (736), and "changed intention" (743–44), he has now put away. For the former interpretation, which is supported by some of the scholia, see Lewis Campbell, *Sophocles: The Plays and Fragments*, 2 vols. (Oxford: Clarendon, 1879–81; repr. Hildesheim: Olms, 1969), 2.71. For the latter interpretation, see esp. Frederick H. M. Blaydes, *The Ajax of Sophocles* (London: Williams and Norgate, 1875), 170, and A. F. Garvie, *Sophocles, Ajax* (Warminster: Aris & Phillips, 1998), 75: "after his anger."

66. See also Josephus, *Ant.* 7.153 (the penitent David is reconciled to God); 7.295 (reconciliation with God depends on turning over Saul's sons to the Gibeonites for punishment); and Philo, *Praem.* 166–167 (three intercessors to plead for

reconciliation with the Father). That Yahweh is easily reconciled does not mean, however, that he is always reconciled; see Josephus, *Ant.* 3.315; 6.143–144, 151.

67. For the use of ἱλάσκεσθαι and διαλλάσσω together, see Plut., *Thes.* 15.1. For reconciliation "by prayers and sacrifices," see Pl., *Menex.* 244a.

68. Bash, *Ambassadors for Christ*, 155, is absolutely on target on this point: "the Sender was usually in a situation of weakness, need, vulnerability or dependence and it was the Sender's situation which gave rise to the embassy."

69. Compare Aelius Aristides, *Or.* 2.396, where Prometheus is depicted as ascending to heaven, where he speaks with Zeus as "an ambassador on humanity's behalf."

70. Paul's particular formulation here appears to be unique. Jewish texts that use the term "reconciler" of Moses (Philo, *Mos.* 2.166: διαλλακτής; Josephus, *Ant.* 3.315: καταλλάκτης) do so in regard to Moses' role as intercessor with Yahweh on behalf of the sinful Hebrews, and they do not apply the term "ambassador" to Moses in this regard. They differ sharply from Clem. Alex., *Protr.* 10.110.3 (160,15 Marcovich), where Clement calls Christ διαλλακτής without any regard to intercession and joins that term with σπονδοφόρος, the Greek term for the one who brings proposals for a truce or peace treaty. Paul's depiction is closer to the idea of the gods seeking to bring about reconciliation between warring humans, but Paul changes it so that he is the envoy whose mission is to bring the word of God's act of reconciliation to humanity. Paul is fundamentally a proclaimer, not an intercessor, though he does cast the proclamation in the form of an appeal (2 Cor 5:20). For the more common Greco-Roman idea, see esp. Dio Chrys., *Or.* 38.18: "men go unarmed into an armed camp as envoys to sue for peace and it is not permitted to wrong any of them, the belief being that all messengers in behalf of friendship are servants of the gods" (trans. LCL). See also Aristophanes, *Av.* 1532–33, 1587–88; Josephus, *Ant.* 15.136, and Plutarch's (*Mor.* 329C) description of Alexander the Great as the divinely sent "reconciler" (διαλλακτής) of the entire world. Compare Pl., *Leg.* 941a. For the idea of god wanting to end the war of pleasure and pain by reconciling these two opposites, see Pl., *Phaed.* 60c.

71. It should be noted that formal reconciliation ceremonies typically included sacrifices offered to the gods in thanksgiving for the peace treaty as well as oaths that were sworn over animals that had been sacrificed (see, e.g., Dion. Hal., *Ant. rom.* 6.95.3). Therefore, sacrifice was not only a traditional part of the reconciliation process in international affairs but also an essential element in the formal ratification of the alliance. For the use of oaths in international affairs, see John T. Fitzgerald, "The Problem of Perjury in Greek Context: Prolegomena to an Exegesis of Matthew 5:33; 1 Timothy 1:10; and *Didache* 2.3," *The Social World of the First Christians: Essays in Honor of Wayne A. Meeks*, eds. L. M. White and O. L. Yarbrough (Minneapolis: Fortress, 1995), 156–77, esp. 167. On the association of temples with reconciliation, see n. 64 above.

72. See, for example, Josephus, *J. W.* 1.92. See also Sophocles' *Ajax*, where Athena's anger (656, 757, 777) ceases once Ajax commits suicide.

73. See also Aeschylus, *Sept.* 908, where the iron sword (and/or Ares) is called their "reconciler" (διαλλακτῆρι), and the discussion of "the theme of the iron as arbiter between the brothers" by William G. Thalmann, *Dramatic Art in Aeschylus's **Seven Against Thebes*** (New Haven: Yale University Press, 1978), 72–4.

74. The meaning of καταλλαγαί in *Sept.* 767 is disputed, with some scholars favoring "settlement" and others "reconciliation." I believe that both meanings are present. I accept the argument of G. O. Hutchinson, *Aeschylus, **Septem contra Thebas*** (Oxford: Clarendon, 1985), xxvi, xxix, 169, 194, that, in the missing plays of Aeschylus, Oedipus's curse mentioned "iron" and spoke of the "reconciliation"

of his sons. Therefore, the chorus in *Sept.* 767 is referring primarily to the "grievous 'reconciliation' prophesied by the curse," and is contending that it now "is being brought to fulfillment" (169). Yet I also think, as other scholars contend, that the adjective "heavy" is suggestive of the "hefty price" paid for the brothers' reconciliation. My rendering ("heavy reconciliation price") is an attempt to combine both connotations of the term. For discussion of this difficult passage, see William Linwood, *A Lexicon to Aeschylus* (London: Taylor and Walton, 1843), 59–60; F. A. Paley, *The Tragedies of Aeschylus*, 2d ed. (London: Whittaker and Co., George Bell, 1861), 296; Augustus Sachtleben, *Septem contra Thebas, A Tragedy of Aeschylus* (Boston: Dennet, 1864) 130; and the references in note 57 above. For a play on the verb καταλλάσσειν as meaning both "to exchange" and "to reconcile," see the saying of Matreas of Alexandria in Athenaeus, *Deipn.* 1.19D.

75. Milgrom, "Sacrifices and Offerings," 768. On the reparation (guilt) offering as essentially a monetary payment that compensates for damages, see Milgrom, *Leviticus 1–16*, 327–8. For a more extensive discussion of the reparation offering, see his *Cult and Conscience.*

76. *DCH* 4.457; see also BDB 497.

77. B. Lang, "כפר, etc." *TDOT* 7.301.

78. Ibid.

79. See also the Hebrew Bible texts in which God is the subject of *kipper* and Lang's discussion of divine atonement in *TDOT* 7.300–1.

80. See Dion. Hal., *Ant. rom.* 6.49.5 for "not accepting (δέχεσθαι) the reconciliation." To confirm a reconciliation (7.19.1; 7.27.1; 7.32.3) is to act in such a manner as to demonstrate its reality.

81. On 2 Cor 6:3–10, see John T. Fitzgerald, *Cracks in an Earthen Vessel: An Examination of the Catalogues of Hardships in the Corinthian Correspondence,* SBLDS 99 (Atlanta: Scholars, 1988), 184–201. Although envoys were supposed to be free from harm during the negotiations following the declaration of a truce (Dio Chrys., *Or.* 38.18), the reality was often quite different (Dion. Hal., *Ant. rom.* 5.34.1; Josephus, *Ant.* 15.136; Bash, *Ambassadors for Christ*, 106). Paul's *peristasis* catalogue in 2 Cor 6:4–10 thus reflects the reality of his role as an "abused ambassador."

82. See the essays in *Friendship, Flattery, and Frankness of Speech: Studies on Friendship in the New Testament World*, ed. J. T. Fitzgerald, NovTSup 82 (Leiden: Brill, 1996).

83. The roots of this formula in the friendship *topos* have long been recognized by New Testament scholars. See Victor Paul Furnish, *II Corinthians: Translated with Introduction, Notes, and Commentary*, AB 32A (New York: Doubleday, 1984), 367.

84. See, for example, LSJ 401 (s.v. διαλλάσσω, III) and 899 (s.v. καταλλάσσω, II), and G. Abbott-Smith, *A Manual Greek Lexicon of the New Testament*, 3d ed. (Edinburgh: Clark, 1937), 109 (s.v. διαλλάσσω, 2) and 236 (s.v. καταλλάσσω). See also Spicq, *TLNT* 2.262: "For pagans and Christians alike, *reconciliation* is the action of reestablishing friendship between two persons who are on bad terms, to replace hostility with peaceful relations." The Latin words *reconcilio* and *reconciliatio* likewise indicate the act and fact of the restoration of friendship and good relations; see, e.g., the *OLD* 1584, where *reconcilio* is defined as "[t]o bring back into friendship."

85. See esp. David L. Balch, "Political Friendship in the Historian Dionysius of Halicarnassus, *Roman Antiquities*," *Greco-Roman Perspectives on Friendship*, ed. J. T. Fitzgerald, SBLRBS 34 (Atlanta: Scholars, 1997), 123–44.

86. Peter Marshall, *Enmity in Corinth: Social Conventions in Paul's Relations with the Corinthians*, WUNT 2.23 (Tübingen: Mohr-Siebeck, 1987).

87. See esp. Alfons Fürst, *Streit unter Freunden: Ideal und Realität in der Freund-schaftslehre der Antike*, Beiträge zur Altertumskunde 85 (Stuttgart: Teubner, 1996). The breakdown of friendships could become so serious that it resulted in death; see now Elizabeth S. Belfiore, *Murder among Friends: Violation of Philia in Greek Tragedy* (New York: Oxford University Press, 2000).

88. My analysis of Paul's use of reconciliation language supports the position that 2 Cor 2:14–7:4 is neither a digression nor part of an originally independent let-ter sent to Corinth. This important unit functions to undergird his efforts to reconcile the Corinthians to himself and is a crucial component of his appeal to them for reconciliation.

89. On confidence as a consequence of reconciliation, see above for the discussion of *PMich.* VIII.502, where Gemellus seeks reconciliation with his brother Valerius so that he may make use of the latter's confidence.

90. For Greco-Roman texts in which the divine acts to end conflicts among humans, see n. 70 above.

91. The presence of the friendship motif in connection with the idea of reconcili-ation is occasionally noted in commentaries on 2 Corinthians, but it is rarely emphasized. See, for instance, the brief comment by C. K. Barrett, *A Com-mentary on The Second Epistle to the Corinthians*, HNTC (New York: Harper & Row, 1973), 180.

92. Although reconciliation terminology is not present in 2 Cor 5:21, it should be noted that the basic idea of "exchange," which is central to the verb καταλ-λάσσειν, is continued in 5:21.

93. William Barclay, *The New Testament: A New Translation*, 2 vols. (London: Collins, 1968–69), 2.72. See also his *New Testament Words* (Philadelphia: West-minster, 1974), 164–8. The strong link between friendship and reconciliation is also rightly emphasized by Breytenbach, *Versöhnung*, 23, 47, 52–3, 61, 180, 223.

Contributors

Loveday Alexander is Senior Lecturer in New Testament in the Department of Biblical Studies, University of Sheffield.

Philip S. Alexander is Professor of Post-Biblical Jewish Literature and Co-Director of the Centre for Jewish Studies at the Department of Religions and Theology, University of Manchester.

David E. Aune is Professor of New Testament and Christian Origins in the Department of Theology, University of Notre Dame.

John M. G. Barclay is Professor of New Testament and Christian Origins in the Department of Theology and Religious Studies, University of Glasgow.

Troels Engberg-Pedersen is Lecturer in New Testament in the Department of Biblical Studies, University of Copenhagen.

John T. Fitzgerald is Associate Professor in the Department of Religious Studies, University of Miami.

Dale B. Martin is Professor in the Department of Religious Studies, Yale University.

Wayne A. Meeks is Woolsey Professor Emeritus of Biblical Studies in the Department of Religious Studies, Yale University.

Margaret M. Mitchell is Associate Professor of New Testament at the Divinity School and the Department of New Testament and Early Christian Literature in the Division of the Humanities, University of Chicago.

Stanley K. Stowers is Professor in the Department of Religious Studies, Brown University.

Henrik Tronier is Lecturer in New Testament in the Department of Biblical Studies, University of Copenhagen.

Index of Ancient Sources

Non-Biblical Writings

Hebrew Bible/Old Testament(Septuagint)

New Testament

Index of Personal Names

Index of Subjects

accommodation, Pauline (1 Cor 9:19–23), 197–214 passim; possible influences on this account, 198–9, 298; and motif of divine condescension, 202–14 (*See also* condescension); as interpreted by Tertullian, 202–3, by Clement, 203–5, by Origen, 208–10, by John Chrysostom, 211–12; as modeled on Christ, in Origen, 210, 306–7, and John Chrysostom, 212

acculturation (and adaptation and assimilation), 11, 130, 136, 138; patterns of Jewish and Pauline immigration, 129–38; and disassimilation, 132–5; and apologetic historiography, 288, 289; in recent scholarship, 290

adaptability, 199–200. *See also* accommodation

alternative social formations, in Hellenistic philosophies and Paul, 94–5

ambassadors, ancient notion of, 316–17, 324

anthropology, Pauline and Hellenistic, 165–6, 238–9; in Paul tangential to eschatology, 166–7,190–6; basically undeveloped in Paul, 190–1; more dualistic in 2 Cor 4:16–5:10 than in Romans 7, 238–9

anti-Semitism, in German scholarship, 263–4

apocalypticism, Jewish; as interpretive, cognitive structure, 10; as wrongly securing Christian uniqueness, 22; basic to Paul's worldview, 167; itself a Hellenistic idea, 167 and 165–96 passim; space (Enoch tradition) and time (Daniel tradition) in, 174–5; in the Enoch tradition, 175–80 (*See also* 1 Enoch); eschatological dimension (time) derived from spatial dualism, 178–80, 191–2, 193; its form in Paul (1–2 Corinthians): its cognitive role, 181, 193, 194–5, in comparison with the cosmologies and epistemologies of Philo and 1 Enoch, 182–4, and reversal of values, 184–6, and social intervention, 186; its function in Paul's description of his heavenly ascent (2 Cor 12), 187–9; as a narrow, time-limited construct, 218; its form in 2 Cor 4:16–5:10, 220–39. *See also* postmortem destination and judgment

Arnold, M., *See* Judaism/Hellenism divide

Arnold, T., and Judaism/Hellenism divide, 269

asceticism, in Hellenistic philosophies and Paul, 91, 280

Babata archive, 274

Barr, J., *See* Judaism/Hellenism divide

Baur, F. C., and "either/or" thinking, *See also* Tübingen school

Biblical Theology Movement, 270–1; and Judaism/Hellenism divide, *See* the latter

body, as container or vessel of the soul, 311

body of Christ, as an interpretive entity (1 Cor 12), 186–7; its function in Paul's account of the resurrection (1 Cor 15), 189–94

Boman, T., and Jewish vs. Greek thought, 273

Christianity, Pauline; and Hellenistic philosophy, 7–8, 12–13, 81–102; and Jews and Gentiles, 14–15; and comparable groups, 81–9, 277, 283

cognition, as a fundamental category in Philo, apocalypticism and Paul, 165–96 passim

condescension (*synkatabasis*), in Greco-Roman sources, 205, and Philo, 205–8. *See also* accommodation

context, Paul's versus his background (or environment),1–2, 21, 241, 316; and etic perspective, 2, 12

conventionality, lack of; of Hellenistic philosophies, 90–1, 281; and of Paul, 91

conversion, in Hellenistic philosophies and Paul, 91–2; rhetoric of, 280

2 Corinthians, its structure, 258–9; its composition, 311, 325

cosmology, new Hellenistic, 228, 314

culture, as an interpretive category, 59–61, 79, 272; against Christ, 271

diairesis, as a Platonic interpretive method, *See* Philo; in Paul (1 Cor 12), 186–7

distinctiveness, of Christianity, 5, 21

Ellis, E. E., and the Biblical Theology Movement, 270. *See also* Judaism/Hellenism divide

emic and etic perspectives, 9–10, 11–13

1 Enoch, as a representative of spatially oriented apocalypticism, 174–5; cosmology and mode of revelation, 175–6; spatial and physical dualism, not ontological or conceptual dualism, 176; Logos-like role of interpreting angel, 176–8; normative, value-reversing role of heavenly world, 177, 179